Towards the Day
After Tomorrow

Towards the Day After Tomorrow

Essays on Humanity's *Teloi* and the *Eschaton*

P. H. Brazier

Foreword by
Justyn Terry

WIPF & STOCK · Eugene, Oregon

TOWARDS THE DAY AFTER TOMORROW
Essays on Humanity's Teloi and the Eschaton

Copyright © 2020 P. H. Brazier. All rights reserved. Except for brief quotations in critical publications or reviews, no part of this book may be reproduced in any manner without prior written permission from the publisher. Write: Permissions, Wipf and Stock Publishers, 199 W. 8th Ave., Suite 3, Eugene, OR 97401.

Wipf and Stock Publishers
199 W. 8th Ave., Suite 3
Eugene, OR 97401

www.wipfandstock.com

PAPERBACK ISBN: 978-1-5326-6021-4
HARDCOVER ISBN: 978-1-5326-6022-1
EBOOK ISBN: 978-1-5326-6023-8

Cataloging-in-Publication data:

Names: Brazier, Paul, author. | Justyn Terry, foreword writer

Title: Towards the day after tomorrow : essays on humanity's teloi and the eschaton / P. H. Brazier.
Description: Eugene, OR : Wipf & Stock Publishers, 2020 | Includes bibliographical references and index.

Identifiers: ISBN 978-1-5326-6021-4 (paperback) | ISBN 978-1-5326-6022-1 (hardcover) | ISBN 978-1-5326-6023-8 (ebook)
Subjects: LCSH: Eschatology. | Abortion—Religious aspects—Christianity. | Simpsons (Television program) | September 11 Terrorist Attacks, 2001. | Just war doctrine. | Barth, Karl. | Christianity and law. | Religion and science. | Epilepsy.

Classification: LCC BR115 B732 2020 (print) | LCC BR115 (ebook)

Manufactured in the U.S.A.

For Hilary

Contents

Foreword by Justyn Terry / ix

Acknowledgements / xiii

Illustrations / xv

Introduction / 1

Part One:
Towards an Understanding of the Arrival of the End Times / 25

Chapter 1.
A Delayed Nativity . . . What If ? The Eschaton Prefigured / 27

Part Two:
Towards an Understanding of the Emergence of the End Times / 39

Chapter 2.
Karl Barth: "*Krisis*," War, & Expressionism—
an Eschatological Encounter / 41

Chapter 3. A Human-Generated Eschaton:
Objectification in the Slave Trade, the Holocaust, and Abortion—
the Delusions of Religious Atheism / 75

Chapter 4. The Just War Theory and the 9/11 Wars:
A Biblical and Eschatological Consideration. / 121

Chapter 5. *Postmortem Status Purgatus*:
A Simpsons' Eschatology:—Towards a Lewisian Understanding
of Eternal Life and Human Rebellion / 149

Chapter 6. The God of the Epileptic:
Postlapsarian Exile, Affliction, and the Sufferance of Salvation / 189

Conclusion / 225

Bibliography / 233

Mediaography / 243

Indices / 249

Sectional Contents / 267

Foreword

One of the characteristics of our secular age is that we are disinclined to think much about death or what might lie beyond it. We tend to occupy our days with such frenetic activity that little time remains for such apparently idle speculation. Even the less active moments of our lives tend to be filled with the sights and sounds of entertainment, leaving little scope for reflection on the meaning of life, the reality of death, and the events which might lie thereafter. This is an age preoccupied with the present, and it has strikingly little interest in the past or the future. We are so busy with today, that we give little thought for tomorrow, let alone the day after tomorrow.

Towards the Day after Tomorrow: Essays on Humanity's **Teloi** *and the* **Eschaton** is a protest against such a mind-set. It is a collection of occasional theology papers that have been developed into a multifaceted reflection on the nature of the *eschaton*, the last things, with a view to what they imply for humanity's *teloi*, our purpose and end. It offers a wide-ranging discussion of matters related to the four last things in particular: death, judgement, heaven and hell, topics much in need of greater attention from the church and the world.

This book deliberately sets alarm bells ringing to draw attention to the perils in which we stand. Unless there is a new seriousness about these vital but largely neglected topics, we might be habitually behaving in ways that would be unacceptable if we understood the end with greater clarity. To start calling his readers to pay attention to the *eschaton*, Dr Brazier offers a parable that retells the story of the nativity of Christ as if it had been unexpectedly delayed. It also involves some unfamiliar characters and some unexpected places. All this gets us thinking afresh about how the birth of the Messiah is the beginning of the end, a breaking in of the future, which will usher in the *eschaton* in due course. Like the entrance of the brass section in an overture, the first coming of Christ as saviour alerts the world to the second coming of Christ as judge, the anticipation of which can also feel very much like a delay.

Attention then quickly turns to the second part of the book, the heart of it, where Brazier begins to develop an understanding of the end times. To do so, he begins by examining the thinking of the Swiss reformed theologian Karl Barth and his wrestling with "'Krisis,' War, & Expressionism." Barth's own protests about the First World War and his outrage that his German theological professors were in open support of it resonate strongly in this chapter. Here we also see an engagement with Barth's views on art through the eyes of an author trained in the fine arts. When Barth rejects modernist art, Brazier makes clear that he is not rejecting all forms of art, as is well known from his having Grünewald's altar piece above his desk. But he is deliberately using his theological lenses to warn his readers off artistic expressions whose messages might lead us astray.

In chapters 3 to 6, we move on to issues of the application and ethics of the eschaton to the slave trade, the Holocaust and abortion, and the objectification of human lives that they entail. It all leads to a strong refutation of the claims of what Brazier calls "Religious Atheism," which he describes as, "a belief system that defines another group of people as non-human, or sub-human, and open to exploitation and destruction" (p. 75). The following chapter continues on an ethical note with a discussion of just war theory in the light of the *eschaton*, arguing that, in a post 9/11 world, it is hard to conceive of what could possibly be considered a just war. Then Brazier uses his literary skills to engage with popular culture, offering a light-hearted discussion of the Simpsons, to see what eschatology is portrayed in that long-running animation sitcom. This is what Brazier calls "theological media studies," where he asks: What do we see in these well-known characters that might give us a fresh perspective on death and the hereafter? Finally, we arrive at the last main chapter, which is a very moving engagement about living with the challenges of epilepsy.

Throughout this book, Brazier is clear about why these topics matter: they really are life-and-death issues, some of which have touched him very personally. His parents' attempt to abort him on at least two

Foreword

occasions, together with his father's frankness that he was sorry these medical interventions had not succeeded, have clearly left their mark on Paul Brazier. His very ability to live and write this book is a testimony to his view that such abortions should simply not be available. Also, the severe epilepsy suffered for so many years by his wife, Hilary, to whom this book is dedicated, is a daily reminder that matters of life and death should be treated as everyday subjects, and not left to those whose profession requires their engagement with them.

Brazier approaches these topics from the perspective of a traditionally minded creedal Christian. He is not constrained by the expectations of political correctness, and writes with great passion, using strong words where he feels they are necessary, and recommends several controversial positions. His very willingness to address these largely taboo subjects means we should not be too surprised about that. Even the occasionally rhetorical tone is largely an echo of the writing of Karl Barth, who is the theologian who plays the largest part in shaping this whole project. We also hear the voice of Colin Gunton, who chaired not only the Department of Theology and Religion at King's College, London, but also its weekly Research Institute for Systematic Theology—and the long lunches that followed—where most of this material first appeared.

Throughout this collection, Brazier brings his theological and philosophical training to bear, and draws on his knowledge of the fine arts and his experiences of suffering. Many times, his contrast of secular and Christian views of death and all that lies beyond brings the subject matter alive in powerful ways. This ensures that the book speaks not only to other academics, but also to anyone who is willing to pay attention to these vital topics. He draws on wide and diverse reading, but his work is largely accessible to a wide audience, with only sections of part two being technically demanding.

This is a frank and provocative book—especially on the issues of contemporary neo-paganism or secular-liberal humanism, and practices like abortion, about which Brazier feels so strongly. Few are likely to agree with him on every point. However, this freedom from the familiar constraints, which affect even academia, should not be seen as a justification for not reading it; quite the opposite. It is an attempt to shake us into thinking seriously about topics that we might be tempted to leave well alone for fear of causing unnecessary upset. Some upset is surely necessary if we are truly to express the self-giving love revealed

IN THE HIGHEST DEGREE

in Jesus, which caused considerable upset two millennia ago. These important issues demand this kind of attention. Human flourishing depends on a right eschatology. Without it, there is a danger of ever greater dehumanisation and objectification of the human race. We really do need to think seriously about tomorrow, and the day after tomorrow, if we are to live well today.

The Revd Dr Justyn Terry

Vice-Principal,
Wycliffe Hall,
University of Oxford

Acknowledgements

A work such as this has complex rights and acknowledgements.
None of the art works cited are reproduced. Links to websites which will give an illutration/reproduction to look at should be checked for legitamation. The link/recomendation assumes no right of reproduction by the website cited.

Acknowledgment and thanks is given to the C. S. Lewis Co. Pte., for permission to quote from the following works used.

THE PROBLEM OF PAIN by C. S. Lewis copyright © C. S. Lewis Pte. Ltd. 1940.

GOD IN THE DOCK by C. S. Lewis copyright © C. S. Lewis Pte. Ltd. 1970.

MIRACLES by C. S. Lewis copyright © C. S. Lewis Pte. Ltd. 1957, 1960.

THE MAGICIAN'S NEPHEW by C. S. Lewis copyright © C.S. Lewis Pte. Ltd. 1955.

Extracts reprinted by permission.

Extracts quoted from works in German, such as those by Karl Barth, are my own translation.

Extracts from the Bible are as cited in the text (NRSV, KJV, NIV, et al) though in most instances are my own traslations from the original Greek text:

Extracts from the Bible used with permission:

IN THE HIGHEST DEGREE

Revised Standard Version of the Bible, copyright 1952 [2nd edition, 1971] by the Division of Christian Education of the National Council of the Churches of Christ in the United States of America. Used by permission. All rights reserved.

New Revised Standard Version Bible, copyright 1989, Division of Christian Education of the National Council of the Churches of Christ in the United States of America. Used by permission. All rights reserved.

New Revised Standard Version Bible: Anglicized Edition, copyright 1989, 1995, Division of Christian Education of the National Council of the Churches of Christ in the United States of America. Used by permission. All rights reserved.

THE HOLY BIBLE, NEW INTERNATIONAL VERSION®, NIV® Copyright © 1973, 1978, 1984, 2011 by Biblica, Inc.™ Used by permission. All rights reserved worldwide.

Nestle-Aland, Novum Testamentum Graece, 27th Revised Edition, edited by Barbara Aland, Kurt Aland, Johannes Karavidopoulos, Carlo M. Martini, and Bruce M. Metzger in cooperation with the Institute for New Testament Textual Research, Münster/Westphalia, © 1993 by Deutsche Bibelgesellschaft, Stuttgart. Used by permission.

A word of thanks must go to the various members of the Research Institute in Systematic Theology at King's College London, department of Theology and Religiious Studies, down the years, for the questions that followed the presentation of a paper, which through multiple reworkings and expansion gave rise to the papers here published—and thanks to the participants in the often heated debates carried out over lunch following the seminars; and thanks therefore to Professor Christoph Schwobel and the late Professor Colin E. Gunton for founding the Research Institute in Systematic Theology in 1988.

Illustrations

Including illustrations of all the paintings and drawing cited in the second essay, etc., would have been prohibitive not just on cost for a theology book, but also in terms of the byzantine complexity of rights and permissions: ownership not just of a work of art, but the photographic rights are complex and multi-layered (galleries, universities, photo agencies, photographers, media groups, variations according to which country the work is reproduced in, etc . . .). This list here contains hyperlinks to the world wide web of all the paintings and drawings referred to. If this book is being read in an e-book/kindle edition, depending on your devices settings, these links should be live.

Most of the works cited can be viewed in The Web Gallery of Art (pre twentieth century)
https://www.wga.hu/

The Web Gallery of Art

See also, Wikiart: a Visual art Encyclopedia:
https://www.wikiart.org/

Wikiart

See also Google Arts and Culture
https://artsandculture.google.com/

Google Arts and Culture

If you are reding from a hard copy (i.e.a paperback book) go to this webpage where there are hyperlinks for all the works concerned:

http://www.cslewisandthechrist.net//toward-the-day.html

IN THE HIGHEST DEGREE

Essay 2
Karl Barth: "*Krisis*," War, & Expressionism— An Eschatological Encounter

PRE-TWENTIETH CENTURY

Matthias Grünewald

　Khan Academy: Isenheim Altarpiece

　Wikipedia: Isenheim Altarpiece

Masaccio (Tommaso di Ser Giovanni di Simone)

　Khan Academy: The Trinity.

　Wikipedia: The Trinity

Hans Holbein the Younger

　MavCor Centre for the Sudy of Material & Visual Cultures of Religio Holbein, "The Body of the Dead Christ in the Tomb"

　Wikipedia: Holbien, "The Body of the Dead Christ in the Tomb"

El Greco ("The Greek"—Doménikos Theotokópoulos 1541–1614)

　Wikipedia: El Greco

　El Greco: Works

　El Greco: "The Vision of Saint John" ("The Opening of the Fifth Seal") The Metropolitan Museum of Art

Vincent Van Gogh

　Van Gogh, "Wheat Field Under Threatening Skies" (The Van Gogh Museum)

　Wikipedia: "Wheat Field under Threatening Skies"

Edvard Munch

　Munch, "The Scream"

Illustrations

GERMAN EXPRESSIONISM I:
DIE BRÜCKE AND *DER BLAUE REITER*

Franz Marc

Franz Marc, "Blue Horse"

Wikipdia: Franz Marc

Emild Nolde

Emil Nolde, "The Prophet"

Wikipedia: Emil Nolde

Georg Grosz

Georg Grosz, see a Collection of Grosz's paintings

Olga's Gallery: Georg Grosz

Otto Dix

Otto Dix, see Wikiart

Otto Dix, "The Skat Players (formerly entitled, "Card Playing War Cripples")

GERMAN EXPRESSIONISM II:
GERMAN ROMANTICISM

Caspar David Friedrich

Caspar David Friedrich: website, complete works

Caspar David Friedrich, "Man and Woman Contemplating the Moon"

Man and Woman Contemplating the Moon: Staatliche Museen zu Berlin

Caspar David Friedrich, "Memorial Monument to Goethe"

The best solution here is to search Google images with artist and title.

Max Klinger, "Christ on Mount Olympus"

The best solution here is to search Google images with artist and title.

IN THE HIGHEST DEGREE

GERMAN EXPRESSIONISM III: MAX BECKMANN

Max Beckmann

The Wikipedia page for Max Beckmann has access to most of his works and other websites with illustration

Wikipedia: Max Beckmann

See also MoMA (The Museum of Modern Art, New York) for examples of all the works by Beckmann cited

Max Beckmann: MoMA

Also, examples of Beckmann's work at the Guggenheim (New York)

Max Beckmann at the Guggenheim

A specific Wikipedia page on Max Beckmann's "Die Nacht"

Max Beckmann, "Die Nacht"

For a complete compendium of Beckmann's works:

Google Arts & Culture: Max Beckmann

MODERNISM

Otto Hoyer, "In the Beginning was the Word"

Google Arts and Culture

OTHER WORKS

Rogier van der Weyden

National Gallery (UK): Rogier van der Weyden

Wikipedia: Rogier van der Weyden

Raffaello Sanzio da Urbino

Wikipedia: Raphael's Entombment (Deposition)

Essay 6
The God of the Epileptic: *Postlapsarian* Exile, Affliction, and the Sufferance of Salvation

William Blake

William Blake, "Newton" (Tate Gallery, London)

Francisco Jose de Goya y Lucientes

The Sleep of Reason Produces Monsters

All of these website were live and active in September 2019 when this list was compiled.

Blasted, and Damaged,
Broken and Regrown,
Humanity, like an old Ash tree,
Survives and Moves,
Growing Unnervingly,
Towards its Fate.

P. H. Brazier, "*The Tree of Life*" Oil on Linen, 23.6 x 15.7 in.

Introduction

"We must work the works of him who sent me while it is day; night is coming when no one can work."
JOHN 9:4 (NRSV)

"... Judas immediately went out. And it was night."
JOHN 13:30 (NRSV)

Several of these essays started life as papers presented to the Research Institute in Systematic Theology at King's College London. These seminars were held weekly, in term time, on the Tuesday morning, and featured papers presented by post-doctoral researchers and visiting lecturers/professors from colleges and university departments. The one-and-a-half-hours were split more or less evenly between the presentation of a paper and then a question-and-answer session. Therefore the paper was restricted to c.6,000 words.

In some instances some of the papers presented here were subsequently published in journals (usually necessitating shortening). Here are revised and much extended editions from the original papers, usually reflecting the questions asked by those attending, and dealing, systematically, with all the issues involved in the subject of the paper, which time and space mitigated against in the original presentation (and likewise space mitigated against lengthening when published in journals). Therefore, many of these papers have tripled in size to 15,000 words or more so as to develop the argument fully, extend the evidence submitted, give relevance to the questions asked at the seminars.

The majority of these papers are, in genre, academic theology and philosophy: pertinently, systematic theology. That is, involving the tools and techniques of philosophical analysis, through extensive questioning; systematic in the sense that theological truth is presented in an orderly, rational, and coherent manner, relating to the Christian faith. There are in addition some elements that can best be described as story, analogy, parable, and even as humor (sometimes somewhat acerbic, critical humor, even satire; these elements complement the systematic analysis, they illuminate). Some of these elements presented here were shared and discussed over an extended lunch in the refectory at King's College London after the seminars. Most Christians fail to see the humor in the Bible, indeed fail to see how humor can have a parabolic/analogic role to play in illumining God's truth; indeed C. S. Lewis noted in correspondence to a Mr. Lucas that he had learned from his wife, Joy Davidman—who had been born and raised an American Jew—how God's chosen people see humor in the Hebrew Bible (the Old Testament) where we Christians do not. Or we fail to perceive the paradoxical humor in a religious context.[1] These elements point to a form of narrative theology.

The value of systematic theology is in its attempt to gauge, analyze, and formulate propositions about God's truth. Parable, narrative, and analogy are also very important in conveying God's revelation and truth. The Prophet Nathan could expose King David to the truth of his actions by setting the king's adultery and the wasting of Bathsheba's husband in a story: a parable. Therefore, Nathan could identify a deeper level of truth than he could by merely stating the situation in the first person, by confronting David directly with the bare facts: such deeper truths are by their very nature theological. Where there is an element of parable, even humor, such theological excursions are minimal but are conceived of as sharp, probing, and pertinent exercises in theology and ethics. Therefore, in systematic theology, proposition, argument, and reason are key, they are of fundamental importance; but humor and narrative also have their place.

I. THE END TIMES: THE DAY AFTER TOMORROW

The Eschaton

What connects these essays is humanity's *telos*, its ultimate end—fed by numerous, disparate, and often contradictory *teloi*, a confusion of aims and progress generated by *fallen* humanity's chaotic and willful

---

[1] Lewis writing to Mr Lucas, Dec 6, 1956. Lewis, *Collected Letters, Vol. III*, 814–15.

Introduction

progress through history—and therefore the *eschaton*. The *eschaton* (from the Greek for "last" or "final things": *eschatos*; *eschatē*; *eschaton*) is, in Christian theology, the four last things: death, judgment, heaven, and hell. Whether applied individually to people as they die or to the end of the world is debatable, but we will all face death, followed by judgment—God's judgment—which decides our eternal fate: heaven or hell. We live in what appear to be the end times, that is, given the wars, rumors of wars, and the chaos of human society today, it appears that the end is near. Though it is important to remember that this was also the perception in the decades following the Reformation, and into the seventeenth century, especially in the context of the English Civil War: a period referred to as, "The world turned upside down."[2] Whatever God's timeframe is for the *eschaton*—and mere mortals are not entrusted with that knowledge (Mark 13:22; Matt 24:36)—we live in our relationship with the risen and ascended Christ *in the end times*, as if this is *the end times*. And the end times?—they are coming, the day after tomorrow, before we know what is happening . . . and night falls.

Multiple Ends

Given the Greek origins of the word,[3] there will be different, sometimes competing theories (Zoroastrianism, Baha'i, Rastafarian, Norse, Hindu, Buddhist, Aztec, Inca, Astrological, Transhumanist, Hegelian, Marxist, National Socialist, philosophical, sociological, psychological, . . .), about an *eschaton*, about end times and ultimate destination: and how we get there—teleology. However, the Judeo-Christian model is the direct result of revelation: how God Almighty, *El Shaddai*, the Lord, YHWH, will define and initiate the end of all things.

---

2   Originally from Acts 17:6, the phrase became common currency, derived from a published broadsheet, a folk ballad, entitled "The World Turned Upside Down," dated to the English Civil War and the Commonwealth. The folk ballad was a protest against the policies of the Parliamentary forces. In subsequent decades and centuries it widened in its criticism of the chaos unleashed on society, and was adopted by the developing left in politics; however, the original song and complaint focused on Oliver Cromwell's censorship and banning of Christmas!

3   Defined as "the divinely ordained climax of history," in 1935, by the Protestant theologian C. H. Dodd (1884–1973) from Greek *eskhaton*, neuter of *eskhatos*—the last, the furthest, the uttermost. Some see the Greek as, "The final event in the divine plan; the end of the world." See Dodd, *The Bible and Its Background* (1935); Dodd, *The Bible and the Greeks* (1935); Dodd, *The Parables of the Kingdom* (1935).

TOWARDS THE DAY AFTER TOMORROW

In the first half of the twentieth century, theologians and Bible scholars of various persuasions invented various terms to encompass their personal theories (speculative theologoumena) as to the *eschaton* being here and now (present hope), yesterday (restricted to Jesus' ministry), or solely in the future (*postmortem*): Realized Eschatology; Consistent Eschatology; Inaugurated Eschatology; Thoroughgoing Eschatology; Futuristic Eschatology; . . .). Many of these theories were driven by a sublimated fear of judgment, which their theory conveniently disposed of. Many twentieth-century theologians and philosophers who embraced a modern or liberal approach defined the *eschaton* in abstract, worldly, non-spiritual terms: demythologized, secularized, where the *eschaton* was about hope in *this* life and the negativity we find in other people, disapproval that judges and restricts our self-fulfillment—this is, of course, individualistic (and for many reflected the vanity of identity politics). Eschatology, in this context, can only be understood as an expectation of imminent events (sometimes initiated and acting as a result of God's incarnation: therefore, also, immanent).[4] On a more collective or societal basis, political commentators talk about a "secular *eschaton*," or "a species transition *eschaton*" (i.e., the crisis and death of a social order . . . or even of a civilization . . . or even the somewhat confused ideas from Transhumanists).[5] While various religious sects try to "imminentize the *eschaton*"—reducing or marginalizing, ultimately denying, the supernatural in an attempt to foreshadow or bring forward the end of all things to the present, to the "now," that moment of time which is for some all we can know—many talk of *the end of history*[6] (i.e., humanity has reached its zenith and can go no further, though it is difficult not to

---

4   For a general introduction and survey of this way of thinking, see, Sauter, *What Dare We Hope?: Reconsidering Eschatology.*

5   See *The Blackwell Guide to the Philosophy of Religion*, Pt. 4 Religion and Life, Ch. 11 Human Destiny, 245–65, specifically, 262.

6   As far as I am aware, this observation was coined by the free-market economist Francis Fukuyama. See, Fukuyama, *The End of History and the Last Man* (1992), developed on from his 1989 essay "The End of History?" Fukuyama claimed that the position Western humanity had reached in the late 1980s formed the endpoint of a sociocultural evolution, giving rise to the final form of human government. However, thirty years on this Western liberal democratic (consumerist) model is changing beyond Fukuyama's perceptions the world over and is under pressure and threat: Brexit, Donald Trump, fiscal chaos in the EU, resurgent nationalism, Vladimir Putin, Al Qaeda-Taliban-Islamic State, global warming and climate change, environmental degradation . . . !

Introduction

conclude that they are talking about Western, liberal humanity, assuming that the political elite and educated classes in the US and Europe represent all of humanity, all that there is to humanity, all that can be achieved by humanity), meanwhile the public generally—fed by disaster movies, apocalyptic drama series—speculates on "global catastrophic risk" and the "secular chaos" that would ensue, stories that echo something of an *eschaton*.[7] Does much of this chaotic speculation derive from sublimated guilt issuing from the abandonment of Christianity in the West?

What Is Certain?

The intellectual and popular culture speculation about multiple end times is a fragmentation of God's story, a dilution, embracing a wide range of often contradictory human/cultural meanings and interpretations; this, from an orthodox Christian perspective, and not to put too fine a point on it, in its refutation of God's revelation, is heterodox: it can only fairly be considered to be heresy. But we *are* meant to know something of what our end will be: we will die, we will be judged—heaven or hell awaits us with open arms, but we know not when, or how all will end. Even in this context, various modernist academics and clerics—depending on their acceptance of the supernatural and numinous . . . or not—often reduced the *eschaton* to just two concepts: death and heaven. This conformed, in a related manner, to popular religion. Many who might best be described as conforming to a contemporary Western form of faith, may subscribe to a *postmortem* nothingness (though defining nothing, or "no-thing," or "no *particular* thing" is fraught with difficulties), or they may subscribe to a more conventional belief, though still flawed, whereby when the individual dies he or she automatically finds him- or herself in a pleasant and warm embracing, non-threatening and inclusive, heaven, indeed a republic of heaven. However, there are two certainties in life. One is that we will die; the second is that we cannot escape God's judgment. This latter is the one absolute point of ontic inclusivity, which mocks the Western liberal obsession with identity politics and inclusivity (which is in many ways veiled exclusive tribalism): no one can escape, or delay, facing God, whatever their religious beliefs. We do not necessarily have control over the manner or time of our death; we cannot forestall or dictate the

---

7   See *The Blackwell Guide to the Philosophy of Religion*, Pt. 4 Religion and Life, Ch. 14 Religion and Politics, 305–26.

terms of God's judgment on us, we cannot plea bargain, however much we may desire favor and acceptance: but God's judgment is a forgiving judgment, if we can face it in uninhibited terms, stripped of all condition and pretense on our part. To do otherwise is to embrace hell in preference to heaven.

In many ways these essays and parables are about people and the world during what may be termed the post-historic era, which will witness the bringing in of God's judgment as civilized order begins to crumble: this may be seen as a divinely ordained preface to God's overt reign (biblical and apocalyptic), immediately preceding the end of the world: this end may be months in coming, or years, or decades . . . .

Judeo-Christian Revelation

Therefore, a key proposition is that the Judeo-Christian revelation on the *eschaton* is central to this work (and to all humanity—past, present, and future—whatever "time" there is left): Hebrew-Jewish eschatology focuses on proceedings and events in "the end of days" (*aḥarît ha-yāmîm*) as revealed in the Bible, but also in intertestamental Jewish thought, and the Jewish tradition that parallels the church. Whose name is written in the book of life? This should be the question to perplex humanity; that recording by name is the future informing us in the here-and-now of what will be—a form of realized eschatology. In this, the Book of Daniel complements the Book of Revelation. This reflects the dialectic that stands unresolved between the Judaism that continued after the Jesus-event and the witness of the believers (the apostles *et al.*) who wrote the New Testament, and those in the text that bear witness to the Jesus event, *who were Jews* (Paul, Stephen, John, Peter, Luke *et al.*): this does represent a dialectic that can only be resolved in the *eschaton*.[8]

---

8 The writers of the New Testament did not think of themselves as belonging to a different religion from the Old Testament authors. They all saw themselves as Jewish followers of the God of Israel. The New Testament authors, however, believed that Jesus was the Messiah who had inaugurated the new age. The danger here is anachronism: reading later Jewish-Christian issues back into biblical texts. The tensions between the pre-Jesus Jewish texts (Old Testament) and the texts by Jewish Jesus-followers (New Testament) developed into a dialectic reflected in later Jewish-Christian beliefs. We err to project the later Jewish-Christian parting of the ways back into a NT text.

II. AIMS AND OBJECTIVES

The aim of these essays is to demonstrate the diverse and divisive, socio-political and religio-cultural "*krises*" that bedevil humanity as it staggers teleologically into the *eschaton*. Perhaps this may stimulate and endorse discussion and (re)acceptance of a traditional/orthodox understanding of the *eschaton*—through a multi-perspective approach, framed by the discipline of systematic theology—aimed not just at the churches but a wider religious understanding, and also to inform the secular powers that now govern in the West. One consistency that might, to a greater or lesser degree, be demonstrated is how the world (John 15:18–19) works against the teleological progress of humanity towards salvation.

Objectively, "*Towards the Day after Tomorrow . . .*" consists of a series of essays analyzing, emphasizing, the human teleological "*krises*" leading up to the *eschaton*. This analysis focuses on the chaos and contradiction that is projected back into time from the end time. As a volume of essays, it is characterized by the breadth of subject and content unified by the orthodoxy of theological analysis, and the traditional model of the *eschaton* the work is grounded in. The *eschaton* is not looked at in disinterested, seemingly impartial, abstract terms, but examined in what theological sense we can make of how we (through the chaos of humanity's multiple *teloi*) are drawn into the end times, however long or short the delayed parousia may be.

We cannot justifiably separate Jewish and Christian revelation on the *eschaton* into their separate religious identities: an understanding of both as one entity, as a fusion, underpins this volume of essays: Hebrew as well as, Christian.

What unites these essays is the confused and sometimes contradictory *teloi*, which humanity generates as it limps in encroaching darkness towards its ultimate end. Therefore, each essay may seem to focus on a particular aspect of the teleological movement towards the *eschaton* and may seem to demonstrate a character different to the other essays: this is because of the actual confused, random, and conflicting socio-cultural beliefs and actions of tribal society—whether religious of otherwise

III. EXPLANATIONS, QUALIFICATIONS

A few terms and concepts do need to be explained, for various reasons, before we proceed. Some readers may not appreciate the full meaning and use of the terms used here, indeed some terms are used with widely different meanings according to which church denomination or academic grouping uses them. Furthermore, some concepts I have used for years and it cannot be assumed that all readers will assume the meaning inherent in their use (such as the pairing of freemasonry and feminism).

The Authority of the Bible

While much of the Bible is written in analogical and metaphorical language, it is imperative to remember that underpinning Scripture is God's truth, certainly about humanity and the human condition, and people's *teloi* and end goal. Scholars may analyze the words of Scripture, they may assert with confidence how a biblical book was constructed and developed, altered, by various authors, but the text has an authority that transcends the assorted writers/compilers.

Creation, Fall, Incarnation, Resurrection, Second Coming, and the Four Last Things

The heart of the Christian faith, the basics, are in some ways summarized by the creation and the *fall* into original sin set out in the Book of Genesis; by the incarnation-crucifixion-resurrection-ascension-second coming of God in Christ, as recorded and portrayed in the New Testament; specifically for our purposes the four "last things" from the Book of Revelation as well as the Gospels: apocalypse reveals the *eschaton*. Some of this may be obvious but it contradicts many modern theologians and churchmen, who have watered down the faith. First, God created everything out of nothing and sustains it. Second, that humanity, through its own fault, disobeyed God and was "infected" by original sin; furthermore we brought this on ourselves, and the predicament we find ourselves in is perilous. Third, God became incarnated as a human being, Jesus of Nazareth, the Christ, who was crucified for our sins and was resurrected, all to atone for our fall into original sin and restore us to a right relationship with God. Fourth, that this same Jesus Christ will return to judge all at the end of the world: death, judgment, heaven, and hell.

Atheism–Theism

A common misconception in society generally is that there is a quantifiable difference between religious people (usually assumed to be

Introduction

Christians) and self-proclaimed atheists. This has led to the simplistic argument that believers are saved, unbelievers damned. Belief, faith, can make a difference to the final outcome of a human life, but that is no guarantee of heaven. Only after death will we be truly known *as we are* (1 Cor 13:12) and therefore how we are to be judged. The Russian prophet and writer Dostoevsky posited a paradox, something of a puzzle: at times the person may claim to be atheistic, yet exude a sound understanding of God and eternity; at other times the individual may proudly believe, and scorn atheists, but exhibit a religious pride that appears to place him or her far from the love of God. At times, the person will claim atheism and die far from God (and from a traditional Western perspective face condemnation and an eternity in hell); at other times, the person may exhibit sound faith and be saved. What Dostoevsky posits is the risks of religion: bad religion condemns; good religion saves, proclamations of belief-unbelief may not always point to the final destination of each human. The pertinent question when we come across a declaration of atheism is, *which* God does the character not believe in? Likewise we may ask, *which* "god" is it that such-and-such a person claims to believe in, and will swear absolute allegiance to?

Law, the Moral Code, . . . and Human Responsibility

A fundamental axiom that underpins the Bible and this study is that there is a divinely ordained law—a natural law—that applies to humanity. Therefore, we can and do err, and this error constitutes sin; we contradict the will of God, we injure ourselves and others, and the environment. What is more, these errors—sin—can accumulate and set the human on a particular path that will change the person, and can lead, eschatologically, to heaven or hell. Therefore, many of us are not as we should be, our decisions are not unethical—amoral—or without value.

Contemporary Western societies and government implicitly reject the concept of natural (or God-given) law, substituting with their own legislation, which they then consider to be moral and good. The Russian writer (and Soviet dissident) Aleksandr Isaevich Solzhenitsyn understood this only too well from his experience of a dictatorial totalitarian Soviet-Marxist regime:

> At the present time it is widely accepted among lawyers that law is higher than morality—law is something which is shaped

> and developed, whereas morality is something inchoate and amorphous. This is not the case. The opposite is true: morality is higher than the law! Law is our human attempt to embody in rules a part of the moral sphere which is above us. We try to understand this morality, bring it down to earth and present it in the form of law. Sometimes we are more successful, sometimes less. Sometimes we have a mere caricature of morality, but morality is always higher than law.[9]

Morality is therefore above the law, and the law (enacted by human, state, legislatures) is often immoral (as judged by *El Shaddai*, YHWH); Atheists can claim to be moral, but from a Christian perspective, all good and right morality—including that of the atheist—issues from God..

God's moral law is fixed and immutable, yet subject to compassion and forgiveness issuing from the crucifixion-resurrection. Human law is variable, relativistic, and tribal: a common aphorism amongst the establishment and in Britain (the Westminster elite) from the early eighteenth century was that law was not fixed but a process. This elite invented or repealed laws at will to suit itself: autonomous ethics projected onto society as heteronomous.

Hegemonic Tribalism

For the last three hundred years or so, though essentially following the religious nihilism that constituted the English Civil War in the middle decades of the seventeenth century, the dominant religious story that has underpinned the body politic in Britain has in effect been hegemonic tribalism. The "official" religious canvas may have been Christian (i.e., Henry VIII's Church of England)—leastwise till the post-WWII era—but we live now in a post-Christian world that many see as anti-Christian). The current dominance of identity politics epitomises this rebellion. The two chief religio-political identities since the early eighteenth century may be named as Freemasonry and Feminism, and in the last two generations LGBTQ+ identity; since the late 1960s various seemingly obscure identities have also demanded respect and their share of the worldly success:

---

9   Aleksandr Isaevich Solzhenitsyn, *Warning to the West*, 45–46. These comments are from the first of three speeches given 30 June, 9 July and 15 July 1975 in Washington, DC in response to the award (1970) of the Nobel Prize for Literature. Though he spent much of his life imprisoned in a Soviet labor camp, he was deported from the Soviet Union in 1974.

Introduction

"Goths," "politicized vegans," with new identities seemingly being added every year. Though unlikely bedfellows (in particular, freemasons and feminists) they have set the religio-political agenda, which ensures that those who identify as such have more than their fair share of power and authority, status and wealth, that any criticism is stymied, with increasing legislation designed to oppress those outside their religio-tribal identity. In religious terms these identities are fluid and may appear to many as ideologically worlds apart, polar opposites, but they are complementary: they enhance each other. The aim of all is self-promotion, in many cases self-worship (hence the dominance of gender and sexuality issues, indeed dozens of self-proclaimed gender identities). The objectives for many may be different, but the result is the same. They can be seen, to a greater or lesser degree, as Machiavellian. All define the good in their own image and expect others to fall in line. All have sought to dominate the establishment, the political *status quo*, in one way or another. For example, feminists have been in the ascent since the late 1960s, while freemasons appear to be in decline: but the result is the same, despite their manifold differences. Eschatologically, the *telos* is defined by reference to self, and is self-reverential: salvation is in the here-and-now with a "god/goddess" being invoked—or not—if necessary, for endorsement and self-promotion. For all, morality and ethics are fluid and relative: again, autonomous ethics projected onto society as heteronomous—the end justifies the means. And their ethics are to a greater or lesser degree post-Christian. Is there a unifying religious identity that can be applied to these various tribes? Consider neo-pagan secular-liberal humanism?

Neo-Pagan Secular-Liberal Humanism

As deeply entrenched as the pagan religion of ancient Rome, neo-pagan secular-liberal humanism is a polytheistically syncretistic, self-reverential, self-referential religion that expounds relativistic, autonomous, consequentialist ethics and worships an infinite number of "gods," resulting in no-god. This is the religion of neo-pagan secular-liberal humanists, founded in the 1960s implicitly and anonymously originating in contradiction to what was taken to be the prevailing Christian religion and culture in Britain, Western Europe, and America at the time, though as a form of anti-Christian rebellion elements of this religion had been building for some time, especially in the Enlightenment, and before that in the English Civil War, and prior to that in Henry VIII's sequestration of the church for the legitimization of his own sexual predilections and gender politics. Like the freemasons, the exponents of neo-pagan secular-liberal humanism hide behind a veil of un-named secrecy. Christianity has been pushed—progressively over the last fifty years—into taking its place alongside other religions, where all are subservient to the beliefs of the secular nation state: "We don't do God" stated a leading director of strategy and communications in the British government (1997–2010).[10]

Why pagan? Strictly speaking in the sense of outside of the Judaeo-Christian revelation and faith. However, an important distinction needs to be made between pre-Christian and post-Christian paganism. C. S. Lewis[11] commented that where it was often being asserted (in the immediate post-WWII years) that Britain was "slipping . . . descending . . . regressing"[12] into paganism, he was quite adamant:

> When grave persons express their fear that England is relapsing into Paganism, I am tempted to reply, "Would that she were." For I do not think it at all likely that we shall ever see Parliament opened by the slaughtering of a garlanded white bull in the House of Lords or Cabinet Ministers leaving sandwiches in Hyde Park as an offering for the Dryads. If such a state of affairs came about, then the Christian apologist would have something to work on. For a Pagan, as history shows, is a man eminently convertible to Christianity. He is essentially, the pre-Christian, or sub-Christian, religious man. The Post-Christian man of our own day differs from him as much as a divorcée differs from a virgin. The Christian and the Pagan have much more in common with one another than

---

10   See, "Campbell interrupted Blair as he spoke of his faith: 'We don't do God,'" See: https://www.telegraph.co.uk/news/uknews/1429109/Campbell-interrupted-Blair-as-he-spoke-of-his-faith-We-dont-do-God.html.

As powerful as a Soviet apparatchik or political officer, Alastair Campbell was noted to utter this on several occasions to steer the topic of conversation with the media or with other world leaders and government representatives, away from religion, even publically censoring the Prime Minister Tony Blair.

11   C. S. Lewis was amongst the first to coin the term "post-Christian" at a time when Britain still perceived its civic pageantry and public religion, and its people, as Christian, first using the term "post-Christian" publically in an address on November 29, 1954: Lewis's inaugural lecture at Cambridge, Nov. 29, 1954. C. S. Lewis, "*De Descriptione Temporum*," 9–25.

12   Lewis, "Is Theism Important?" 136–38.

either has with the writers of the *New Statesman*; and those writers would of course agree with me.[13]

"Pagan" therefore refers to this form of religion and religious myths from outside of, in our instance, the Jewish and Christian traditions. It is important to remember that the term "pagan" is not necessarily used with derogatory intent, nor as a term of abuse. Traditionally the term simply referred to those peoples and cultures outside of the Jewish and Christian traditions: that is, Oriental, Middle Eastern, Indian, and European tribes and nations, but particularly in the ancient world (Greek and Roman philosophy and literature, religion, and mythology) and especially the religion and mythology of the North European tribes (Celtic, Norse, etc.), with whom the name pagan is most often associated. Ancient paganism was an open religion, though blind *in varying degrees* to God, and God's purposes, though open in degree to *God's revelation* (as C. S. Lewis realized and analyzed in-depth.)[14] Ancient paganism was pre-Christian, but ever moving towards the complete revelation of God in Jesus Christ. In the West today, neo-pagan refers not so much to a regression into ancient pre-Christian paganism but transformation into a new post-Christian paganism. Essentially the difference between a pre-Christian pagan and the contemporary post-Christian pagan is one of movement, experience, and meaning (hence Lewis's analogy with a virgin and a divorcee): the pre-Christian or ancient pagan was *moving towards* in his/her theistic beliefs; the post-Christian or neo-pagan is *moving away* in his/her atheistic beliefs and liberal indulgence.

Neo-pagan is liberal in the sense of freedom from rules and regulations (though not anarchistic, believers/practitioners merely invent their own rules), it is in essence secular, and focuses on the human, even when invoking "gods"/"goddesses," and is evangelical in the sense of the promotion of identity politics (often through state legislation). It is humanist in the sense that although these people are innately religious, they espouse a rationalist outlook, a system of belief characterized by a primary importance to human rather than divine or supernatural matters. Although essentially from the Renaissance (where human needs and values were considered before God), today's Western,

13   Lewis, "Is Theism Important?" 138.
14   See, for example, P. H. Brazier, "C. S. Lewis and Christological Prefigurement," 742–75.

contemporary humanism is now deeply secular (i.e., rejecting religious or spiritual matters, not subject to or bound by religious rule) considering the needs of the individual as more important than traditional religions and religious beliefs. At the heart of neo-pagan secular-liberal humanism is sexual freedom, sex and sexuality raised to something of an intense emotional high; religion is then invented to complement and complete the enjoyment of this sexual freedom.

Liberal and Modernism

"Liberalism" is often seen as a contentious and problematic word—often it appears to generate an emotional response, may be considered pejorative, and may also be invoked in an equally subjective manner. In this work, the words "Liberal" and "Liberalism" with an initial capital letter are used strictly in the context of theological Liberalism in the church: this is a position that more often than not denies (but not always) the incarnation and resurrection, seeking to promote the idea of Jesus of Nazareth as an ordinary human being; furthermore, a Liberal theological position may not believe in God (with a capital "G") but happily allow people to believe in "gods" of their own making, their own invention (this is a position that can be identified with some l/Liberals in the nineteenth century, as well as in the twentieth and early twenty-first centuries).

Much that constitutes theological Liberalism since the eighteenth century has claimed freedom not only from traditional dogmas and creeds but also in the analysis of and value accorded to Scripture. Such theology was to a large degree formulated in the light of what were considered advances in the natural sciences and philosophy—the spirit of the Age of Reason and the Enlightenment. In this work, when cited with a lower case initial letter ("liberal"), the term refers to liberalism in politics, society, and culture generally, in ethics and morality, in the nineteenth and twentieth centuries. Therefore, a distinction needs to be drawn between Liberalism as a theological movement or belief system and what is often euphemistically called a liberal perspective in society generally. The term "Modernism"/"Modernist" can be seen in very much the same context as Liberalism, and philosophical atheism.

Introduction

1970s Liberal Anglican

In essence a form of identity politics, the term "1970s Liberal Anglican" appears to have been coined locally, here in South-West London, by a Church of England priest writing to *The Church Times*,[15] where he identified himself as such and lamented how the progress represented by his education and training as "*a 1970s liberal Anglican*" was being eroded. The priest was looking back nostalgically at his theological education and formation in the 1970s, where the gospel was re-written to accommodate the socio-sexual, cultural-political revolution of the late 1960s. This also encompassed a Liberal theological agenda that questioned the supernatural, the divinity of Christ, and the authority of the Bible, and refuted most of the propositions within the Creed. Politically *1970s liberal Anglican* proclaimed the advancement of left-wing politics, governmental control of charity and the good in society (funded by taxpayers), and an LGBTQ+ agenda, along with an ever numerous legion of other forms of identity politics.

IV. PART ONE
TOWARDS AN UNDERSTANDING OF THE ARRIVAL OF THE END TIMES

A Delayed Nativity . . . What If? The Eschaton Prefigured

The first essay here is a parable, which is to be considered narrative theology: the incarnation—on the nativity. So why start a book about the *eschaton* with the nativity? Because the coming of the Christ into the world, God in human flesh, is quite literally the begin of the end. God despaired of humanity and allowed it to go its own way (Acts 14:16; cf. Rom 1:24–25?), but God now has entered into the human world, intimately; the grey, imprecise middle-ground is thrown into sharp focus: light and shadows, black and white. This is the preface to the *eschaton*: Christ has come to separate out, sift (Judg 7:4; Isa 30:28; Amos 9:9; Luke 22:31), thresh (1 Chr 21:20; Isa 27:12; 28:28; 41:15; Hos 10:11; Mic 4:13; 1 Cor 9:10), to judge and assign, to forgive those who are able to be

---

15   Revd Andrew Wakefield (1956–2016), Letter to *The Church Times*, July, 21 2006; see also, on the perceived decline and threat to 1970s Liberal Anglicanism, Revd Maggie Guillebaud, Letter to *The Church Times*, Aug, 13 2008. See also, https://en.wikipedia.org/wiki/Liberal_Christianity.

forgiven: this is at the heart of Christology. To some, the theologian Karl Barth's Christology is too realized: that is, over-realized eschatology—because a Barthian position is that in coming into the world, and being sacrificed, Jesus Christ answers completely the problem of sin. Colin Gunton paraphrasing Barth on the significance and importance of the incarnation commented,

> For Barth this is realized eschatology because the end in the form of Jesus Christ really has come amongst us—this is in such a way that the human situation and condition is changed forever. The coming of Christ changes the situation and condition of humanity universally. Every single human being would be in a different place had He not come. This realized eschatology applies to everyone whether or not they accept it: this is God with us and this is universal—it means everyone, even though only the Christians seem on the surface to accept this . . . . In many ways this is the language of a realized eschatology—the end has come, almost . . . . It is a realized eschatology but it is only a beginning; it is a realized eschatology that also has a future eschatology to come.[16]

Human sin and death is nailed to the cross, Jesus of Nazareth, the Christ of the triune God, is the one to be punished and killed, sin is therefore over: what is there left? Hence the importance of the incarnation as the beginning of the end, but also the question that some theologies may be over-realized. What is left for the human to do? The judgment from the end times is in the here-and-now. This, it is often agreed amongst orthodox and traditional theologians, is over-realized, because we surely should work out our salvation in this life, *through faith*; or we reject our salvation in this life: all becomes clear upon our death. That clarity is a form of the judgment of God on us and it is clear that we may end up in heaven . . . or in hell. So the beginning of the end is with the incarnation, and the condition of God's arrival: the nativity, the occasion of Christ's birth.

The point of this first essay, "A Delayed Nativity—What If? The *Eschaton* Prefigured," is to assert the starting point of the *eschaton*, and how miraculous it was. There are countless tiny miracles, unexpected events, often outside of human control or interference, that for hundreds of years led to this single momentous point in time, a point that could have so easily have gone wrong, or been delayed by the most obscure of events.

---

16   Gunton, *The Barth Lectures*, 149, 156–58.

Introduction

A butterfly flapping its wings off the coast of West Africa may indeed trigger a series of apparently random events that leads to a hurricane over the Caribbean.[17] God did not charge into creation and impose God's-self; therefore despite the attempts by evil to subvert salvation, God did enter to start the end process, but came quietly, surreptitiously, subverting the powers of this world. Perhaps this was like a game of chess, where one player—God—has to quietly plan, achieve an advantage towards the point of incarnation, without the other player—Satan—realizing fully, and consistently, what is going on, so that he can be outsmarted, even if at certain stages Satan believes he has won. Given the length, and complexity of human history that God worked through to achieve this moment of incarnation, to bring in the beginning of the end, a delayed parousia is but small compared to the eons of earth and human history.

"A Delayed Nativity" is narrative theology, a story based on the idea, "What if circumstances had dictated a delay in the incarnation?" The three-thousand-year history of the ancient Hebrew people and the Jews is of paramount importance, but even the Romans had their role—unknowingly—to play (and if we read the Old Testament it is clear that the ancient Hebrews were not always obedient to God's will, but over time, they did conform, gradually, leading eventually, after much molding and persuasion, to the point of the incarnation). We noted earlier Colin Gunton on Barth, on the coming of the Christ, that "every single human being would be in a different place had *He* not come,"[18] therefore this parable places human history as diametric to history as we know it, but still the Christ comes, and events converge. This story is offered as a consideration of just how miraculous the incarnation/nativity was as an historic event, and how it demonstrates the beginning of the end of all things. The events in this story could be seen to have happened in our reality (a differing timeline?), or on another world in a far-flung corner of the galaxy, where similar humanoids needed redeeming! A considerably

---

17   Invented by the American meteorologist Edward N. Lorenz (1917–2008), the Butterfly Effect highlights the possibility that small causes may have momentous effects. See: http://www.scholarpedia.org/article/Butterfly_effect).

Also, "In chaos theory, the butterfly effect is the sensitive dependence on initial conditions in which a small change in one state of a deterministic nonlinear system can result in large differences in a later state:" Boeing, "Visual Analysis of Nonlinear Dynamical Systems: Chaos, Fractals, Self-Similarity and the Limits of Prediction." *Systems* 4.4, 37.

18   Gunton, *The Barth Lectures*, 156.

shorter version of "A Delayed Nativity" was originally published locally, at the church my wife and I attend, as part of some study notes on the nativity for a theology discussion group on January 9, 2012.

V. PART TWO
TOWARDS AN UNDERSTANDING OF THE EMERGENCE OF THE END TIMES

Karl Barth:
"Krisis," War, & Expressionism—An Eschatological Encounter

A serious doctrinal essay that is in effect an exercise in systematic theological media studies (the medium being Fine Art[19]), Karl Barth owed as much to the artistic movement of Expressionism in Central Europe in the first third of the twentieth century as to any theological and philosophical influences from the eightieth and nineteenth centuries. As a young Swiss Reformed Church minister, in a poor working-class parish, in the heart of war-torn Europe, Karl Barth, reacted passionately against the stagnant, stable, and condescending malaise of nineteenth-century liberal neo-Protestantism he had been schooled and trained in. Poverty, bad industrial relations, and the First World War blew apart the lukewarm religiosity of the *status quo.* Along with his friend and fellow minister Eduard Thurneysen, he set about a revolution in eschatological thinking: "*Krisis,*" judgment, the victory of God over the power of evil—ideas, concepts, and realities that focused these young rebel minds. Expressionism in the visual arts parallels and influences this eschatological existential angst and "*krisis.*" A rebellion that focuses on Barth's commentary on the *Epistle to the Romans* (*Der Römerbrief,* 1919 and 1921). Here we find the seeds of the mature Barth's eschatology, even his over-realized eschatology, as it is sometimes critiqued. That Barth is considered stylistically an Expressionist is nothing new, however, here we focus not on his theological language (and the parallels in central-European literature), but the contemporary Expressionistic visual arts. This paper addresses two questions: To what extent is Barth's use of Expressionism part of the prevailing *zeitgeist* in the visual arts? Secondly, was Barth an iconoclast? Considering Barth's work in an artistic-cultural

---

19   Why Fine Art in particular? In the 1970s, I studied at art college, culminating in a B.A. Hons degree in Fine Art; then to teach for six years in a London art college.

Introduction

context (the visual, fine arts) shows how his uncompromising criticism of modernism (both artistic and theological) in both the Expressionistic style of *Der Römerbrief* and the classical German of the *Kirchliche Dogmatik* was in many ways prophetic, and formed a crucial part of his evolving eschatology (a doctrine that paralleled the "*krisis*" in war-torn Europe, especially in the inter-war years), the influence of which can be seen in his mature work.

The original edition, the genesis of this paper, was presented fourteen years ago to the Research Institute in Systematic Theology at King's College London on 23 November 2004; a shortened edition was then published in the German periodical, *Zeitschrift für Dialektische Theologie*.[20] This edition is much extended, expanded, and updated with new research.

A Human Generated Eschaton:
The Slave Trade, the Holocaust, and Abortion—
The Delusions of Religious Atheism

Death is central and primary to the *eschaton*. Ultimately we are in God's hands and cannot avoid death. When humanity takes control of death the results are more often than not demonic: whether death is self-inflicted or forced onto others constitutes a tyranny—where the perpetrators then invent socio-cultural, religio-political justification for their actions. This is a paper about what used to be called man's-inhumanity-to-man (though it is important to remember the salutary truism that *women are no better than men; men are no worse than women*: gender wars are usually highly selective in rendering the other sex inferior or more culpable than the self-righteous accuser). This paper is about the human capacity to objectify, to dehumanize, and to create beliefs and politics to justify inflicting death in the form of mega-holocausts (often achieved using chemical weapons, onto others, to pass judgment on others, define and denigrate by spurious tribal criteria, then to use, abuse, and kill: this is a human-centered pseudo *eschaton*, issuing from the *fall*, original sin. This is to usurp God's judgment (Rom 12:19; cf. Deut 32:35: *eritis sicut Deus*). A theology of death is analyzed here relating to three post-Reformation mega-holocausts, (all three had been framed legally and with popular

---

20   Brazier, "Barth and Expressionism—Some Further Considerations," (2005) 34–52.

"democratic" support): first, slavery, the Western slave trade in the sixteenth to nineteenth centuries; second, the holocaust of the Jews in the 1940s by the Nazis; and third, the holocaust of the unborn—abortion—in the later twentieth century and early twenty-first century.

The original much shorter edition of this paper was presented to the Research Institute in Systematic Theology at King's College London on June 16, 2009, then to be published in the Dominican journal, *New Blackfriars* in 2011.[21] This edition loosely based on the original paper is much extended, expanded, and updated.

The Just War Theory and the 9/11 Wars: A Biblical and Eschatological Consideration

The attacks on America by Al Qaida on September 11, 2001, ushered in what many refer to as the 9/11 wars—a global conflict between the West and the Middle East, between the resurgence of paganism in North America and Europe (and some of their former colonial lands, globally), on the one hand, and a revitalized fundamentalist Islam wherever it may manifest itself globally. It is often said that the first casualty of war is truth. If this is so, then the second casualty of war is righteousness. In response to 9/11 Western leaders subverted the Christian Just War Theory and turned it from a *Limited Defensive Response* to a *Pre-Emptive Absolute Response*: if threatened, get your response in quick, absolute destruction on the perceived enemy before the first shot is fired. War is a prefigurement of the *eschaton*; indeed, according to Scripture, war will usher in the *eschaton*; but humanity often subverts the death and judgment of war to its own ends. Given this new, re-defined just war theory, how does it stand up to a biblical, theological, and eschatological analysis? How will the West stand up to this sifting (Judg 7:4; Isa 30:28; Amos 9:9; Luke 22:31) when faced by the judgment of God, how righteous is the West in its global policies? From a strictly Christocentric perspective the only option is to turn the other cheek when threatened, to pour shame on the terrorists, in an attempt to generate reconciliation; from an eschatological perspective we must hold our nerve, hold on to a reasoned and considerate response, weigh the consequences of our actions before Almighty God, the Lord.

---

21   Brazier, "A Theology of Death: The Slave Trade, the Holocaust and Abortion— The Delusions of Religious Atheism." *New Blackfriars* 92.1039 (2011) 285–307.

Introduction

However, the modern/liberal West's redefined just war theory asserts that you get your retaliation in first or you don't survive.

"The Just War Theory and Terrorism: A Biblical and Eschatological Consideration" was presented to the Research Institute in Systematic Theology at King's College London on June 29, 2010, then to be published in *The Evangelical Review of Society and Politics* in 2012.[22] This edition is much extended, expanded, and updated.

A Simpsons' Eschatology:
Towards an Understanding of **Postmortem Status Purgatus**— *Eternal Life and Human Rebellion*

"A Simpson's Eschatology" is a serious doctrinal essay that is, in effect, an exercise in systematic theological media studies (the medium being animated film). It is aimed at examining the eschatological *telos* of humanity, and the stubborn willful myopia of unrepentant people. Theological media studies is still, to some extent, in its infancy, and still regarded as somehow inferior to actual or real theology, especially systematic theology. Churches will hold discussion groups around a film or a television program or a book (most Church of England parishes run a book club—which is grounded in theological media studies!) discussing what theology can be read from a program, and assessing how the medium (film, TV, or a book) may help or hinder Christian discipleship, and so on. Popular culture is endemic and deeply influential: often for bad reasons. The American animated series *The Simpsons* is widely misunderstood. It is not simply a comic presentation of American life. It is—I believe—actually a picture of hell, . . . or is it purgatory? Or in the absence of purgatory, *purgation* (1 Cor 15:52?), or is it a no-man's-land between heaven and hell? These are those who do not realize they are dead, who won't let go of this life and have rendered themselves unfit for heaven, and languish in what appears to be an upper level of hell . . . or the fringes of heaven? Do some who are changed move into heaven? But are these heaven-bound a woefully small number, whereas the overwhelming majority languish in this hellish state with no way out, unable to lay down their crowns (Rev 4:10)?—only to sink eventually deeper and further into hell? *Postmortem status purgatus*: or judgment, purgation, and the loving

---

22   Brazier, "The Just War Theory and the 9/11 Wars: A Biblical and Eschatological Consideration." *The Evangelical Review of Society and Politics* 6.1–2 (2012) 107–28.

purposes of God, "A Simpson's Eschatology" is intended as a humorous doctrinal examination of how the human defines its end result—framed by its teleology—eschatologically. *The Simpsons* should be seen as a parabolic warning to viewers of the dangers of eschatological judgment and humanity's *postlapsarian* default position, whereby we stubbornly define our final resting place (i.e., a doctrine of infernal voluntarism[23])—unless we accept God's forgiving judgment and what the translation to heaven involves.

Originally sketched-out for presenting to the Research Institute in Systematic Theology at King's College London (and discussed with some of the doctoral students over lunch after a seminar, c. 2010–11!), a couple of paragraphs about the characters from *The Simpsons* as lost souls featured in a review article in the journal *Sehnsucht*,[24] but the paper here was only recently completed.

The God of the Epileptic:
Postlapsarian Exile, Affliction, and the Sufferance of Salvation

Epilepsy can inform and shape—perhaps subtly, subliminally—an individual's implicit understanding of eschatology (this will often seem to be different to the eschatological beliefs of the average academically impartial, seemingly disinterested and neutral, theologian whose brain is not epileptic). An epileptic will often demonstrate certain nuanced details in his/her thought arguably giving a more dynamic and truer understanding of the eschatological reality that humanity occupies, and the judgment that we all will face. In many instances, epilepsy can still be considered to be something of a taboo subject, along with death: as a seizure builds, the sufferer is gripped by a sense of crisis, which can affect anyone close by, observing. More pertinently, does the condition of epilepsy allow the triune God to impart, to generate in the mind, a sounder eschatological understanding than many ordinary people demonstrate? Contrary to the popular view that epilepsy is an unfortunate illness that occasionally troubles the individual, a consideration of

---

23   Buenting (ed.), *The Problem of Hell: A Philosophical Anthology*. See also, Sickler, "Infernal Voluntarism and 'The Deep Courtesy of Heaven,'" 163–78.

24   Brazier, "Review Essay: Hell and Damnation, Freedom and Responsibility. Joel Buenting, (ed.), *The Problem of Hell: A Philosophical Anthology*, and, Jordan C. Ferrier, *Calvin and C. S. Lewis: Solving the Riddle of the Reformation*." *Sehnsucht* Vol. 7/8 (2013–14) 123–33.

epilepsy and the profound effect the condition has on the mind of an epileptic is crucial in understanding eschatological theology. How recurrent seizures affect the precise nature of theological beliefs is an open question yet to be examined. However, epilepsy may under certain circumstances be considered to be eschatological because epilepsy can foster dualistic, binary thinking, and as such leads to an inclination towards an eschatological way of seeing the world; in addition, there is a sense in many epileptics of the need for urgency in decision making, in dealing with a crisis, a sense that everything is coming to a head, that judgment is coming (these thoughts often precede seizures of varying intensities). This may be considered a particular interpretation of eschatology when most people do not concern themselves with the crisis of life and the risk of eternal judgment. Epilepsy can lift people out of a worldly complacency. Such beliefs are profoundly eschatological and, to a degree, dualistic: light and dark, heaven and hell, good and bad, ecstatic and nihilistic, either-or: in a word, dialectic. Dualism, issuing from the epilepsy, accounts—in part—for this paradoxical antinomy. Epilepsy is not an inconvenient illness that occasionally disables the individual. An epileptic brain operates differently from a so-called "normal" brain. Epileptically conditioned beliefs significantly alter the superficial religious background (characterized by a relatively trite theological anthropology). Why? First, all epileptic seizures constitute a near-death experience: everything goes, then the brain slowly "re-boots," and the mind becomes aware of itself again, and tries to piece together the shattered sense of identity and reality. Second, epileptics are often forced into the position of outsiders. People around epileptics fear a seizure, not just because they do not know how to cope with it, but it unnerves them—they fear losing their own mind, not being in control, and they fear the risk of death (SUDEP: sudden unexplained death from epilepsy). Outsiders, like lepers in the biblical world of Jesus, or the blind, the lame, the disabled, who were ostracized from the Jerusalem temple cult and religion, either love Jesus, or loath him: the gospel sees such matters in terms of light and dark, either-or, angels or demons, heaven or hell. Such is the case with epileptics, even if the condition is relatively well controlled. It may be speculated that this is why the marginalized, the afflicted, the suffering outcasts, saw Jesus and responded strongly, either one way or the other. They did not respond to Jesus with indifference (as did the two thieves crucified either side of Jesus: *Yeshua, Messiah, Lord*: Luke 23:39–43). Post seizure, the world still remains the same, but there has been a change in the person; this is movement, either the movement towards salvation or, for some, a movement away from salvation into damnation. This can be seen as an existential eschatological crisis, conditioned by epilepsy, by the seizure. This suffering, this affliction, is to a degree—though certainly not always—a form of Christlikeness that separates the individual from polite society, even respectable religious classes, and often renders irrelevant the Western obsession with consumerism and fashionable identity politics.[25]

Originally a much shorter edition of this paper was presented to the Research Institute in Systematic Theology at King's College London on October 30, 2007 (unpublished); this edition is much extended, expanded, and updated. I am currently working on developing the subject of theology and epilepsy into a book: *Sacred Disease : Wounded Healer: The God of the Epileptic.*

---

25   Hilary, my wife, has severe, complex, and intractable temporal-lobe and generalized epilepsy. She was in hospital with the epilepsy when we met in 1982, to marry six months later. Thirty-seven years on we still carry the epilepsy, which needs constant attention, of being aware, as seizures are unpredictable.

PART ONE
TOWARDS AN UNDERSTANDING OF THE ARRIVAL OF THE END TIMES

1

A Delayed Nativity ... What If?
The *Eschaton* Prefigured

*Therefore the LORD himself shall give you a sign;
Behold, a virgin shall conceive, and bear a son, and shall call his
name Immanuel.*

ISAIAH 7:14

*... Mary was greatly troubled at his words and wondered what
kind of greeting this might be. But the angel said to her, "Do not be
afraid, Mary; you have found favor with God. You will conceive
and give birth to a son, and you are to call him Jesus. He will be
great and will be called the Son of the Most High. The Lord God
will give him the throne of his father David, and he will reign over
Jacob's descendants forever; his kingdom will never end."*

LUKE 1:29–33

I. A BIBLICAL HOLOCAUST

The Barley harvest was gathered in. Crucially there was just enough left over to pay the tax. The Romans were due in two weeks and just as plans were being laid to celebrate, to feast and sing and dance in thanks to the Lord God, a stranger appeared in Nazareth. It was Ruth. No one had seen her for what must have been four years. She looked old, weary, belying the seventeen harvests she had witnessed. Her mother wept and screamed in joy, and in shock at what she saw. The signs of face paint were just discernible, Ruth having scrubbed and scrubbed her skin raw to erase the traces of what indicated her status as a sex-slave. Taken in lieu of taxes her parents could not pay to the Romans, they had wept in fear as to what would become of her as their thirteen-year-old daughter rode away on a horse, behind a centurion, her small arms wrapped around his waist. She had been taken for General Felix. But now she was back. She stood frightened and alone, sick and nauseous as the abuse she had suffered for four years swept over her; she looked at the faces of the people she had grown up with. The town shunned her. Her mother screamed and shunned her. The rabbis passed her by, as though she did not exist. They knew what she was; her protestations that every time was rape fell on deaf ears: she had been owned by General Felix and he did with her as he pleased—as a thirteen-year-old child, and now as a young woman. But she could take no more of the obscene depravity of her benefactor. She ran away. She crept out in the dead of night and stole away pretending to be one of the servants: then walked, barefoot, wrapping herself round with a filthy, discarded horse blanket, walked the two hundred miles home to Nazareth, avoiding the main roads and skirting round villages and towns, scavenging what she could to eat. This had taken her over two months. Within days of her absence Felix had sent troops to Nazareth to search for her: they found her not. But the Nazarenes feared what would happen if she did return.

Ruth had returned. The neighbors wanted her away, anywhere but in Nazareth—before news got out and Felix's troops returned. She stayed in her parents' house, never straying out. As an unclean she was not allowed by the local Rabbis into the synagogue. Rumors were rife; excrement was thrown at the house. And then they came. General Felix had caught word from his spies of Ruth's return. The cohort rode in and went straight up to the house; Ruth was taken, bound, and thrown over the back of a horse, behind the centurion, who ordered the massacre from the saddle. And her parents, and the other seven children, were run-through with the sword and the house torched. They did not stop there. Troops ringed the small town. No one could escape. Every house was burned; all the inhabitants put to the sword. In a small house on the outskirts lived Joachim and Anne, and their daughter. At the sound of the slaughter and with the acrid stench of burning flesh they hastily gathered together a few belongings and made for the door intending to go into the woods. But the troops, who had ringed the town, stopped them. Six-year-old Mary tried to hide in her mother's skirts. Joachim blocked the doorway. He was cut down first. Anne pleaded on her knees—she knew from her vision that Mary was to be someone special, very special, to the LORD—but to no avail: Anne and Mary were both slaughtered and the house torched....

II. TWO MILLENNIA LATER

The days were short, darkness fell all too soon. As the rain turned to sleet and the biting wind cut through the rags wrapped around the women, many of them with infants strapped to their backs, the tradesman's entrance was finally opened for them. They went in, gathered their buckets and mops, dusters and polish, empty black plastic bags for rubbish, ready to start the night's work.

Mary knew her time was near, but like the other women, the untouchables, she had to keep working. Later, Joseph had finished his night-shift on the building site so he came to meet her. He waited outside the corporate concrete, steel, and plate-glass building till she appeared. Clearly things were not right; she was beginning to go into labor. But where could they go? The office block she cleaned, with nearly two dozen other women, was next door to the Temple of Diana. This massive temple had stood for hundreds of years, on the site of successive Roman temples. Dedicated to the goddess Diana, and in alignment with the Temple of Apollo, the Temple of Diana was atop of Ludgate Hill, in the City of Londinium.

Joseph shepherded Mary with all the care he could muster over to the demonstration outside and to the side of the Temple of Diana. All of the demonstrators were Roman citizens—no one else would have been allowed to demonstrate—indeed, two weeks earlier, a Jewish preacher (recognized by the Star of David tattooed, by law, on his forehead) had actually stood on the steps of the temple and read aloud from the Book of the Prophet Isaiah. He preached that one was coming after him whose sandal latch he was not worthy to undo, he that was to come would baptize them with water and with fire! This prophet was known, and mocked with amusement, but now, to do this on the steps of the goddesses' temple . . . ! Members of the Praetorian elite rushed him, hacked him down immediately with their traditional short Roman swords, then shot him in the head. The demonstrators—demanding changes to the land ownership conditions, and the rights to personal wealth, for Roman citizens suffering a heavy tax burden—had been interrogated to know if they had supported this Jew-prophet. The city of Londinium was one massive building site—in preparation, barely thirty years away, for the two thousandths anniversary of the final conquest and subjugation of Britannia, under Emperor Claudius. Two triumphal arches were under construction at each side of Ludgate Hill, one in remembrance of the Emperor "god" Claudius, the other for his general, Aulus Plautius.

III. BEHOLD, A VIRGIN SHALL CONCEIVE, AND BEAR A SON, AND SHALL CALL HIS NAME IMMANUEL (ISAIAH 7:14)

Joseph and Mary asked the demonstrators for shelter: could they take them in? Mary was now in labor. But they refused, leastwise, a small group who often dominated the debate refused them entry into the tented encampment, precisely because of what had happened to the prophet, whose blood still stained the steps of Diana's Temple. No untouchables were allowed into the demonstrators encampment, certainly no Jews—by law, by decree!

A middle-aged man, immaculately dressed, wearing an expensive suit, his sallow complexion giving him away as a Greek, his clothes and manner that of a financier, a banker, hated by the demonstrators, this man sidled up to them, surreptitiously whispering to them, "Come. Now. Quick, I can give you shelter." They walked round behind the demonstrator's encampment, to the rear of a tall stainless steel building. "No!" said Joseph, "No, we can't go in there!" It was The Exchange. All Roman banking and financial transactions focused onto this one building. All transactions were scrutinized, approved, or rejected, for the whole of Britannia. This delayed matters financial—this was one of the complaints by the demonstrators, the state control of the market, the state subsidy of the market (although the luxury that they were allowed to hold their demonstration, being Roman citizens, while others would have been executed for demonstrating, was lost on them). Nicolaides the Greek reassured them. He worked in the Exchange, a city trader and banker, he could get them into the basement through a small rear door: "You must come, look, your wife is about to drop!" So as clandestinely as possible, they entered the tiny rear door, descending three flights of stairs, Nicolaides unlocking and entering a door into a store room, spreading out sacks and computer printout papers for Mary to lie down on. She insisted on turning, to kneel on all fours, as the labor pains gripped her.

1. A Delayed Nativity . . . What If?

"Don't worry," said Nicolaides reassuringly, "No one can hear us down hear."

Mary's screams were loud; but no one came. Eventually, as Joseph held her, she gave birth. It was quick, as was expected for a sixteen-year-old, the long hours of physical work, cleaning, helping. And she brought forth a son, her first-born, and named him Jesus, as the Angel Gabriel had commanded when, nine months earlier, he had visited her on the tented encampment, the Jewish ghetto, around the banks of the River Lea, East of Londinium. The puzzlement at this virginal conception from God being matched by Joseph's initial rejection of her, till her prayers were answered and Gabriel had visited Joseph.

IV. FIRST VISITORS

"Sshh!" ordered Nicolaides. There were clearly sounds coming from the stairwell. The door opened gradually. A voice called out in a whisper, "Here, they're here." A tall elderly African Jewish women came in followed by some eight others, all cleaners. "I knew it, I knew it! The dream, my vision was too clear, too real, I knew the savior, the Christ, was to be born tonight, I knew this was the place, here, here!" In they came. They offered gifts, an old anorak to wrap around the babe, a bar of chocolate—for Mary! Mary rested; while the cleaners worshipped the babe. "It is thousands of years since the prophets spoke, but they are never wrong, nor the angel in your vision," a young cleaner commented, no more than a girl herself, "We are saved! Lord, now we can go in peace, your word has been fulfilled."

V. EXODUS

Nicolaides the Greek came back, he had been scouting around: "You must go. There are Praetorians in the upper floors of the building and around the precinct. They must suspect something. Come, we must all go. The Governor fears the old prophecies, and he has informers!" The women cleaners helped Mary up, petting the babe! They all followed Nicolaides' lead. Everything went smoothly until they exited the building, but as they rounded the corner next to the encampment (they were still illegally within its precinct) they ran into two Praetorians. Joseph stood between them and Mary. He was hacked down immediately, then a Taser thrust into his mouth to fry his brain with 2000 volts. The women gathered around

Mary wailing and pleading, throwing themselves at her feet and the feet of the Praetorians, thereby impeding their thrust at Mary. Nicolaides spoke hastily to the demonstrators at the rear of the encampment—"You owe me! Now, give us a distraction, I have to get the young woman away with her baby! Come, you owe me!" Nicolaides, among others, was the focus of the demonstrator's hatred, but he had helped them, had secretly supported them. For a few seconds they paused, thought, but knew they had to respond. They hurled rubbish, sleeping bags, pots and pans at the Praetorians, more of whom had arrived. Amidst the melee Nicolaides slipped his arm round Mary, ushered her away as she looked back at Joseph's slaughtered body. The distraction had worked, but many of the cleaners, with infants carried on their backs paid the price. The infants were ripped off them and speared, slashed, cut-through there and then, many of the women being shot through the Star of David tattoo on their forehead. The demonstrators, being Roman citizens, were chided by the Praetorians, but left alone to continue with their illegal, but fashionable, demonstration. Initially they had rejected Mary, yet they had then saved the Christ!

VI. REFUGEES

Nicolaides helped Mary and the baby Jesus into the boot, the trunk, of his limousine—apologizing profusely that it had to be so. Being a Greek financier and a Roman citizen, he was waved through all checkpoints. At his house in North Londinium Mary washed, changed, and fed Jesus, then climbed into the rear-facing seat behind the grill in Nicolaides' other vehicle (a large utility estate car, the front part was for him, and his kind; any untouchables, were behind the grill). Now he could transport her as a servant without questions being asked.

Mary sat quietly weeping, rocking gently back and forth, holding on to the baby Jesus, wrapped in swaddling rags gathered by the women who had visited her after the birth. She watched the rain and the road as it disappeared behind her, facing rear, as London dissolved behind her first into mist, then rain. They travelled northward. Was this really how it was meant to be? Nine months earlier after the unexpected visitation from Gabriel—was he really an angel, he looked so ordinary—her annunciation has been proved by the fact she was holding a newborn babe, *the* newborn babe. And then there had been her visit to cousin Elizabeth. Mary wept for

1. A Delayed Nativity . . . What If ?

Joseph. He had rightly questioned her pregnancy: how could she be with child if she truly had not slept with a man? He had been rightly angry. Is this why he now lay dead, slaughtered? She had been to visit Elizabeth on the outskirts of Glevum—properly, *Colonia Nervia Glevensium*—where they owned and ran an estate, a fruit farm, serving this retirement resort for the officials, the elite, that formed the Roman civil service. Elizabeth knew—and had greeted her arrival in such a strange manner, praising her as the mother of her Lord! Elizabeth was pregnant also; they agreed that Mary should stay with her till the birth. But no, Zechariah's dream vision pointed to Mary going back to the Lea Valley, betrothed as she was to Joseph, to sort out with him what was happening: Zechariah was convinced it would be alright. She had returned, Joseph had been besides himself with the sight of her full pregnancy; but then he changed, one morning he appeared at her parents' house full of reconciliation. He had confided in her his dream, his vision: all she said was indeed true: the virgin shall bear a child, his name was to be Jesus, and he would save his people from their sins. But now he had died: he had saved Jesus from the Praetorian Guard. They drove on; Mary silently wept for Joseph, and gave thanks to the Lord for her safe delivery, for Jesus, and for Joseph's sacrifice. They drove all the next day and night, along the Ermine Way to Eboracum York, then on along Dere Way to Coria, stopping to eat, and for Mary to clean and change Jesus. Even when they reached the frontier post at the recently re-built Hadrian's Wall (now a sixty-foot-high steel and concrete barrier) Nicolaides' credentials saw them through—they were clear of Rome! Now in Caledonia (the land of the Scots and Picts—outside of the Roman Empire—but part of the Scania Lands, stretching to the ice-wastes of the north), he had friends who could get them West into Dál Riata—the three-thousand-year-old Celtic kingdom, occupying the Hebrides, the Western coast of Caledonia, and the mountainous Northern part of Hibernia known as the Ulster Province. They stayed for a two weeks in Dál Riata, an independent kingdom, but owing allegiance to Rome in exchange for protection, whereby Nicolaides' credentials could guarantee their safety and passage slowly north through the islands, eventually onto a fishing boat, then to the Faroe Islands where finally they could stop and rest. Nicolaides the Greek had been born in Alexandria, an ancient Greek community on the Egyptian coast, as such he knew the Hebrew Scriptures, but did not fully understand them, or the prophecy regarding the Christ. But he had grown up with Greek Jews, knew the story, trusted Mary implicitly, and knew in his heart this was right.

VII. MAGI

After resting up on the Faroe Islands they shipped across further into the Scania Lands, navigating fjords to reach deep into the land to register at the regional capital, Bergen, which held a large Jewish community. Here they were visited by three Sages, Norse Shamans who knew who and what Mary's child was. They had studied all the Scriptures, they had observed the stars, the planetary movements, which confirmed the stories they knew from their own tradition, the stories of God being incarnated to save humanity. They stayed here, overlooking fjords at the invitation of the Sages, which gave Mary three years of peace and quiet to nurture and raise the infant Jesus into a little child.

VIII. MIGRANTS

Then, on Nicolaides' advise and urging, as the locals began to suspect there was something special and different about the child, they moved on: moving on, never settling in any one place for any length of time, ever moving. Nicolaides cared for Mary—now outside of Roman jurisdiction—giving to her the status of a senior housekeeper (the highest status for women who were not Roman citizens, working for a Roman citizen, conferring on her certain rights: the right not to be enslaved by Rome). International Roman banking allowed him to fund their travels through a world of empires. The first and most powerful was, of course, that of Rome (covering Europe, but also the Great African Desert, and the East Coast of North America and its hinterlands). But the world consisted of other empires, including the Scania Lands (from the Germanic states to the Arctic) and the Slav Empire (also known as Rus), bounded by Rome and the Ural mountains. As they journeyed, they met travelers from the Chinese and Indian Empires, which covered Asia east of the Ural mountains. When traversing the Scania lands and into the Slav Empire, the young Jesus even met and talked with Jews from the Great African Empire—the largest on earth, with its capital in the ancient citadel of Zimbabwe—that encompassed Africa south of The Great African Desert, but also the North and South American continents, and the Central Americas. These fellow-travelers encountered by Jesus were orthodox,

1. A Delayed Nativity . . . What If?

believing, and practicing Jews who were Africans, Native Americans, and who were yearning for the Messiah's redemption; all respective of ethnic and religious origins—both slave/servant and free—had the status and rights of citizens of the African Empire. Nicolaides business contacts drew in a personal assistant from the Maori Empire, encompassing The Great Pacific Ocean, all its islands, including the land of the Aborigines, and from the Persian-Arab lands. It was as though representatives of the peoples of the world were coming to see the Christ, *incognito*, but they were just ordinary people, not high-and-mighty leaders, kings, queens, emperors, or religious leaders.

Mary must get Jesus to the Eastern Mediterranean. Nicolaides knew this was the riskiest part of the venture. What used to be the ancient Kingdom of Israel had been a wasteland for nineteen hundred years: a no-go area, devoid of civilization, just nomadic tribes, some Jewish, and the ruins of Jerusalem, and other cities: razed by the Romans, but still occupied and controlled by them. While they resided in a large town in the Ural Mountains, Jesus was taken to a synagogue, and presented to the elders. Jesus grew strong, and knew the Scriptures, he spent untold hours talking with the Rabbis and elders, waiting for the day he could arrive in Palestine: Israel, the eternal Israel beckoned.

IX. ARRIVAL

Nicolaides—who was not a young man—grew ill, contracting tuberculosis, and died. His wealth could not be left to Mary, his housekeeper. This would have been possible had she been from a different tribe or people, but under Slav law, although Jews were not classed as untouchables, they were not citizens. Mary was on her own again. Mary knew that Zechariah and Elizabeth, with their son John, had migrated from Glevum to Palestine—officially, sanctioned by Rome, to run an olive plantation. Mary knew that there was some mystical connection between Jesus and John that was to happen, that had to work out: it was divinely ordained and the years of travel, migrating around the Roman Empire, were in part for this encounter to take place. But what? How? When? Now, back as a working domestic, she had to make her way with Jesus south out of the Land of the Slavs and eventually into Babylonia, attaching herself to a nomadic caravan as a servant, with Jesus apprenticed as a tent maker and repairer, and learning the skills of a carpenter from the older master craftsman in the caravan. Jesus became a respected craftsman amongst the builders and architects around the Tigris and Euphrates rivers, and they were sorry to see him go. They had been treated well, and had been part of the disparate Jewish community; for the years they lived around the Babylonian rivers, Jesus earned well, and Mary could finally retire and just keep her own house.

Back in Londinium the Roman Empire celebrated the two thousandth anniversary of the conquest of Britannia. Thousands of miles away, Jesus, being nearly thirty years of age, was ready to embark on his ministry and mission, to shed his blood for Israel's redemption and the atonement of humanity. As he arrived at the border post on the Jordan River with Mary, and other relatives, they were both searched, questioned, interrogated— their papers checked (having paid handsomely for their visas, work permits, and identity papers at a Roman consulate in Syria); finally, they entered the promised land. They walked slowly over a pedestrian suspension bridge. On the other side they were escorted through the gates of the barbed-wire perimeter—it was as though the whole of the Kingdom of Israel, what was left of it, was now a concentration camp. Then they took the road to Bethlehem. They walked. The road lined with crucifixions—every half league, one man, or a woman, or a child, alive, dying, or a rotting corpse: Jews whose only crime was to read the Scriptures in public (often reciting the Mosaic Law, which contradicted the pagan Roman practices, especially sexual practices), or they had been guilty of asserting their identity as God's chosen people, or worse, claiming the promised land from the Nile to the Euphrates had been given to them by *El Shaddai, YWHW: Almighty God, the Lord*, to form the Greater Israel, a promise witnessed in the Hebrew Scriptures, promised to Abraham, and to Abraham's son Isaac, and to Isaac's son Jacob. All had been transported from all over the Roman Empire, to die here: publicly executed. As Jesus walked, he observed each crucified person, prayed for each, and walked on contemplating his own ministry, and his own end; Mary could just hear his voice, quietly, almost at a whisper, say "My people, my people! . . . Oh, Israel what have they done to you . . . !"

X. MINISTRY

A Rabbi who had journeyed with them from Syria, and knew who and what Jesus was asked him, "When will you start? When will you begin preaching, healing? Help us, Lord!" "Start?" retorted Jesus, "Start—this is the beginning of the end, my brother." But aren't you going to destroy the Romans, liberate Israel, restore the Kingdom of Israel, institute the Greater Israel? Jesus smiled at him; Jesus loved him. "The Kingdom of God is within you. Can you not know it? Know God? My mission is already well advanced, but you cannot begin to conceive of the wonders to come. Israel will indeed be glorified; but first there will be great suffering, my child: the end is coming, and coming soon, but first . . . ."

They arrived at Bethlehem—the City of David—at nightfall, and began the search for somewhere to stay, sleeping temporarily overnight in a stable attached to an inn, till the search for accommodation could begin in earnest in the morning, then once rested and settled, to travel north along the banks of the Jordan to visit Zechariah and Elizabeth's plantation, then to find their son, John the Baptizer . . . .

PART TWO
TOWARDS AN UNDERSTANDING OF THE EMERGENCE OF THE END TIMES

2

Karl Barth: "*Krisis*," War, & Expressionism— An Eschatological Encounter

Whoever acknowledges me before others, I will also acknowledge before my Father in heaven. But whoever disowns me before others, I will disown before my Father in heaven. Do not suppose that I have come to bring peace to the earth. I did not come to bring peace, but a sword. For I have come to turn . . . .

MATTHEW 10:32–35

SYNOPSIS

With the advent of the First World War, and facing the poverty of his parishioners, the young Swiss Reformed Church minister Karl Barth, reacted passionately against the stagnant, stable, and condescending malaise of nineteenth-century liberal neo-Protestantism, which he had been schooled and trained in. War blew apart the lukewarm religiosity of the *status quo*. Along with his friend and fellow minister Eduard Thurneysen, he set about an eschatological revolution: "*Krisis*," judgment, the victory of God over the power of evil, all focused these young rebel minds. Parallel to them was the movement of Expressionism in the visual and literary arts that informed and drove their rebellion against their teachers and the tired theological establishment: Barth's commentary on the *Epistle to the Romans* (*Der Römerbrief*, 1919 and 1921) being described by the Catholic theologian Karl Adams as a bombshell thrown into the playground of the theologians. Here we find the seeds of the mature Barth's eschatology, even his over-realized eschatology, as it is sometimes critiqued. That Barth is considered stylistically an Expressionist is nothing new, however, when observing Barth's work and his use of theological language, commentators have in effect avoided the visual arts, focusing on a literary genre and parallels. Therefore, this paper addresses two questions: To what extent is Barth's use of Expressionism part of the prevailing *zeitgeist* in the *visual arts*? Was Barth an iconoclast? By examining Barth's theological use and admiration for mediaeval and Renaissance art, and Expressionism, we can assert that it was modernism that Barth objected to, not the visual arts *per se*. Therefore, he was no iconoclast, though he expressed severe reservations about the distraction of art in church buildings. Considering Barth's work in an artistic cultural context (the visual, fine arts) shows how his uncompromising criticism of modernism (both artistic and theological) in both the Expressionistic style of *Der Römerbrief* and the classical German of the *Kirchliche Dogmatik* was in many ways prophetic, and formed a crucial part of his evolving eschatology, the influence of which can be seen in his mature work.[1]

I. INTRODUCTION

War ushers in the end times. Although no single particular war over the last two thousand years has triggered the actual *eschaton*, the situation has got worse over the centuries. There are more people alive today in the world than have lived in the past. So obviously the situation of conflict has magnified. And then there is the state of modern weaponry: enough nuclear weapons, chemical/biological/nerve agents, stockpiled to wipe out humanity, indeed to destroy life as we know it on the planet. War issues from a crisis: in a word, failure, which then generates deeper crises. Pertinently, certainly for Karl Barth, *krisis*, from the ancient Greek for "decision" (often forced decisions), is characterized by determination and judgment, trial, conviction/sentence. If so then there is accusation, quarrel, and dispute, causing a turning point or *decisive moment* from which affairs either improve, or worsen into the end.

II. REVOLUTIONARY THEOLOGY IN THE MAKING

The conflagration that was the First World War triggered a *krisis* in many young people's thinking in central Europe: the Swiss theologians and young ministers Karl Barth and Eduard Thurneysen among them. A brief reminder: although he studied theology at the universities of Berne, Berlin, and Tübingen, it was at Marburg, much to his father's displeasure, that Barth felt at home—particularly under the tutelage of the liberal Wilhelm

---

1 For details of and access to all the works of art discussed here: http://www.cslewisandthechrist.net//toward-the-day.html
See also note at beginning of this book: Illustration.

2. Karl Barth: "Krisis," War, & Expressionism

Herrmann and the influence of Albrecht Ritschl and Adolf von Harnack. Initially working as assistant pastor to the German-speaking church in Geneva (1909–11), he then served for ten years in the small industrial town of Safenwil in the Aargau (1911–21). During this time he became progressively disillusioned with his education in nineteenth-century neo-Protestant liberal theology and took the best part of these ten years to reform his beliefs. As a liberal, Barth's understanding of sin, as such, was sociological. Liberal neo-Protestantism was a very hierarchical and moralistic religion; sin, as such, had, to a large degree, been secularized into social ethics—this effectively limited Christianity to what is often considered to have been a moral code welding society together.[2] Once he began working in the industrialized region of Safenwil, Barth became heavily politicized: sin became very real. He perceived it in the oppressive attitude of the factory managers and owners to the workers. Here we have the seriously political sermons, the involvement with trade unions, articles written against the bourgeois complacency of the wealthy classes, the involvement with Swiss Religious Socialism: Barth was labelled by his congregation as the red pastor or comrade Barth.[3]

Around this time Eduard Thurneysen introduced Barth to Hermann Kutter—the prophet of Swiss Religious Socialism. In meetings with Kutter, Barth learned to speak the word "God" with reverence, to emphasize the separateness, the distance, the otherness of God, which was implicit in the much-used phrase, the kingdom of God:

> From Kutter I simply learnt to speak the great word "God" seriously, responsibly, and with a sense of its importance. Kutter represented the insight that the sphere of God's power really is greater than the sphere of the church and that from time to time it has pleased God, and still pleases Him, to warn and to comfort his church through the figures and the events of secular world history.[4]

---

2   See Rupp, *Culture-Protestantism: German Liberal Theology at the Turn of the Twentieth Century*; also, Fischer, *Revelatory Positivism? Barth's Earliest Theology and the Marburg School*; see also Reardon (ed.), *Liberal Protestantism*.

3   Busch, *Karl Barths Lebenslauf, Nach seinem Briefen und autobiographischen Texten*, 60–71.

4   Busch, *Karl Barths Lebenslauf*, 88. Busch is quoting from an interview between Barth and H. Fischer-Barnicol from 1964, and from "Nachwort," in *Barth, Schleiermacher-Auswahl*, 293.

These meetings with Kutter are of crucial importance in the development of Barth's critique of religion—a critique that is built on this doctrinal separateness, this distinctiveness of God, a God above all human gods, who is wholly other and cannot be domesticated into religion. However, it is important to remember that this is a criticism of religion *per se*, and is generated by and in the service of the gospel: if there is true and valid religion it is in the service of proclaiming and promoting the gospel— true religion is from the gospel and transcends mere religiosity. Barth's politicized criticism of religion/church also fed into what is now termed the year of the new starting point: 1915. Ingrid Spieckermann[5] and Bruce McCormack[6] both see 1915 as important in Barth's development away from liberalism. McCormack categorizes this new starting point as *critically realistic* in the sense that "God is now seen as a reality complete and whole in itself apart from and prior to the knowing activity of human individuals."[7] God, for Barth, was no longer to be seen in terms of nineteenth-century German religion—that is, "in contrast to the idealistic tendency of the Ritschlian School to treat God as a postulated source of the moral ought."[8] Crucially, Barth began reading the troubling, existential, eschatological novels of the Russian prophet and writer Fyodor Mikhailovich Dostoevsky, introduced to him by Thurneysen. Barth's understanding of sin begins to become theological—or more pertinently, sin is defined by and in relation to this God of otherness. From the Blumhardts,[9] Barth learned to believe in a spiritual reality peopled by angels and demons, contrary to the humanist religion he had been schooled in, which in its extreme form even denied Jesus Christ's divinity, and thereby the doctrine of the Trinity. Here in the war he could see an eschatological reality devouring people, wasting communities, killing,

---

5   Spieckermann, *Gotteskenntnis: Ein Beitrag zur Grundfrage der neun Theologie Karl Barths.*

6   McCormack, *Karl Barth's Critically Realistic Dialectical Theology: Its Genesis and Development, 1909-1936.*

7   McCormack, *Karl Barth's Critically Realistic Dialectical Theology*, 129

8   McCormack, *Karl Barth's Critically Realistic Dialectical Theology*, 129

9   Johann Christoph Blumhardt (1805-80), the nephew of Christoph Gottlieb Blumhardt (1779-1838), founded the Protestant Basel Mission. From 1852 he worked at Bad Boll near Göppingen, which became a center for charismatic missionary work. Christoph Friedrich Blumhardt (1842-1919) took over the work of his father as the Director of Bad Boll and became a Social Democrat Party MP. See: Thurneysen, *Christoph Blumhardt.*

2. Karl Barth: "Krisis," War, & Expressionism

where the only answer was in Jesus Christ: God incarnate, crucified and resurrected for our salvation, to bring us out of this mess.

Amidst the chaos of industrial relations in Safenwil and in the wider eschatology of the First World War, Barth and Thurneysen discovered the work and witness of Johann Christoph Blumhardt: *Jesus ist Sieger*. Blumhardt, from his ministry in Möttlingen in 1843, dealt with two women suffering from demonic possession. The conventional theology regarded this as a delusion—merely some sort of psychiatric problem. But Blumhardt took it seriously, and healed the women by casting out the evil spirits—through prayer, through the power of the Holy Spirit: Jesus was the victor! Demon possession is so often mentioned in the New Testament, but was dismissed amongst the intellectual bourgeois liberal classes. Such a victorious encounter over evil was directly the result of Jesus's ontological status as the Son of God. Blumhardt had been pulled into a charismatic healing ministry, something that did not happen amongst the polite educated classes in modern Europe.

> I mean, this sort of thing just did not happen in the nineteenth century. People, Protestants, on the whole had ceased believing in miracles. That's the interesting thing, you see, here in the middle of the skeptical nineteenth century where one writer has said so pervasive was the Newtonian mechanistic worldview that theology had become almost impossible (I am over-Romanticizing), you see the belief in miracles was certainly not by any means universal and here it has happened! But the interesting thing is, of course, this demonic cry "*Jesus is the Victor*," that gives Barth his theme. Anyway that is an interesting tale and it just shows how Barth is a great thinker; you see, he just takes up themes from all over. Blumhardt recounted that the shriek was *Jesus ist Sieger*, variously translated as *Jesus is the Conqueror* or *Jesus is the Victor*.[10]

This is a profound eschatological reality, an eschatological battle, which profoundly influenced Barth's development.

---

10   Colin Gunton, comments from a lecture course on Barth at King's College London: B406, A Selected Modern Theologian—Karl Barth, 2000–2001, transcription of a lecture course delivered at King's College, London, Wednesday 4th October 2000, "Lecture 2. Barth's Development up to Romans." The lecture course, which was something of an internationally acclaimed annual event, was posthumously published as, Gunton, *The Barth Lectures* (2007); see 207–8.

Crucial in Barth and Thurneysen's development was the discovery of the Russian prophet and novelist Fyodor Mikhailovich Dostoevsky,[11] from whom they learnt how evil and sin was balanced by the grace and forgiveness won by Jesus Christ on the cross: *Jesus is the victor* (the Blumhardts). However, it is the influence of the contemporaneous artistic movement in central Europe of Expressionism that we are to consider here.

III. BARTH AND EXPRESSIONISM

That Barth is considered stylistically an Expressionist is well established and accepted. That his early work is considered Expressionistic is recognized in the scholarly tradition, so why some further considerations? Because when examining Barth's early work commentators write on artistic style in cinema, literature, music, but in effect eschew the visual arts. This paper seeks to address two questions: First, to what extent is the style, form—and to a degree the content—of Barth's move away from nineteenth-century neo-Protestant liberal theology (circa 1911 to 1921) part of and influenced by an Expressionist movement in the visual arts (as well as in literature, music, indeed culture generally)? Second, was Barth an iconoclast? Answering the first question will show how his work is indeed part of a wider cultural movement, but Barth is deeply skeptical of the aims and objectives of the Expressionist painters—but not painters from the mediaeval and Renaissance periods (some of whom are classified as Expressionistic, precursors to modern Expressionist art). However, he soon moves away from the *zeitgeist* to assert the pre-eminence of the *Deus dixit*, the revelation of the crucifixion and resurrection of God incarnate: Christ at the center of humanity. Regarding the accusation of iconoclasm, a central aim of this paper is simply to refute a widely assumed belief that Barth had an aversion to religious art, especially in church buildings. By examining Barth's theological use and admiration for mediaeval and Renaissance art—something he shared with his friend and theological colleague Eduard Thurneysen—we can assert that it was *modernism* that Barth objected to, not the visual arts *per se*. Therefore, he was no iconoclast, though he expressed severe reservations about the distraction of art in

---

11   See Brazier, *Barth and Dostoevsky: A Study of the Influence of the Russian Writer Fyodor Mikhailovich Dostoevsky on the Development of the Swiss Theologian Karl Barth, 1915–1922*. Also, Brazier, *Dostoevsky: A Theological Engagement*.

2. Karl Barth: "Krisis," War, & Expressionism

church buildings. By looking at Barth's work in cultural context we can see how his uncompromising criticism of modernism (both artistic and theological, philosophical and socio-cultural) in both the Expressionistic style of *Der Römerbrief* and the classical German of *Kirchliche Dogmatik* was in many ways prophetic, given the developments in central Europe circa 1925 to 1945, and how his adherence to the self-revelation of God in Christ Jesus meant he was something of a voice crying in the wilderness.

Stephen Webb, in *Re-figuring Theology: The Rhetoric of Karl Barth*, is the foremost scholar to have analyzed Barth's Expressionistic style.[12] I do not intend to depart from anything Webb has established, simply to add to his conclusion by examining Barth in relation to the visual arts.

IV. WHY EXPRESSIONISM?

First, what is Expressionism? Essentially a modern-art movement in poetry and painting, Expressionism originated in Central Europe—essentially Germany—in the early twentieth century. The aim was to re-present the world from a subjective perspective, distorting reality to conform to feelings and ideas, by focusing on generating images to portray emotion and spirit, concepts and thoughts. Physical reality is then secondary. Expressionism was particularly avant-garde in the years prior to the First World War; post-war it developed a darker side amongst the survivors of the trenches; however, its popularity developed with the Weimar Republic, especially in the decadent quarters of Berlin. Expressionism could be found in a wide range of mediums: painting and literature, theatre and film, also music, dance, and architecture.

The observation by critics of Barth's Expressionism starts with the publication of the first edition of his commentary on the apostle Paul's letter to the Romans: *Der Römerbrief* (1919). In 1926, the Roman Catholic theologian Karl Adam commented, "Barth's *Römerbrief* hit immediately in its first appearance—August 1919—like a bomb on the playground of the theologians, comparably in its effects with the encyclical on antimodernisation of Pope Pius X."[13] *Römerbrief* (1st ed.)[14] was a wake-

---

12   Webb, *Re-figuring Theology: The Rhetoric of Karl Barth*. Webb examines Expressionistic literature and cinema (in particular *Das Cabinet des Dr Calgari*) and some examples of paintings that influenced Barth's Expressionism.

13   Adam, "Die Theologie der *Krisis*," 271–86.

14   The first edition of Barth's commentary on Paul's letter to the Romans—*Der Römerbrief*—(written between the summer of 1916 and August 1918, and published in

up call following on from the apocalyptic catastrophe of the First World War. It was Hans Urs von Balthasar who first really examined the proposition that Barth's style in this move away from nineteenth-century neo-Protestant liberalism was Expressionistic, though the accusation was initially levelled, derogatively, by Alfred Von Harnack shortly after the publication of *Römerbrief* (1st ed.) in 1919. Webb neatly summarizes how Harnack was "Probably the first person to call Barth an Expressionist. . . . He used the term to mean that Barth was unscientific."[15] Harnack entered into correspondence with Barth not long after the publication of *Römerbrief* (1st ed.), a correspondence that established just how far from his liberal heritage Barth had progressed. Wilhelm Pauck, writing on Barth as early as 1931, commented on the dangers of Expressionism, about how it was formed through the revolt of young people against authority. He comments how terrifying the awakening was in the war and its aftermath: revolutions, famines, foreign oppression, inflation and a general breakdown of the economic order. Further, how for youth there was only one attitude to take: mistrust the world, express your own self. Pauck shows how Barth was not alone in his interpretation, though the others were far from orthodox. Wilhelm Pauck, writing in 1931, on the existential *krisis* for the Germans who had survived the slaughter of the First World War, noted how a youth movement sprang up "as a revolt of young people against the civilization of the big cities and which had developed into a rebellion against the authority of the elders of school, of church and home, and which seemed justified."[16] However, he continues, the reality, post-war, was terrifying: revolutions, famines, foreign

---

the summer of 1919) is hereafter referred to as *Römerbrief* (1st ed.). The rewriting of *Der Römerbrief* as the second edition (written between October 1920 and September 1921, and published in the September 1922) is hereafter referred to as *Römerbrief* (2nd ed.). The title *Der Römerbrief* will be used when referring to both first and second editions, or subsequent editions of Barth's commentary on Paul's letter to the Romans: Karl Barth, *Der Römerbrief* (Erste Fassung 1919) (edition 1985); Karl Barth, *Der Römerbrief* (Zweite Fassung 1922) (1999); ET: Karl Barth *The Epistle to the Romans* (trans. Sir Edwyn Hoskyns, 1933).

15   Webb, *Re-figuring Theology*, 183; Webb draws on Rumscheidt, "The Correspondence between Harnack and Barth" (PhD diss., 1967).

16   Pauck, *Karl Barth: Prophet of a New Christianity?* 18. Rare and out-of-print, an online edition can be consulted at: https://archive.org/details/karlbarthprophet012001mbp.

2. Karl Barth: "Krisis," War, & Expressionism

oppression, inflation, and a general breakdown of the economic order. This was summarized for the youthful survivors in one word: mistrust.

> Mistrust the world as it is and the power that permeates it—express your own self. The magic of the romanticism of self-expression could furnish the only salvation. Expressionism in literature and art; mysticism and the occult exercises of Theosophy and Anthroposophy in religion; communistic, socialistic, democratic ideologies in politics; abandonment of the old rules of sexual relationship and married life—all these reveal the age of disillusionment, when man returned from the world, which he thought he could conquer, to find only his own self, seeking hope and relief in the seemingly unbounded dreams of his soul.
>
> Yet this life was no revival, it did not bring relief. It was rather the expression of despair. It supposedly provided an escape from a destroyed world and also from a cultural turmoil. Actually men merely retreated from their wider, secular selves into the secret chambers of the soul and its hidden, partly unspeakable longings. The world they had built was in upheaval and ruin: where else could they go—but to themselves.[17]

The responsibility, for Pauck, and for Barth, had been in the arrogance of the Western progress that had driven Europe in the nineteenth century:

> This was the last, most pathetic, most tragic phase of a period of civilization which in amazing feats of progress had tried to prove that man was to rule the world and that it was his. At the end—man was alone.
> . . . It furnishes despair and respite. It is a crisis, and a crisis is a turning point.[18]

Barth, particularly in *Römerbrief* (1st ed.), is as Expressionistic as many of the German and Swiss youth who rebelled against the collapse of civilization during the First World War, and likewise the watchword of *krisis* rang from his work as much as from secular writers, painters, and film makers. But Barth saw the solution to this *krisis* in the orthodoxy of the Christian faith, in gospel truths. Other Expressionists—religious or otherwise—merely sank into despair then nihilism, often suicide. Barth's Expressionism is set apart from this by his outwardness. Eberhard Jüngel

---

17   Pauck, *Karl Barth: Prophet of a New Christianity?* 19.
18   Pauck, *Karl Barth: Prophet of a New Christianity?* 19–20.

commented, "These early writings spoke not only with the Expressionist language of their time but also with a vigorous recklessness that emphasized the new."[19]

V. BARTH'S USE OF AN EXPRESSIONIST STYLE, TROPE, & IDIOM

So what can be said of Barth's early style: it has been likened to a stuttering machine gun in its uncompromising assertions, it is full with ambiguity, paradox, negation, it celebrates apparent contradiction, it glories in dialectic to undermine all human efforts, particularly religious. As Barth was to comment later in *Kirchliche Dogmatik*, the revelation of God is the abolition of all religion; that is, religion as the attempt by humanity to justify and to sanctify itself before a capricious and arbitrary picture of God.[20] It is important to note that the German word Barth used is *Aufhebung*, which is an abolition or rescindment, a revocation or cancellation, but also, simultaneously, a lifting, an uplifting. Barth almost certainly used *Aufhebung* with a dialectical meaning: religion is both the highest most important enterprise of humanity, yet its failures mean its abolition before the gospel. Colin Gunton has commented on *Der Römerbrief* that, "[T]he impact of this book is more important than its content. . . . The Barth story is that he felt like a man climbing a dark church tower and instead of grabbing the handrail he grabbed the bell rope and awakened the countryside. It had an immense impact throughout Europe."[21] Theology is, therefore, at its best, kerygmatic. Colin Gunton, again,

> The problem, for many, is Barth's assertive style—he does not seem to argue, merely assert. Barth does not argue people into faith, but nor does Mozart, and that is the model for Barth. Barth is simply displaying the beauty of God's Word. Barth was one of the first in the modern period to take up and comment on the beauty of God. This was then taken over and taken further by the critics and those commenting on Barth's work: Hans Urs Von Balthasar, notably his work on theological aesthetics. Barth's assertive style

---

19   Jüngel, *Karl Barth, A Theological Legacy*, 12.
20   Barth, *Church Dogmatics, Vol I/2 The Doctrine of the Word of God*, See Ch. 2, §17.2 "Religion as Unbelief."
21   Gunton, *The Barth Lectures*, 25.

2. Karl Barth: "Krisis," War, & Expressionism

does make it difficult for mild-mannered establishment Anglicans to cope with.[22]

Hans Urs von Balthasar correctly distinguishes the classical German of *Kirchliche Dogmatik* from the vibrant Expressionism of *Der Römerbrief* and quite rightly asserts that this is more than a stylistic difference: "an inherent part of this language is the cry of one who has seen something that no one else around him has seen. Perhaps in this existentialism, Barth was trying to express the inexpressible, to bring the eternal flow of time to a standstill. Perhaps he was deliberately trying to bring ridicule on himself by seeking,"[23] and here Balthasar quotes Barth's Tambach Lecture, "to catch a bird in flight, well knowing that motion itself, divorced from the thing in motion, becomes just a theme, a thing."[24] Furthermore, "For Barth, the encounter with revelation inevitably raised the question of style in theology. He knew that the task of theology was not only to say something about the content of revelation but also to convey to us how utterly, stupendously dramatic the event was that is now reaching our ears. It is . . . theological Expressionism, especially in methodology."[25] And, quoting Barth's *Römerbrief* (2nd ed.), Balthasar continues, "We find ourselves in the highly unusual situation of having to speak about that of which we cannot speak . . . '[O]ur location is no real standpoint at all but a mathematical point on which we cannot gain any footing.'"[26]

From the time of Barth's appointment as Honorary Professor of Reformed Theology at Göttingen we see in effect the beginning of the maturing of this rebellious, angry existential young theologian/

---

22   Gunton on Barth, "Lecture 6. The Basis, Task and Situation of Theology," 1st November 2000. See Gunton, *The Barth Lectures*, 97–109.

23   Balthasar, *Karl Barth, Darstellung und Deutung seiner Theologie* (1951). ET: Balthasar, *The Theology of Karl Barth—Exposition and Interpretation* (translated by John Drury), 31f. Balthasar quotes from Karl Barth "Der Christ in der Gesellschaft" (the so-called *Tambach Lecture*—address delivered at Die religiös-soziale Konferenz, The Conference on Religion and Social Relations, held at Tambach on the 25th September 1919) published in Barth, *Das Wort Gottes und die Theologie*, 33–69. ET: "The Christian in Society" translated by Douglas Horton, in *The Word of God and the Word of Man*, 272–327.

24   Balthasar, *Karl Barth, Darstellung und Deutung seiner Theologie*, 31f.

25   Balthasar *Karl Barth, Darstellung und Deutung seiner Theologie*, 82–83. Balthasar quotes from *Römerbrief* (2nd ed.), 12f.

26   Balthasar *Karl Barth, Darstellung und Deutung seiner Theologie*, 82–83. Balthasar quotes from *Römerbrief* (2nd ed.), 99 & 128.

pastor, but not a dimming of his assertive style: his mature work is as uncompromising and assertive, still as vibrantly eschatological, but drenched in the forgiveness of Christ.

Stephen Webb examines in depth not just the early work but Barth's mature work also. Webb sought to understand the priorities, particularly in Barth's early work, likewise the role of rhetoric in his assertions: "Theology in its attempts to make deep truths clear and to defend its own legitimacy has always had a stake in rhetoric."[27] (Remembering, as Webb notes, that Aristotle defined rhetoric as closely aligned to the art of persuasion.) We are therefore dealing with first-order religious language—not reflective, not academically neutral, not disinterestedly hermetic, but declaratory, persuasive, kerygmatic. Barth's detractors immediately accused him of rhetoric and subjectivism: theology to his critics could only be academic, disinterested, impartial, apparently agnostic. However, as Webb and others have shown, Barth is something of a theological poet.[28] Yes his language is explosive and inflammatory, again not something disputed: "in his early work Barth pushes theology to dialectical, paradoxical and contradictory limits."[29] Furthermore, Webb, quoting *Römerbrief* (2nd ed.), comments:

> Barth could make pronouncements on God with the most confident enthusiasm, portraying grace as a shattering disturbance, an assault which brings everything into question. In fact, when Barth speaks of God's grace as a lightning bolt, both illuminating and destroying human existence at the same time, the reader today can only think of Barth's work itself, and the effect it had on the theology of its day. The contour of this anxious writing wavers between bombastic exclamations and cunning retractions. The resulting mixture is often explosive.[30]

Barth is therefore symphonic, architectonic, but the result is, as John Bowden has noted, a hymn of praise to the goodness of God.[31] This does not detract from the point that Barth's style is intentionally provocative, as was the cultural phenomena of Expressionism: both represent a culture in crisis. Barth acknowledged this in a later preface (1926) to *Der*

27   Webb, *Re-figuring Theology*, 1.
28   Webb, *Re-figuring Theology*, 4.
29   Webb, *Re-figuring Theology*, 4–5.
30   *Webb, Re-figuring Theology*, 5f.
31   Bowden, *Karl Barth, Theologian*, 13; quoted in Webb, *Re-figuring Theology*.

2. Karl Barth: "Krisis," War, & Expressionism

Römerbrief: "When I wrote the book, did I simply put into words what was everywhere fashionable—especially in Germany after the War?"[32] Furthermore, he added that it was his intention to swim against the tide, to bang on the doors, to rail against everything human, in particular religion: "there are definite and obvious parallels between Romans and other currents in German culture, and the Expressionist analogy serves to bring those shared traits into focus. Barth came to see that his theological style was, to a significant extent, a reflection of the style then dominant in the arts."[33]

But does the Expressionist dictum completely fit with Barth's style and aims? Expressionist painters were certainly not kerygmatic, they offered no solution to this *krisis*. They did, however, repudiate a superficial naturalism, they were passionately anti-realistic, they refused to imitate, thereby they attempted to get to what underpinned reality, the hidden sense that transcended, to identify that which pointed beyond. In this sense their agenda could be considered as Platonic—even broadly theological. However, the slogan of the movement—particularly from the groups *Die Brücke* (*The Bridge*) and *Der blaue Reiter* (*The Blue Rider*), and oft quoted in academic works on Expressionism[34]—was, *Die Welt ist da, Es wäre sinnlos, sie zu wiederholen* (the world is there, it would make no sense to repeat it). Webb:

> There is a panicked urgency in Barth's writing.... It is as if Barth thought that by piling up enough negative proclamations about God, some positive truth could finally be reached. However, negations can serve as only shaky foundations at best, and this is the source of much of the anxiety and panic the reader is forced to feel in the text. Can Barth's Sherman-like march through the battlefields of a defeated liberal theology leave anything but destruction in its wake?[35]

Krisis is therefore the ruling metaphor or trope. It is sometimes said that method is in short supply; but is this really so? Suffice to say that Barth soon moved on in terms of methodology and style into the classical German of his mature work—but the work on *Kirchliche Dogmatik* is still as assertive

---

32   *Römerbrief* (2nd ed.), ET, 21f.
33   Webb, *Re-figuring Theology*, 11.
34   See, Eberle, *Max Beckmann Die Nacht—Passion ohne Erlösung*.
35   Webb, *Re-figuring Theology*, 17.

and uncompromising as his youthful work, it is as kerygmatic, and it is equally eschatological. Both Barth's theology in *Der Römerbrief* and his work in *Kirchliche Dogmatik* are grounded in the unknowability of God from a human perspective (caused by original sin), an unknowability that dissolves human religion, leaving the primacy of the *Deus dixit*: God's self-revelation in Christ.

VI. EXPRESSIONISM: THE VISUAL ARTS

So, what did Barth approve of in the arts—particularly, the visual arts? Barth made various comments in his mature work, which we will examine later, particularly on the use of visual arts in Protestant churches. He is fully aware of Expressionistic paintings contemporaneous to his year of the new starting point (1915), through to *Römerbrief* (2nd ed.), and likewise earlier paintings from the later mediaeval period and the Renaissance, which are considered to be a precursor to modern Expressionism. However, at the heart of Barth's aesthetic of the visual and plastic arts is *The Crucifixion* from Grünewald's *Isenheim Altarpiece*.

VII. MATTHIAS GRÜNEWALD AND HANS HOLBEIN THE YOUNGER

Matthias Grünewald's *The Isenheim Altarpiece* (completed 1515) is a complex series of images, double doors and center panels with three views: first, the crucifixion; secondly, the annunciation, nativity, and resurrection; thirdly, the patron saints of the foundation.[36] Painting, for Grünewald, was not about hidden laws of beauty, as it was for many Italian Renaissance artists. No, for Grünewald art's sole purpose and function was to glorify God and inform about God's truth through revelation: the sacrifice of God's only Son on the cross for our salvation: suffering comes before resurrection and glory. Art was therefore was didactic, kerygmatic, it served the economy of salvation and atonement; therefore it served the proclamation of the church. This was the aim of virtually all religious art in the Middle Ages, providing a sermon in pictures, proclaiming, as

---

36 Matthias Grünewald (b.1470/80, Würzburg, d.1528, Halle), *The Isenheim Altarpiece*, completed 1915, oil on wood, 269 x 307 cm, (location Musée, d'Unterlinden, Colmar). *The Isenheim Altarpiece* was undertaken for the hospital chapel of Saint Anthony's Monastery in Isenheim in Alsace; it is a carved shrine with two sets of folding wings, three views, and multiple images.

2. Karl Barth: "Krisis," War, & Expressionism

many mediaeval manuals on painting stated, the sacred truths in the form of events recorded in the Bible as taught by the church (not far really from Barth's *Kirchliche Dogmatik*). Most mediaeval art is characterized by multiple-point perspective, used as a theological technique—for example, Masaccio's *The Trinity* (c.1425–28), which used a system of spatial illusionism, and a conception of time and space that transcended the material, yet dealt with the very stuff of temporal reality[37]—not the single-point perspective of Renaissance painting. Grünewald's *Crucifixion*, at the center of *The Isenheim Altarpiece*, is as bleak, barren, and desolate as any Good Friday sermon: we see the horrific results of human sin, *the fall* writ large, the distorted body, the hands writhing in pain. We are reminded of the sentence spoken by Christ in the crucifixion from the English mediaeval mystery plays: "All this I suffered for thy sake—Say, man, what suffered thou for me?"[38] For Grünewald, John the Baptist stands with the *Agnes Dei*, the symbol of the lamb carrying the cross and pouring out its blood into the chalice, his bony finger emaciated from service points to the Christ and above are written the words from John's Gospel: "*illum oportet crescere me autem minui*" ("He must increase, but I must decrease," John 3:30). The figures at the foot of the cross are disproportionately smaller. Grünewald rejected the emerging and developing Renaissance principle of correct proportion, he varied figures according to their innate importance *eschatologically*, to reflect an inner meaning (a technique used consistently since the very earliest period of Christian art, especially in the catacombs in Rome): proportion was governed by God, not by superficial appearance. Coupled with the stark Expressionistic, even existentialistic, nature of this image, all is governed by a biblical-ecclesial kerygmatic principle. Next to Christ in importance are the figures of John the Baptist and the two Mary's (with, presumably, John the beloved disciple supporting Mary the mother of Christ, Mary Magdalene being the other figure). The meaning and proportion of the four figures at the foot of the cross is that they are less than Christ and any meaning their existence holds is in Christ. The church is represented by John the

---

37   See, Aiken "The Perspective Construction of Masaccio's 'Trinity' Fresco and Medieval Astronomical Graphics."

38   York Cycle, Play 47: "The Mercers, The Last Judgment, Christ speaking in Judgment," lines 275–76, circa fourteenth century: Happé (ed.), *English Mystery Plays*, 642. Online text, University of Michigan: http://quod.lib.umich.edu/c/cme/York/1:50?rgn=div1;view=fulltext. See also, Peter Happé (ed.), *English Mystery Plays* (1975).

Baptist—he is the signifier, but he points away from himself to Christ. Barth commented, "We think of John the Baptist in Grünewald's painting of the crucifixion, with his strangely pointing hand. It is this hand which is in evidence in the Bible."[39] Barth discovered Grünewald's *Crucifixion* around the time he was writing *Römerbrief* (1st ed.),[40] and from that point on he always worked with a reproduction of it above his desk in his study so that whenever he raised his eyes from writing he beheld this image of Christ, and the figure of John the Baptist kerygmatically representing what Barth himself believed he was called to do. In a similar vein, we see Holbein's *The Body of the Dead Christ in the Tomb* (1521), which was valued by Barth's theological colleague and friend Eduard Thurneysen, an image shared and respected also by Barth: again we see the utter degradation, suffering, torture, and the reality of death hoisted onto Jesus Christ the Son of God by those he came to save: this is art but it is also a sermon, it is existentialist, Expressionistic, shockingly kerygmatic.[41] Is this not the *eschaton* breaking in?

VIII. EL GRECO, VINCENT VAN GOGH AND EDVARD MUNCH

Expressionist artists/painters are cited by Eduard Thurneysen and Karl Barth in their correspondence,[42] likewise Barth cites artists in his addresses, and in *Der Römerbrief*.[43] They also betray a respect for

[39] Barth, Karl "Biblische Fragen, Einsichten und Ausblicke" (address delivered at the Aarau Student Conference, 1920) in *Das Wort Gottes und die Theologie*, 70–98. ET: "Biblical Questions, Insights and Vistas" translated by Douglas Horton, in *The Word of God and the Word of Man*, 51–96.

[40] See, for example, *Römerbrief* (1st ed.), 164 & 620; *Römerbrief* (2nd ed.), 117 & 141.

[41] Hans Holbein the Younger (b.1497, Augsburg, Germany, d.1543, London) *The Body of the Dead Christ in the Tomb* 1521, oil on wood, 30,5 x 200cm, Kunstmuseum, Öffentliche Kunstsammlung, Basle.

[42] See for example, "Barth writing to Thurneysen, 25 März 1918;" also, "Barth writing to Thurneysen, 3 Juni 1919;" and "Barth writing to Thurneysen, 28 Dezember 1920," in Karl Barth, *Karl Barth-Eduard Thurneysen Briefwechsel Band I 1913-1921* (1973). See also, "Barth to Thurneysen, 7 Juli 1922 (Rundbrief)," in Barth, *Karl Karl Barth-Eduard Thurneysen Briefwechsel Band II 1921-1930* (1973).

[43] Barth writing on these artists in *Römerbrief* (1st ed.): for example, Albrecht Dürer (164, 620), Matthias Grünewald (164, 620); see also Michelangelo Buonarotti (496, 633), August Rodin (84) also comments on the dramatist Henrik Ibsen (507) and poet/writer Friedrich von Schiller (26f, 31, 35, 39, 48, 78–81, 85, 130, 228, 280, 291,

2. Karl Barth: "Krisis," War, & Expressionism

mediaeval and Renaissance painters. Thurneysen refers to the sixteenth-century painter El Greco ("The Greek"—Doménikos Theotokópoulos 1541–1614), a painter, sculptor, and architect of the Spanish Renaissance:

> We are thinking of the remarkable, elongated, and animated figures in the paintings of El Greco, or the variously attacked creations of the Expressionists, which are often with good reason compared to Dostoevsky's work. The obvious dislocations and distortions of these figures can hardly be due to defective vision, as some have surmised for El Greco. Most probably these painters also have seen something of that deep tendency of life toward the beyond. "This mortal must put on immortality." (1Cor. 15:53.)[44]

Form is distorted in El Greco's work so as to convey a deeper meaning, as in *The Opening of the Fifth Seal* (1608–14; from The Revelation to John 6:9), where there appear to be multiple picture planes, with several systems of perspective, most of which have vanishing points outside of the picture: in art-historical terms this is often termed Catholic Conceptualism (evident even in El Greco's landscapes—for example, the heavily charged *View of Toledo* (1597–99) as distinct from the tight super-realism of much Protestant seventeenth-century art—for example, Vermeer.

Both Barth and Thurneysen used the concept of multiple vanishing points outside of a picture as a metaphor of the eschatological resolution of all outside or beyond this world, this reality.[45] Both cite Expressionism where the resolution of lines of perspective are in a *Fluchtpunkt* outside of the picture; in addition, the physical appearance of people is not according to expectation but is a reflection of the inner psychological state and truth of the person. These examples provide Thurneysen with an analogy for the closure of the dialectic between God and humanity—only in eternity is the antinomy resolved.[46] Therefore, the utter realism of Dostoevsky's literary perspective is analogous with the perspective of a painting that

---

325, 352f, 355, 380, 383, 388, 396, 417, 435, 494, 496, 607, 610, 624f). Barth writing on these artists in *Der Römerbrief* (2nd ed.): Matthias Grünewald (117, 141); see also Michelangelo Buonarotti (247. 249) and writers Friedrich von Schiller (482) and Tolstoy (428, 478, 508).

44   Thurneysen, *Dostojewski*, 35.

45   "Fluchtpunkt" (vanishing point), the point where all lines of perspective converge, in an apparent contradiction of Euclidean geometry. See, Thurneysen *Dostojewski* (1921), 35–36, 45, 53, 58.

46   Thurneysen, *Dostojewski*, 35–36.

can only be resolved in the vanishing point (*Fluchtpunkt*) outside of the picture plane, outside of this reality, the other side of this life, this world. Eduard Thurneysen also goes further into the visual analogy of lines of perspective meeting outside of the picture plane because two parallel lines will never meet, according to Euclidean geometry, yet have the appearance from human perspective of converging as they disappear into observable reality. Again, Barth and Thurneysen will argue that in eternity they will meet in the same way that all the irreconcilable antinomies of suffering and evil on earth in this life will be resolved in eternity.[47]

Nineteenth-century precursors to German Expressionism included Vincent Van Gogh's *Wheat Field under Threatening Skies* (1890), which is heavily psychological and distorted (even more so when one knows that Van Gogh shot himself and died a matter of hours after painting the scene); likewise Edvard Munch's *The Scream* (1893), which represented the psychological state of the individual, not the outward appearance of reality.

IX. GERMAN EXPRESSIONISM I: *DIE BRÜCKE* AND *DER BLAUE REITER*

Grünewald is nowadays considered a forerunner of Expressionism for reasons we have briefly alluded to above: the nature of the painting, the distortion of form for the sake of a deeper meaning, et cetera. German Expressionism began in the early years of the twentieth century with the work of two groups, *Die Brücke* and *Der Blaue Reiter*, where painters such as Franz Marc and Wassily Kandinsky liberated themselves from traditional representation by using distortion and vibrant unrealistic color in their painting to express what they consider a deeper, truer meaning. Consider Franz Marc's animal paintings, for example *Blue Horse* (1911), or Emil Nolde's religious paintings, for example *The Prophet* (1912).

With the First World War Expressionist painters and writers developed a much darker, more existential character—the cruelty of the war was reflected violently in the work of Max Beckmann, Otto Dix, and Georg Grosz. They could not avoid observing the eschatological chaos that the evil in humanity had unleashed. Max Beckmann worked for the German army's medical corps during the war, sketching the horrors on the front line—for example, *The Morgue* (1915). Following

---

47   Thurneysen, *Dostojewski*, 35–36.

2. Karl Barth: "Krisis," War, & Expressionism

a nervous breakdown, his paintings became harsher, expressively distorted, and filled with symbolism reflecting the immorality of human behavior. Georg Grosz (1893–1959) experienced the horrors of war in the trenches—for example, Georg Grosz, *Grenade* (1915)—this deepened his intense loathing for German society. Discharged from the army for medical reasons, he produced savagely satirical paintings and drawings that expressed his despair, hate, and disillusionment. Otto Dix (1891–1969) was injured and witnessed suffering on both fronts, represented in his work, for example, *Artillery Duel* (1917). After the war he developed left-wing views and his paintings and drawings became increasingly political; he was angry about the way wounded and disabled ex-soldiers were treated—for example, *Card Playing War Cripples* (1920). These are Barth's contemporaries, they shared his political views, his anger at the bourgeois hypocrisy of nineteenth-century liberal neo-Protestantism, and he shared with them, as with many of the younger generation of the intelligentsia in Germany and Switzerland, a desire to change, to rebuild from the nihilism of the First World War. However, he did not approve—theologically and in terms of the Christian life—of the solution posited in their work: this solution was no solution. The Expressionist painters in effect identified *the fall* (or more pertinently, the consequences of original sin), however, their own confused, syncretistic agnosticism prevented them from naming it thus or pulling back from its effects in their own lives. This Expressionist solution of no solution merely echoed Nietzsche's assertion that in looking into the abyss, the abyss will look back, the result was/is despair, and many of them were swallowed by the abyss. Barth realized this. In *the Tambach lecture* he even stated that he and others held an aversion to the work of the Expressionists, this is despite the value of such pictures in illustrating the plight of humanity, the depraved and sinful human condition. Barth commented,

> However strong our aversion may be to the work of the modern Expressionistic artists, it is more than clear that for these men the chief concern is the essence, the content, the referring of the beautiful to life's unity, in contrast to that art for its own sake which prevailed during the last generation, but neither, after all, can cite precedent with certainty in Raphael or Dürer.[48]

---

48   Barth, "Der Christ in der Gesellschaft," 46f.

Eberhard Busch notes in his biography of Barth how he often met with young poets, writers, artists, and how his personal acquaintance with the writer Hermann Hesse led him to comment negatively.[49] Barth, writing to Thurneysen, noted:

> ... I met Hesse there, a sculptor Hubachers, a poet ... and some Statisten [theatrical extras?]. I endured the embarrassment of the situation, it was grim and I was somewhat unprepared! The conversation with Hesse took place previously. Again I was astounded at the pietistic narrowness of these artists. Evidently they are mostly preoccupied with the problems of their private existence: "I order things so as to find my way through a rather heavy life, okay." That is the argument of all arguments. I invited him to omit at least all the polemics. He manipulated rather lively against namely Lenin, Ludendorf and other contemporaries; however, he gave in finally to that which he would already grasp, that is, to my *Weltanschauung*. But also there must be room for such question marks. Shortly after, the man was not just overpowering but with little teaching to say. Hubacher (the sculptor) is without a worldview much more reasonable.[50]

X. GERMAN EXPRESSIONISM II: GERMAN ROMANTICISM

German Expressionism, despite its apparent contrast with nineteenth-century German romanticism, shared something of a human-centered approach to religion and religious art, both shared a common heritage in the world of Friedrich Schleiermacher (1768–1834), Johann Wolfgang von Goethe (1749–1832), Georg Hegel (1770–1831), et cetera. For example, the mystical and misty pantheism of Casper David Friedrich's *Man and Woman Contemplating the Moon* (1824) or the neo-classical religious iconography, devoid of all Christian reference, of *Memorial Monument to*

---

49   Busch comments further how he had already made the acquaintance of two other artists in his brother-in-law's house, and saw more of them later: these were the sculptor Hermann Hubacher and the painter Cuno Amiet (who belonged to the Dresden Die Brücke group—including Ludwig Kirchner, Erich Heckel, Emil Nolde, and Max Pechstein). See, Busch, *Karl Barths Lebenslauf, Nach seinem Briefen und autobiographischen Texten*, 137–38.

50   "Barth writing to Eduard Thurneysen June 20, 1921," see: Barth, *Karl Barth—Eduard Thurneysen Briefwechsel Band I 1913-1921*, 497.

2. Karl Barth: "Krisis," War, & Expressionism

Goethe contemporaneous with Schleiermacher's religion of feeling. Such idiomatic imagery perhaps reached its height in German civic religious art, where Jesus Christ was often reduced to a mere human presented with neo-classical pagan imagery derived from Greek and Roman culture: for example, the early painting of Max Klinger—*Christ on Mount Olympus*, which presented Jesus as a pale-skinned, blonde-haired, blue-eyed wise Germanic religious leader conversing with young Greek men and women (in the mold of Strauss' Christology?—anti-Semitic religious atheism, perhaps).

XI. GERMAN EXPRESSIONISM III: MAX BECKMANN

Arguably the foremost Expressionist painter, Max Beckmann's work was known by Barth, and it may be argued exerted an influence of sorts on him during the writing of *Römerbrief* (1st ed.) (1919). Much of the second part of the first chapter entitled "*Die Nacht*" ("The Night") reflects similar aims and objectives, also theological anthropology and a profound understanding of the despair of the human condition, which can be seen in Beckmann's painting, also entitled *Die Nacht* from 1918. The second part of chapter one of *Der Römerbrief* entitled "*Die Nacht*,"[51] is prefaced by Romans 1:18: "The wrath of God is being revealed from heaven against all the godlessness and wickedness of men who suppress the truth by their wickedness." In his own translation from the Greek, Barth added to the final clause, "those who hold the truth imprisoned in the chains of their unrighteousness."[52] Anyone familiar with the opening chapters of Paul's Epistle to the Romans will be aware that the apostle goes to great lengths to establish the problem of humanity, the desperation that the fall brought, the depravity and sadism of the human condition, and only then offers God's solution in Christ. Beckmann's painting posits the same problem—humanity is represented by the darkness of the night, embroiled in the perversion, sadism, and despair of *Die Nacht*, but he offers no solution. This is true essentially of the other German Expressionists: they could recognize only too well the desperation of humanity—and remember

---

51 In *Römerbrief* (1st ed., 1919) the sub-sections of "*Die Nacht*" ("The Night") are entitled "Der Abfall" ("The Trash") on Romans 1:18–21, and Der Sturz (The fall) on Romans 1:22–32. In *Römerbrief* (2nd ed., 1922) these sub-section titles are changed to "Ursache" ("it's the reason," "the cause") and Wirkung ("its effect" or "operation").

52 *Römerbrief* (1st ed. 1919), 24.

that both Barth and Beckmann were working during the desperate final years of the First World War parallel to the Marxist revolution in Russia—but the only solution the Expressionist painters and writers could offer was the secret chambers of the soul and its hidden, partly unspeakable longings."[53] Is this not in the same mold as Schleiermacher's religion of feeling? Perhaps. Max Beckmann's *Die Nacht*, though based on and inspired by a brutal crime, is not simply an illustration, a pictorial representation of an event. It takes an event—the torture, abuse, and murder of a small family by a group of criminals who broke into their flat one night—and projects the deeper underlying meaning onto a picture that encapsulates what was happening to European civilization at that time during the later stages of the First World War.[54] Like the chapter entitled "*Die Nacht*" in *Der Römerbrief*, what results is symptomatic of the human predicament and how humanity is preying on itself, destroying itself as it tries to justify itself. The same image can be seen in the war poetry of Wilfred Owen and Siegfried Sassoon.[55] Beckmann's *Die Nacht*, like the work of Grünewald and El Greco, is not composed around single-point perspective, there are several scenes layered, overlaid, juxtaposed, so as to take the emphasis away from reality, the real event—which according to the Expressionist dictum already exists (*Die Welt ist da, Es wäre sinnlos, sie zu wiederholen*)—thereby to invoke a wider, deeper meaning reflecting the depravity of human behavior: the gang's invasion of a family flat on the micro scale, the collapse of European civilization during the First World War on the macro. Barth, from *Römerbrief* (2nd ed.), on the night, and its causes commented:

> And so in us the light has become darkness, and the wrath of God is now inevitable: "They became vain in their reasonings and their senseless heart was darkened."* The barrier is now a barrier, and the "No" of God is now indeed a negation. Bereft of understanding and abandoned to themselves, people are at the mercy of the dominion of the meaningless and pointless powers of this world; for our life in this world has meaning only in its relation to the one true God.

53 Pauck, *Karl Barth: Prophet of a New Christianity?* 19

54 For a piercing description and analysis of Beckmann's *Die Nacht*, see Lackner *Max Beckmann*.

55 For example, Wilfred Owen *Anthem for Doomed Youth*, also, Siegfried Sassoon, *The Rear-Guard*, and from *Attack!* See Gardner (ed.), *Up the Line to Death—The War Poets 1914-1918*, 136-37, 129-30, 142.

2. Karl Barth: "Krisis," War, & Expressionism

... Dark, blind, uncritical, capricious, mankind becomes a thing in itself. Heartless, merciless, perceiving without observing or understanding and therefore empty, void, is our thought: thoughtless, observing without perceiving and therefore blind, is our heart. Fugitive is the soul in this world and soulless is the world, when men do not find themselves within the sphere of the knowledge of the unknown God, when they avoid the true God in whom they and the world must lose themselves in order that both may find themselves again.

This is the Cause of the Night in which we are travelling, wandering: this also is the Cause of the Wrath of God which has been manifested, revealed, over our heads.[56] [* Barth quoting Romans 1:21b]

XII. ZEITGEIST

Bruce McCormack in Karl Barth's *Critically Realistic Dialectical Theology*[57] has shown how Barth's developments—the making of an outsider, the genesis of a dialectical theology in reaction to the liberal neo-Protestant theology of his teachers against the shadow of a process eschatology as characterized by *Römerbrief* (1st ed.), which then develops through *Römerbrief* (2nd ed.) into the consistent eschatology of his work in the 1920s (essentially the rediscovery and analysis of his own Reformed heritage, then to form the foundations of his mature work in the shadow on an *anhypostatic-enhypostatic* Christology)—operated against and were conditioned in reaction, to a degree, to the prevailing socio-cultural-political climate in central Europe: war, revolution, fragmentation. This is an eschatological *zeitgeist* and, yes, Barth is moved by the spirit of the times, but the pre-eminence of the *Deus dixit* following the year of the new starting point (1915) meant that his work moves, gradually, away from the spirit of the times: yet the urgency of this eschatological *zeitgeist* remains. This becomes clear as his work develops through the 1920s and he begins to put theological space between himself and many of the other dialectical theologians who begin to flirt with the religious ideas being

---

56   *Römerbrief* (2nd ed.), 25. (My translation.)

57   McCormack, *Karl Barth's Critically Realistic Dialectical Theology, Its Genesis and Development 1909–1936*. See in particular, Pt. I, §. 4 Theology in a Revolutionary Age, 184–203. See also, Raabe (ed.), *The Era of German Expressionism*.

generated around the National Socialists (remembering that the Nazis were in many ways a continuation of the *zeitgeist* of the immediate post First World War angst). By the end of the 1920s fractures had appeared between Barth and many of the other adherents to *Dialektische Theologie* (for example, Gogarten, Bultmann, and Brunner—not forgetting the prevailing importance of the philosopher Heidegger). The rise of National Socialism in Germany and the manner in which many of his colleagues supported the idea of the Blood-and-Soil religion of the Nazis led Barth to distance himself from many of the so-called supporters of *Dialektische Theologie*. Though not part of this circle of dialectical theologians, Wilhelm Stapel (1882-1954)—writer, journalist, and translator, noted as a Protestant German Nationalist, who supported the National Socialists—is a name all but forgotten from this period. A dangerous name who in effect scripted the religious mythology for the National Socialists; his works included, *Der christliche Staatsmann* (*The Christian Statesman*), *Die drei Stände* (*The Three Conditions*), a new translation of the *Parsifal* and *The Heiland* (*The Savior*), he also worked on the concept of Heathen Imperialism in which he saw the will of the German people as synonymous with the will of "god" (his "theism," as such, drew much from a simplified reading of Hegel and Nietzsche, but equally from the pagan Norse myths popularized by Wagner!).

By the late 1920s, the point had been reached where Barth broke off relations completely with theologians who once had been his colleagues, in particular Gogarten.

XIII. BARTH & CREATIVITY

To return to art and creativity: why Grünewald? Because for Barth this is art that is *self-effacing*, it points to God (remember that most mediaeval art is anonymous—particularly illuminated manuscripts—unlike modern art it points away from the artist/sculptor/illustrator). The figure of John the Baptist epitomizes Barth's theory of art—the elongated finger that points to the Christ, therefore art must not point to itself but to God. Barth loved Mozart's music: "they can say what they like about my theology but they must leave Mozart alone" is a comment often attributed to Barth. In his study in Bruderholzallee 26, Basel, from 1955, Barth had two portraits, one of Mozart the other of Calvin, hung on the same level above two doors, and he would take great pleasure in explaining to visitors that both

2. Karl Barth: "Krisis," War, & Expressionism

were on the same level.[58] Of course, this betrays something of a modern weakness in Barth: portraits can be taken to represent the modern obsession with the individual, with celebrity, the romantic artist, the cult of the individual. Hanging, say, the title page from Calvin's *Institutes* and the opening page from the score of a Mozart opera would have been, perhaps, more appropriate.

Therefore we may ask, why Mozart? Does Mozart's secular music point to God?—in a way, yes, because Mozart's creativity, his genius, does not appear to be of the natural world, and immediately evokes the other, the beyond. Mozart's genius was such that he would often wake up in the morning with a complete symphony or piano concerto in his mind—all he had to do was write it down. Roger Penrose, the mathematician and cosmologist, commented on Mozart's genius that this was the ability to think outside of time;[59] Mozart's creativity was therefore not contained by or issued from the temporal. But why not the visual or plastic arts? Is this because music is the purest form of abstract art, and if so it points beyond? Can this be said of the visual/plastic arts? Is this not possible because the visual/plastic arts deal with matter—the very stuff of reality? But why is music exempt—it needs material reality in the form of voices, instruments. So are we moving towards conceptualism as the ultimate art form, acceptable before the gospel? Provided the concepts/ideas point towards God? Though such a statement raises the question, which God? Therefore, such concepts/ideas must in some way reflect the givenness of the revelation of the *Deus dixit*. Because, it may be argued, much music does this already, we have to pass over, regrettably, looking at Barth's love of Mozart in any depth.[60]

XIV. BARTH THE ICONOCLAST?

Some of Barth's comments in his mature work caused the charge generally of iconoclast to be raised against him—that is, his apparent complete

---

58   See Busch, Karl Barths *Lebenslauf*, 423.

59   Kelly et al., *Irreducible Mind: Toward a Psychology for the 21st Century*. See Ch. 7 Genius, specifically 487f. for Mozart, and Penrose's comments. In the context of the work as a whole, the authors note (on the back cover), "Practically every contemporary mainstream scientist presumes that all aspects of mind are generated by brain activity. We demonstrate the inadequacy of this picture by assembling evidence for a variety of empirical phenomena which it cannot explain."

60   See Barth, *Wolfgang Amadeus Mozart*.

rejection of visual art and images as idolatrous. So what did Barth actually write?[61] The danger for Barth of visual images, art, even music, lies in the second commandment: "You shall have no other gods before me. You shall not make for yourself an idol in the form of anything in heaven above or on the earth beneath or in the waters below. You shall not bow down to them or worship them" (Exod 20:3–5a). Webb comments that often it may be concluded that, "Barth's entire theology, which pits the dialectic of the heard Word against the illusory identity of appearance and reality, can be considered as essentially anti-aesthetic and iconoclastic."[62] However, Barth did not object, as we have seen, to the visual arts in a relatively secular context—consider his liking of Renaissance Christian art as evidenced from his discussions with Eduard Thurneysen, or his daily use of Grünewald's *Crucifixion* as an *aide memoire* of what Christ had done for humanity. But herein lies a danger: contemplating a work of Christian art in a gallery, or a reproduction in a book or on the wall at home is one thing, the presence and use of such pictures and statues in a church building is another. There is always the danger when worshipping in a church building of the focus or object of our prayer and worship falling onto a temporal object—for our minds constantly want to latch onto the concrete, the visible, the temporal and corporeal. In an essay entitled "The Architectural Problem of Protestant Places of Worship,"[63] Barth comments on these problems; he endorsed the recommendation of a circular place of worship "because it shows that church buildings are designed to be places for the preaching of the Word of God and for the prayer of the assembled community," further that there should be a simple wooden table at the center for the purposes of preaching, communion, baptism. He comments that, "Since the organ and choir are accessories appreciated to a greater or lesser degree and may in principle be dispensed with, they should not appear in the field of vision of the assembled community."[64] What of the visual arts:

---

61   Webb, *Re-figuring Theology*, cites most of the material from Barth's mature work that led to the charge of iconoclast being raised, and details of the accusers; my acknowledgement is to Stephen Webb for pointing me in the direction of this material from *Church Dogmatics, Dogmatics in Outline*, etc.

62   Webb, *Re-figuring Theology*, 183 (n. 37). See also Webb, Ch. 1, §. 3, 8–14, and §. 4, 17–18.

63   Barth, "The Architectural Problem of Protestant Places of Worship," 92–93.

64   Barth, "The Architectural Problem of Protestant Places of Worship," 93.

2. Karl Barth: "Krisis," War, & Expressionism

> Images and symbols have no place at all in a building designed for Protestant worship. They too can serve only to dissipate attention and create confusion. It is only the community met together for worship in the strict meaning of the word—that is for prayer, preaching, baptism and the Lord's Supper—and above all the community in action in everyday life, which corresponds to the reality of the person and work of Jesus Christ. No image and no symbol can play that role.[65]

So, only the community in action in everyday life corresponds to the reality of the person of Jesus Christ: this is what we are all founded in, grounded in, not necessarily religious affiliation. Church is about people, community, not objects or buildings—a fundamental ecclesiological axiom that we tend to forget. Therefore, Barth has no place for what he terms extraneous ornamentation. Webb comments that Barth was aware of his iconoclastic tendencies[66] and quotes his defense from the *Kirchliche Dogmatik*, which warns against the danger of becoming "Philistines or Christian iconoclasts in the face of human greatness."[67] Commenting on the destruction of heathen and pagan temples by early Christians, he noted how "after a time the storm of iconoclasm was succeeded by a fresh form of artistic decoration," therefore supplanted by idols, statues, and stained glass. Barth commented on the problems of Christianity and art, from §17 of *Kirchliche Dogmatik*:

> Devaluation and negation of what is human may occasionally have a practical and symbolical significance in detail, it can never have any basic or general significance. We cannot, as it were, translate the divine judgment that religion is unbelief into human terms, into the form of definite devaluations and negations. . . . But we must still accept it as God's judgment upon all that is human. It can be heard and understood, strictly and exactly as intended, only by those who do not despair of the human element as such, who regard it as something worthwhile, who have some inkling of what it means really to abandon the world of Greek or Indian gods, China's world of wisdom or even the world of Roman Catholicism, or even our own Protestant world of faith as such, in the thoroughgoing sense of that divine judgment. In this sense the

---

65   Barth, "The Architectural Problem of Protestant Places of Worship," 93.

66   Webb, *Re-figuring Theology*, 9f.

67   Barth, *Church Dogmatics*, I/2 §17, subsection 2 "Religion as Unbelief," specifically 298f.

> divine judgment, which we have to hear and receive, can actually be described as a safeguard against all forms of ignorance and Philistinism. . . . [I]n the sphere of reverence before God, there must always be a place for reverence for human greatness. It does not lie under our judgment, but under the judgment of God.[68]

Writing in *Dogmatics in Outline*, Barth elaborates that it is because of the aseity, the sovereignty, and the freedom of God that all the other gods and idols "collapse into dust, and He remains the only One. 'I am the Lord thy God . . . thou shalt have no other gods before Me.'"[69] Furthermore (from *Dogmatics in Outline*):

> And the Second Commandment also becomes quite clear then: "Thou shalt not make unto thee any image nor any sort of likeness. Thou shalt not bow down to them nor worship them." . . . God has Himself done everything in order to present Himself. How should man make an image of Him after He has presented His likeness Himself? A well-intentioned business, this entire "spectacle" of Christian art, well-intentioned but impotent, since God Himself has made His own image. Once a man has understood "God in the highest," it becomes impossible for him to want any imagery in thought, or any other kind of imagery.[70]

So, Barth is guilty of skepticism, theologically, towards human artistic endeavor generally, also whether there is any ultimate value to Christian art specifically, because God has given us his own image in Jesus Christ, but he is not necessarily an iconoclast. Thus, we may conclude that Barth commencing his working day listening to a piece of music by Mozart, and looking on Grünewald's *Crucifixion* before starting work at his desk, was a form of contemplation. He was contemplating what God had done to redeem humanity, whilst listening to the beauty of God's inspiration and creativity focused through the frail sinful human being that was Mozart—not venerating the picture as if it was God, or believing the intense aesthetic response to the music was a "god" of sorts. Therefore, we must acknowledge that there is a thin line between contemplation

---

68   Essentially, Barth *Church Dogmatics*, I/2 §17 300. See, "Im Raum der Ehrfurcht vor Gott wird die Ehrfurcht vor menschlicher Größe immer ihre Stelle haben müssen: sie unterliegt Gottes, sie unterliegt nicht unserem Gericht," Barth. *Kirchliche Dogmatik*, I/2 §17 328.

69   Barth, *Dogmatiks in Grundriss*, §.5 Das Gottesverhältnis und der Grund des Handlns, 49f.

70   Barth, *Dogmatiks in Grundriss*, 40–41.

2. Karl Barth: "Krisis," War, & Expressionism

under certain circumstances and veneration—that is, the worship of a human crafted product in the place of God, or as surrogate for God. We may presume that it is this capacity for veneration in humanity to which Barth objects, quite rightly: but he does not object to contemplation or reverence (*Ehrfurcht*). It is difficult to refute the accusation that Barth is being patronizing—he can trust ordinary Christians with art in their homes, but not when they go to church; he is strong enough to resist the temptation of idolatry himself, but they may not be. But, as Barth asserted in *Kirchliche Dogmatik*, any objection to the displacement of the word of God by art, design, and craft, "does not lie under our judgment, but under the judgment of God," and, ironically, the 1930s saw one of the greatest iconoclastic purges of art in all history—the piles of painting, sculpture, literature, smashed and burnt by the Nazis caused the iron-bar finger-crushing Byzantine iconoclasm of the eighth to the ninth centuries, and the hammer-wielding church vandalism of the Protestant Reformation in the sixteenth century, to pale by comparison.

XV. MODERNISM?

Is Barth right or merely prejudiced in his rejection of much of the visual/plastic arts? Or does this apply to modernism? It would appear the latter—that he objected to modernism, and art in churches. What actually happened to the German Expressionists? The movement as such transmuted into the *Neue Sachlichkeit*—the bohemian decadence of the Weimar Republic—many of the Expressionists then underwent an ideological shift over to the social realism of German National Socialist art, offering what were, in their own way, religious paintings (often in the form of mass-produced graphics, such as postcards or cigarette cards). And then there is Hermann Otto Hoyer's painting of Hitler addressing, converting, the people (in the 1920s, the early days of National Socialism) entitled, *In the Beginning was the Word* (no known date: circa late-1920s?) with its direct take on John's Gospel: Hitler, rather than Jesus Christ, is presented as the Word of God.[71] Ironically the Nazis condemned Expressionism as degenerate.[72] The experiment in National Socialist art is

---

71   My acknowledgement for the Nazi illustrations is to Bytwerk, *Bending Spines: The Propagandas of Nazi Germany and the German Democratic Republic*.

72   Max Beckmann was eventually branded a purveyor of degenerate art by Hitler, sacked from his teaching post in 1933, fled to Amsterdam in 1937, then settled in America, dying at the age of sixty-six years in 1950.

a reflection of the politics of Nazism. It is deeply eschatological—a *krisis*-driven revolution where death becomes glorified, but it is demonic in origin, not pneumatological, it is an evil inversion of God's *eschaton*: it is not holy and divinely authored.

It is important to note that most mediaeval and Renaissance artists held to a faith that the German Expressionists—whose religious beliefs were by and large syncretistic if they declared any—did not. This surely shows through in their work. Around 1916 to 1917 Beckmann experimented with the Christian subject matter of mediaeval and Renaissance art. As the Beckmann scholar Didier Ottinger has commented, "For a while Beckmann had thought that primitive art, and faith in a renewed Christianity might prove a crucible for the emergence of new collective values."[73] However, Beckmann concluded that he had taken the wrong track and regarded this experiment as an illusion for, what he termed, obsolete myths. These paintings included, *Christ and the Woman Taken in Adultery* (1917), *Adam and Eve* (1917), and *Resurrection* (1918). In the case of Beckmann's *The Descent from the Cross* (*Kreuzabnahme* 1917), which was based explicitly on *The Descent from the Cross* by the fifteenth-century Flemish painter Rogier van der Weyden, both paintings appear to reflect the lifestyle and beliefs of the artists. Does Beckmann's *Descent* say more about him as an alienated modern liberal than it does about Mary's anguish, grief, and realization of the momentousness of the death of the Son of God? Perhaps van der Weyden's *Mary*, like Grünewald's figure of John the Baptist, points beyond the self to the object of faith and the knowledge of the death of the Son of God? Does Beckmann's existential alienation show through in his work, and thereby disallow him to raise his art—even when explicitly religious—to the level of the great mediaeval and Renaissance masters? By comparison we can see the problem of insularity and individualism in many twentieth-century Expressionists and Existentialists where nothing is deemed to exist except one's own perception, nothing exists beyond individual consciousness. It is surely this that shows through when comparing Beckmann's *Kreuzabnahm* with van der Weyden's *The Descent from the Cross*. Barth, as we have seen already, commented in his *Tambach Lecture* how neither the German Expressionists nor the nineteenth-century German romantics

---

73   Ottinger, "Beckmann's Lucid Somnambulism," 137.

could "cite precedent with certainty in Raphael or Dürer."[74] He regarded the art of Raphael and Dürer on a different level, theologically, to German Expressionism, despite the fact that the Expressionists wanted to refer to the beyond, the transcendent, a glimpse of the *eschaton*. Therefore, Raphael's *Entombment* (1507; the burial of Christ after the descent from the cross) provides a suitable comparison: the figures are not floating ethereally as in an El Greco, they are very real, muscular, truly flesh and blood, yet the scene is shot through with the transcendent because of what it is: Who is this dead man? What did he do? How did he die? Why did he die? Why are the people carrying the body so overcome with real grief as they struggle to complete their task? The world in Raphael's *Entombment* is precious, good, yet *fallen* and sinful, and every blade of grass echoes with the transcendent: with God's reality. And with what is to come.

So Barth was not inherently prejudiced against the visual/plastic arts. His objections were, first, to the misuse of visual images and sculpture in church buildings; second, related to modernism and liberalism—as they were in theology! For Barth, Grünewald and Mozart epitomized what the arts *should* be about: they should point away from the human self and towards the *Deus dixit*—for example, the figure of John the Baptist in Grünewald's *Crucifixion*. Is this so with Mozart? It was with Michelangelo—he implicitly believed and trusted in the God and Father of Jesus Christ, and knew of his creative reliance on the Holy Spirit. Both Michelangelo and Mozart were naively, even childishly, reliant on their faith to allow them to be creative and to point beyond self—even at the expense of order in their own lives. Barth at the time of writing *Der Römerbrief* was certainly very critical of bourgeois worldly comfort, as he saw and bore witness to a perennial eschatological *krisis* in society and culture. And we may certainly posit that neither Grünewald, Michelangelo, nor Mozart lived in bourgeois comfort! Neither did Beckmann—but did Beckmann have the faith of Grünewald, Mozart, and Michelangelo? It is faith and/or a lack of faith that is the litmus test when it comes to the judgment of God, *postmortem*.

XVI. CONCLUSION

So, Barth looked on and contemplated Grünewald's *Crucifixion* each morning, before starting work. This was clearly not venerating! Then he

---

74   Barth, "Der Christ in der Gesellschaft," 46f.

turned to his own work—like John the Baptist pointing to Christ on the cross. So Barth would have approved of a picture—say a painting—which pointed the observer towards the *Deus dixit*, the revelation, atonement and salvation wrought by God in Christ Jesus. Such art is therefore theologically ontological: it can point towards a reality that exists outside of, independent of, human imaginings, especially religious imaginings. But it is also intimately linked to humanity because the Word was incarnated and humanity is the object of this atonement/salvation. A few years ago the National Gallery in London held an exhibition for the millennium entitled *Seeing Salvation*, consisting of images of Jesus Christ. The title was deliberately provocative—it was not meekly, inanely, called "pictures of an important religious leader," the title prevented the exhibition being like a display of Buddha statuettes. The exhibition organizer wanted to provoke, to make the public consider who this person was, and why he died. For example, Jesus Christ's question to Peter: "Who do you say that I am?"[75] Perhaps Barth would have approved of this exhibition if he saw the works pointing to the *Deus dixit*?—in contrast to his disapproval of religious art in church buildings. Indeed, the setting is important, the building (a gallery) can be considered to be theologically neutral, allowing the visitors (not a congregation) to observe, consider, ask questions, and leave either closer to God in Christ, or further away. The decision, issuing from their response to the paintings, is theirs and theirs alone, the responsibility for that decision is in the general scheme of things "religious," yet it carries with it the eschatological promise of their final destination: heaven or hell! The measure of good art work from the gospel perspective is then perhaps in the public response: good Christian art will deflect the human response from itself and towards Christ. Perhaps this is how Barth saw Christian art functioning. The key to Barth's response to the visual arts is possibly as we saw earlier in his *Tambach Lecture*: that art for its own sake is as deadening and destructive as religion for its own sake, and that—as he commented—there is a world of difference between the aims and art of Raphael and Dürer, on the one hand, and the German Expressionists, on the other, despite the Expressionists concern for the inner essence. From a gospel perspective there is not much to choose between the art of the Expressionists and the broadly Schleiermachian art of the nineteenth-century German romantics that preceded them, or the superficial and propagandist art of the National

---

75   See, Matt 16:15; Mark 8:29; Luke 9:20.

2. Karl Barth: "Krisis," War, & Expressionism

Socialists that followed. We have not touched upon the use and theory of icons in the Orthodox traditions, nor have we examined Barth's doctrine of beauty. There is indeed much in the *Kirchliche Dogmatik* on the beauty of God in itself, and as the measure of all humanity (including creativity). Does Barth address a theology of art?—probably not.[76] But he does consider the beauty of God in a way many other theologians fail to. For example, "God is beautiful, divinely beautiful, beautiful in *His* own way, that is *His* alone, beautiful as the unattainable beauty yet really beautiful."[77] Colin Gunton, commenting on Barth's understanding of God's beauty wrote, "Barth is not concerned to argue any more than Mozart is concerned to argue, Mozart just plays. I think that is Barth's aim: to play on the revelation of God so that its truth and beauty will shine. He is a very aesthetic theologian."[78] Gunton also noted,

> Barth makes the point that theology has to a degree marginalized, or steered clear of the beauty of God. Protestant theology certainly has—although he does draw on a number of the Protestant dogmaticians to get his concept of glory from; Catholic theology has, he says, really until the nineteenth century, when it rediscovered it. And of course Von Balthasar who wrote a book on Barth based his first major seven-volume work; in fact, he called it *The Glory of the Lord* (in translation) and clearly drew on Barth for this. Von Balthasar too has some sour words for both Catholics and Protestants—but particularly Protestants because they can't have a doctrine of God's beauty. And Barth here wants to say that there is nothing wrong, nothing un-Protestant about having a doctrine of God's beauty and there is some great stuff there. But he happily draws on the Catholic tradition to speak of the beauty of God, people like Augustine.[79]

The danger is always that art is merely a reflection of the society that produces it (the *zeitgeist* writ large). For example, conceptual Brit Art (from the end of the twentieth century into the early twenty-first century) in the

---

76 It will be noted that I have deliberately avoided the theologian Paul Tillich on art—precisely because so much has been written on him and also that Barth is in many ways diametric to Tillich on art and creativity (especially with regards to natural theology). Further, Barth and the visual arts is a relatively unexplored area.

77 Barth, *Church Dogmatics*, I/1, 650.

78 Gunton on Barth, Lecture 5: "The Decade after Romans" (2), 25th October 2000. See, Gunton, *The Barth Lectures*, 76–96.

79 Gunton on Barth, Lecture 9: "The Being of God as the One Who Loves in Freedom," 29th November 2000. See Gunton, *The Barth Lectures*, 134–37.

UK: Damien Hirst's, statement about how incomprehensible death is to something living represented by a dead shark in a tank of formaldehyde; Tracey Emin's tent with the names of the myriad people she has slept with pasted inside; or Gilbert and George's large human phallus sculpted from human faeces (which was incidentally banned from exhibition not on grounds of morality and decency by the London Borough of Southwark, but on grounds of health and safety!). If all art is unavoidably a reflection of the society that produces it then perhaps German Expressionism was indeed a true reflection of central European society during and after the First World War, which adds even more justification to Barth's objections. And if the measure of art is whether it draws you to God, then again, this must be qualified by the question, "Which God?" If, as was the case with the National Socialists, Hitler was raised up to a divine level comparable to the Roman emperors (remembering that school children in Nazi Germany prayed not *for* Hitler, but *to* Hitler), and if you then commission artists to produce work to promote Hitler and all he represents then, ergo, you are in effect doing this for this "god" (note the lower case), as Hitler is then this "god," this pagan divine. The Holocaust then becomes an eschatological burnt sacrifice, an offering, to the demonic pagan "god" that Hitler's followers believed him to be. The efficacy of Barth's position—starting and ending with the *Deus dixit*, also the refutation of natural theology as the ground for a doctrine of God—then becomes clear. To return to the comment we quoted from Colin Gunton about how Barth's work is simply displaying the beauty of God's word, it is surely salutary to conclude with Mother's Teresa of Calcutta's comment about how the work of her missionaries caring for the poor, the sick, the dispossessed, was simply about doing something beautiful for God. Perhaps doing something beautiful for God is one of the highest theological justifications for art, but this must be framed by sound doctrinal beliefs: yes, it does matter what we belief and how we behave?

3

A Human-Generated *Eschaton*: Objectification in the Slave Trade, the Holocaust, and Abortion— The Delusions of Religious Atheism

> *"How long, O people, will you turn my glory into shame?*
> *How long will you love delusions and seek false gods?"*
> PSALM 4:2

> *"For I have no pleasure in the death of anyone,*
> *declares the Lord God; so turn, and live."*
> EZEKIEL 18:32

> *"Yet you brought me out of the womb; you made me trust in you,*
> *even at my mother's breast. From birth I was cast on you;*
> *from my mother's womb you have been my God."*
> PSALM 22:9–10

SYNOPSIS:

If death is an element of the *eschaton*, what happens when humanity usurps the God-given order of death followed by judgment? Humanly conferred judgment, leading to death, is tribalistic, despite the apparent veneer of civilized, polite behavior. A central belief amongst many of the secular-humanist and self-confessed atheistic critics of Christianity specifically, and religion more generally, is that "religious" people will eventually oppress and even kill their opponents; however, they fail to apply this proposition to themselves, to their own anti-theistic religiosity and to the tribalistic hegemony that validates and approves: *zeitgeist*. The aim of this paper is to explore how an Enlightenment-led theology of death is rooted in religious atheism, a belief system that defines another group of people as non-human, or sub-human, and open to exploitation and destruction. In terms of contemporary identity politics and Western liberal democratic principles this is comparable to a form of objectification. Whether *forced* or *voluntary*, this objectification has led, since the Reformation, to three Enlightenment mega-holocausts (de-humanized destruction and slaughter on an industrial scale): through the slave trade, through the holocaust of the Jews, and now through abortion. The roots of this are in the judgmental religious terrorism evidenced amongst Roman Catholics and Protestants in the Reformation, though it must be acknowledged that the element of dehumanizing objectification is a particular characteristic of the Age of Reason and Enlightenment-spawned religious atheism (seen in the associated mega-holocausts, and now continued into the post-Enlightenment, and modernist-postmodernist cultural identities). Initially we can identify and define objectification (whether forced or voluntary), and thereby theological objectification, "otherness," (as an element of our theological anthropology—as an attempt to redefine a person's God-given ontology); then we will deconstruct a doctrine of religion, and outline some defining principles. We must then consider the ontology of Jesus Christ as very God and very man (noting the conclusions of the seventh-century theologian Maximus the Confessor, as compared to a Manichaean aversion to flesh and blood). This will lead to a consideration of Inca child sacrifice as an example of religious justification for a theology of death. Finally we may consider Cain and Abel as establishing the framework for a human-generated *eschaton*. This has resulted, inevitably, in a revival of ancient pagan sacrificial practices: human and animal sacrifice, but in particular child sacrifice, now on an industrial scale; this is blood shed to idols, in the place of Christ's atoning sacrifice: a demonically-driven pagan inversion to Christ's atoning and complete sacrifice. This paper concludes that religion may be bad, atheism worse, but religious atheism is to be seen as the worst of all options: we must trust in the blood of the lamb, the one true living God incarnated as *Yeshua the Nazarite*, the Christ who was fully human and at one with humanity from the moment of his conception. We must not put our trust and our faith in the blood of Enlightenment pagan sacrifices numbering tens of millions.

I. INTRODUCTION

The *eschaton* is in God's hands. We have no control on the timing of our death and our judgment at God's hands, nor ultimately the absolute decision as to our existence, *postmortem*, in heaven or in hell. We can affect out ultimate end, our fate is in our hands, but our ethical decisions are often to the detriment of our own well-being and ultimately our salvation; if we try to control our life's destiny, if we reject God's will for us, we usually end up condemning others. The aim of this paper is to explore how an Enlightenment theology of death is rooted in religious atheism, a belief system that beguiles and deludes a particular group of people into believing that they are right and proper, absolute and

3. A Human-Generated Eschaton: Objectification

universal, and often kind and considerate, liberal and good, in subjecting a group of people to *ante-mortem* judgment, and in consequence, death. They consider whatever death is foisted onto people as essential and beneficial to all, whether they have invented a "god," "goddess," or an "infantile and regressive godlet," or no "divine patron," to validate and justify their actions.

II. CREATION AND OBJECTIFICATION

Although the Genesis creation story asserts that we are caretakers of the world, stewards of creation (Gen 1:26–28), we have taken nature, the world, everything we can see, and laid our hands on the power of life and death: objectifying all as though we were somehow separate and independent of creation, of the world. The key word in Gen 1:26 (in the Septuagint) is *archetōsan*, a literal translation would be "let them [humanity] control," often rendered in translations as "dominate" creation, the world.[1] What is the warrant for this?—"Then God said, 'Let us make humankind in our image, according to our likeness; and let them have dominion over the fish of the sea, and over the birds of the air, and over the cattle, and over all the wild animals of the earth, and over every creeping thing that creeps upon the earth'" (Gen 1:26, cf., 9:2; Ps 8:6–8). This verse from Genesis is taken by some to claim that Christianity promotes ecological destruction due to the Genesis command to "subdue the earth" and "have dominion" (KJV/AV and NRSV), and because it is seen as anthropocentric. The words *katakyrion* and *archetōsan* should rightly be seen not as domination and *destruction* but as stewardship and, yes, *control* (Septuagint, my translation) and *rule* (NIV). To many it is the technological basis of the Age of Reason and the Enlightenment, and not the Judaeo-Christian tradition, that may be seen as having initiated climate change and the despoiling of the earth (though many Jews and Christians see no problem in following the initiative of Enlightenment-led scientists and technicians in this). The pilot of an aircraft does not fly the plane to its limits, till the wings tear off and it crashes. The pilot knows s/he is in control, but dominating and destroying the plane only harms her/him. A more organic example is with the relationship between a rider and a horse. Yes, the horse needs breaking in, training, but once broken and controlled the horse can achieve things it could never have dreamt of.

[1] *The Septuagint*, 1851 edition compiled by Sir Lancelot C. L. Brenton.

The relationship between horse and rider is symbiotic, not objectifying and domineering. Why is this relevant?—because this paper is about humanity taking this power of dominion and destruction over creation *for its own ends*, effectively usurping the *eschaton* in the form of judgment and death: objectifying. But this power and right of domination and destruction issues not from the Hebrew Bible and the gospel, but from science and technology, often driven by a mistrust of God amongst the religious at best, an explicitly self-proclaimed atheistic agenda at worst. As a result humanity has claimed the right of control and dominion, life and death over all. This is objectification; that is, the process or manifestation of objectifying, separating, and asserting independence and judgment over another, whether animate or inanimate, organic or inorganic. We identify and conceive, then we reduce and objectify, and in the process demean, belittle, and ultimately use, and dispose of. This is *postlapsarian* humanity: right and wrong is objectified and controlled and redefined to our ends, because we took and ate of the fruit of the tree of the knowledge of good and evil. To classify and regard—driven by hegemonic power—a person as an object or a thing is to dehumanize, that is, "the act of disavowing the humanity of others."[2] This often takes the form of regarding a person as a mere object of sexual craving: women (and men) regarded and controlled by men and women as sexual objects. Drawing on the work of the philosophers Martha Nussbaum and Rae Langton, objectification occurs when some of the following statements are applied to a person.

> **Instrumentality**: treating the person as a tool
>
> **Denial of autonomy**: treating the person as lacking in autonomy or self-determination
>
> **Inertness**: treating the person as lacking in agency or activity
>
> **Fungibility**: treating the person as interchangeable with (other) objects

---

2 Nussbaum, "Objectification," 281.

3. A Human-Generated Eschaton: Objectification

Violability: treating the person as lacking in boundary integrity and violable, "as something that it is permissible to break up, smash, break into."

Ownership: treating the person as though they can be owned, bought, or sold: enslaved

Reduction to body: the treatment of a person as identified with their body, or part of his/her body alone. Often involving the denial of soul.

Reduction to appearance: the treatment of a person primarily in terms of how they look, or how they appear to the senses.

Denial of subjectivity: treating the person as though there is no need for concern for their experiences or feelings.

Silencing: treating the person as though they are mute.[3]

There are times when an individual will adopt for him- or herself some of these categories, but this is voluntary and part of the implicit social rules, e.g., keeping quiet and anonymous during a concert or at the theatre. The roles of a servant or domestic worker often involved some of this categories. But often a line is crossed, and these criteria are conveniently set aside and ignored.

III. "OTHERNESS:" THEOLOGICAL OBJECTIFICATION

Relating closely to and part of our theological anthology, theological objectification is the attempt to redefine a person's ontology before God: if he or she is no longer to be regarded as fully human then the normal ethics derived from the Judaeo-Christian tradition (the theological ground) no longer apply. Put simply, this is the redefining of our neighbor as "other," not one of us. There is nothing in the gospel to justify this theological objectification. From a secular-humanist perspective objectification has

---

[3] For details of these classifications see, Nussbaum. "Objectification," 253; and Langton, *Sexual Solipsism*, 228–29.

been much discussed amongst feminists, sociologists, psychologists, and left-wing/liberal politicians since the socio-cultural-sexual revolution of the 1960s. There is, however, amongst the pronouncements of these activists, politicians, and academics evidence of confusion, of contradiction, even of duplicity. Abortion, which we will examine theologically in this paper, is an obvious example. A central principle of the socio-cultural-sexual revolution of the late 1960s, abortion (along with sexual freedom, and the legalization of paraphilic sexual activities) involves objectification of the unborn child by its mother—the developing child though waiting to be born is defined as other—by women who themselves often complain at being objectified as sex objects. What this confusion and duplicity involves and represents is a theological distinction between *forced objectification* and *voluntary objectification*. Objectification—a denial of full God-given humanity, amongst other principles—is *forced* onto the unborn child, or a criminal to be executed, or an enemy in war against his/her will, whereas suicide in its manifold forms, assisted or voluntary, involves *self*-objectification. It is therefore clear that the aims and goals of objectification can appear confused and contradictory when assessed against theological anthropology and ethics: is capital punishment right or wrong? Women will voluntarily choose to prettify themselves for the attraction of men (or homosexuals of both genders for the same-sex other?), therefore is this vanity a form of self-objectification, or are there additional factors involved? Or does it issue from confusion of will where it is difficult to prove that the individual does make an impartial free-will decision, objectifying for gratification of her/his own sexual desire, the craving to copulate? If there is confusion then perhaps we must assert that there is apparently no possibility of a free and untainted, impartial and willed decision since the *fall* into original sin, unless the individual is possessed by the Christ through baptism by water and the Spirit. Or does objectification issue from a hardened, demonically driven, willfulness, reveling in its cruelty and evil? Whither free will, when objectification ultimately involves judgment and death?

IV. THE NEW ATHEISTS & THE NEW MORALITY

We will all face death: we will die. This appears to be the natural course of events for *postlapsarian* humanity. We will then all be subject to God's righteous and forgiving judgment—if we can repent and call upon that

3. A Human-Generated Eschaton: Objectification

forgiveness, if we can accept being forgiven. But what happens when humanity—driven by tribalistic identity politics (a consequence of the *fall* into original sin, as we now languish East of Eden)—usurps God's judgment? Such an appropriation condemns people in this life, subjecting them to pseudo-legalistic killing. This is the *eschaton* sequestrated and appropriated, usurped, taken, arrogated, assumed—and demonic in its intent. Despite the image of superficial kindness and liberalism projected by these Western societies, such a theology of death is promoted by an oligarchic elite dedicated in their celebrity status towards proclaiming an atheistic revolution to support this *ante-mortem* tribal death.

Recent governments (especially in Britain) have looked to intellectual atheists for the framework and justification for this approach. Richard Dawkins and Phillip Pullman are an example of a contemporary intellectual trend amongst so-called New Atheists.[4] They have proposed in their writings that the exponents of all religions will eventually oppress and even kill their opponents, that religion *per se* should be done away with, as peaceably as possible. Dawkins has reiterated this accusation throughout his career, however, some of the New Atheists have openly expressed support for using violence as a means of combating militant Islamists, some of them also call for rescinding the tolerance of religious belief formerly characteristic of Western liberal democracies.[5] This anti-God, anti-religion proposition is essentially derived from two works: Pullman's explicitly atheistic anti-Narnia mythology aimed at children, entitled *His Dark Materials*,[6] and Dawkins short anti-religion polemic *The God Delusion*, which though lacking in any extended argument or considered systematic theological analysis, has none the less sold, like Pullman's work, millions of copies world-wide. Dawkins contends that a supernatural creator almost certainly does not exist and that faith

---

4   Others include the journalist and literary critic Christopher Hitchens (who describes himself as an "anti-theist"), the philosopher A. C. Grayling, the journalist-writer Sam Harris, the novelist Martin Amis, and the author and screen writer Ian McEwan. However, John Gray has now published criticizing the nature of the atheism promulgated by the New Atheists (where he is very critical of the New Atheists and recommends a form of atheism that has a certain mystical slant to it). See Gray, *Seven Kinds of Atheism*, 2018

5   Dawkins, *The God Delusion*.

6   Pullman, *His Dark Materials*, consisting of *Northern Lights* (1995), *The Subtle Knife* (1997), and *The Amber Spyglass* (2000).

qualifies as a delusion—as a fixed, false belief.[7] Whilst Pullman advocates the death of God, Dawkins jumps from point to point across numerous disciplines simply to propose that anyone who claims to believe in a "god," or those who are religious, are deluding themselves: there is no God for the New Atheists, and religion is always theistic, and therefore delusory, a psychological sickness. Superficial though their treatises are, Pullman and Dawkins do implicitly acknowledge, quite correctly, that something is wrong with religion, that religion can be considered as human-generated. But are the New Atheists immune from being religious? Despite their disbelief in an objective God, the belief system of the New Atheists is religious and bears the hallmarks of a religious mindset: Richard Dawkins is an evangelical atheist.

John F. Haught has attempted to categorize the beliefs of the New Atheists. First, apart from nature and humans, there is nothing else; in addition, nature is to be seen as self-originating.[8] Second, the universe has no point or purpose; therefore nothing exists but natural causality.[9] Third, all features of humanity can be explained by recourse to Darwinian processes.[10] Fourth, in religious terms, faith in God has produced only evil in society, and in terms of ethics, morality does not necessitate belief in a "god."[11] This reductionist hermeneutic in effect denies personhood and the why of our consciousness:

7 Dawkins, *The God Delusion*, 5.

8 That is, an accident with no inherent meaning?

9 Yet the existence of something as specific as causality implies something other.

10 Here is the Achilles heel of the New Atheists generally, and Richard Dawkins specifically: Darwinism has been slowly eroded of veracity over the last thirty-five years by geneticists and biologists. The more scientists have analyzed genetics, investigating what actually is going on in each cell and how DNA works, the more the basic theory of random mutation being the engine of evolution has become redundant. Darwin got it wrong: thus stated an article in the journal *New Scientist* (see, Lawton, "Uprooting Darwin's Tree," 34–39). The only safe proposition, I assert, is: *Evolution, yes; Darwinism, no*. Darwin's theory was guesswork, and it does not tally with the sheer complexity and wonder of creation in the form of the action of DNA, transgenerational epigenetics, accelerated evolution, biological plasticity, quantum biology, all evidenced through scientific analysis of the cell! See, for a full survey of the scientific evidence and progress, Brazier, "Towards an Understanding of the Ontological Conditions Issuing from Original Sin" (2016). When Dawkins wrote that "faith qualifies as a delusion—as a fixed false belief" (Dawkins, *The God Delusion*, 5), what he most properly spoke of was his own pseudo-religious faith in Darwinism.

11 Haught, *God and the New Atheism*, xiii–ix. A characteristic here is that the religio-cultural belief system of the so-called New Atheists is typically postmodern in that

3. A Human-Generated Eschaton: Objectification

> The modernist worldview starts with the presupposition that the prime thing is inanimate cold matter just bouncing around with no values and then comes up with the problem of how by some weird series of coincidences this accidental little bit of delusory personhood happened to pop up inside our skulls, that's the way round it goes. So for the modernist worldview, we are always the slightly weird exception to everything else—and the problem.[12]

Malcolm Guite, speaking here, succinctly points out how what we are made of is not what we are: to focus only on our physical constitution—the unwinding of DNA in the genome, the interaction of chemicals that constitute inanimate matter—denies the "irreducible mystery of my I-am-ness."[13] This I-am-ness is personhood and it is personhood, full humanity, that the reductive "enlightened" New Atheists seek to deny: selectively. The Roman Catholic religionist Tina Beattie, in *The New Atheists: The Twilight of Reason and the War on Religion*, has produced a sound critique of the arrogance and the lack of systematic rigor in the anti-God agenda of the New Atheists. For example, Beattie sympathizes with the New Atheists hostility to fundamentalism, but argues that they have fallen into the trap of their own self-generated, we may even assert self-righteous, fundamentalism. Despite their avowed atheism, the New Atheists belief in the innocence and goodness of their anti-theistic, pseudo-religious belief system is not new.

V. THE MODERNIST-ATHEISTIC SIN

Defining another group of people as non-human, or sub-human, and open to exploitation and destruction is the essential basis of this socio-political theology of death. It is theological because it usurps God's righteousness, it pre-empts the first two elements of the *eschaton*—death and judgment—and reverses them: judgment and then killing! This is grounded in objectification. As we noted earlier, women (often self-

---

not all subscribe to all the unwritten clauses in this anti-theistic proto-creed. Therefore, some or all of what Haught asserts applies to the various New Atheists as individuals.

12   Revd Malcolm Guite, Chaplain of Girton College Cambridge, speaking on the BBC1 documentary, *The Narnia Code* (broadcast on Thursday 16 April 2009, 23:35). This can be viewed at: http://www.bbc.co.uk/programmes/b00jz2qp#broadcasts .

13   Revd Malcolm Guite, speaking on the BBC documentary, *The Narnia Code* (2009).

defining as feminists) routinely complain about being "objectified"—turned into sex objects—by men,[14] yet they not infrequently objectify the unborn child so as to kill him or her in an abortion clinic. State-sanctioned legislation somehow makes this acceptable. This illustrates the double-standards and inherent contradictions to the patrons of this theology of death; double-standards grounded in objectification.

This pseudo-eschatological objectification—the action of degrading someone to the status of a mere object, usable, destructible—has led, inevitably, since the Reformation, to a revival of ancient pagan sacrificial practices. I intend to show how although the New Atheists are quite correct in their criticism of human-centered religion they are blind to their own religiosity and the level of sacrificial death that the belief system their work has grown out of demands. The New Atheists are as deluded as many clerical or priestly elites down the centuries in believing that their own religio-cultural mind-set is innocent and beneficial to humankind.

VI. RELIGION AS UNBELIEF

First we need to establish some working definitions: of the Enlightenment and of religion. Secular liberal humanists today will often invoke the Enlightenment with confidence, with religious certainty, exhibiting a glazed-eyed emotionalism akin to veneration. In broad terms, the Enlightenment was a period in Western philosophy and cultural life, science and technology, essentially in the eighteenth century, in which reason was elevated to be the principal source and authority, the ground for decision-making. Indeed, the human capacity for willful decision-making was regarded as foundational. Intellectuals, by and large, during the Age of Reason, the Enlightenment, were seen by many to reject a traditional religious perspective, substituting it with what they saw as humanity's innate capacity to deal with life from its own strength through the faculty of reason. Echoing the ancient Greek, pre-Socratic philosopher Protagoras, this eighteenth-century, Western, male, oligarchic elite confidently proclaimed that man was the measure of all.[15] And a

---

14 See, Fredrickson and Roberts, "Objectification Theory."

15 "*Pantōn chrēmatōv metron estin anthrōpos tōn men ontōn hōs estin tōn de ontōn hōs ouk estin.*" (Man is the measure of all things: of things which are, that they are, and of things which are not, that they are not.) See, Hermann Alexander Diels (1848–1922), a German classical scholar known for his work compiling a collection of quotations from and about pre-Socratic philosophers. Protagoras' statement that humanity (*anthrōpos*)

3. A Human-Generated Eschaton: Objectification

definition of religion? There is in effect no generally agreed definition of religion. From Middle English (from Old French) or from Latin *religio*, "obligation," "reverence," religion for many is seen as the belief in and worship of a superhuman controlling power, especially a personal God or the "gods"; to others religion is a particular system of faith and worship with no particular "god"; for yet more, being religious is simply an interest or pursuit followed with great devotion. The term is used with widely different meanings—especially by the New Atheists. Marcus Tullius Cicero—Roman philosopher, politician, lawyer, orator, political theorist, consul, and constitutionalist—defined *religio* as the giving of proper honor, respect, and reverence to the divine, by which he meant the "gods."[16] According to Cicero such *religio* was a dutiful honoring of the "gods," as distinct from a superstition, an empty fear of them.[17] Cicero's definition implies an object: theistic religion will invoke God, or the "gods," as the object of religious practice (though this object may only be in the mind of the believer). In addition, religion may embrace non-theistic belief systems from Buddhism to Marxism, or from football to popular culture, or for that matter the tribal totems of identity politics, all of which exhibit the characteristics often associated with objectively theistic religions. The Enlightenment was innately "religious," and spawned religious systems from deism to Freemasonry. Perhaps any philosophy of life that exhibits a worldview of sorts and that embraces some notion of right and wrong is in some way implicitly religious. Certainly, according to postmodern relativism, almost anything can count as *religion*, any lifestyle statement as *religious*.

Karl Barth distinguished, dialectically, between religion and revelation. In stressing the sovereignty of God, Barth denied, to a degree, knowledge of God through human effort. Therefore, *all* religion was a human activity: for Barth, God could only be "known" by God's self-revealing, through revelation, in Jesus Christ. And the truth of this could only be accepted by faith. Religion at its best was to be seen as

---

is the measure of all is summarized and reiterated by Plato in his *Theaetetus*, §152a, however, a full quotation is given by Sextus Empiricus (c. second–third century BC) in *Adversus Mathematicos* (*Against the Mathematicians*), §7.60.

16   Cicero, *The Nature of the gods*, 2.3.8; and Cicero, *The Orations of Marcus Tullius Cicero, Volume IV: The Fourteen Orations against Marcus Antonius; The Treatise on Rhetorical Invention; The Orator; Topics; On Rhetorical Partitions, Etc.*, 2.53.161.

17   Cicero, *The Nature of the gods*, 1.4.2.

a *flawed* human response to the self-revelation of the one, true, living God. Therefore, Barth asserted that we live under the divine judgment, God's judgment on all religion: "Apart from and without Jesus Christ we can say nothing at all about God and man and their relationship one with another."[18] Ironically, and given our *postlapsarian* predilection for objectification, God, in seeking our salvation, objectifies God's triune being in the person of Jesus of Nazareth, the Christ. What happens to Jesus is what happens to the victims of tribalistic objectification: judgment and slaughter. This leads to our salvation, leastwise, it opens up the potential for salvation for the righteous and sinners alike, yet it condemns the objectifiers, the dehumanizers. The objectifiers are exposed eschatologically to be not-at-one with Christ but at one with personified evil: Satan, Lucifer, the *fallen* angel. There is no argument, no appeal; the objectifiers are what they are, and will be exposed as such in the *eschaton*.

The proposition from the New Atheists that all religions are of human invention and are self-serving is therefore—in a Barthian context—true. Likewise, the proposition from the New Atheists that all religions will oppress and even kill their opponents is, to a degree, true. If, like Barth, we are to regard religion *per se* as idolatrous, as unbelief, because it perpetually falls short of the unknowable *aseity* of the one, true, living God revealed in Jesus of Nazareth, the Christ, then what do we classify as religion? Is belief in God, or for that matter a "god," an essential axiom of religion? No; for there is the phenomena of religious atheism. By comparison, Barth saw the self-revealing of God—the paradoxical dialectic of an unveiling-veiling—as the abolition of all religion.[19] This unveiling-veiling dialectic implies that we can never get religion right, even if we claim to be Christian. Therefore, the New Atheists don't take their criticisms of religion far enough: they fail to criticize their own religion, their own religious atheism, their innate self-reflective and self-reverential religiosity.

---

18 Note Barth's use of *Aufhebung* we cited earlier. See, Barth, *The Church Dogmatics*. See: §17 The Revelation of God as the Abolition of Religion I/2, 280; §25 The Fulfilment of the Knowledge of God II/1, 3; §26 The Knowability of God II/1, 63; §. 27, The Limits to the Knowledge of God, II/1, The Doctrine of God, specifically, 179–256. Specific reference is made to I.2, 299 and IV.1, 45.

19 Barth, *The Church Dogmatics* I/2, §17 The Revelation of God as the Abolition of Religion I/2, 280.

3. A Human-Generated Eschaton: Objectification

VII. ENLIGHTENMENT DEATH 1.
THREE MEGA-HOLOCAUSTS

If the New Atheists proposition is correct, that all religions will oppress and even kill their opponents, and if we can look at church history and see how Christians, whether lay or a priestly elite, have defined and measured people by certain criteria—whether tribalistic or according to identity politics—externalizing them and subjecting them to exclusion and ultimately to torture and death, and if this behavior is innate to *postlapsarian*—and therefore, by definition—religious humanity, then although we will be able to point to this same proposition in Western, Enlightenment, modern, and postmodern religion—whether self-consciously atheistic or assertively theistic—we must start with its evidence in an explicitly Christian context, given the historic identity of Christianity with Europe over the last fifteen hundred years.

VIII. ENLIGHTENMENT DEATH 2.
A PSEUDO-"CHRISTIAN" THEOLOGY OF DEATH

An Enlightenment theology of death essentially grew out of the religious terrorism of the Reformation. We can look at Henry VIII's macho religio-political tyranny as almost comical, but for the suffering and death it visited on the English people. The same was true when his daughter Mary came to the throne, attempting to reverse the Protestant revolution of her brother Edward VI (with the disenfranchisement and torture/oppression of Catholics), subjecting the English to a tyranny of burnings, oppression, torture, and death in the name of religion. The same can be said of Calvin's dictatorial theocratic rule of Geneva. But we must look specifically at the actions of the Roman Catholic church: for example, the burning alive of men, women, and children because they refused to stop reading the Bible in English (or translating, or printing and distributing the Bible in the vernacular). The belief was in the equality before God of the so-called heretics, therefore for his or her own good the soul of such an individual needed cleansing with fire. In addition, there was the religio-political necessity to stop the spread of Bible reading and study outside of the authority of the church's control, which itself was related to the issue of indulgences and priestly power. In the 1520s, the Inquisition in Seville would often hold a three-hour, intensely religious and emotional Mass, then go out and supervise an *auto-da-Fe* (literally an act of faith—the burning alive at the stake of usually a hundred so-called heretics); the perpetrators were utterly convinced of the rightness of their actions, they acknowledged the full humanity of the victims and many of this priestly elite wept as they looked on.[20] The religious roots of burning the victim alive at the stake were pagan, as was the Protestant response—hanging, drawing, and quartering. The roots of burning alive would appear superficially to lie with the wicker man amongst Celtic tribes and the Middle Eastern and Indian dualist religions whose priests were convinced that, whether alive or dead, certain people needed cleansing fire to redeem them, for the soul to escape the body. When this is translated to the curia and the Inquisition, or for that matter Protestant sects in the New World obsessed with the threat of witches and witchcraft, the protagonists had, in effect, taken possession of the judgment and vengeance of God, hence usurping Christ's righteousness, acting as if they were God: *eritis sicut Deus*. One of the last victims of this pseudo-"Christian" theology of death was Thomas Aikenhead, a twenty-one-year-old Scottish student executed in 1697 for blasphemy in promulgating atheistic views and for denouncing the Bible.[21] Secular liberal humanists today never cease to sanctify Aitkenhead and proclaim him as evidence of the primitive and superstitious nature of religion.

For the followers of the Enlightenment, reason replaced religion, reason without revelation, to a degree; it was within this atheistic, pseudo-religious agenda that we can identify the origin of a theology of death. But whereas the victims of the Inquisition and other pre-Enlightenment "Christian" theocracies were deemed equally human and in need of purification unto death to be saved (in varying degrees according to the

---

20   The Russian novelist Dostoevsky, writing in the 1870, recounted an example of Calvinists in Geneva weeping as they execute a young man for his crimes. The story—based on fact, from a pamphlet translated into Russian—is recounted by an atheistic rebel, Ivan Karamazov. The young man in question is converted to Christ whilst in prison, and when he is led out to the scaffold: "They all walk or drive to the scaffold in procession behind the prison van. At the scaffold they call to Richard: 'Die, brother, die in the Lord, for even thou hast found grace!' And so, covered with his brothers' kisses, Richard is dragged on to the scaffold, and led to the guillotine. And they chopped off his head in brotherly fashion, because he had found grace." Dostoevsky, *The Brothers Karamazov*, Bk. 5 Pros and Contra, ch. 4 Rebellion, 239–40.

21   Thomas Aikenhead (1676–97), a student from Edinburgh, was indicted in December 1696 and executed on 8 January 1697 for blasphemy; Aikenhead is recorded as having pleaded for mercy during the trial and attempted to recant his views, but was sentenced to death by hanging.

prevailing religious culture), the victims of an Enlightenment theology of death were deemed *sub-* or *non-*human and therefore as usable and disposable as the rest of creation. Certain groups, when defined as sub- or non-human, became of no more value than animals or plants, or the earth itself, to be used and wasted as the elite saw fit. It is important to remember that if the earth is to be destroyed through pollution and environmental degradation it is not a religious elite or priestly caste that have taken on itself the knowledge and power to destroy the earth, but scientists, technocrats, and engineers, whose beliefs are grounded in this Enlightenment axiom that humanity is the measure of all things. It is generally acknowledged that the numbers executed by and through the Reformation were probably in the tens of thousands across Europe, though objective evidence and accurate written records are scarce. Post-Reformation, the level of death meted out by the exponents of these human-centered religio-political belief systems has measured in the tens of millions. For example, there have been three Enlightenment-led mega-holocausts since the Reformation. Why mega-holocausts? Because the destruction and slaughter has been on a *mass* scale, and religiously motivated, according to the vain belief that the "god/goddess/godlet" subscribed to was demanding a sacrificial burnt offering akin to the Hebrew burnt offering, a theistic holocaust.

IX. ENLIGHTENMENT DEATH 3.
SLAVERY: "AM I NOT A MAN AND A BROTHER?"

The first Enlightenment-led mega-holocaust was of the West Africans: slaves. Men, women, and children from West Africa were objectified, defined as sub-human, usable and disposable: enslaved. Respectable society in Britain—with endorsement from the Church of England in certain quarters—deemed this "reasonable," acceptable, and economically unavoidable, indeed highly beneficial to the British economy. It is important to remember that this trade already existed in Africa—with West African tribe enslaving West African tribe, and Arabs travelling across the Sahara Desert to purchase the commodity. However, the British slave traders simply ratcheted-up this trade into a mega-holocaust, using the technological developments of the Enlightenment. Napoleon was right, the English were a nation of shop keepers and traders. They did not capture and enslave, they merely travelled to the West African coast and purchased humans already enslaved by humans, though it is important to remember that they caused a hundred-fold increase in the tribal enslavement already endemic amongst the indigenous population.

The dehumanization of West Africans enslaved by the British was enshrined in law. There were often violent clashes between slaves and overseers, especially in the docks. In one case in the seventeenth century (a test case as it would be termed today), a sailor from a ship docked in Jamaica killed an African slave in a drunken dockside brawl. He was not charged with murder but with gross damage to the slave owner's property. He had to pay compensation equivalent to the value of replacing the slave (indenture to the plantation owner for ten years labor—however, he jumped ship and escaped). His crime was not considered to be the killing or murder of another human being. If a ship crossing from Africa to the West Indies was foundering in a storm the crew was allowed to do what they would on any other ship—ditch some of the cargo overboard to lighten the load and to save the ship.[22] West African slaves were considered cargo, not passengers, they were just another commodity; alive or dead they were thrown overboard to prevent the ship from foundering. They were then claimed on insurance as *cargo*, not passengers, not human beings, each unique, made in the image of God.[23]

As the body count climbed (more than fifteen million), finally—after a couple of hundred years—people's consciences fought for a ban: the slogan or catch phrase of the abolitionists was "Am I Not a Man and a Brother?" which was antonymous of the dehumanization policy of the Enlightened Europeans. English philosophers from the Age of Reason saw the slave trade as justified, reasonable, and beneficial according to the criteria of the ruling oligarchic elite. Slavery in pre-Civil War America, as also was the annihilation of Native Americans in the mid-West in the late nineteenth century, is related to and part of this holocaust, which was defined essentially along similar racial lines, as are the numerous other examples of racist-driven apartheid or ethnic cleansing, whether theistically or atheistically grounded, characterized by this principle of objectification/dehumanization. Thomas Jefferson, the third US

---

22   An ancient practice recorded in the Bible: Jonah 1:5b; Jonah's commitment to the deep, however, is for other reasons—his perceived sin; therefore his sacrifice is to save the lives of the crew and the ship.

23   See: Gen 1:26–27; 3:17–19; 5:1–2; & 9:6; Deut 10:17–19; 22:6–7; Isa 7:23–25; Ps 8:3–8; Matt 5:48; Rom 3:23; 1 Cor 11:7; 2 Cor 4:4; Phil 2:6; Col 1:15; Heb 1:3; Jas 3:9.

3. A Human-Generated Eschaton: Objectification

president, epitomizes the Enlightenment's approach to religion and slavery. The Statute of Virginia for Religious Freedom granted pluralistic equality for all religions yet effectively denied religious truth, asserting one truth—Jefferson's highly individualistic deistic beliefs. Jefferson claimed to oppose slavery but owned and controlled many slaves on his estates, and benefitted from them all his life.[24]

Therefore, racism is to be seen as the denial and/or refutation of another's humanity given that we are all of the same race: the human race. A white race does not exist, nor a red race, a yellow or a black race: there is but one race, the human race. We need to avoid the confusion of tribal racist stereotypes.

X. ENLIGHTENMENT DEATH 4. THE HOLOCAUST OF THE GOD'S CHOSEN PEOPLE

The second mega-holocaust inspired, to a degree, by the Enlightenment was the holocaust of the Jews: again, an oligarchic elite defined a particular group of people as sub-human and then non-human, disposable. In a few years this holocaust claimed over six-and-a-half million lives. Again, those who ruled, who democratically passed the laws (the 1953 Nuremberg Race Laws, enacted by a democratically elected National Socialist—Nazi—government), considered this reasonable. If some men or women were considered useful as slave labor then they were worked to death (therefore, this human-generated *eschaton* became *judgment*, then *hell*, then *death*). The others were simply, systematically, herded into the gas chambers, killed, then processed for whatever was of value. The National Socialist religion, essentially scripted in the late 1920s by Wilhelm Stapel, was derived from pagan religion, from ancient German and Norse mythologies, selectively rewritten, adapted to suit the National Socialist racist agenda. This multiplicity of "gods" and "goddlets" denied the God of the Jews and sought to recast Jesus as a Caucasian, Aryan, Enlightened European.[25] However, in addition to its pagan religious roots

---

24   For The Statute of Virginia for Religious Freedom, see: https://en.wikipedia.org/wiki/Virginia_Statute_for_Religious_Freedom.

25   Wilhelm Stapel (1882–1954), writer, journalist, and translator, was noted as a Protestant German Nationalist who supported the National Socialists and was crucial in formulating their religious mythology and anti-Semitism. Stapel poured scorn on German Christians who opposed Hitler but also on those who offered qualified support by endorsing the brotherhood fostered by the Nazis. See Stapel, *Der christliche Staatsmann—eine*

National Socialist religion—or religio-politics—also has impeccable Enlightenment credentials: National Socialism evolved, to a degree, from nineteenth-century German thinkers such as Nietzsche, Feuerbach, and implicitly from Hegel.[26]

But the churches also had their part in these mega-holocausts. The Methodist church in Germany initially praised Hitler because he had made the trains run on time. Lutheran Christian SS guards in the concentration camps held prayer meetings to thank their "lord" for giving them the opportunity of solving the problem, as they saw it, of the Jews. The Church of England implicitly endorsed the slave trade: in the eighteenth-century, Anglican priests refused to baptize the children of African slaves in the Caribbean because it would imply equality with the slave masters. Ironically the Roman Catholic missions in the New World were against slavery. In 1537, Pope Paul III issued the encyclical *Sublimis Dei*, proclaiming the Native American Indians (from across all the Americas: North, Central, and South) to be truly human beings with the full intellectual and moral capacity to become Christian and therefore Rome outlawed slavery. In contradiction to *Dum Diversas* (1452) and *Romanus Pontifex* (1455)—which granted the right of taking the "natives" of newly discovered lands as perpetual slaves, because according to the Aristotelian-derived anthropology humans were in three groups (Asian, Africans, and Europeans) and therefore the "Indians" of the New World

---

Theologie des National-sozialismus (1932). See also Stapel, *The Heiland* (1932). He worked on the concept of "heathen imperialism" in which he saw the will of the German people as synonymous with the will of "god" (his "theism" as such drew much from a simplified reading of Hegel and Nietzsche, but equally from the pagan Norse myths popularized by Wagner!). See Stapel, *Die drei Stände Versuch einer Morphologie des deutschen Volkes* (1941).

26   Whether it was true or not, there was an apposite scene at the end of the BBC historical drama called *Conspiracy*, detailing the infamous 1942 Wannsee Conference. The SS General Reinhard Heydrich, with Machiavellian skill, plots with his fellow Nazis the final solution (the annihilation of the Jews) and then sits down to listen sensitively to the most soul-piercingly beautiful music by Schubert (the 2nd movement of the String Quintet in C) as if nothing was wrong, as if what had been achieved was the highest of truth. The Wannsee conference took place on 20 January 1942, in a villa at Wannsee on the outskirts of Berlin. The German High Command, under General Reinhard Heydrich (SS-Obergruppenführer, Chief of the Reich Security Main Office (RSHA) and Deputy Reichsprotektor of Bohemia and Moravia), was convened under the direct orders of Hitler to draft the procedure for the so-called Final Solution. The meeting only lasted an hour and a half, sealing the fate of millions of European Jews. The film/docudrama *Conspiracy*, which accurately followed the one surviving copy of the minutes of the meeting was broadcast in 2001 on BBC1. See: https://en.wikipedia.org/wiki/Conspiracy_(2001_film)

3. A Human-Generated Eschaton: Objectification

were to be classified as "dumb brutes" outside of and different from humanity—*Sublimis Dei* (1537) accepted them as fully and equally human because it was found that they could hear the gospel and be converted to Christ (or could make a willful decision to reject the gospel), but what was important was that they could respond in a way that an animal or bird could not. Therefore, for the Roman Catholic Church, the definition of being a human being, equal to all others, was the capacity to respond freely to God's truth about the human condition, and the revelation of salvation through Jesus Christ. Whether an individual responded positively or negatively was of no consequence to their ontic status, the fact they *could* respond was a hallmark of their humanity, and therefore protection against enslavement. *Sublimis Dei* stated,

> The enemy of the human race, who opposes all good deeds in order to bring men to destruction, beholding and envying this, invented a means never before heard of, by which he might hinder the preaching of God's word of Salvation to the people: he inspired his satellites who, to please him, have not hesitated to publish abroad that the Indians of the West and the South, and other people of whom we have recent knowledge should be treated as dumb brutes created for our service, pretending that they are incapable of receiving the Catholic Faith.
>
> ... [N]otwithstanding whatever may have been or may be said to the contrary, the said Indians and all other people who may later be discovered by Christians, are by no means to be deprived of their liberty or the possession of their property, even though they be outside the faith of Jesus Christ; and that they may and should, freely and legitimately, enjoy their liberty and the possession of their property; nor should they be in any way enslaved; should the contrary happen, it shall be null and have no effect.[27]

The ultimate sanction under *Sublimis Dei* was for the enslavers to be excommunicated: cut-off from God's grace, the church, and condemned to hell (i.e., realized eschatology in the form of *ante-mortem* judgment). During the Reformation there was a clash between Roman Catholic missionaries and the profit-driven venture capitalism of the colonialists and conquistadores. The Jesuit missionaries saw all peoples as needing to be converted and saved, all were equal before God. If the Indians rejected

---

27   Extracts from, *Sublimis Dei*, encyclical on "The Enslavement and Evangelization of Indians," issued by Pope Paul III, 29 May 1537, accessed at, http://www.papalencyclicals.net/Paul03/p3subli.htm. Para 3, & 4b.

the call of Christ, rejected conversion/salvation, they were still fully human and equal, because they had made an informed human decision.

It was in the Protestant and Reformed churches that the colonialists and empire-builders were to find a belief system to complement their dehumanizing greed. It is in the Protestant countries that the churches develop a belief system to justify slavery, by objectifying, by classifying, the native peoples of Africa, Asia, the Americas, as sub-human or non-human. The principle of objectifying to dehumanize continues today and is, ironically, taken up by what we may term secular-liberal humanists (representing the dominant and majority religio-political belief system in Britain and most Western countries).

XI. ENLIGHTENMENT DEATH 5. THE SILENCE OF THE ABORTED

What of the third Enlightenment-inspired mega-holocaust? This is the holocaust of the unborn: the victims of abortion (and, related, embryonic stem-cell harvesting). Again, a particular group of people are defined as sub-human or non-human and usable, disposable: objectified by their mothers: encouraged by society at large and its institutions—the media, the political world, the law, educational establishments, and medical professionals. The silence from this third holocaust is deafening: no child survives. Slavery and discrimination against the Jews has always existed; women have always sought to abort a so-called "unwanted" pregnancy—the ancient Celts and the Anglo Saxons knew of certain plants where the leaves would trigger menstruation and therefore abortion.[28] However, since 1967 in Britain and

---

28   The ancient Ballad Tam Lin records this. The iconography and content of the ballad is accepted as going back to pre-Norman conquest England and Scotland—many of these ballads originate in the oral tradition that spawned Beowulf. Margaret, a princess, becomes pregnant by Tam Lin, a young man possessed by the Queen of Elves. A serving maid tells her of "*A herb in the merry green wood, that'll twine thee babe from thee*," so she searches out the herb: "*And she hadn't pulled a herb in that merry green wood, A herb but barely one, When by her stood young Tam Lin, Saying, Margaret leave it alone, Me love, Saying Margaret leave it alone.*" Margaret a Christian princess plans to kill her unborn child; Tam Lin, who is due to be paid as a tithe to hell by the Queen of Elves, stops her! He says, "*Oh how can you pull that bitter little herb, That herb that grows so grey, To take away that sweet babe's life, That we got in our play, Me love, That we got in our play.*" Child, *The English and Scottish Popular Ballads* (10 Vols. 1882–98). See, Vol. I, Ballad 39 "Tam Lin", 335–58. Other ballads cite the consequences of abortion and infanticide as execution and burning in hell, for example, "The Cruel Mother" (Child no. 20, Vol. I, 218–27, medieval in origin) and "Mary Hamilton" (Child no. 173, Vol. III, 379–400,

3. A Human-Generated Eschaton: Objectification

1973 in the USA, abortion procedures have received state sanctioning. There is a contemporary myth that all theology must be impersonal and academically disinterested. If you hold to this myth you will I hope forgive a personal testimony that makes the theological arguments highly pertinent. Prior to state sanctioning of the third Enlightenment mega-holocaust in Britain in 1967, a small number of children survived abortion and knew it, because their parents had the gall to tell them that they had tried to kill them in the womb as unwanted. In the early 1950s my parents purchased under-the-counter medicine from a chemist's shop/drug store to trigger an abortion, on the premise that they could not afford another child, and when this failed, ensured that I knew of this on numerous occasions as I grew up. I was one of the lucky few. Since the late-1960s the holocaust has been complete—no child survives. Should I have been killed in the womb so as to silence all opposition? Though an embryo of a few weeks gestation may seem insignificant, it holds the complete life and loves, strengths and weaknesses of a person—in potential. Should I, and many others, have never been? Everything that I am was there in my mother's womb when my parents attempted to kill me in 1953. No, I was not a meaningless cluster of cells, take my word for it, my testimony is true, and no I wasn't waiting for a soul to be given to me to make me human, neither was I waiting to be born so I could claim human rights or citizenship.

Why has this third Enlightenment mega-holocaust arisen? Abortion is, for many, defined by the so-called "right to choose." However, this is a misnomer: the woman's right to choose actually lies in the initial decision whether to mate or not. However, in rape cases there is no willful decision to mate; the problem then is who is to be executed for the crime, the act of rape?—is the rapist to be executed, or is the unborn child to be executed for the offence of coming into being? Biologically, pregnancy goes with mating; is it to be classified as an unwanted side-effect? Western governments interpret a women's "right to choose" as relating to the decision of life or death over another human being, but do not extend this right to other citizens who seek to damage, exploit, or destroy other human beings (through dehumanized-objectification). It is this existential autonomously defined "right to choose" that, theologically, undergirds all three Enlightenment mega-holocausts: *eritis sicut Deus*: humanity acting as if it was God. If we are to defend a woman's "right to choose" an abortion then we have no

---

sixteenth century, based on a real event at the Stuart court in Scotland).

moral basis to criticize the Nazi's "right to choose" whether the Jews lived or died? Neither have we any moral basis to criticize the "right to choose" claimed by the British slave traders over our African brothers and sisters. We cannot pick and choose which crimes against humanity we endorse or repudiate. The "right to choose," which is a gender-based, non-inclusive, discriminatory, sectarian proposition, is a license to kill another human life: justified through their objectification. As a man, many women would say I have no right to comment, but I comment not as a man but as the survivor of an abortion. If I cannot speak, then the Jews who survived the holocaust must remain silent and not criticize the religio-political beliefs of their persecutors. The problem with the pro-choice lobby is that they are not liberal or inclusive enough: if they were liberal and inclusive they would grant equal human rights to the unborn and recognize the right to life from the moment of conception of a fully en-souled human life. Whatever the consequences, once life has started only God the creator, whose one complete sacrifice has atoned for our sins, has the right to end it—if we try to solve these problems ourselves we only make matters worse (Rom 7).[29] Every abortion, every death of a child unborn, is a cry before God of innocent blood, wantonly spilled. These are my brothers and sisters in Christ, these my real blood relatives, for I survived but they were wasted:

> Whoever destroys a life, it is considered as if he destroyed an entire world.
> And whoever saves a life, it is considered as if he saved an entire world.[30]

29   "We know that the law is spiritual; but I am unspiritual, sold as a slave to sin. I do not understand what I do. For what I want to do I do not do, but what I hate I do. And if I do what I do not want to do, I agree that the law is good. As it is, it is no longer I myself who do it, but it is sin living in me. I know that nothing good lives in me, that is, in my sinful nature. For I have the desire to do what is good, but I cannot carry it out. For what I do is not the good I want to do; no, the evil I do not want to do—this I keep on doing. Now if I do what I do not want to do, it is no longer I who do it, but it is sin living in me that does it. So I find this law at work: When I want to do good, evil is right there with me. For in my inner being I delight in God's law; but I see another law at work in the members of my body, waging war against the law of my mind and making me a prisoner of the law of sin at work within my members. What a wretched man I am! Who will rescue me from this body of death? Thanks be to God—through Jesus Christ our Lord! So then, I myself in my mind am a slave to God's law, but in the sinful nature a slave to the law of sin." Rom 7:14–25, NIV.

30   *Jerusalem Talmud*, Sanhedrin 4:8 (37a). The Talmud is considered an authoritative record of rabbinic discussions on Jewish law, Jewish ethics, customs, legends, and stories. It consists of the Mishnah, a record of oral traditions, and the

3. A Human-Generated Eschaton: Objectification

By comparison to this axiomatic wisdom from the Talmud, Stalin is reputed to have said that one death is a tragedy, a million a statistic. We must not be blinded by the numbers: the scale of this third holocaust now outranks the other two. A conservative body count for the Western world stands at eighty million since state sanctioned liberalization in the late 1960s,[31] but the West considers it reasonable behavior—*reasonable* according to the self-referential principles of the Enlightenment and the self-reverential beliefs of postmodern relativism.

XII. ENLIGHTENMENT DEATH 6. DEFINING PRINCIPLES

There are certain important defining principles to these three mega-holocausts that we need to identify.

First, the principle of objectified dehumanization is rooted in both prejudice and in scientific naturalism. According to scientific naturalism, all matter is equal; there is no inherent difference between a fertilized egg and the greatest artistic or scientific genius. If this proposition is followed through, then whatever consciousness we have is an accident of evolution. According to a Darwinian-inspired, or grounded, scientific naturalism, all flesh is equal—equally valid and equally invalid. However, the exponents of the principle of objectified dehumanization fail to follow this through logically and invent prejudiced principles to separate out some humans from the herd as sub- or non-human.[32] However, what of the victims within the Soviet state? Marxist-Leninist pseudo-religious

---

Gemara, which comments upon, interprets, and applies these oral traditions.

31   Given that in Britain the last publically issued figure (2015) cited 8.2 million abortion from the point of the 1967 abortion act, given that the most recent statistic per year for the USA was 1.3 million (2005), given that these levels per head of population are similar across all countries in the Western world, then we may assume a figure of two million abortions per year. Assuming a base line in 1967 of 10% of these figures (statistics are not available for the late 1960s but many women were queuing up to receive the new state-sanctioned abortions), then given the exponential growth it is reasonable to propose a figure of eighty million children slaughtered in the last fifty years across Western nation states. See UK Government, Office for National Statistics: https://www.ons.gov.uk/.

32   Many evangelical atheists argue in the context of the stem-cell debate, that it is right to dissect, analyze, and harvest stem-cells from people in their embryonic state because there is no innate value to life, and yet they constantly beseech us to value *conscious human* and *intellectual* life: again, the selective dehumanization principle.

atheism wasted the lives of over a hundred million, for example, in the farm collectivization program of the 1930s and in the Gulags; however, Marxism defined all people as equal: those who offended against the Soviet state (like those defined as heretical by the Roman Catholic church), were equally and fully human but in need of severe punishment and/or correction to redeem them before the state (or in Rome's case, before the church). Marxist-Leninism did not, in principle, subscribe to the dehumanization principle. However, the Soviet state enjoyed punishing, torturing, and wasting citizens for their own good, and for the common good (defined as the Communist Party!) before the religion of Marxist-evangelical atheism.

Second, each mega-holocaust operates peacefully and democratically within a nation state and its environs/colonies. The British Empire's slave traders straddled the world exploiting and dehumanizing, imposing a *pax britannica*, imitating the Roman Empire's *pax romana*. The 1935 Nuremberg laws passed by the democratically elected National Socialist government defined the Aryan race and objectively de-humanized and excluded Jews and others from citizenship; Hitler wanted nothing more than to be left in peace to pursue his agenda of turning Europe into an Aryan colony free from sub- or non-humans; it was the allies that declared war. Therefore, I have not included the victims of the two World Wars amongst other twentieth-century conflicts here (all-out war has few principles, and an innate disrespect for life). The exponents of these three mega-holocausts invent dehumanizing religio-political criteria, and then merely want to go about their business peacefully without interference from outside.

Third, that technology and scientific developments issuing essentially from the Enlightenment, the so-called Age of Reason, have been essential in generating the high levels of death within each holocaust: modern medical procedures allow for the sheer scale of unborn children killed, likewise, the Nazis struggled during 1941 and 1942 to develop and perfect the technology to facilitate a large scale of killing and processing of the corpses in the concentration camps.[33] The Nazi holocaust would

---

33   In early 1942 gas vans (mobile gas chambers) were invented to replace the mass shooting of Jewish populations, but were deemed "inefficient." They were invented because in 1940–41, in the Polish ghettos, amongst other occupied territories in Eastern Europe, ordinary German soldiers were used simply to shoot vast numbers of Jewish men, women, children, and babies. This caused profound psychological sickness (PTSD?)

3. A Human-Generated Eschaton: Objectification

have failed without the American company IBM supplying them with the business machine technology to handle the massive logistic and bureaucratic demands of the Holocaust.[34] Advances in ship design and construction, methods of navigation, along with the expansion of a Royal Navy (ships manned by enslaved—press-ganged—sailors!) supplied and maintained globally, for the protection of British interests, all led to the growth of the slave trade on an industrial scale.

Fourth, *onus probandi*, the burden of proof, teleologically, should be for the perpetrators to prove that the object of their killing is not human, whereas West Africans subject to enslavement, and European Jews, victims of the holocaust, were effectively put in the position of having to prove that they were human and equal. And today, *onus probandi*? Unborn children are presumed to be less than human unless they can prove otherwise. *Sublimis Dei* placed the burden of proof on the enslavers, who could not prove their slaves were sub- or non-human.

Fifth, duplicity and double-standards, a vice that is endemic to all humanity. This is in effect a polite way of identifying what could be considered to be a position of hypocrisy—that is, the practice of claiming to have higher standards or more laudable beliefs than is the case. In the eighteenth century, African slaves in the Caribbean practiced herbal abortion so that they did not give birth to children who would be enslaved, whilst at the same time taking an anti-slavery position. Secular liberal humanists live under the illusion that they are kind and soft-hearted, and do no-one any harm, yet endorse abortion on an industrial scale, promote assisted suicide, and many other components of a culture of death.

A recent example of this duplicity and double standards is in the "Black Lives Matter" movement in the USA and in Britain. A number of African Americans were shot dead during confrontations with the police, so activists start demonstrating, coining the racially specific and divisive phrase, "Black Lives Matter." By identifying double-standards within the Black Lives Matter movement, no criticism is intended of the root belief of the movement (i.e., that so-called black people matter as much as so-called white people). The movements problem is that they are arguably not taking their core belief seriously enough. Theirs is a legitimate

---

amongst the soldiers who spent every waking hour each day shooting, non-stop. This was not defensive war, defensive killing, and thus contradicted the soldiers' code of honor, so to speak.

34 See, Black, *IBM and the Holocaust*.

protest. American society does not treat black lives with the same value it treats white lives. The data behind such a claim is overwhelming. Yet terminations carried out on African American and Hispanic women constitute year-on-year two-thirds of America's, up to one-and-a-half million annual abortions: that's two "black" lives for every "white" killed. If "Black Lives Matter," truly matter, and are as valid as tribal, so-called, "white" lives, why are the activists not campaigning outside abortion clinics about one million African American and Hispanic children being slaughtered every year on an industrial scale? Why are they not criticizing their own people for killing so many? The principle of dehumanized-objectification contradicts a belief in equality across the human race.

XIII. AN HYPOSTATIC UNION 1. WITHOUT CONFUSION

What we have identified so far is an underlying principle, that of denying humanity to others, objectifying others as sub-human, then non-human, allowing the protagonist to use, abuse, and kill at will: this was applied to West Africans by the British slave traders, it was applied by the Nazis to the Jews (and the slaves, Gypsies, and homosexuals), and today by neo-pagan secular-liberal humanists and the New Atheists to unborn children. There are, of course, many other examples of ethnic cleansing, tribal wars, and slavery that reflect this principle of dehumanization, however, given its current status as approved by Western societies and governments—on an industrial scale—we need to consider what the theology is behind both the endorsement and the repudiation of this third Enlightenment mega-holocaust, and how these arguments relate to the other two Enlightenment mega-holocausts.

XIV. AN HYPOSTATIC UNION 2. IMMEDIATE ANIMATION

This dehumanization principle is endemic in humanity. We may argue that the early church began to deny it—to assert the full humanity of all, *in Christ*. For example, the apostle Paul extending the gospel to the gentiles, or encouraging Philemon to take Onesimus, the runaway slave and convert, back on equal terms, whereby master and runaway slave

3. A Human-Generated Eschaton: Objectification

were to stand within the church as one and the same.[35] However, the church failed to develop this precedent for centuries; the churches failed to assert the complete unity of brotherhood and sisterhood throughout all humanity, throughout each and every life, as an immovably axiomatic principle. The principle of absolute equality comes into perfect effect with the *eschaton*: all will come before Christ in judgment regardless of tribal stereotypes, irrespective of gender or wealth, of ability and talent, notwithstanding good or bad deeds, religious identity will not benefit, all will be subject to the same judgment, and its eschatological consequences. Theologians have taken various positions over the last two thousand years: asserting and reasserting full humanity in the face of slavery, pogroms, infanticide, indeed anything that denigrates and dehumanizes. This appears a never-ending task; the fight all the time is against a demonic *zeitgeist*, which always appears good and beneficial, right and proper: hence the domination in the West of a perfect belief in the right and necessity of abortion (just as the perfect belief in the right and necessity of the Holocaust in the National Socialist elite and the German people c.1935 to 1945).

The seventh-century patristic theologian Maximus the Confessor (c.580–662) worked out a systematic theological justification for the full humanity of each person from the point of conception, although this was in the context of the incarnation, and in refuting the monothelite (one-will) position.[36] Maximus's ontology of the human is intertwined with his Christology: if Christ, as God incarnate, is fully human and at one with us then Jesus Christ must have been fully human from the point of conception.[37] The second person of the Trinity was incarnated human,

---

35   The Letter to Philemon. See: specifically 1:15–16.

36   Monothelitism originated in Armenia and Syria in the early seventh century. Monothelitism taught that Jesus Christ had two natures but only *one will*. Orthodox Christology taught that Jesus Christ has two wills—one human and the other divine—each corresponding to the two natures, human and divine. Derived from the Greek for "one will," a monothelite position denies the Chalcedonian position on how the divine and human interrelated equally in balance in the person of Christ incarnate. By the end of the seventh century, it was defined as heretical.

37   See Maximus the Confessor, *Ambigua, 2*, in, Migne, ed., *Patrologia Graeca*. See *Ambigua* 2.42, in, Vol. 91, 1324C. See also, 2.7, in, Vol. 91, 1101A; also, references to Maximus in Vol. 3 & 4. For a modern translation see, Berthold (ed.), Maximus Confessor: *Selected Writings*. For modern scholarship on Maximus and these issues see, Balthasar, *Cosmic Liturgy*, and, Cooper, *The Body in St Maximus Confessor*. An excellent summary of these body-soul-conception questions can be found in, Saward, *Redeemer in*

therefore there cannot have been a time—when incarnated—that he was not human.³⁸ On the question of the moment at which soul and body are united, Maximus wrote in the *Second Ambigua* to contradict earlier teachings (for example, the Origenist—though not necessarily Origen's own—position, teaching that the soul exists before the body) and to deal with certain ambiguities in Gregory of Nazianzus' writings. Maximus rejected both earlier teachings, asserting, Christologically, that soul is created by God and infused into the body *in the very instant of conception*.

Jesus Christ must have been human *from the point of conception*. There cannot have been a time after fertilization when Christ was not human but some form of sub-human animal life, and if there is a time after fertilization when we are not human (i.e., not en-souled), if we are not human from the moment of conception when Jesus Christ was, then we are not completely at one with Christ and therefore our salvation is imperiled because Christ does not fully share our humanity. This is apart from the fact that each and every human is genetically human from the point of conception. Humanity may attribute a different status to each human in the first few weeks of life in the womb, but this does not alter what they are before God: human ontology is divinely bequeathed, a gift, it is not selectively defined by the human will or by political necessity.

In human terms, the origin of each person had been established according to rather spurious grounds by Aristotle, amongst other ancient Greek philosopher-scientists. An Aristotelian proposition, endorsed by Aquinas, was that the humanity and personhood was not there from the moment of conception, some other animal life was. Aquinas takes this further and asserts delayed ensoulment, or postponed animation (that the soul is only given to the human after several weeks of development in the womb).³⁹ However, this position must be seen as flawed and wrong in

---

the Womb, 3–21.

38   This is not to deny the question of the *logos asarkos–logos ensarkos*; however, this is not immediately relevant to the developing argument of this paper.

39   The idea of delayed ensoulment has been used by certain modernist religious professionals—so-called *1970s liberal Anglicans*—in the Church of England to justify abortion, though none will actually identify and define when ensoulment takes place; the point is clearly movable and defined by the needs of the individual woman to justify aborting. Some American Episcopalian priests, comparable to *1970s liberal Anglicans* and issuing from the socio-cultural, religio-politico, revolution of the late 1960s, will claim ensoulment does not take place till the moment of birth, therefore late—last minute—abortion is thus justified, according to their neo-gnostic belief system.

3. A Human-Generated Eschaton: Objectification

the light of scriptural revelation and theological argument. Maximus the Confessor asked what the moment of the incarnation reveals:

> It confirmed what he already believed on other grounds, namely, that the rational soul of man, which is not generated by the parents, is created immediately by God and infused into the body at the moment of conception (in modern jargon, the doctrine of "immediate animation").[40]

For Maximus, contrary to a drift amongst many church theologians by the seventh century, who were beginning to see a human as a soul using a body, he reasserted the scriptural axiom that all men and women are a unity of soul and body: a psychosomatic whole (i.e., from the NT Greek, *psyche* and *sōma*). Maximus uses the term *eidos holon*, a "complete whole," a "complete entity," or, *ekplērōsis*—completeness. The Greek *holos* implies that something is simultaneously a whole and a part, hence Maximus's uses of the term evokes dialectic and paradox—the soul and body are simultaneously parts and a whole, a complete entity, yet separately divisible and identifiable. *Holos* also states that something is a whole in itself, altogether, as well as a part of a larger system:[41] the psychosomatic unity of soul and body that is a person is autonomous, to a degree, yet exists and subsists in God. This wholeness is from the beginning, from the moment of conception: what is true for humanity is true for the Christ. What is true for Jesus born of Mary is true for all men and women. If Christ Jesus' soul was not the result of immediate animation, then his humanity is optional; furthermore, Maximus identified that behind the theory of later ensoulment was a Manichaean aversion, a loathing, a repugnance, for associating the higher elements of the human—the intellect, and so on—with the messiness of sex and bodily fluids.[42] This Manichean aversion begins to deny the incarnation, deny that the Word

---

40   Saward, *Redeemer in the Womb*, 8, 13–21.

41   In terms of twentieth-century philosophy, a *holon* is simultaneously a whole and a part and refers to phenomena that are whole in themselves, but are also part of a larger system. A *holon* is embedded in larger *holons*, which influence it whilst it influences the greater. A model of this is sub-atomic particles, molecules, matter and objects, and the universe.

42   Maximus the Confessor, *Ambigua* 2.42, in *Patrologia Graeca*, Vol. 91, 1337B–1340B. In postmodern, *neo pagan secular-liberal humanist* terms, this repugnance is translated into a refusal to accept that sexual intercourse is, in many ways, primarily about creating a new person, a new life: postmodern secular-liberal humanists divorce pregnancy from the act of copulation.

was made flesh: delayed ensoulment points to a docetic Christ, a Christ who *seems* to be human, fleshly, but is really only inhabiting a human form temporarily, and selectively. Delayed animation asserts a part-time Christ, not fully at one with us.

In terms of the concept of delayed ensoulment, The Revd Dr Gordon Dunstan, Professor of Moral and Social Theology at King's College London from 1967 to 1982, a self-confessed liberal and an establishment Anglican, was influential in scripting the ethics of divorce (contrary to Scripture), and in providing a theological basis for downgrading the status of the embryo by claiming ensoulment did not happen until late in pregnancy (a proposition derived, as we have seen, from pagan Greek philosophy). Dunstan did not define or give a specific point in the life of the unborn child; however, this in turn fed into the 1984 Warnock report, the 1990 Human Fertilization and Embryology Act, and the Lords' Select Committee on Stem Cell Research. However, his position was based "on a mistranslation of scripture, mistaken biology, and a misrepresentation of the Christian tradition."[43] Dunstan, despite his liberal Anglican credentials, proof-texted: he took one verse out of context from Exodus, which was essentially about economic compensation for causing a miscarriage in a woman, and formulated a doctrine of late ensoulment, backed up by Aristotle's (pseudo-)scientific theories, and Aquinas's flawed philosophical arguments. The verse Dunstan quotes reads thus: "When people who are fighting injure a pregnant woman so that there is a miscarriage, and yet no further harm follows, the one responsible shall be fined what the woman's husband demands, paying as much as the judges determine. If any harm follows, then you shall give life for life . . ." (Exod 21:22–23). Exodus 21 sets the rate of compensation for causing a miscarriage early in pregnancy as lower than the rate for causing a miscarriage late in pregnancy. Dunstan argues that the higher rate of compensation indicates delayed or late ensoulment. Therefore, he gave the theological green light to embryo research, selective in vitro fertilization, and, leading on from that, a theological justification for early abortion. However, it is this economic compensatory factor that tends to characterize ancient religio-political legal systems—particularly in Middle Eastern tribes, African societies, etc. If you deprive a man/patriarch of a child that would have grown up to work for the extended family and look after the parents in

---

43 David Jones, "Dunstan, the Embryo and Christian Tradition," 10.

the old age then recompense is necessary. This is why, I would suggest, all of Exodus 21 (not just one verse) focuses on apparently just, measurable recompense, rather than an escalation of hatred and vengeance. This has nothing to do with so-called ensoulment, delayed or otherwise.

But more than this, a doctrine of immediate animation means that all the victims of the Enlightenment mega-holocausts are fully human and at one with the rest of humanity (and, importantly, with Christ), and not separated out into a non-human sub-species.

XV. AN HYPOSTATIC UNION 3. THE FULL HUMANITY OF THE CHILD-PERSON FROM CONCEPTION

Western liberal democracies generally define the start of a human life at the point of birth (though there is confusion about the state of a child in the womb depending on its age and development). The question of personhood doesn't enter into the debate. Scripture defines the start of a human life as from the womb and therefore we may assume, the moment of conception. The Psalmists proclaimed the full existence of a human life from the moment of conception, and how this life related to God: "Yet you desired faithfulness even in the womb; you taught me wisdom in that secret place."[44] Furthermore, the very process of creation and gestation was blessed:

> For you created my inmost being;
>   you knit me together in my mother's womb.
> My frame was not hidden from you
>   when I was made in the secret place.
> When I was woven together in the depths of the earth,
>   your eyes saw my unformed body.
> All the days ordained for me were written in your book
>   before one of them came to be.[45]

The prophet Jeremiah takes this further. God knew the child in full personhood: "Before I formed you in the womb," the Lord commands, "I knew you, and before you were born I consecrated you."[46] John the Baptist was filled with the Holy Spirit whilst in his mother's womb—this was

---

44   Ps 51:6.
45   Ps 139:13, 15–16.
46   Jer 1:5.

part of his full humanity.⁴⁷ The apostle Paul was set apart even from his mother's womb.⁴⁸ If this is true of John the Baptist and the apostle Paul it is equally true of all people. It is equality before God that is the touchstone of the argument against the Enlightenment mega-holocausts; it is equality that the Western secular liberal humanists and the New Atheists claim to believe in, assert as axiomatic, yet fail to practice. Scripture shows us that theologically discriminating against people according to racial-tribal stereotypes, slave or free, male or female, born or unborn, or discriminating on grounds of lifestyle or behavior, is wrong before God in Christ: reductionist objectification-dehumanization should be seen as anathema, as a thing devoted to evil.

XVI. THE THEOLOGICAL ROOTS OF THE THIRD ENLIGHTENMENT MEGA-HOLOCAUST

The theological roots of the three Enlightenment mega-holocausts can be found in Genesis 3: the *fall* from grace, the descent into the original sin, and the subsequent and consequent repetition from this first or original sin: humanity has taken on to itself all decision making, having eaten of the fruit of the tree of knowledge of good and evil—proto humanity's (Eve, and Adam's) sin was to choose, to be invited by personified evil to claim the right to choose, but to make wrong decisions, the wrong choices. This right to choose is self-referential and issues from the *fall* from grace— this right to decide, to override God's will for humanity, is at the heart of original sin. Humanity no longer lives in God's grace, hence when it believes it is doing the good it is not, it fails. But it does not acknowledge this failure; it deludes itself by judging others, convincing itself it is right, doing good, while indulging in the evil it claims to repudiate:

> I do not understand my own actions. *For I do not do what I want, but I do the very thing I hate.* Now if I do what I do not want, I agree that the law is good. But in fact it is no longer I that do it, but sin that dwells within me. For I know that nothing good dwells

---

47   "Even before his birth he will be filled with the Holy Spirit" Luke 1:15 (NRSV). "He will also be filled with the Holy Spirit, even from his mother's womb." Luke 1:15–16 (NKJV).

48   "But when He who had set me apart, even from my mother's womb, and called me through His grace . . ." Gal 1:15 (NRSV).

3. A Human-Generated Eschaton: Objectification

within me, that is, in my flesh. *I can will what is right, but I cannot do it. For I do not do the good I want, but the evil I do not want is what I do*. (Rom 7:14–19, also, 7:20–25.) (My emphasis.)

How does this relate to the Enlightenment mega-holocausts? The author Philip Pullman is generally counted amongst the New Atheists. Pullman's trilogy of books for the children of secular-liberal humanists, *His Dark Materials*, are in effect implicitly religious—atheistic mythology for postmodernist Westerners, an inversion of the implicitly Christian agenda of C. S. Lewis's Narnia books. Pullman's *His Dark Materials* pursues a pseudo-theological program, which is teleological, but the eschatological framework is self-defined: we simply arrive at a bourgeois, Western, liberal, consumerist lifestyle devoid of God or wider meaning as ultimate reality. In his work, Pullman claims that all religions become powerful and assertive enough to kill their opponents (true, to a degree). But Pullman, like Dawkins, fails to follow this through theo-logically, and to see it is a deep *postlapsarian* flaw in *all* humanity. A central thesis in *His Dark Materials*, which Pullman makes much of, is that the church systematically tortures and kills children. It can be fairly asserted that this has only happened in an extreme minority of cases, and even then it is questionable as to whether such action was indeed Christian. There is, however, a contemporary religion that has consistently, systematically, in accordance with autonomous consequentialist ethics, killed upwards of one-and-a-half to two million children per year, geographically located in the Western sphere of influence (North America, Western Europe, Australasia, etc.): this religion is the dominant religion in the West—this religion is neo-pagan secular-liberal humanism. The founding of this movement occurred, it may be argued, in 1967, the same year as the Abortion Act in Britain (and the liberalization/legitimization of homosexuality: sexual freedom raised to something of an intense emotional high was an essential component of neo-pagan secular-liberal humanism). And love?—Love was a warm, cozy feeling, essentially a cloying sentimental attachment issuing from the sexual freedoms: this form of love (essentially the ancient Greek loves of *eros*, justified by *philia* and *storgē*), if generated, in turn legitimized the ever-more-bizarre forms of sexual practice that had generated this cloying sentimental attachment in the first place. Pregnancy—being with child—was unwanted: neo-pagan secular-liberal humanists argued that they did not want to be ruled by their biology (so why did they mate/copulate in the first place? Why did they give in to their biologically generated sexual desires?). Abortion therefore became a religious act, guaranteeing their freedom to belief in a neo-pagan secular-liberal humanist lifestyle. The very word "pregnant/pregnancy" is in itself a form of objectification: prior to its use/invention, the phrase was "with child." Derived from the Latin—i.e., late Middle English: from Latin *praegnant-*, probably from *prae* "before" with the base of *gnasci* "be born," by the fifteenth century, *praegnantem* (nominative *praegnans*, originally *praegnas*)—there was an implication that pregnancy led to birth, and was taken to mean "with child," however, in the modern world it is taken to mean an objectified condition affecting, for better or for worse, the woman. That is, either blessing her, or threatening her. And if the latter, the condition must be done away with: removed, cut-out, destroyed—aborted. (Pregnant in the modern world can also mean "full of meaning or significance," again, morally neutral: a blessing or a threat, that is, objectified neutrality.)

This is the religion of the New Atheists. These children were killed as part of the third Enlightenment mega-holocaust. These are millions of children who have been killed, their lives cut short, for, yes, religious reasons. Is it not a Freudian perspective that what we deny in ourselves we then project onto others? It is certainly the condition of the *fall*, of original sin, that we project onto others flaws and faults we deny in ourselves because we have taken onto ourselves the decision-making—the "right to choose"—having metaphorically eaten of the fruit of the tree of the knowledge of good and evil. An underlying concept that should be in any criticism of such atheistic apologetics is that religion is bad, but atheism is worse (particularly when fed by the illusion of the *zeitgeist*); a principle that we invoked earlier and that underpinned Karl Barth's acerbic criticism of religion in the service of the gospel, where Barth is merciless on human religiosity, whichever "god" such religion claims to believe or not believe in. Pullman has commented that, "My books are about killing God,"[49] yet his readers are blind to the holocaust of the unborn, which they implicitly endorse. Indeed, the heroine of Pullman's *His Dark Materials*, the freedom-loving, autonomous-ethics pursuing Lyra Belacqua, will call on abortion when she grows up if, to ensure her sexual freedom, she does not want to be "with child." Such an action

---

49 Quoted by Steve Meacham, from an interview with Philip Pullman. See, Meacham, "The Shed Where God Died."

3. A Human-Generated Eschaton: Objectification

would be entirely in keeping with Pullman's aims, objectives, his thesis and the character.

The theological roots of the Enlightenment mega-holocausts lie in a theology of death where humanity, through original sin, deludes itself into believing it is doing the right, the good, when it is sinning and committing evil atrocities. This is so when enslaving and working to death West Africans, or when seeking to annihilate the Jews in gas chambers, or when killing the unborn.

XVII. THE RELIGIOUS ROOTS OF THE THIRD ENLIGHTENMENT MEGA-HOLOCAUST

The so-called right to choose is seen as a central tenet of the disparate and often contradictory pseudo-religious beliefs of neo-pagan secular-liberal humanists (including the so-called New Atheists). Abortion and feminism are heavily politicized issues and belief systems that are closely related because some of the founding matriarchs of feminism saw abortion as necessary to free a women's body from what was perceived to be the tyranny of childbearing and childbirth: abortion was intimately entwined with sexual freedom. This is postmodern, post-Christian, and thereby related to the social, cultural, and religious revolutions that started in the late 1960s, and as this revolution, Western in origin, has developed pace it now seeks the evolutionary mutation of the churches—and therefore the gospel—into a religion that complements this neo-pagan secular-liberal humanist revolution. This leads to what many see as the paganization of the gospel generally, the Church of England specifically.[50] Many liberal

---

50   Positions taken by Anglicans across the world are—predictably—varied, contradictory, and often vague. Contrary to Revd Dr Gordon Dunstan's casuistical attempts to dehumanize the unborn child, a 1980 statement by the Anglican church asserted that the fetus has the right to live and develop as a member of the human family, classifying abortion as a great moral evil. However, in a typical Anglican fudge it then asserted that the right to life does admits some exceptions. The Episcopal Church in the United States of America (ECUSA) adopts a pro-choice stance, passing a resolution at its triannual General Convention that reiterates a woman's right to choose, furthermore they opposes any government that limits a woman's right to choose. (see: http://www.episcopalchurch.org/3577_37993_ENG_HTM). However, America's pro-choice position, which now results in at 1.1 to 1.5 million abortions per year, is inadvertently racist. Why? Because year on year approximately two-thirds of American abortions are performed on the children of African American and Hispanic/Latino women.

Anglicans will echo a strong denial of a forensic legalistic atonement theory.[51] Why? Because arguing that Christ's death on the cross is the reconciliation of God and humankind through a sacrificial death, penal substitution, this leads, so many *1970s* liberal Anglicans[52] will politely offer ruefully, to Christians killing each other and justifying capital punishment. Progressive liberals, *1970s* liberal Anglicans amongst others, look at Christian history and quite rightly are shocked at the level of carnage visited by one group of Christians on another but are then blind to the level of killing that results from the third Enlightenment mega-holocaust. Liberals echo the critique of American feminist theologians that penal substitution amounts to cosmic child abuse, the Father visiting punishment and death on the Son (this criticism, however, hinges on the degree of Trinitarian individuation subscribed to), yet at the same stroke of the pen they will champion a women's "right to choose." The level of killing—Christian on Christian—in past centuries is small in comparison to the number of children killed by the Enlightenment mega-holocausts, particularly in the twentieth century.

So what is happening here, can we explain this in terms of a theory of religion? It relates very closely to how, through faith, we believe in Christ's atoning sacrifice and how much we accept the cross and all that is eschatologically contained in the crucifixion: we can trust in Christ's atoning sacrifice, including the element of penal substitution, or we can substitute with our own sacrifices, our own blood offerings. Ironically, many 1970s Anglican liberals deny any element of penal substitution but they then endorse what is in effect the revival of pagan child sacrifice in the third Enlightenment mega-holocaust. Many so-called 1970s liberal Anglicans are correct when quoting Hebrews that the churches have often failed to truly accept that Christ's sacrifice on the cross is full and complete, that Christ's sacrifice does away, to a degree, with morality and legalism. Therefore, in the past, church leaders have implicitly failed to place their trust, fully, in what God in Christ has done for them on the cross because they have visited judgmental violence on others. Today, is it not so that liberal Anglicans, American Episcopalians, postmodern neo-pagan secular-liberal humanists, and the assorted New Atheists reject, for various reasons, the substitution element in the crucifixion only to revive and endorse pagan child sacrifice in the third Enlightenment mega-holocaust in its place? This becomes a humanist pseudo-substitution atonement theory: we must kill to protect ourselves and our values and beliefs, beliefs that must surely be seen as implicitly religious. The state

---

51   See Finlan, *Problems with Atonement*.

52   See: https://en.wikipedia.org/wiki/Liberal_Christianity.

sanctioning of the third Enlightenment mega-holocaust on an industrial scale is to be seen as the revival of pagan child sacrifice.[53]

XVIII. *QHAPAQ HUCHA/CAPACOCHA*: INCA PROTECTIONIST CHILD SACRIFICE— THE *ESCHATON* PREFIGURED

One of the best documented examples of child sacrifice was in the ancient Inca kingdom, practiced to prevent the world ending: the rationally held religious belief was that the world would be consumed by elemental chaos, earthquake and storm. The sacrifice of a child prevented this. Inca child sacrifice probably amounted over the time of the Inca Empire to no more than three to five children per year, if that. Knowledge and understanding about Capacocha (trans: "real obligation"), the sacred Inca ceremony of human sacrifice, is essentially from two sources: the accounts written by Jesuits in the sixteenth and seventeenth centuries, and from each newly discovered mummy. The ritual sacrifices were intricate and of great importance. The sacrifice had to be of a child—for purity (including physical perfection). The worship of mountains as "gods," and the elaborate burial procedures involved, elevated the status and ontology of the sacrificed child to that of a deity, at one with the "gods." The sacrifice was usually that of a chieftain's child or even the offspring of the Inca Emperor—these people were considered to be descendants of the sun "god." The child to be sacrificed would be fed a maize alcohol (*chicha*) to numb pain from exposure and the altitude. Liturgical ritual at the place of the cairn on the mountain top led to the child being enveloped in ceremonial clothing and incarcerated in the cairn-tomb, guarded by sacred artefacts, and left to die of exposure. According to the Jesuitical records/accounts, this was done to appease the "gods," and to prevent the world collapsing into chaos.[54] The Inca practice

---

53   In this context, vivisection (again something that has been ratcheted up to an industrial scale since the late 1960s) is to be seen as the revival of pagan animal sacrifice. Did not ancient pagans sacrifice animals and children to stop the world ending—they believed so. The Romans sacrificed wild dogs as a cure for mildew—a fungal disease—that affected wheat; today in a vain attempt to find cures for an escalating range of diseases, often created through our lifestyle indulgence, hundreds of thousands of animals are subjected to levels of tortuous experimentation the scale of which would perhaps have shocked our ancestors.

54   For a general introduction see, "Child Sacrifice in Pre-Columbian Cultures." https://en.wikipedia.org/wiki/Child_sacrifice_in_pre-Columbian_cultures   (accessed Nov 30, 2016).

of child sacrifice—*Qhapaq hucha* (often named as, *Capacocha*)—was undertaken during the calendar of important events, such as the death of an emperor (the *Sapa Inca*) or during a famine. Children (six years of age being the youngest, fifteen being the oldest, according to discovered corpses) were elected because they were considered to be the purest of beings to be offered to the "gods." The child was appareled in rich jewelry and clothing, having been fed-up over the preceding months; hundreds of valuable objects were buried with these children. The priests removed the children to mountains for sacrifice. "Upon reaching the burial site, the children were given an intoxicating drink to minimize pain, fear, and resistance. They were then killed either by strangulation, a blow to the head, or by leaving them to lose consciousness in the extreme cold and die of exposure."[55]

Inca child sacrifice was undertaken with thought, consideration, and religious seriousness; it was undertaken with piety and surrounded with liturgical conviction, with utter persuasion that the course undertaken was right (comparable with a Roman Catholic *auto-da-Fe*, or the Calvinistic Scottish elders execution of Thomas Aikenhead?). My mother was persuaded of the rightness of my father's request that they should sacrifice me: because they could not afford another child, my sacrifice would have (theoretically) prevented their world and economy from collapsing.[56] When the under-the-counter medicines failed, my father went back for more, after all, once these "gods" have demanded sacrifice there is no appeasing them until they have drunk of a child's blood. But the pharmacist was on his summer holiday—so my father had to wait for his return. This time, after

---

55   See, Reinhard. "A 6,700 metros niños incas sacrificados quedaron congelados en el tiempo," 36–55. "Early colonial Spanish missionaries wrote about this practice but only recently have archaeologists . . . begun to find the bodies of these victims on Andean mountaintops, naturally mummified due to the freezing temperatures and dry windy mountain air." Wikipedia, *Capacocha*, https://en.wikipedia.org/wiki/Capacocha (accessed Nov 30, 2016). See also, Andrushko et al., "Investigating a Child Sacrifice Event from the Inca Heartland," 323–33; Besom, *Of Summits and Sacrifice*; Ceruti, "Human Bodies as Objects of Dedication at Inca Mountain Shrines* (North-Western Argentina)"; Reinhard, "Sacred Mountains, Ceremonial Sites, and Human Sacrifice among the Incas," 1–43.

56   If my parents' aim in attempting to sacrifice me—that they could not afford another child—had been true, then surely I would have died of starvation or exposure within the first few weeks after being born? No, what they suffered from was relative consumer poverty: they did not want to allocate money to my upbringing that they preferred to spend on themselves.

3. A Human-Generated Eschaton: Objectification

a second dose, my mother bled for two days. But I survived.[57] I thank God that I know the details (both from my parents—as my father chided me for failing to die in the womb!—but also from discussion with my mother's two life-long school friends, when I was seventeen years of age). After all is said and done I know how Isaac felt!

Following the abolition, as such, in the Old Testament of human/child sacrifice in the Abraham and Isaac episode (Gen 22:1–24), child sacrifice was outlawed for the Hebrews—God's chosen people—and was considered to be one of the worst of all crimes before God. The Book of Leviticus specifically outlaws child sacrifice to the "god" Molech: "Child sacrifice profanes the name of the Lord" (Lev 18:21). The prophet Ezekiel laments that the people of Israel sacrificed their children:

> And you took your sons and daughters whom you bore to me and sacrificed them as food to the idols. Was your prostitution not enough? You slaughtered my children and sacrificed them to the idols. In all your detestable practices and your prostitution you did not remember the days of your youth (Ezek 16:20–21).

The evidence of child sacrifice amongst the ancient peoples of Israel and the abomination that this was before the Lord God is at its most explicit in Psalm 106:

> They worshiped their idols, which became a snare to them.
> They sacrificed their sons and their daughters to demons.
> They shed innocent blood, the blood of their sons and daughters,
>   whom they sacrificed to the idols of Canaan,
>   and the land was desecrated by their blood.
> They defiled themselves by what they did; by their deeds
>   they prostituted themselves.
>
> Psalm 106:36–39

---

57   I have suffered from Ménières disease (tinnitus, vertigo, and deafness) all my life. This is a disease which is supposed to come on in adults (usually in their twenties), it is not known in children. Because I was born at the end of January 1954, my conception would have been, for arguments sake, on 1 May 1953. If the chemist was on his summer holiday between my father's first purchase and the subsequent second dose of the illegal aborting medicine, this would point to sometime between mid-July and the end of August (this was the traditional time for the English middle-class professionals to take their single annual holiday in the 1950s). An unborn child's brain-nervous system is highly sensitive and susceptible to environmental damage—especially from chemicals—during the period two-and-a-half months to four months into development in the womb: was this Ménières type disease inflicted on me by the aborting chemical weapons?

Pagan sacrifices—whether children or animals—were undertaken to appease the "gods" and to prevent the end of the world on a communal scale. Whatever the aims, an important part of pre-Enlightenment pagan child sacrifice was that the child was fully human. By comparison the three Enlightenment sacrificial mega-holocausts work by reducing or denying the full humanity of the victims, although in the case of the sacrificial offering of the unborn, postmodern relativism ensures this denial varies with each death, and any contradictions are ignored. For example, stem cells are harvested from what is defined as a sub- or non-human embryonic person, because they are considered to be of immense value to curing diseased and corrupted adults (the sacrifice of the embryonic person to prevent the end of the world of the sick adult is a central principle of neo-pagan secular-liberal humanist sacrifice). However, not only are the stem cells of value because the embryonic person is fully human, they are harvested as of immense value because the embryo is actually super-human—it contains characteristics that transcend the merely mortal nature of adult humanity (which again confirms the pagan religious ground underpinning such sacrificial practice). Whatever the individual aims, these Enlightenment mega-holocausts are sacrificial because they are undertaken to stop the world ending. Millions of West Africans were sacrificed as slaves to promote to promote and fulfill, to enrich a pseudo-*eschaton*: heaven-on-earth for the British Empire. The Nazis sacrificed the Jews in slave labor camps and in the gas chambers in part because they prevented the purity and fulfilment of their Aryan world. The third Enlightenment mega-holocaust is individualistic and lacks the communal element that characterized ancient pagan sacrifice, though both seek to prevent the world of the individual or the community ending. The third mega-holocaust is characterized by autonomous consequentialist ethics; Inca child sacrifice was characterized by heteronomous communitarian ethics.

XIX. CAIN AND ABEL

The tide of secularization in the West, which has increased immeasurably since the late 1960s, has led Christian groups once considered hostile to each other (Evangelicals and Roman Catholics, for instance) to huddle together in a form of relative unity in the face of a postmodern, neo-pagan secular-liberal humanist society dominated by consumerism

3. A Human-Generated Eschaton: Objectification

and an agenda obsessed with lifestyle and individual identity politics, a society justified not by Christ's atoning sacrifice but by protectionist killing (in recent times, the Iraq-Afghanistan wars, abortion, stem-cell research, vivisection, suicide, euthanasia, Islamist suicide bombers, etc.): the boundaries between the various theologies of death that constitute these Enlightenment mega-holocausts are, in postmodern relativistic terms, blurred. This is a culture of death, which in the last forty years appears to have overturned and rejected, inverted, everything that was characteristic of a Christian society.[58] In rejecting Christ's propitiatory atoning sacrifice, in rejecting penal substitution, in rejecting the concept of punishment, and therefore the completeness of Christ's death on the cross, the West has generated and endorsed the revival of pagan sacrifice on an industrial scale. The exponents look to the splinter in the eye of the historic church whilst ignoring the tree trunk of pagan sacrifice in their own eye. If the churches have been insufficient representatives of Christ's atoning sacrifice in the past, does not the secular, liberal, humanist delusion make their faults pale by comparison?[59]

---

58   Pro-choice abortionists, particularly in the USA, call for plurality—the idea that different views should live alongside each other without attempting to contradict each other. This was a central tenet in Barack Obama's election campaign relating to the issue of abortion and stem-cell research. However, this is a recent phenomenon. Is the question of the third Enlightenment mega-holocaust, as with the first two (the slave trade and the Holocaust), simply a question of opinion? No. The measure is the level of death subscribed to—the level of protectionist killing. The slave trade and the Holocaust of the Jews demanded a level of death rarely seen before; the same is true with abortion since state sanctioning. The resulting delusion inverts the truth. For example, most of the New Atheists are really only journalists or novel writers, but are Machiavellian experts at handling the media and cultivating a media image. A common accusation levelled at the churches in America by these oligarchic elites is that they should not oppose abortion but welcome it as part of the spirit of liberation that was evident in the civil rights movement and amongst abolitionists in the nineteenth century. This was a charge laid by the commentator and TV media historian Simon Schama in his active role in the 2008 US presidential campaign. To link the abolitionists' campaign against the slave trade with the pro-choice-abortion lobby is a delusionary inversion. The abolitionists—for example, William Wilberforce—opposed the enslavement and death of Africans from an Evangelical perspective; the pro-life lobby often oppose abortion from a Roman Catholic-Evangelical perspective: in both cases abolitionists and anti-abortionists oppose death, oppose protectionist killing, arguing for equality before God. The measure of right or wrong is in the level of death subscribed to. Pluralism, in this instance, merely endorses death.

59   Cf. Matt 7:3–5 and Luke 6:41–42.

How do we respond to this theology of death? The Swiss theologian Karl Barth outlined the eschatology of this in his second commentary on Romans in the context of the 1917 Marxist revolution that had just taken place in Russia, and in relation to Dostoevsky's Grand Inquisitor. Barth stated that the revolutionary (and have not the Enlightenment-led mega-Holocausts been part of a social revolution that constituted a pagan rebellion against the Lord?) is not the Christ who stands before the Grand Inquisitor, but is, contrariwise, the Grand Inquisitor sitting in judgment on those he/she decides need correcting, using, abusing, disposing of, according to need?

> The revolutionary must, however, own that in adopting his plan he allows himself to be overcome by evil. He forgets that he is not the One, that he is not the subject of the freedom, which he so earnestly desires, that, for all the strange brightness of his eyes, he is not the Christ who stands before the grand inquisitor, but is, contrariwise, the grand inquisitor encountered by the Christ. He too is claiming what no man can claim. He too is making of the right a thing. He too confronts other men with his supposed right. He too usurps a position which is not due to him, a legality which is fundamentally illegal, an authority which—as we have grimly experienced in Bolshevism, but also in the behavior of far more delicate-minded innovators!—soon displays its essential tyranny.[60]

Therefore, we may postulate that when Catholics stood before Protestants and were executed (for instance, in the Thirty Years War) they were at one with Christ. Likewise, when Protestants, or so-called heretics, stood before the Inquisition and were burned alive they were also at one with Christ—the perpetrators being of the devil because they usurped the righteousness of God and acted *eritis sicut Deus*? Are all such perpetrators, whether the British stave traders, the Nazi SS guards at the death camps, or today's abortionists at one with Pilate in judging and condemning Jesus, or Herod in the Massacre of the Innocents?[61] There is no space for compromise here—either we are the victims at one with Christ, or we are the perpetrators at one with Pilate and Herod. We are all either Cain or Abel: humanity, not God, defined this dualistic distinction. Like Cain's sin, the Enlightenment holocausts are intertwined with pseudo-religious,

---

60 Barth, *The Epistle to the Romans*, 505.
61 John 18:31 and Matt 2:16–18.

self-justification. In the Enlightenment mega-holocausts the protagonists focus on the base elements of the human—uncontrolled and indulgent passion—as Cain did in killing Abel. The story of Cain and Abel is about acceptable and unacceptable sacrifice, good and bad religion. Cain rejects God's wisdom and makes a sacrifice of his brother: this human solution to the question of right religion has echoed through the Enlightenment mega-holocausts. Cain and his spiritual progeny exhibit selfishness, jealousy, and aggression; they are divorced from the higher "human" nature characterized by altruistic love, they reject God's judgment on their innate religiosity, therefore they reject the wisdom of God. In so doing they dehumanize first the object of their religious hatred, then they dehumanize themselves (for example the exponents of apartheid in South Africa and in the United States in the decades after the Second World War). By dehumanizing, by classifying some people as sub- or non-human, the elite merely dehumanize themselves. Therefore, we may ask, "To what degree do the protagonists close themselves off to the redeeming influence of the Holy Spirit?" The measure is always death—the degree to which death, and dehumanization, is subscribed to and used as an attempt at protectionist self-justification. This is why—to explore the "theo-logic" in Barth's axiom—the revolutionary is not the Christ, the lamb, the victim, before the Grand Inquisitor, but was the oppressor, dehumanizing his or her victims. Therefore, a crusade, or jihad, against such holocausts merely endorses this theology of death. It is wrong and anathema to firebomb abortion clinics, vivisection laboratories, it is evil to assassinate doctors who perform abortions. Have I made it clear enough? Such actions merely play into their hands: those who live by the sword die by the sword and no one is righteous. Being Pharisaic or puritanical merely generates self-righteousness and the impossibility of living up to the law. All we can do is speak out, even if this leads to censorship and persecution, to draw a line, to try to persuade people through argument, through God's truth, to refuse to sanction the escalating body count in the multitudinous Enlightenment-led holocausts that have plagued the world for more than three hundred years.

XX. CONCLUSION

Humanity is excellent at convincing itself of the rightness of any course of action it wishes to follow and inventing religious justification for such action. We must always acknowledge that there is distance between God in Christ and our religion, because we are fallen (religion issuing from the *fall*, to take the place of the immediate relation with God that humanity had before they sinned). If religion is inexorably corrupted and we will all face eschatological judgment, then ethics is all that is left. We may assert we have faith in Christ, but this does not necessarily validate our ethics (Matt 7:21, 25, specifically vv. 31–46). We must recognize this space—otherwise how do we explain the sins of the church?

Blindness: we condemn in others what we refuse to acknowledge in ourselves. The American politician Sean Spicer commented how Hitler did not use chemical weapons on his own people; the liberal West immediately condemned him in social media, official statements, *et al.*, because Hitler had used chemical weapons: on the Jews, amongst others—in the gas chambers.[62] Spicer was wrong. But the critics were oblivious to the fact that children killed in abortion clinics are slaughtered using chemical weapons: the means of death is a chemical; it is a weapon in that it is "a thing designed or used for inflicting bodily harm or physical damage, a means of gaining an advantage or defending oneself" (OED). The critics in America—those who form the majority of Americans who are happy with the slaughter of up to one-and-a-half million children each year through acts of willful abortion—were correct in their observation of Spicer's comments but denied in themselves what they condemned in others.

So what is the answer? There is only one answer, to repent and accept Christ's forgiveness wrought through his atoning propitiatory sacrifice. We have barely begun to understand and accept the completeness of Christ's atoning sacrifice. The punishment and the price for the alienation and distance caused by sin has been paid. However, it is Isaiah writing hundreds of years before the cross who established this axiomatic truth—"He was pierced for our transgressions, he was crushed for our iniquities; the punishment that brought us peace was upon him, and by his wounds we are healed."[63] To paraphrase and extend the apostle Paul's inclusive

---

62 See BBC News, online: http://www.bbc.co.uk/news/world-us-canada-39573063; http://www.bbc.co.uk/news/world-us-canada-39580120.

63 "Who has believed our message and to whom has the arm of the Lord been revealed? He grew up before him like a tender shoot, and like a root out of dry ground. He had no beauty or majesty to attract us to him, nothing in his appearance that we should desire him. He was despised and rejected by men, a man of sorrows, and familiar

3. A Human-Generated Eschaton: Objectification

eschatological sociology of the cross, Christ's punishment was in the place of, and related to, all humanity, whether Greek or Jew, slave or free, male or female, and whatever racial or tribal classification we wish to impose on people, but also born or unborn, all, regardless of culture, religion, lifestyle, or behavior. We will all, equally and inclusively, be raised in judgment by Christ. We must trust in the blood of the lamb, for therein lies God's forgiveness, we err to trust in the blood of Enlightenment pagan sacrifices, if we can face what we have truly become, where such forgiveness is eschatological.

---

with suffering. Like one from whom men hide their faces he was despised, and we esteemed him not. Surely he took up our infirmities and carried our sorrows, yet we considered him stricken by God, smitten by him, and afflicted. But he was pierced for our transgressions, he was crushed for our iniquities; the punishment that brought us peace was upon him, and by his wounds we are healed" (Isa 53:1–5).

4

The Just War Theory and the 9/11 Wars: A Biblical and Eschatological Consideration

Come and see the works of the LORD,
the desolations he has brought on the earth.

He makes wars cease to the ends of the earth;
he breaks the bow and shatters the spear,
he burns the shields with fire.

"Be still, and know that I am God;
I will be exalted among the nations,
I will be exalted in the earth."

PSALM 46:8–10

SYNOPSIS:
It is considered that war will usher in the *eschaton*, and there is good biblical precedent for this. The relationship between war—armed conflict fighting, even confrontation—and the *eschaton* has inevitably led humanity, in diverse times and places, to vainly believe that they are pre-empting the *eschaton*, by launching a "holy war": claiming God's approval and authority. Traditionally the churches have responded to a call to arms with caution: who really is righteous? But what of oppression? A cautious response is seen in a just war theory: *jus ad bellum* and *jus in bello*. Here, a defensive war may be seen as the lesser of two evils, a compromise. But how do we limit and contain death and destruction? How do our actions stand before God in the *eschaton*? War is grounded in eschatological judgment and death. Is war a form of realized eschatology? In recent years there have been calls to rewrite the just war theory for a war on terror, part of the so-called 9/11 wars. Just war theories abound; they are not necessarily Christian; however, it is necessary to consider a Christian response in the sixth commandment. Is biblical theology rather than philosophical disputation now an appropriate ground for considering

the justice of a war on terror? From scripture we find three war ethics: pagan, Hebrew, and Christian. Which path characterizes the so-called war on terror? The answer is in objective facts, statistics: actions, not intentions. A Christocentric categorical imperative asserts that there are moral absolutes, which the Bible and church tradition attest to. Any consideration of the war on terror must therefore be from the eschatological context of Jesus' sayings and commands: the return of the Landlord to the vineyard to settle accounts and weigh all according to his righteous judgment, the danger being of religious practice where we are unreconciled—to God, and each other. This paper concludes that it may be justifiable to re-write the just war theory from a neo-pagan secular-liberal humanist standpoint, however, from a biblically informed eschatological perspective it cannot be justified.

I. INTRODUCTION

Early on after the 9/11 attacks on America, and in the subsequent years, there have been calls to re-write or extend the just war theory in response to terrorism. The so-called 9/11 wars are quantifiably different to the two twentieth-century world wars and are seen as a culmination of terrorist atrocities enacted since the late 1960s (though terrorism has a much longer history). These post-1960s attacks are often (but not exclusively) seen as a form of global cold war between the West and the predominantly Muslim Middle East. September 11, 2001, marked a turning point, in many ways, of this sporadic global terrorist war: the attacks on America by fundamentalist Muslim terrorists serving the religio-military organization Al-Qaeda, the subsequent American invasion of Afghanistan and Iraq, and the consequent terrorist attacks in various cities throughout the world (London, 7/7; Madrid, Mumbai, et al.), and in recent years ideologically inspired terror attacks in the West by trained military cells related to Islamic State (IS) or simply inspired by lone citizens in the West, motivated by support for IS. The demand to re-write or extend the just war theory in response to terrorism has echoed from military quarters, but also, pertinently, from some within the churches,[1] and from elected leaders within Western governments.

1   Essentially from some British and American Presbyterian, Baptist, and Evangelical churches, though not from the catholic-established churches. Many of the Church of England bishops were categorically against the invasion of Iraq, but were noticeably silent about the invasion of Afghanistan. See the BBC News website for a report on the bishops' stance on the eve of the invasion of Iraq: "Church of England bishops have made their most outspoken criticism yet of plans for military action against

4. The Just War Theory and the 9/11 Wars

When talking about the war on terror initiated by the United States in 2001 in response to 9/11, what exactly do these calls for a rewritten and re-structured just war theory entail? We can deduce three principles: first, strike back harder, more destructively and more decisively than the antagonist; second, act, strike, pre-emptively if a threat is perceived (this involves a serious suspension of human rights and freedoms); third, colonization: take over countries that give shelter and succor to terrorists and attempt to convert the citizens away from the belief system that has led to the war in the first place. Do these three principles now constitute a post-Christian secular just war theory?—indeed, a neo-pagan secular-liberal humanist just war theory?

What is the just war theory and how does it relate to these three principles? What is the theological—more pertinently biblical—basis for a just war theory? Indeed, what is a Christian approach to war and peace? We need to look back prior to the Age of Reason, and prior to the formulation of the essentially mediaeval Catholic-Christian just war theory and see what scripture in the form of biblical theology can tell us.

II. JUST WAR THEORIES: AGGRESSION AND JUSTIFICATION

Just war theories abound; they are not necessarily Christian. Any nation or tribe will invent theories and principles to justify aggression and war—either as a pre-emptive offensive strike, or in defense. Such theories will often invoke religious justification, claiming to be in accord with the will of some "god" or "idol." In 2010, Radovan Karadžić at his trial at the International Criminal Tribunal for the former Yugoslavia (ICTY) in The Hague, following the UN indictment, claimed his actions in the fragmented former Yugoslavia in the early 1990s were "holy and just."[2]

Iraq with one of them accusing the government of acting as judge, jury and executioner. They repeated their view that an assault on Saddam Hussein would unacceptably lower the threshold for war and said it could not be morally justified. . . . 'There is absolutely nothing new now which would justify us going over the awesome threshold of war,' Bishop of Oxford Richard Harries said." See, http://news.bbc.co.uk/1/hi/uk/2659673.stm

2   "He [Radovan Karadžić] spends two days outlining his case—that Bosnia's Serbs were acting in self-defense against a Muslim elite who wanted total power in Bosnia. 'I will defend that nation of ours and their cause that is just and holy,' he says. He dismisses some of the most infamous features of the Bosnian war—the massacre at

Adolf Hitler's *Mein Kampf* was, in effect, a just war theory; it justified in neo-pagan religio-political terms the actions of the Nazis invading and subjugating Europe and attempting to annihilate the Jews. Karl Marx's *Das Kapital* is often seen as a justification for the class war. The *pax romana* was in effect a just war theory, that is, peace and prosperity within the Roman Empire was achieved by a brutal crackdown on dissent and any military attempt to challenge Roman authority (and thereby the Roman "gods": the use of crucifixion on a vast industrialized scale ensured that any rebellion was short-lived, for hitting back hard served as a warning to others. Conceptualizing, formulating, and defining acceptable criteria for aggression, subjugation, and war would appear to have evolved with the development of nation states, often characterized by racial and cultural (i.e., tribal) identity. But where does the concept of the "just" come in? Is the concept of the "just" integral to a religious perspective, or is it simply a protectionist assertion of tribal identity? Is the invention of justifiable criteria for war necessary to placate conscience? The theory of a "just" war is often associated with a Roman Catholic doctrine of military ethics. However, the idea of containing and channeling, of ethically justifying, all-out war was a concern of Graeco-Roman writers. For example, Plato (c. 428–347BC) was concerned about the rightful conduct of war, and the importance of virtue and restraint in warfare.[3] Cicero (106 BC–43 BC) argued that military action had unambiguous aims and objectives, in particular how and when to fight, but also how different adversaries should be tackled and how they should be treated after the cessation of hostilities: "The only excuse, therefore, for going to war," wrote Cicero, "is that we may live in peace unharmed."[4] A doctrine of military ethics grounded in a just war theory as we have received it is essentially the work of

---

Srebrenica, the siege of Sarajevo, the detention camps—as 'myths,' designed to arouse Western sympathy for the Bosnian cause." Record of the trial from March 1, 2010, reported by the BBC News website, 4 March 2010. See: http://news.bbc.co.uk/1/hi/world/europe/8332276.stm. Accessed May 2010 and February 20, 2017.

3   See, for example, the Alcibiades and Laches dialogues. See: Plato (trans. W. R. M. Lamb), *Plato in Twelve Volumes*, Vol. 8. Text available online at: http://www.perseus.tufts.edu/hopper/text?doc=Plat.+Lach.+178a&redirect=true

4   Cicero, *De Officiis* (1913). See: Bk. 1, §. XI, quotation from 34. For an online edition, see: http://www.constitution.org/rom/de_officiis.htm.

4. The Just War Theory and the 9/11 Wars

Augustine of Hippo[5] and Thomas Aquinas.[6] However, there have been many others who have attempted to square the circle, close the dialectic, between war and peace from a just and equitable perspective.[7]

III. JUST WAR THEORIES: A THOMIST THEORY

Aquinas opens with the basic statement that all wars are illegal: "It would seem that it is always sinful to wage war. Because punishment is not inflicted except for sin. Now those who wage war are threatened by Our Lord with punishment, according to Matthew 26:52: 'All that take the sword shall perish with the sword.' Therefore all wars are unlawful."[8] However, Aquinas then goes on to outline acceptable criteria whereby the concept of a just war is underpinned by certain basic beliefs: first,

---

5   Augustine, in *de civitate Dei* (*The City of God*, completed work published 426) is essentially the first Christian writer to attempt to develop a just war theory; that is, what are the conditions that make war acceptable? 1) war can only be acceptable if it is for a "just cause" and a "good end," not for self-gain or for domination; 2) a war that is just can only be fought by a legitimate authority, such as the state; 3) the primary motive should be peace, a peace only achievable through a state of temporary violence. See Augustine, *The City of God*, Bk. V, ch. 22 "The Duration of Wars and Their Outcome . . . ," 216–18; also, Bk. XIX, ch. 7 "Human Society Divided by Differences of Language. The Misery of War, Even When Just," 861–62.

6   Thomas codified three criteria, derived essentially from Augustine, for a just war: a) right authority—sovereign government, not individuals or groups have the right of authority; b) a just cause whereby wrongs are avenged, including restoration of land unjustly occupied or seized; c) right intention, that is, the advancement of good and/or the avoidance of evil. See Aquinas, *Summa Theologica*, Second Part, of the Second Part (SS) (QQ.1–189) Treatise on The Theological Virtues (QQ.1–46), On Charity (QQ.23–46) Question. 40 – OF WAR (FOUR ARTICLES): Article. 1 – Whether it is always sinful to wage war? Article. 2 – Whether it is lawful for clerics and bishops to fight? Article. 3 – Whether it is lawful to lay ambushes in war? Article. 4 – Whether it is lawful to fight on holy days?

7   For example, from the patristic and medieval period, Ambrose (337/340–397), Augustine of Hippo (354–430), Thomas Aquinas (1225–74), and Stanislaw of Skarbimierz (1360–1431). From the period of the Renaissance and Reformation Francisco de Vitoria (1492–1546), Francisco Suarez (1548–1617), Alberico Gentili (1552–1608), Hugo Grotius (1583–1645), and Baron von Pufendorf (1632–1694); from the Age of Reason and the Enlightenment, John Locke (1632–1704), Emerich de Vattel (1714–67), Immanuel Kant (1724–1804), and John Stuart Mill (1806–73); and from the modern to contemporary period, Paul Tillich (1886–1965), Reinhold Niebuhr (1892–1971), and H. Richard Niebuhr (1894–1962); these are amongst a plethora of philosophers and theologians of various persuasions and of numerous nationalities.

8   Aquinas, *Summa Theologica*, (P(2b)-Q(40)-A(1)-O(1).

that taking human life is wrong (we will come to the distinction between murder and lawful killing later), however, tribes and nations have an obligation of security, protection, and preservation. This is a duty of defense, and raises questions of justice. Warfare must be just and not for colonization or for punishment; intervention must be to protect life rather than take it; likewise—the principle of comparative justice—the injustice suffered by one nation or peoples must significantly outweigh that suffered by the aggressor. The legitimate authority to wage war, for Thomas, lies with kings (and therefore governments, public authorities, or trans-national bodies—for example NATO or the UN), provided the aim and cause is just or that warfare corrects a suffered wrong. Right intention is just; economic or material gain is not. He then tackles the question of the probability of success: lives should not be lost in a futile cause, or where disproportionate measures are used to achieve a small or limited victory. Finally, war should be a last resort: all peaceful, diplomatic, and feasible alternatives must be shown to be exhausted. By comparison we may ask, is pacifism just? It may not seem so to the oppressed. At times measured force and violence may be the only justifiable means of defense.

IV. JUST WAR THEORIES: THE JUST

Before we continue we need to decide whether the use of the term "just" is justifiable (!); for that matter, under what terms and definition is it being invoked?

Traditionally the concept of justice is considered to be a philosophical theory, therefore the concern of philosophers—then preserved in legal terms—by which what is seen as fairness is administered. However, justice varies from culture to culture, politic to politic, religion to religion. Divine command theory argues that justice issues from the "gods," or God: more pertinently, divine command theory says that X is just because God/the gods says it is just. It is God's decision, in other words, that makes things good or right or just. And doing justice or acting justly is simply the administration of what is "just," especially by the impartial adjustment of conflicting claims or the assignment of merited rewards or punishments.[9] The just is then defined as "having a basis in or conforming to fact or reason," [being] "faithful to an original," [and/

---

9   Merriam-Webster Dictionary:https://www.merriam-webster.com/dictionary/justice. Accessed Feb 20, 2017.

4. The Just War Theory and the 9/11 Wars

or] "conforming to a standard of correctness," [thereby] "acting or being in conformity with what is morally upright or good."[10] This leads to the concept of "just rewards" or "just punishment" but there is an element of circularity between the "just" leading to justice, or justice grounded in the just. This circularity was countermanded by invoking natural law, which was common in the patristic and mediaeval period, but natural law becomes a problem with the Age of Reason, the Enlightenment, difficulties aggravated by modernism, postmodernism, and where philosophers, lawyers, and politicians fear anything that is God-given, and therefore outside of the control of their hegemony.

And who do we take to be the justified before God, according to the Gospels and in particular the apostle Paul's theology? Does a just war make us righteous before God? In printing, justified text—like this—is balanced and equal on each side: all right and correct! So does a just war, despite the contradictions inherent in violence, make all sides equal, balanced, fair, and "just"? No. If one thinks one has a just cause, according to the theory, then one also thinks that one's opponents do not have a just cause. One does not think that all sides are equal.

V. JUST WAR THEORIES: A ROMAN CATHOLIC PERSPECTIVE— *JUS AD BELLUM* AND *JUS IN BELLO*

In Christian terms, specific criteria and conditions were defined by which kings and rulers could decide a) if it was just to go to war, and b) the conditions under which a war could be fought. So is war just, or permissible? Is the concept of the just equitable with the good? From a broadly Christian perspective, and in the context of a doctrine of military ethics, a just war theory is grounded in the proposition that going to war is the lesser evil, but this implies that war and violence is still evil, just the lesser of two evils. From a Roman Catholic perspective, the just war theory (invoked on an annual basis all over Europe in the Middle Ages), as we have come to know it, was defined by and in relation to God in Christ: issuing from reasoned (logos) philosophy. Therefore, in the Christian West, before the development of neo-pagan secular-liberal humanism, rulers and governments of all persuasions were implicitly recognizing

---

10   Merriam-Webster Dictionary: https://www.merriam-webster.com/dictionary/just. Accessed Feb 20, 2017.

and defining war as evil and wrong, but a regrettable necessity when the criteria of the theory were met.

It has been very easy to create a non-Christian justification for war and conquest. For example, the Viking[11] lifestyle made a "god" out of war: justified by the expansionist blood-lust war ethic of the Vikings—rewarded with entry to Valhalla, the Viking "heaven" (which was in reality a region of hell), characterized by fighting and blood-letting, rape and subjugation, mutilation, drunken revelries, and feasting—along with other "pagans" and "barbarians." There are times where attempting to justify war can seem ambiguous and irrational. For example, how difficult in practice is it to keep to the rules of engagement scripted for justification? Are attempts to govern the declaring of war and the conduct of war by ethics impossible? In many ways, this was confirmed by the Anglo-Saxon term berserk, applied to the Viking, whereby the warrior was taken over by an irrational bloodlust and could not stop hitting out at anything and everyone, slashing and slaughtering.[12]

According to the Roman Catholic doctrine, there are two elements: *jus ad bellum* (the criteria whereby war is justified) and *jus in bello* (the manner in which war is conducted according to certain ethical criteria). According to *jus ad bellum* (the right to go to war), warfare must be just and not for colonization or for punishment; civilians must be in imminent danger, intervention must be to protect life rather than take it. The injustice suffered by one nation or peoples must significantly outweigh that suffered by the aggressor; therefore, we have the concept of legitimate authority (governments, public authorities, or trans-national bodies—for example NATO or the UN—may wage war given just cause, right intention: correcting a suffered wrong is good; economic or material gain is not). But there are various complicating criteria as to the good: the probability of success must be weighed and taken seriously; lives should not be lost in a futile cause, or where disproportionate measures are used

---

11   Vikingr: *freebooter, sea-rover, pirate, viking*, which usually is explained as meaning properly *one who came from the fjords*.

12   As an adjective, *berserk* implies out of control; wild or frenzied. As a noun, *berserk* (also *berserker*) referred to an ancient Norse warrior who fought with frenzy; in reference to ancient Norse warriors, *berserkers* fought with furious violence. The word derives from Old Norse *berserkr*, probably from *bjorn* "bear" with *serkr* "coat"; it has been suggested that warriors performed a war dance wearing bearskins to imbue them with the bear's strength before battle. The word has also been explained as being from *berr* "bare" (i.e., without armor).

4. The Just War Theory and the 9/11 Wars

to achieve a small or limited victory; all peaceful, diplomatic, and feasible alternatives must be shown to be exhausted; the degree of destruction and violence used must not exceed the threat, or the suffering experienced by an occupied people (proportionality). According to *jus in bello* (how to conduct war), the first principle is of distinction, whereby war should be directed at military forces and combatants, and not civilians; the bombing of residential areas that exclude military targets is excluded, likewise indiscriminate acts of terrorism, or reprisal against civilians, are considered unjust; which raises the question of proportionality. The principle of proportionality dictates that an attack cannot be launched on a military target in the knowledge that the civilian injuries would exceed the anticipated military advantage. Likewise, there is the complementary principle of military necessity: the principle of minimum force dictates that war must lead to the defeat of an enemy, the destruction of military targets only; there must therefore be an attempt at a limitation of death and destruction.

VI. JUST WAR THEORIES: A SECULAR-MODERNIST PERSPECTIVE?

In recent years, and in many ways resulting from the nature of war in the twentieth century, a third category has been added—issuing essentially from secular theorists—which addresses how a war is ended, and how a just peace is achieved: *jus post bellum*. For example, peace treaties, reparation, reconstruction, war crimes trials, and so forth. The concept of the right of self-defense is often seen as complementary to a just war theory, however, they both differ by degree of emphasis. *Jus post bellum*—literally, "the law after the war"—defines the cessation of hostilities. In the twentieth century, secular theorists (for example, Gary Bass, Louis Iasiello, and Brian Orend) formulated a post-conflict addition to the just war theory. The theory of *jus post bellum* concerns justice after a war. Termination of hostilities may take place if there is evidence that the original cause is now satisfied, if the cause has now been solved. Termination of hostilities may take place if the aggressor accepts/negotiates terms of surrender/cessation. Termination of hostilities may take place if a war becomes unwinnable, or the aims for going to war cannot be achieved without using excessive force. Termination of hostilities may take place if the aim and objective change to revenge. Both sides—the victor as much as the original perpetrator—must be willing to allow their forces to be subject to impartial investigation (i.e., for war crimes). The terms of peace must be made by a legitimate authority, and the terms must be accepted by a legitimate authority (but what constitutes a legitimate authority, given that authorities are in effect self-referential: they create their own authority?). Is it valid to differentiate between political and military leaders, and between combatants and civilians. Measure and punishment is to be aimed at those responsible for the conflict. Truth and reconciliation will often be more important than punishment. Any terms of surrender must be proportional to the rights that were initially violated.

However, in neo-pagan secular-liberal humanist terms this degree of emphasis appears to have allowed for a greater or lesser use of force and the re-scripting of ethics to suit the situation. Often this justifies the use of force as retaliation by any necessary means: the end justifies the means. Ethics—or more pertinently, ethical conundrums and objections—must be phrased as relative, subjective, and variable, whilst having the appearance of "law" and "respectability," "permanence" and "rightness," even if the ethics for war in one situation appear contradictory to a new situation a few years later. (Essentially this is a war ethic for a consumer society.)

VII. CONFLICT

Conflict between the Christian West and Islam is centuries old (though ironically this conflict has become much worse since the secularization agenda of the late 1960s); much of the antagonism is historic (the Crusades) and is rooted in fundamental religious difference issuing from the revelation in Christ. However, since the mid-nineteenth century this age-old antipathy has changed due to the drift into secular-liberal humanism in the West and a perception by Middle Eastern Muslim nations of their oppression and exploitation. Since the late 1960s this "war" has taken the form of industrialized terrorism (for example, the hi-jacking of passenger airliners, random shooting, sometimes chemical attacks, and suicide bombers). This was initially perpetrated by heavily politicized nominally Muslim groups in the 1970s, wedded to a Middle Eastern form of Marxist dialectic. From the late 1980s a form of fundamentalist Islamic religious dogma replaced the Marxist dialectic.[13] The reality

---

13   See Pastor, *Terrorism & Public Safety Policing*; Pape, "The Strategic Logic of

faced by ordinary citizens is that they are essentially relatively innocent bystanders caught between the military issues and the protracted and ongoing political realities (essentially since the break-up of the Ottoman Empire,[14] and the reliance on Middle Eastern oil by the West). This fuels age-old resentments by factions and tribes and nations characterized by a keen sense of the salient features of the historic situation.[15] But amidst this welter of discussion and thesis, politicking and policy, nothing seems to change—except the situation has worsened. Talk of "rights" and "legalism" only makes the situation worse.[16] Western forces were entrenched in what many saw as an unwinnable "armed conflict" in Afghanistan and Iraq, while the Taliban merely bide their time waiting for the West to depart. Little has changed since the British Empire attempted (and failed) to subdue Afghanistan in the mid-nineteenth century. Human history is characterized by, for C. S. Lewis, money and poverty, war and ambition, prostitution and sexual degradation, the class struggle, empires, and slavery. Lewis takes this further: original sin is the key to history; civilizations and cultures grow up, often founded on sound principles, good laws are formulated, but something always goes wrong, "some fatal flaw always brings the selfish and cruel people to the top and it all slides back into misery and ruin."[17]

VIII. WAR & PEACE 1: AGGRESSION & SIN—SANITY

If political theorizing, reasoned philosophical disputation, and Machiavellian scheming are not going to offer a solution to age-old conflicts then what will? Should a Christian take up arms and fight, kill, in these conflicts? What has scripture, the Christian theological tradition, and—all importantly—Jesus Christ got to say about war? Few if any countries claim to be "Christian" in any robust sense. So whatever Christians decide about what they should do, countries will decide on different criteria. Even if some countries do want to sign up to Christian just war principles, most countries would not. Most are non-Christian.

Suicide Terrorism"; Hoffman, *Inside Terrorism*; Sageman, *Understanding Terror Networks*.

14   See Itzkowitz, *Ottoman Empire and Islamic Tradition*; Said, *Orientalism*; Lewis, *Istanbul and the Civilization of the Ottoman Empire*.

15   See Lewis, *Islam and the West*; also Chaliand, *The History of Terrorism*.

16   See Benton, *Law and Colonial Cultures*.

17   Lewis, *Broadcast Talks*, 49.

But is it that simple? What of civil wars, warring neighbors, warring families—theft, aggression, sin? What of the war that rages in all of us between different elements of our personalities? Or the war we all wage to stay on the right side of sanity when anger boils up in us?

IX. WAR & PEACE 2: LORDSHIP & OBEDIENCE

The sixth commandment (Exod 20:13) is often quoted by pacifists as a prohibition on all killing. Traditionally, this is stated simply as, "Thou shalt not kill." However, the Hebrew word *rātsach* (pronounced *rah-tsakh'*), should be more accurately translated as "Thou shalt not commit an illegal killing." *Rātsach* is properly a primitive root meaning "to dash in pieces," that is, to kill another human being, especially to murder, on impulse, put to death in anger, irrationally. *Rātsach* evokes an irrational act, an unmeasured response—to strike out destructively with no consideration whether the other person lives or dies, to slay, to exterminate, to destroy. This is the sin of Cain (Gen 4:1–16, specifically 8b). Properly speaking *rātsach* applies to an illegal killing. The nearest we have in English is the word murder (that is, as a noun and a verb, the unlawful premeditated killing of one person by another), though perhaps manslaughter better describes the impulsive act, whereas murder in modern Western nations is often categorized as pre-meditated; however, here we have a problem. The difficulty here is that national governments—secular, liberal-humanist governments—define what constitutes legal and illegal killing. Legality for the ancient Hebrews was defined by and in relation to God—to YHWH, the righteous LORD—hence the divine permission for the Hebrews to defend themselves, on numerous occasions, against the invading Philistines *et al.* The response from the ancient Hebrews was in obedience to YHWH, God, the personal Lord, the eternal self-existing one. This was no impartial deity, but the one true God, who expected right behavior, who benevolently dictates the terms of morality and ethics and expects his chosen people to behave as such: war and justice were part of this heteronymous ethic, given, revealed, serving salvation history.

In the ancient Near East, the armies of the tribes and nations that surrounded the ancient Hebrews believed that they were led by their "gods." The Hebrews carried the divine presence in the form of the Ark of the Covenant—which contained the law given by YHWH—onto the battlefield (Num 10:35–36; 1 Sam 14:18). Therefore, because God could not be conquered, any victory was ascribed to YHWH, triumph and conquest reflected God's will for his chosen people; a defeat was ascribed to the faithlessness of the Israelites. However, for the ancient Hebrews, different categories of war were distinguished: *milhemet hovah* (obligatory war), was considered by some as identical with *milhemet mitsvah* (war commanded by God); and *milhemet reshut* (permitted war). One only has to consider the dynamic account of apocalyptic war contained in one of the Dead Sea Scrolls (the "War Scroll") to consider the implications of this; or the apocalyptic tension only resolved through war in the Book of Daniel (also in Revelation in the New Testament). In the State of Israel today Jewish scholars debate whether Jews should serve in non-Jewish armies in wars that do not directly affect Israel: the majority decided that the principle of *dina' de-malkhuta' dina'* (the laws of the country are to be observed) obliges Jews to serve.

X. WAR & PEACE 3: JUSTICE

But what does Jesus Christ require?—born to the House of David, son of Mary with impeccable Jewish heritage and credentials: very God and very man. How do the "gods/godlets" of war measure up against the revelation of the one true living God of the Hebrews and the Lord and Father of Jesus of Nazareth? It is salutary to note amidst the theistic-atheistic religious tribalism that goes under the panoply of mainstream religion in the West generally, Christianity-aChristianity specifically, that "Jesus wasn't actually a Christian. He was a temple worshipping, kosher-keeping, circumcised, first-century Jew, who loved the book of Isaiah and called God 'Abba.' . . . [He was a respecter of] God's promises as laid out in the Hebrew scriptures."[18]

Jesus of Nazareth, the Christ, his requirement is embodied in the law of love—cited on numerous occasions in the New Testament generally, the Gospels specifically. The question then is how do you define love? The obvious answer is in the Greek word *agapé* (self-giving, self-denying, disinterested, altruistic love). Therefore, do we just sit back and do nothing

---

18   Revd Giles Fraser, speaking on the "Thought for the Day" three-minute broadcast, as part of the *Today* news and current affairs radio program on BBC R4 (Mon–Fri, 06:00–09:00am; Sat, 0700–9:00). Broadcast, Jan 1, 2018, 07:47–07:50. See, https://www.bbc.co.uk/programmes/p00szxv6. Archive of recordings: https://www.bbc.co.uk/programmes/p00szxv6/clips.

when darkness and evil engulf our neighbors, ourselves? The Lutheran pastor and theologian Martin Niemöller commented—

> First they came for the communists, and I did not speak out—
> because I was not a communist;
>
> Then they came for the trade unionists, and I did not speak out—
> because I was not a trade unionist;
>
> Then they came for the Jews, and I did not speak out—
> because I was not a Jew;
>
> Then they came for me—
> and there was no one left to speak out for me.[19]

It was, in effect, for situations similar to this that the church evolved a just war theory. Does this not represent an apparently irreconcilable dialectic between war and peace, defense and aggression, commission and omission? If we take up arms to defend, we sin in our slaughter and destruction of others; yet if we do nothing our sin is that we are complicit in the evil and destruction? This element of commission-omission is embodied in the General Confession in the Church of England Book of Common Prayer: "We have left undone those things which we ought to have done; And we have done those things which we ought not to have done. And there is no health in us."[20]

XI. WAR & PEACE 4: A SPIRITUAL BATTLE

The just war theory identified not only armed conflict between or among nations or groups of people, but also an intense protracted struggle not involving arms/weapons: "soldier of Christ" (*miles Christi*) and the "army of Christ" (*militia Christi*) engaged in spiritual combat with evil (the hymn Onward Christian Soldiers comes to mind: "marching as to war ...," but not engaged in physical violence).[21] The majority of Christians

---

19   Martin Niemöller (Friedrich Gustav Emil Martin Niemöller, 1892–1984), Lutheran pastor theologian, speaking before the Confessing Church in Frankfurt on 6 January 1946 about the rise to power of the National Socialists. See, https://en.wikipedia.org/wiki/First_they_came.

20   The General Confession, Morning and Evening Prayer, The Church of England Book of Common Prayer, 1662.

21   *Onward Christian Soldiers* (originally entitled, *Hymn for Procession with Cross*

have accepted armed conflict as characteristic of life in a world as yet not fully redeemed. Christians may, therefore, morally participate in a just war according to the guidelines laid down in the tradition; by contrast, Christians must not take part in unjust wars. In essence, Augustine, working from the ideas of his teacher Ambrose of Milan, defined the principle of the lesser of two evils. A Christian could take up arms or participate in war if the evil of war was less than the evil that would result from not taking up arms (the lesser-of-two-evils principle). A just war therefore can only be defensive, never offensive or aggressive, although the theory did allow for the reluctant and limited use of force whereby a Christian might be required in charity to serve the needs of an innocent neighbor being attacked. However, the just war theory has been severely tested by contemporary events: nuclear weapons, or the so-called war on terrorism, or wars of liberation, and of course the perverse thinking of a suicide bomber. How far a Christian can participate in war will continue to be a problematic question with relativistic answers: defense is a necessary response to evil; but hostility is a negation of the good.

XII. WAR & PEACE 5: RECONCILIATION

But what did Jesus Christ have to say? Jesus looks at the issue eschatologically: how will we stand when we come before him in judgment at the end of days? Hence, Jesus' emphasis on reconciliation: be reconciled with your neighbor before coming before God or you will both face retribution (Matt 5:23–24; 18:21–35). This, like much of Matthew's Gospel, is about inter-Christian relations. But we also bear a responsibility to those outside of the faith, both on an individual and on a national level: we are our brother/sister's keeper (Gen 4:9), and we will be held responsible (Ezek 33:8–9). Therefore, we must exhaust, utterly, all avenues of reconciliation and making peace before resorting to conflict, worse, to war:

> Owe no one anything, except to love one another; for the one who loves another has fulfilled the law. The commandments . . . are summed up in this word, "Love your neighbor as yourself." Love

---

and Banners) was written by the Revd Sabine Baring-Gould in 1865 for a processional hymn for children walking from Horbury Bridge (where Baring-Gould was curate) to Horbury St Peter's Church near Wakefield, Yorkshire, Pentecost/Whitsuntide, 1865. See, Bradley, The Book of Hymns, 1989, 333.

See also, https://en.wikipedia.org/wiki/Onward,_Christian_Soldiers

> does no wrong to a neighbor; therefore, love is the fulfilling of the law. (Rom 13:8f)

When confronted by the centurion who sought the healing of his servant, Jesus does not use the situation for an anti-war polemic, or a criticism of the military mindset. On the contrary, he praises the military discipline in the centurion's mind that has produced such faith—"Truly I tell you, in no one in Israel have I found such faith" (Matt 8:5–13). And we are told to obey the authorities over us because they are God-given: "render unto Caesar" (Mark 12:17)—so much for rebellions, civil wars, and revolutions.

But to take this issue of reconciliation further, it is this that perhaps is at the heart of how Christians (indeed how all people) should live. Conflict may be inevitable but warring and violence issue from the fall (pertinently the sin of Cain), therefore, it is not how we should live. Ideally, we should live in peace and harmony. Jesus does appear to be talking about conflict between individuals, or small groups, hence the principle that we cannot, must not, ignore of turning the other cheek even when confronting evil (Matt 5:38–42): again, is this because of the eschatological implications? Does this apply to individuals or to nations? How do we extrapolate this ideal onto tribes, countries, nations? Also, we are called to love not just our friends but our enemies (Matt 5:43–48)—a sentiment endorsed by Paul's comments (Rom 13:8f). If we are called to love one another, what sort of love is this? The greatest love of all is altruistic: agape. And agape is the greatest sacrificial love: to lay down one's life for one's friends. Even greater is the love in which one lays down one's life for those one does not even know, giving one's life to protect others from destruction, from warring invaders, or—as on D-Day—to liberate them from evil. The greater love is to lay down one's life in defense against manifold evil. For example, where teenage pilots in the Battle of Britain laid down their lives not even being sure of the consequences of their actions—

> If you keep my commandments, you will abide in my love. . . . This is my commandment, that you love one another as I have loved you. No one has greater love than this, to lay down one's life for one's friends. (John 15:10–13)

4. The Just War Theory and the 9/11 Wars

XIII. A BIBLICAL PERSPECTIVE 1: DOCTRINE, PRINCIPLE, AXIOM

To make any reasoned sense out of the apparently irreconcilable dialectic between war and peace, defense and aggression, and to postulate what an acceptable response to terrorism would be, we need to see what theology we can read from the Bible. That is, what doctrine, principle, and axiom can be read from scripture, to create a biblically charged and informed mindset? If this is done then we find three distinct ethical responses to war and conflict in the Bible. The first is pagan, characterized by ego and desire, religious self-interest, and political domination; the second and third are communitarian, heteronymous, and issue from revelation. On this basis, there were three courses of action following 9/11: one pagan, one Hebrew, and one that is Christian.

XIV. A BIBLICAL PERSPECTIVE 2: THE PAGAN PRINCIPLE: VENGEANCE IN EXCESS

Amongst the pagan nations that surrounded ancient Israel—indeed this is an ethic that can be found amongst tribes and nations the world over—is a war ethic, recounted several times over in the Old Testament, evidenced in the actions of these pagan nations as they preyed on the Israelites. The Hebrews were explicitly forbidden by the Lord God, by YHWH, from following this war ethic as a way of retribution. To give this a name, it is the principle that vengeance is demanded in excess of an equitable, measured, and just response. According to this war ethic, if one goat was stolen, five—on average—were taken as revenge and reparation. If one man was killed, five—on average—were killed in revenge from the murderer's tribe. But when the five were killed, twenty-five were then demanded from the victim's tribe, and so on: this is a blood feud. According to this ethic, hostilities cease when one side capitulates under the pressure of all-out violent war. The victorious side would often then execute hundreds simply as a warning against insurrection, and to celebrate victory. In occupied territories, such as France and Norway during the Second World War, the Nazis ratcheted-up this demand for greater reparation. If one German soldier was killed, a hundred civilians were immediately rounded up at random, and summarily executed; the ratio of reparation was therefore increased from 5:1 to 100:1.[22] If this ethic was applied to 9/11, then the demand would be for a greater number than the three thousand lives lost on 9/11 (fifteen thousand or greater).

The pagan tribalism of a vengeance-in-excess war ethic, this biblical world of retribution and blood-justice, continues to this day. In his book *The Seven Pillars of Wisdom*,[23] T. E. Lawrence (Lawrence of Arabia) recounts the Arab uprising during the First World War, which he in many ways instigated and led, drawing disparate tribes together to attack and evict the Turks: the Ottoman Empire's colonization and subjugation of much of the Middle East. He recounts how one man, Hamed the Moor, kills another (from a different tribe) in a fit of anger. Hamed must be executed to avoid a blood feud: but if the victim's tribe executes then there will be a blood feud. Lawrence as an outsider takes on the role of executioner, thus a blood feud is avoided: "I have no tribe, and no one is offended."[24] Furthermore, realizing how the blood feud would escalate (vengeance in excess), Lawrence writes after the event,

---

22   However, the same can be said for the allies during WW2. On the night of 14 November 1940, the city of Coventry was carpet-bombed by the Luftwaffe (generating a new verb—to "Coventrate"—meaning to destroy an entire city) approximately six hundred people were killed ("In one night, more than 4,300 homes in Coventry were destroyed and around two-thirds of the city's buildings were damaged. . . . A recorded/discovered bodies, lists 568 people killed in the raid (the exact figure was never precisely confirmed), with another 863 badly injured and 393 sustaining lesser injuries." Ray, *The Night Blitz*); Winston Churchill commented that "They have sown the wind, they shall reap the whirlwind." (Hosea 8:7) In return the allies carpet bombed Hamburg beginning on the evening of 24 July 1943 for eight days and seven nights, killing according to cautious estimates fifty thousand. Later in the war the allies carpet-bombed Dresden (13 and 15 February 1945) killing according to cautious estimates twenty-four to forty thousand. For details, statistics, and further references/sources, see, https://en.wikipedia.org/wiki/Coventry_Blitz.

23   Colonel T. E. Lawrence's (1888–1935), *The Seven Pillars of Wisdom* (privately published, 1922; from Proverbs 9:1: "Wisdom has built her house, carved out of her seven pillars") is the autobiographical account of Lawrence's military activities in the Middle East during the First World War; Lawrence of Arabia, as he was styled in later years (*El 'aurens* was his title amongst the Arab tribes), served as a liaison officer to Prince Fisal (*Faisal I bin Hussein bin Ali al-Hashimi*, 1885–1933), having single-handedly generated the Arab rebellion against the Ottoman Turks (allied with Germany) 1916 to 1918. See Lawrence, *The Seven Pillars of Wisdom*; see also Barr, *A Line in the Sand*; also, Rogan, *The fall of the Ottomans*.

24   Thus speaks Lawrence in the film *Lawrence of Arabia*, which although the murder and execution was accurate, added much artistic license to sensationalize the story. It was not Gasim (a real character whom he did rescue from the desert), but

> Then rose up the horror which would make civilized man shun justice like a plague if he had not the needy to serve him as hangmen for wages. There were other Moroccans in our army; and to let the Ageyl kill one in feud meant reprisals by which our unity would have been endangered. It must be a formal execution, and at last, desperately, I told Hamed that he must die for punishment, and laid the burden of his killing on myself. Perhaps they would count me not qualified for feud. At least no revenge could lie against my followers; for I was a stranger and kinless.[25]

In an attempt to frame the West's actions after the 9/11 attacks on America, and in the context of the apparent proliferation of so-called weapons of mass destruction (WMD), politicians, philosophers, theorists, and media pundits in the West scripted a loose—i.e., subjective, relative, and ill-defined—theory, a policy of pre-emptive defense (comparable in some ways with a just war theory), which is a modern interpretation of the ancient vengeance-in-excess principle.

XV. A BIBLICAL PERSPECTIVE 3: THE ANCIENT HEBREW PRINCIPLE: AN EYE FOR AN EYE

An "eye for an eye" (Lev 24:19–21, Exod 21:22–25, and Deut 19:21; in Hebrew, *ayin tahat ayin*) countered the principle where vengeance was demanded in excess of an equitable, measured and just response. Properly considered an eye for an eye was a measured response to an unlawful act, a measured response that limited violence whilst attempting to answer cries for justice. This principle is grounded in the law of equitable retribution; an offence should not generate a greater offence. Retribution is thereby restricted, contained and defined, but in relation to the will of YHWH and the given laws of the Torah: an exact, proportionate, measured, and controlled response was designed to ensure justice and to prevent either the anarchy of lynch-mob vengeance or matters escalating out of control into all-out war. Gandhi is reputed to have said that an eye for an eye makes the whole world blind. Gandhi is objecting to the concept of reparation, which can be seen as stoking the furnaces of resentment.

Hamed the Moor. For the actual account see Lawrence, *Seven Pillars*, Bk 3, A Railway Diversion, ch. 31, 170. For an online edition/complete text, see: Project Gutenberg, http://gutenberg.net.au/ebooks01/0100111h.html#book3

25 Lawrence, *Seven Pillars*, Bk 3, A Railway Diversion, ch. 31, 171.

However, this is not what is happening here. An eye for an eye was specifically given to ensure a restrained, just, and measured response, so that intensification and escalation was avoided. This was (as we noted above in relation to Lawrence of Arabia) why hangmen and executioners developed as hooded anonymous outsiders, separate from society—they had no tribal allegiance, so when one man was executed for the murder of another, no tribe was then offended by the actions of the executioner. Around three thousand lives were lost on 9/11, so according to this ethic, three thousand Al-Qaeda terrorist combatants should have been sought-out, arrested, and after due process of law, executed. Though the reality amongst the ancient Hebrews was more subtle, varied, and complicated: The law also allowed for the "equivalent" to be something other than an exact equivalent. So some crimes could be punished with monetary punishments, say, rather than doing the exact same to the person who committed the crime. But the balanced principle of an eye for an eye—and no more—remained the bench mark.[26] *Ayin tahat ayin* is the principle enshrined in the Old Testament, which the Lord, YHWH, required of the ancient Hebrews to prevent an escalation of conflict whilst providing and guaranteeing justice.

XVI. A BIBLICAL PERSPECTIVE 4: THE CHRISTIAN PRINCIPLE: TURN THE OTHER CHEEK

In the Gospels we find a radical and different approach to that in either the ancient pagan nations or the Pentateuch: to turn the other cheek. We may stop and think, "Why have we been attacked?" "How may we have offended?" "How can we stop the escalation of violence?" Legitimate questions, but this is not necessarily what the gospel injunction is about .This is the New Testament approach, explicitly stated by Jesus Christ in the Gospels. And in case we decide to dismiss this as a one-off Jesus

---

26 In Islam, under *Sharia* law, the eye-for-an-eye principle is raised to a retaliation-in-kind principle, retributive justice: *Qisas*. For example, in Iran recently the man convicted of throwing acid in the face of a woman—Ameneh Bahrami, blinding her (see: https://en.wikipedia.org/wiki/Ameneh_Bahrami)—was convicted and the judge offered *Qisas* to the victim whereby the perpetrator would have had acid—to blind—thrown in his face. At the eleventh hour the victim and her family rescinded the threat of *Qisas*, and offered a pardon.

soundbite that was miss-reported or can be contextually rejected, or whittled away by a hermeneutic of suspicion, the emphasis is clear:

> You have heard that it was said, "Eye for eye, and tooth for tooth." But I tell you, Do not resist an evil person. If someone strikes you on the right cheek, turn to him the other also. And if someone wants to sue you and take your tunic, let him have your cloak as well. If someone forces you to go one mile, go with him two miles. Give to the one who asks you, and do not turn away from the one who wants to borrow from you. You have heard that it was said, "Love your neighbor and hate your enemy." But I tell you: love your enemies and pray for those who persecute you, that you may be sons of your Father in heaven. He causes his sun to rise on the evil and the good, and sends rain on the righteous and the unrighteous. (Matt 5:38–46)

This is not just passive resistance, but complicity to a degree; this is radical. Indeed, the victim is taking control of the situation, but passively. It exudes authority, the authority of the righteous one—who allowed himself to be tortured, then slaughtered on a cross. However difficult this sounds, Jesus certainly practiced what he preached. Luke extrapolates:

> But I tell you who hear me: love your enemies, do good to those who hate you, bless those who curse you, pray for those who mistreat you. If someone strikes you on one cheek, turn to him the other also. If someone takes your cloak, do not stop him from taking your tunic. Give to everyone who asks you, and if anyone takes what belongs to you, do not demand it back. Do to others as you would have them do to you. (Luke 6:27–31)

The apostle Paul talks of blessing those who persecute us, mourning with those who mourn, attempting to live in harmony and leaving no room for pride (Rom 12:14–16)? Should we fight evil with evil? No, we should not take revenge, for revenge—vengeance—is the Lord's prerogative (Deut 32:35; Rom 12:19; Heb 10:30), and we should not repay anyone evil for evil (Rom 12:18–19). If we are attacked we should shame our enemy into retreating: "If your enemy is hungry, feed him; if he is thirsty, give him something to drink. In doing this, you will heap burning coals on his head. Do not be overcome by evil, but overcome evil with good" (Rom 12: 20b–21). If we do not want others to treat us violently, brutally, if we do not want our enemies to kill us, then why do we do this to them?

The principle of turning the other cheek is not without precedent in the Old Testament. For example, "You shall not take vengeance or bear a grudge against any of your people, but you shall love your neighbor as yourself: I am the LORD" (Lev 19:18), and "It is good that one should wait quietly for the salvation of the LORD. It is good for one to bear the yoke ... to give one's cheek to the smiter, and be filled with insults" (Lam 3:26–27 & 30). However, there is an assertive claim to equality, given the socio-cultural context of Jesus's sayings, in turning the other cheek. Greeks and Romans would spar and box, but both participants were deemed equal. When they fought they used fists or the back of the hand. If a master was to strike a slave it was with the palm of the hand—a slap—never the fist or back of the hand, as this would imply equality. By turning the other cheek a slave would be inviting the same punishment but—using the same hand—the slave master would have to use the back of the hand to strike the other cheek, thereby implying equality. By turning the other cheek the slave (or a subjugated nation like Israel under the Romans) was provoking the assailant rather than submitting submissively: "I am your equal, you cannot harm or destroy me in the long term."[27] This is radical. By constantly turning the other cheek, you increase your righteousness before God in Christ, while the assailant builds an ever more complex fictitious world outside of God's grace; by turning the other cheek the victim is inviting the assailant to condemn themselves deeper and deeper into the hell of their own making. This is dynamically radical. Any situation leading to violence should be judged by the eschatological consequences, not for the immediate gain or the short-term consequences.

XVII. A BIBLICAL PERSPECTIVE 5: THE WAR ETHIC FOR A WAR ON TERROR?

Jason Burke, historian and journalist, has travelled to the main theatres of the 9/11 wars, and through painstaking research compiled accurate statistics of casualties: deaths, serious injuries, and destruction of communities, essentially by Western military action, but also by the religious terror foisted on their own people by Al-Qaeda, and other terrorist groups.[28] Burke

---

27 This socio-cultural context was recounted to me by a fellow theologian in the discussion after this paper was presented at the Research Institute in Systematic Theology; he had heard this example given in a lecture by the American Bible scholar Walter Wink, also at King's College London.

28 See essentially, Burke, *The 9/11 Wars*. This is a massive volume—over 700

4. The Just War Theory and the 9/11 Wars

notes, "Throughout the 1990s a vast conflict was brewing. The storm broke on September 11, 2001. Since then much of the world has seen invasions, bombings, battles and riots. Hundreds of thousands of people have died. These are the 9/11 wars."[29] By visiting all local and national governments (and NGOs on the ground), by cataloguing the actual deaths and injuries in villages, towns, and cities, by cross-checking and cross-referencing, Burke catalogues in excess of 250,000 civilians, military, and police killed.[30] If injuries and displacement of civilians (i.e., total destruction of buildings and communities, deaths among refugees) are taken into account, confirmed by a conservative ratio of 3:1, then the total cost in terms of deaths, injuries, and lives wasted through the Western response to 9/11 is now over one million.[31] (However, it is questionable whether the deaths Islamists inflicted on Islamic nations should be in this calculation because they are not part of the West's response to 9/11; however, again, the West's response—the wasting of Iraq and Libya, to name but two countries—has led to Islamist anarchy and the deaths of Muslims in the Middle East.)

So, which biblical war ethic is the war on terrorism comparable to: pagan, Hebrew, or Christian? According to the data compiled this is considerably more than the five lives taken for every one life killed that the pagan tribes surrounding the ancient Hebrews demanded. It is more than three times the level of reparation (100:1) demanded by the Nazis in the occupied territories.

---

pages, around 300,000 words—with detailed accounts of all the 9/11 wars, the Western response to 9/11, and the continued terrorist activities from Al-Qaeda *et al.* A four-page summary of the salient argument and statistics from the book appeared in the British Newspaper, *The Guardian*, August 22, 2011, in the G2 supplement: https://www.theguardian.com/profile/jasonburke; see also, https://www.theguardian.com/world/2011/sep/11/911-books-round-up-review. See also, Burke, Al-Qaeda.

29   Burke, *The 9/11 Wars*, xviii.

30   The detailed statistical information on deaths and injuries can be found in Burke, *The 9/11 Wars*, 503f.

31   Burke notes that although around three thousand were killed on 9/11, the total deaths attributed to Al-Qaeda in the first ten years of the 9/11 wars, the total of civilians killed in terrorist actions directly linked to the Al-Qaeda-affiliated or inspired Islamic militants, "was almost certainly in excess of 10,000, probably nearer 15,000, possibly up to 20,000." Burke, "Counting the cost of the 9/11 wars," *The Guardian*, August 22, 2011, G2, 10.

XVIII. A WAR ON TERRORISM

By its very nature terrorism has little or no respect for life and will kill indiscriminately regardless of perceived innocence or guilt. Indeed, using terror as a tactic relies on the victims—or target—having no understanding of the criteria used by the terrorist: anyone, anywhere, at any time could be a target and could suffer horrendous injuries or death. Terrorism is often defined as the use of fear or terror as a means of retribution or coercion. In terms of its effect on civilians terrorism is similar to carpet bombing. When the town of Guernica was bombed during the Spanish Civil War on 26 April 1937 killing between two hundred and four hundred civilians the term coined was "terror bombing"—aerial bombing of cities and towns is indiscriminate, and terrifying, or terror-generating. The connection with conventional warfare is in the use of violence and injury, intimidation and death, the intention is to create terror and fear for ideological reasons. Far from scripting rules of engagement or just war theories, terrorists will deliberately target randomly: no one can be defined as a non-combatant. Much terrorism may appear reason-less, random: some acts are indiscriminate killings, while others are carefully and methodically calculated in human casualties; it is perhaps one of the closest human inventions to evil that we can perceive. The problem with a so-called war on terror is that it relies on the tactics of the terrorist, it will be fought on similar ideological lines, and it seeks to make the defenders as evil as the terrorist.

XIX. AN ESCHATOLOGICAL PERSPECTIVE

So, what is the theology in this? The incarnation-cross-resurrection can be seen as the central pivotal point in human history. As such this point is the end of time, yet also the beginning: all human history, ante and post, is defined by this central event. Meaning flows from this point: the point of the moment of the death of Jesus Christ on the cross. Yet we live. We live, as Karl Barth referred to it, *Zwischen den Zeiten*, between the times. That is, between the first and the second coming, in a bubble of time constantly inflating between the resurrection and the *eschaton*, the completion of all things. Therefore, everything Jesus said relates to the end of times. All his sayings can only be understood eschatologically. Hence, the categorical imperative for reconciliation—before it is too late. Are not biblical ethics grounded in this transcendent categorical imperative? Is not the

4. The Just War Theory and the 9/11 Wars

Decalogue—the Ten Commandments—likewise grounded in and issuing from this transcendent reality: YHWH, the Lord, requires right action of us, and behind and within YHWH is the universal Christ, the second person of the Trinity, incarnated as Jesus of Nazareth? These moral absolutes issue from and relate to the economic Trinity, which the Bible and church tradition attest to, moral absolutes that will existentially press on us from the pneumatological element of the economic Trinity. These are absolutes that should govern our behavior. But to what extent do our religious egos interfere and deny this imperative?

This transcendent categorical imperative is therefore towards eschatological reconciliation. We have our chance, but the dangers are very real. The key scriptural passage is in Matthew's Gospel, the Sermon on the Mount and the sayings that follow. We are blessed if people insult us, we are blessed if we show mercy and are peacemakers, we are blessed if people utter all manner of evil against us because Jesus is the eschatological fulfilment of the law, and our Father in heaven takes notes and prepares to weigh, to sift, all. This evokes an eschatological reality:

> You have heard that it was said to those of ancient times, "You shall not murder"; and "whoever murders shall be liable to judgment." But I say to you that if you are angry with a brother or sister, you will be liable to judgment; and if you insult a brother or sister, you will be liable to the council; and if you say, "You fool," you will be liable to the hell of fire. So when you are offering your gift at the altar, if you remember that your brother or sister has something against you, leave your gift there before the altar and go; first be reconciled to your brother or sister, and then come and offer your gift. Come to terms quickly with your accuser while you are on the way to court with him, or your accuser may hand you over to the judge, and the judge to the guard, and you will be thrown into prison. Truly I tell you, you will never get out until you have paid the last penny. (Matt 5:21–26)

Given the eschatological context of Jesus' sayings and commands we may cautiously conclude that Jesus is neither a pacifist nor a militarist.[32]

---

[32] For example, the return of the Landlord to the vineyard to settle accounts (Mark 12 and Luke 20) and weigh (Luke 22:31) all according to his righteous judgment (Luke 12:58), the perils of judging others (Matthew 7:1–2; Luke 6:37; John 8:15–16), the dangers of religious practice when we are estranged, unreconciled, from our neighbor in worship (Mark 5:23–26), and the categorical importance of reconciliation because those who are reconciled reflect Christ's commandment and are not judged (John 12:47–48).

It is clear from YHWH's command to the ancient Hebrews that defense was legitimate—if YHWH declared it so. Defense therefore had its place in salvation history. But history ends with the incarnation-cross-resurrection; reconciliation is therefore an imperative if we are to avoid a judgment that condemns us. Hell and damnation are real, and are very real possibilities. Our actions when they contradict the will of God and are in opposition to ethics that can be read from scripture—ethics that should be exercised through a categorical imperative, actions that are contrary to the law of reconciliation revealed though the Christ—these actions have the potential to condemn us before God in Christ in judgment.

In religio-political terms, a war on terror appears to have no concept of reconciliation; furthermore, it appears to be motivated by a pre-Christian and pre-Hebrew war ethic defined by nationhood and boundaries, retaliation and retribution: pre-emptive strike (liberal paranoia?), vengeance in excess of an equitable, measured, and just response.[33] The reality of a war on terror is defined by the offensive war ethic of the pagan nations that surrounded ancient Israel, and not by the defensive war ethic of the ancient Hebrews, or the eschatological realism of Jesus's command to turn the other cheek and to love our enemies. In eschatological reality what has happened between the West on the one hand and Afghanistan-Iraq on the other is not an argument between Christianity and Islam but a row between two warring pagan tribes, each battling—on a global scale—to impose its own religio-political vision on the other. Western neo-pagan secular-liberal humanism is here set against Al-Qaeda, and latterly Islamic State?

X. CONCLUSION

Because of the invasion and subjugation of Afghanistan and Iraq, Al-Qaeda moved (according to media reports) its training camps, its headquarters, and its operations control centers into the mountainous no-man's-land between Pakistan and Afghanistan, also into Kenya, the Sudan, and other tribal territories in Africa, but also to the Far East—Indonesia and the Philippines—and now the Yemen. As Islamic State loses territory, their

---

33 Between c. 800 and 1200 AD the firstborn son of a Viking war lord or chieftain was required to prove himself by not just equaling his father's war conquests and military exploits but by surpassing them; has this happened in recent history in the context of two American presidents (George Bush senior and George W. Bush, his son) where the son has excelled his father's war exploits?

4. The Just War Theory and the 9/11 Wars

combatants merely move into other areas, including Europe, to re-start their mission to form a caliphate. Therefore, the war on terrorism is not against a nation state. The enemy shifts and changes, moves, and disappears into the night, relocates and re-emerges transformed but as dangerous as before. All of these locations are in reasonably peaceful nation states, which then suffer collateral damage (i.e., civilian deaths) through conventional military tactics by the West. This conventional war mentality does not make the West any safer. This is a totally unwinnable scenario, and simply creates yet more recruits from peaceable civilians who wanted nothing to do with Islamists but are driven into terrorism out of a desire for revenge. The war on terrorism can by no means be considered a measured response.

So what was the alternative? Given the precedence of the sixth commandment, and what we can read of these three war ethics from the Bible, then we may ask what is implied by George W. Bush and Tony Blair's war on terror, grounded as we have seen in a pre-Christian pagan war ethic? If George W. Bush was correct in bombing and invading Afghanistan because of the support of the Taliban government for Al-Qaeda and if this invokes and relates to a categorical imperative, then would the British Prime Minister Mrs. Thatcher have been justified in sending the Royal Air Force to bomb the Irish community in New York?—because the IRA bomb that blew up the Grand Hotel in Brighton (12 October 1984), nearly killing the prime minister and the heart of the British government, was paid for by Irish-American dollars. Did not many American senators ideologically support the IRA? Such a bombing raid on the Irish quarter of New York would have been amoral, evil, and ridiculous. But no more ridiculous than invading and laying waste two sovereign nations because terrorists associated with one of those countries had demolished the Twin Towers—symbols of nationhood and freedom—in New York. There is therefore no alternative to the Gospel precedent that Jesus established. (The British government and its anti-terror agencies tracked down the Brighton bomber, who was tried, convicted, and imprisoned, not assassinated by special forces at the behest of a presidential leader.)

So, is it justifiable to re-write the just war theory for a war on terrorism? The answer depends on how you define a just war theory. From a secular-liberal humanist standpoint a just war theory is whatever a given group of people—an oligarchic liberal elite?—want it to be at any given time, for any given situation. However, from a Christian perspective, more specifically from a biblically informed eschatological perspective, rewriting the just war theory to allow for a first strike if there is the threat of terrorism cannot be justifiable; neither can a retaliatory strike that destroys and subjugates a people out of all proportion to the initial act of terrorism be justifiable. From a strictly Christocentric eschatological perspective the only option is to turn the other cheek, to pour shame on the terrorists, in an attempt to generate reconciliation. If both sides war, both are condemned, in probability, to hell; if one side turns the other cheek then at least God can salvage something out of the situation (righteousness lies in turning the other cheek, even though it makes the situation worse for the assailant). The just war theory has been re-written from an essentially secular perspective. Retaliation comes, in principle, before being attacked, and there is no means of offence that is out of bounds, provided the government of the day can put a suitable spin on the affairs. If this is indeed a just war theory it bears little resemblance to the Catholic-Christian just war theory. Indeed, one is tempted to consider this secular just war theory merely an attempt to shelter behind the credibility of the Augustinian-Thomist foundation of a Catholic-Christian just war theory.

In principle, this postmodern, post-Christian, secular-liberal humanist just war theory is the pagan vengeance principle with the level of vengeance killing ratcheted-up: it is a defense obsession that generates vengeance in excess of an equitable, measured, and just response, and is defined by the three principles we postulated at the beginning: strike back harder, more destructively; strike pre-emptively; and colonize to convert the citizens away from the belief system that has led to the war in the first place. Without God, or with false "gods," morality is whatever is necessarily defined; without God there are as a result no limits or constraints on human behavior, ethics become whatever is acceptable to an oligarchic elite at any given time: the end justifies the means, and Machiavellian spin-doctoring defines the ends and the means. If a just war theory is humanistic and relativistic, then it is simple enough to define the criteria, to redefine, modify, rewrite, ad infinitum. But in relation to orthodox Christian doctrine and ethics it cannot be justified, or justifiable, to rewrite the just war theory— for short-term gain—driven by suspicion about invisible enemies in the night with weapons of mass-destruction. Or, more pertinently, given what we can read from Scripture, how can such short-term aggression, such irreconcilability, be eschatologically acceptable before God in judgment in Christ?

5

Postmortem Status Purgatus: a Simpsons' Eschatology:— Towards a Lewisian Understanding of Eternal Life and Human Rebellion

> *The twenty-four elders fall down before Christ who sits on the throne, and worship him who lives for ever and ever.*
>
> *They lay their crowns before the throne and say:*
> *"You are worthy, our Lord and God, to receive glory and honor and power, for you created all things, and by your will they were created and have their being."*
>
> REVELATION 4:10–11

SYNOPSIS

This paper is an exercise in theological media studies, examining the eschatological *telos* of humanity. *Postmortem status purgatus*: the ancient Greeks and Romans held to a truism—what we do in the here-and-now echoes through eternity. What we are, what we make of our life, determines our outcome. Christ's judgment on us then merely reflects, ontologically, what we have made of ourselves, what we have become. (This raises questions about determinism, compatibilism, and an unhindered free will.) This paper is a serious, though humorous, examination of heaven and hell, in the form of *purgation*. That is, in a Lewisian context, we are not positing a third "place" (purgatory): the tree lies where it falls (Eccl 11:3). *Postmortem*, the person either gets used to being in hell, sinking deeper and deeper into its own evolving demonic depravity, or—as it is shriven in its repentance and regret—it becomes more and more acclimatized to facing God and being in heaven. This is all to be seen in the light of the judgment we will all be resurrected to.

TOWARDS THE DAY AFTER TOMORROW

Therefore, this will involve a light-hearted consideration of the *eschaton* in *The Simpsons* (that is, the traditional *eschaton*, death, judgment, heaven, and hell, not the modernist-liberal *eschaton* of death followed by heaven)—and what this can illustrate about the human condition issuing from the *fall* into original sin, balanced by the loving purposes of God's forgiving judgment. Popular culture may seem an academic irrelevance, but millions of people (along with national and local governments and councils) absorb the religious ideas this popular culture promotes, . . . yet how seriously should we take all of this? What value is there in facing evil with humor, hell as the *absurd* contradiction of God's Word (John 1): a *surd*-like evil, a nihilistic *alogos*?

I. INTRODUCTION

Where are we going? The scriptural witness is that the *telos* of all creation is in its transformation, through the *eschaton*, into the eternal heavenly kingdom of Christ. From the forging of God's chosen people, the ancient Hebrew witness, though Mary's "yes," through the incarnation in Jesus of Nazareth, through the crucifixion-resurrection, through the triune realization and witness (the church), through into eternity, this kingdom is God's will for humanity, it is what we are created for. But there is human freedom. We are responsible for what we become through our exercise of free will. When we come before the judgment of God we cannot escape what we have become. It is clear from the Gospels that we cannot avoid the reality of what we have made of ourselves, or more pertinently what we no longer are: "Hell is really about and best defined by a negative, a loss, and not a positive. The damned are defined by what they are not—or are no longer—rather than by what they are."[1]

What we no longer are is a denial of our God-given humanity, the *imago Dei* in us. We may not like it but we define our existence, we are responsible for our *status postmortem*. We hold on to that responsibility with a vice-like grip and yet throw our hands up in horror at the consequences, yelling (in consort with one Bart Simpson), "I didn't do it!"[2] This then leads to humanity inventing its own religious justification. How so? For thousands of years humanity has invented "gods" and "goddesses," pagan divines, heavens and hells, and developed religious speculation as to the ontology of eternal life, but also beliefs and ethics to justify human

---

1 Weems, "Universalism Denied: C. S. Lewis's Unpublished Letters to Alan Fairhurst," 87–98, quote 96.

2 *The Simpsons*, "Bart Gets Famous," 5.12.

5. Postmortem Status Purgatus: a Simpsons' Eschatology

actions in this world. This has led to innumerable human-generated ideas on how we should behave and what we should believe, but also as to the nature of eternal life, reflecting the nature of the human and its teleology. These ideas vary widely from the Valhalla (heaven) of the Vikings (which in all honesty was a region of hell!) and the neo-gnostic beliefs of some Western liberal neo-Buddhists (desperately seeking *postmortem annihilation*?) to the salvation of all—regardless of sin or goodness—in a self-generated, self-reverential, paradisal heaven for modern Western liberals of various religious/irreligious persuasions. Few of these religious ideas give credit to or acknowledge the universal divine right of God to judge people and to decide the fate of creation. But then do not many of these religions do away with God, or the "gods," anyway, leaving their exponents mild-manneredly to proffer, apologetically, a vague unknowable, but friendly and accommodating, divine substance of sorts, which is usually a projection of their sexual desire?

When speaking of the universal right of God we are acknowledging the primacy of Almighty God the Lord—*El Shaddai*, *YWHW*—revealed in *his* purposes and dealings over thousands of years with the ancient Hebrews, finally culminating and made manifest in *Yeshua*—Jesus of Nazareth, the Christ—which leads to the atonement and salvation wrought on the cross: open to all, but realized by few. Further, God elects to be obedient to the God-given natural law humanity is subject to (where a right is a freedom enshrined in law): thus we are all open to a forgiving judgment, if we are prepared to face such a sentence, such a ruling, such a rigor. A sentence, as a legal term, is highly appropriate. In summing-up a trial the judge accurately portrays not just what the accused has done but also, pertinently, what the accused has become. Judgment and sentence is then a pro-active command that simply reflects what the person "is," and is guilty of. A human trial may sometimes—often?—be flawed, but God's judgment is not.

A commonly understood assertion within Greco-Roman religion—indeed in life generally—was that what we *are*, what we have become, what we do in the here-and-now, echoes through eternity. This is not far from the intimations of eternal life given by Jesus Christ, that the righteous abide in heaven while the unrighteous languish in hell, further, that we cannot escape responsibility for our decisions and actions in this life. This philosophically-derived Greco-Roman understanding realized that we are to a very great degree responsible for our lives, our actions, and our beliefs. But the revelation from the Christ indicates that all are subject to the loving judgment of God, that God can pneumatologically change us—if we are capable and able through our own empire-building to face that change. Can we reconcile these two approaches to the *telos* of human life: if what we do in the here-and-now dictates what we are after death does this do away with the eschatological judgment of God in Christ, or are they both complementary? If there is an organic relationship between our self-willed, self-creation—what we in our rebellion make of ourselves—and the judgment of God to forgive us and change us, does this give rise to a persistent concept in parts of the Christian tradition: purgatory?—or more pertinently, *purgation*, a purging, a changing.

From the Gospels it is clear: all people are moving through this life either towards heaven or towards hell. Although the movement may not always be smooth, there will be sudden jumps!—the obvious one being a deathbed conversion, but also being born again (John 3), sudden acts of untold generosity at great risk to ourselves, a faith confession that costs us dearly. And at the point of judgement each person is in heaven or hell.[3] But what of resurrection? The unique revelation of the gospel is that we are all to be resurrected. When? Do the righteous rest in paradise until the general resurrection? Or is resurrection immediate? Is it what the apostle Paul describes as a spiritual resurrection? These are some of the questions that we may explore briefly in this paper examining the concepts of *postmortem status purgatus* in relation to the loving purposes of God's judgment. To this end, we will examine the American cartoon series *The Simpsons*.

II. OH, HELL! . . .

But first, what of hell? Is hell no more than an exclamation, an evocative provocative? Or is there something real, an actuality? Ross Douthat critically tackles the perennial modern belief that hell must not exist . . . must not be allowed to exist (!).[4] Hell, he says, is an essential by-product of

---

3   A pertinent point that I do not intend to discuss here at any length, as it has little impact on the central thesis of this paper, is this: do the dead await judgement at the end of time, all humanity resurrected together, judged together with the initiation of the *eschaton*, or is each individual judged and assigned at the point of death?

4   Douthat, "A Case for Hell." See: http://www.nytimes.com/2011/04/25/opinion/25douthat.html?emc=eta1. Accessed April 25, 2011

5. Postmortem Status Purgatus: a Simpsons' Eschatology

human freedom and judgment. Douthat notes how hell's weakening grip on the religious imagination is a consequence of pluralism, also, that this hellish skepticism issues from the delusions, we might say, of modernity:

> As our lives have grown longer and more comfortable, our sense of outrage at human suffering—its scope, and its apparent randomness—has grown sharper as well. The argument that a good deity couldn't have made a world so rife with cruelty is a staple of atheist polemic, and every natural disaster inspires a round of soul-searching over how to reconcile God's omnipotence with human anguish.... [D]oing away with hell, then, is a natural way for pastors and theologians to make their God seem more humane.[5]

Douthat continues, that to believe in God, but not in hell, is to deny the reality of human choices: if there's no possibility of saying no to paradise then none of our "noes" have any real meaning. Hell makes our decisions real: "The miser can become his greed, the murderer can lose himself inside his violence, and their freedom to turn and be forgiven is inseparable from their freedom not to do so."[6] *Postmortem* judgment, heaven or hell. It may appear dualistic to liberal sensitivities, but the either-or is the key to the *eschaton* from which no one can escape. But what is hell?

There are as many definitions of hell as there are religious perspectives, often confusing and seemingly contradictory. Hell is separation from God, with all that is implied in this state of existence: from the corrosive feeling of regret that will overwhelm the individual through to the torment and agonies, tortures and pain, traditionally involved in this *status*, without hope. Perhaps we may assert that hell is nihilistic. Given that hell is so very nearly nothing (both as no particular thing, as well as being a contradiction of all that is good and real, holy and healthy, righteous and alive), it is of no surprise that hell is riven with legion contradictions, confusion, and sheer hellishness. Like an astronomical black hole, hell perhaps can only be proved in the negative.[7]

---

5   Douthat, "A Case for Hell."

6   Douthat, "A Case for Hell."

7   Astronomical Black holes can only be proved by observing what happens around them: i.e., by studying a black hole's event horizon. See, http://hubblesite.org/reference_desk/faq/answer.php.id=64&cat=exotic
https://www.sciencedaily.com/releases/2018/06/180618141834.htm
https://www.skyandtelescope.com/astronomy-news/black-holes/best-evidence-yet-that-black-holes-really-exist-0505201523/

Hell may be difficult to conceptualize or even—because of its ontology—to prove, but pertinently, we should ask, what is purgation, and how does it relate to heaven and hell?

III. PURGATORY OR PURGATION:
POSTMORTEM STATUS PURGATUS

A growing number of theologians and philosophers in the early twenty-first century are realizing that hell may be defined by a doctrine of infernal voluntarism, with the alternative being voluntary purgation: the damned opt, in accordance with the will of God, for hell: God wills that they have the freedom to opt for hell, though he would prefer their salvation.[8] But does God want them to opt for hell? Is this an example of compatibilism whereby free will and determinism are mutually compatible? Compatibilists define free will as freedom to act according to willed motives without outside hindrance or compulsion from other individuals, institutions, circumstances. This takes no account of original sin. In most Western legal systems—though essentially in the UK and USA—courts of law make judgments, without reference to God or revelation, asking, did a person act of their own free will, or were they compelled consciously or sub-consciously by circumstances? "It is assumed in a court of law that someone could have acted otherwise than in reality. Otherwise, no crime would have been committed."[9] How will we be judged by God? And not just by the evil we opted to do, but also by the good we failed to do. What causes us to make decisions? Are free will decisions still possible, "*post-lapse*" (or "after the fall")? Again, hell is defined by confusion and contradiction.

The saved by comparison are subject, in varying degrees, to *purgation*—a shriven changing, healing—as part of their journey *into* heaven. The saved who need change, a purging, are subject to a voluntary

---

8 Coates, D. Justin; McKenna, Michael. "Compatibilism." *Stanford Encyclopedia of Philosophy*. See also, Podgorski, "Free Will Twice Defined: On the Linguistic Conflict of Compatibilism and Incompatibilism." See also, Salles, "Compatibilism: Stoic and modern," 1–23. Compatibilism was a proposition endorsed by the Stoics, medieval scholastics (e.g., Thomas Aquinas), and by Enlightenment philosophers (e.g., David Hume, Thomas Hobbes).

9 See, *Stanford Encyclopedia of Philosophy*, "Theories of Criminal Law" https://plato.stanford.edu/entries/criminal-law/

agreement (a promise, a settlement, and a covenant) that constitutes a relinquishing of their rebellion; the damned continue in their rebellion. The damned have therefore freely chosen hell before heaven. All who genuinely desire heaven, all who can genuinely *perceive* heaven and not mistake their own pagan rebellion for a projected heaven of sorts (i.e. the Vikings?), will be invited into heaven. This thinking is rooted in the work of a mid-twentieth-century apologist, philosopher, and theologian: C. S. Lewis.[10] Lewis subscribed to a doctrine of purgatory, or more pertinently, *purgation*. This is one of his more Catholic beliefs, which most evangelical readers of his work are puzzled by, though he held to the doctrine for sound reasons.

So what is purgatory? Purgatory is not hell; though for many being in a state of *purgation* will be hellish. According to traditional doctrine, people in hell are not saved: "abandon hope all you who enter here," is the sign Dante placed over the entrance to hell.[11] By contrast the people in purgatory are saved, redeemed by Christ, more pertinently they have accepted Christ's forgiveness, wrought on the cross on their behalf, and in accepting they take the consequences of their actions and beliefs, and the consequence is a cleansing, an emptying: in a word, *purgation*: they are defined by hope. Traditionally this is seen as an image of the spiritual cleansing of a soul in purgatory. In Roman Catholic doctrine, purgatory is a *place* or *state of suffering* inhabited by the souls of sinners who are "expiating their sins before going to heaven" (OED), whereas hell is a *place* regarded in various religions as a spiritual realm of evil and suffering, often depicted as a place of perpetual fire beneath the earth to which the wicked are consigned after death. Both hell and purgatory may traditionally be regarded as places: physical, geographic (in the sense of relating to the arrangement of places and physical features), to a greater or lesser degree, with widely differing concepts throughout the world's religions, and even within the Christian tradition. Or hell generally, purgatory specifically, may be seen as a *state* of mental anguish, a condition of apparent physical suffering, indeed of great torment reflecting the justice and goodness of God. The differences are the degree of mental anguish and suffering experienced by individuals, and that those in purgatory will eventually find their suffering eases as they are translated to heaven. The assumption

10   See Buenting, *The Problem of Hell: A Philosophical Anthology*.
11   Dante, *The Divine Comedy*, Vol. 1 Inferno. Canto 3.9, 89.

is that even the redeemed can sin (i.e., willfully make bad, wrong, decisions in relation to natural law and the will of God) and will still need a degree of change, of purging, after death: having resisted being truly washed in the blood of the lamb during life.

So, is purgatory a place, or is it a state, a condition, or is it a form of noetic torture? A working definition we may postulate for this paper is *postmortem status purgatus*,[12] that is, after death some may find themselves in a state of purging, cleansing, a state of purgation characterized by regret and doubt, of having to face the responsibility they held for their decisions, what they made of their life, wrestling to come to terms with what their life had been. This condition is imposed by the will of God, a state not unlike, yet different from, what they had become in this life, which should lead to repentance and cleansing. This state, condition, position may be characterized by some as an intensely burning (remorse, repentance) for life's mistakes. But is this state real? And what do we mean by "real"? Does purgatory geographically exist? Probably not, though such geography is ultimately about perception and generating mental spatial concepts. Perhaps these are the wrong questions. The correct question, we will see, is, "How long is a moment?"

IV. PURGATORY OR PURGATION: "THE TREE LIES WHERE IT FALLS"[13]

The consistent characteristic of *postmortem* existence for the human is twofold: *First*, the need to be perfect ("Be perfect, therefore, as your heavenly Father is perfect" Matt 5:48), therefore Christ will perfect the human whatever the cost, unless s/he rebels.[14] *Second*, the primacy of the human will, that is, the willful decision by the human dictates the human condition after death. The Catholic side of Lewis believed in and asserted not so much purgatory but the need for *purgation*: none of us will be good enough to face Christ in eternity, we will need to be sanctified and

---

12 That is, a state or condition of purgation, purification, after death: from the Latin, *status*: a position, condition, appointed, to stand, remain, to set-up; and, *purgo*, *purgare*, *purgavi*: purge/excuse; or *purgatus*: cleansed/purified/excused; *postmortem*, after death. *Postmortem status purgatus*: literally—"After the death the position purged."

13 Eccl 11:3

14 Lewis, *Mere Christianity*, 202.

5. Postmortem Status Purgatus: a Simpsons' Eschatology

purified—at the very least changed. Many theologians and philosophers (including C. S. Lewis) can appreciate this position but draw the line at postulating a physical-geographic reality named purgatory, separate from heaven and hell. However, Lewis and others are prepared to postulate a state or condition of purgation. The very nature of heaven and hell is that they the two are diametrically different; the hellish humans subsist in a near-to-nothingness state that makes them unfit for heaven, where heaven is too strong and painful for the self-centered near-to-nothingness of the damned to enter.[15] If purgation is a purification, the spiritual cleansing and strengthening of the human,[16] the washing away of the effects of sin in the human, "washed by the blood of the lamb,"[17] does this imply that salvation is fluid after death? Yes, but this is one-way, those who are translated after purging to heaven cannot back-track (1 Cor 15:50-53; Rev 4:10-11). Does this imply that certain theologians may be marginalizing and relativizing the judgment of God? To this extent C. S. Lewis, for example, is strictly Protestant: "The tree lies where it falls" (Eccl 11:3), its place is assured—there is no purgatory, only heaven and hell. Yet the human can be changed. For Lewis, those who submit to a purifying purgation, and are translated to heaven, have in fact been in the "fringes" of heaven all the time: those who do accept the change and move into deep heaven were in heaven all along, though the pains of purgation felt like hell to them, *for a period of "time."* Those who refuse to let go of their willful possessiveness, who cannot stand the pain of change, are in hell all along, and stay there: "I think earth, if chosen instead of heaven, will turn out to have been, all along, only a region in hell: and earth, if put second to heaven, to have been from the beginning a part of heaven itself."[18]

---

15   From the Middle English, derived from Old French *purgacion*, from Latin *purgatio(n-)*, from *purgare*, to *purge*.

16   A basic ontic principle established and illustrated by Lewis in *The Great Divorce*.

17   In terms of the blood of the Lamb: 1 Cor 10:16; 1 Cor 11:27; 1 John 1:6-9; 5:6; 1 Pet 1:1-2; Acts 5:28; 20:28; Col 1:19-20, 22; Eph 1:7; 2:13; Heb 9:11-15 (specifically 12-14); 10:3-14, 19-22, 28-31; 12:24; 13:11-12, 20; John 6:53-57; 19:33-34; Luke 22:20; 22:44; Mark 14:23-24; Matt 26:27-28; Rev 1:5-6; 5:9-10; 7:14-17; 12:10-11; Rom 3:25-26; 5:9. In terms of a cleansing: 1 Cor 6:11; 1 John 1:7, 9; 1 Pet 1:22; 2 Pet 1:9; Eph 5:26; Ezek 20:38; 22:15; 36:25, 29, 33; 37:23; Heb 1:3; 9:14; 10:22; Isa 4:4; Jer 33:8; John 15:3; Lev 16:30; Num 8:21; 19:9; Ps 51:2, 10; Titus 2:14; 3:5; Zech 13:1.

18   Lewis, *The Great Divorce*, ch. 13.

V. PURGATORY OR PURGATION: HOLD ON A MOMENT... WE WILL ALL BE CHANGED

Is there a biblical precedent for this, and for purgation? The apostle Paul, speaking of the righteous, asserts that we shall be changed:

> What I am saying, brothers and sisters, is this: flesh and blood cannot inherit the kingdom of God, nor does the perishable inherit the imperishable. Listen, I will tell you a mystery! *We will not all die, but we will all be changed, in a moment, in the twinkling of an eye*, at the last trumpet. For the trumpet will sound, and the dead will be raised imperishable, and we will be changed. For this perishable body must put on imperishability, and this mortal body must put on immortality.
>
> 1 Cor 15:50–53 (My emphasis.)

So, how long is "a moment," what duration is "the twinkling of an eye?" Has a period of time elapsed? It cannot be no time at all, for if there is no time at all then, logically, there would appear to be no change. For there is time and space in heaven but such eternal temporality must be seen as different to our perception of earthly time and space. But is our perception of time changed by our circumstances? For a prisoner waiting for sentence to be pronounced, as the fear wells up in his throat, how long are the moments it takes for the judge to be ready? A child in the dentist's chair sees the hypodermic needle move ever closer, slowly towards its mouth, unhurriedly in the hand of the dentist, the dentist pulls at the lips, a single drop of the anesthetic liquid hangs from the point of the needle, the dentist pulls at the gums to select the best spot to inject: all this seems hours of agony to the child who has a deep-seated phobia about the dentist and particularly the anesthetic injection. This moment, of no more than a few seconds, may seem an eternity of anguish. To the unrighteous who still hold back, the impure holding onto their precious sins, still mired in their little empires, their being changed in the twinkling of an eye may seem an eternity of "time," in varying degrees! However, to the righteous, whatever change Christ demands will seem but a moment's discomfort, so brief as to be almost imperceptible, like "the twinkling of an eye." The Greek used by the apostle Paul for "in a moment, in the twinkling of an eye" (1 Cor 15:52) is *atomos* (usually translated as an instant, a moment, indivisible, uncut, an "atom" of time); and, *rhipe* (*hree-pay*: a jerk of the eye, in an instant, sudden almost imperceptible, but noticeable).

5. Postmortem Status Purgatus: a Simpsons' Eschatology

Something happens, there is change, but for the righteous in Christ this will seem but momentary, perhaps like the instantaneous, momentary, mild electric shock from static on a sweater. For the less righteous, this change may appear to drag out—painfully—for a long "time," a very long "time." Whatever it takes, if we are prepared to submit to God *he* will change us, purify us:

> See, I am sending my messenger to prepare the way before me, and the LORD whom you seek will suddenly come to his temple. The messenger of the covenant in whom you delight—indeed, he is coming, says the LORD of hosts. But who can endure the day of his coming, and who can stand when he appears?
>
> For he is like a refiner's fire and like fullers' soap; he will sit as a refiner and purifier of silver, and he will purify the descendants of Levi and refine them like gold and silver, until they present offerings to the LORD in righteousness. Then the offering of Judah and Jerusalem will be pleasing to the LORD as in the days of old and as in former years.
>
> Then I will draw near to you for judgment; I will be swift to bear witness against the sorcerers, against the adulterers, against those who swear falsely, against those who oppress the hired workers in their wages, the widow, and the orphan, against those who thrust aside the alien, and do not fear me, says the LORD of hosts.
>
> For I the LORD do not change; therefore you, O children of Jacob, have not perished. Ever since the days of your ancestors you have turned aside from my statutes and have not kept them. Return to me, and I will return to you, says the LORD of hosts.
>
> Mal 3:1–7a

The day of God's appearing brings judgment and hope, cleansing and salvation. This may happen while we are alive—a form of realized eschatology—some will even be acceptable from the point of death without the need for *postmortem* change (or at the very least, little). But if we refuse—as we have the will to do so—then we condemn ourselves before the judgment seat of Christ.

VI. AN INFERNAL ANALOGY?

C. S. Lewis excelled at presenting complex doctrinal issues in story form—analogical and symbolic narratives—parable-like accounts which narrate an event in real time rather than trying to freeze reality into a doctrinal proposition. Using the genre of analogical narrative Lewis presented complex theological propositions about heaven and hell, faith and grace, predestination and determinism in the form of stories: *The Screwtape Letters*, *The Great Divorce*, *The Four Loves*, and to a degree, *The Chronicles of Narnia*. To an older generation (whose grandparents were born—along with C. S. Lewis—in the late nineteenth century) many of these hell-bent characters are so readily identifiable; but not necessarily so with a younger generation or in contemporary society, which is so diametrically different to the Western mid-twentieth-century society, the time when C. S. Lewis wrote. Perhaps there is a popular television series that inadvertently illustrates humanity's blind ignorance of its fate as it generates its own little socio-political-religious empires, preparing themselves for an eternity in hell?

Hell is not a problem for the redeemed,[19] indeed, in the Parable of Dives and Lazarus (Luke 16:19–31) the saved exhibit no concern for the damned. Hell is not a problem for Satan, or for demons: they have got what they wanted. Hell is a problem for philosophers, and for many of those—following Lewis's supposal—who subsist in hell, but are often unaware either of their death or their damnation. If most of the humans presented by Lewis in "hell" do not realize or acknowledge their state then perhaps a latter-day representation, subconsciously in the spirit of Lewis's *The Great Divorce*, is the American cartoon series *The Simpsons*. At variance to the aims and expectations of the writers and producers, *The Simpsons* is, hypothetically, a vision of hell . . . or is it *postmortem status purgatus*? None of the characters in *The Simpsons* know that they are dead, but they appear fixed for eternity never to grow up or grow old, never to change, never to leave where they live: they subsist in a shallow, meaningless, nihilistic existence where nothing alters, subject to the vicissitudes and vagaries of the life and the person they created (though some characters—a very small number—do appear to move away, leave, die, cease: i.e., translated to heaven . . . or sink in their depravity into a deeper level of the hell they so love and cherish).

Homer Simpson often gets a new job (from a variety of different occupations) but he always ends up back in his fixed *status* working at the nuclear power plant. At the end of an early episode, when Homer returns to his job at the power plant, Mr. Burns has a notice placed on the wall

---

19   See Rev 14:9–12; also Lewis, *Great Divorce*, ch. 13.

5. Postmortem Status Purgatus: a Simpsons' Eschatology

above Homer's work station, which defines the ontology of hell: "Don't forget you're here forever!"[20] No matter what happens to people they can't escape their condition; yet they all try to move on (they try to develop through their own *will*power, they have ambitions, but they are in a fixed state). It is easy to see how characters such as Homer, Marge, Mr. Burns, Smithers, and the Police Chief are condemned to this purgation: held, as they are, between heaven and hell, locked into a hellish existence caused through the fragmented dysfunctional beliefs that have generated their self-determinism.

Many characters suffer terrible life-threatening injuries and seeming death but they are simply restored to how they were, they cannot escape their self-willed damnation, and are too religiously corrupted to see the way out, through Christ, of this hellish purgation.

So, perhaps theologians and philosophers—such as Lewis—are quite correct: many will simply create the reality, *postmortem*, that they are condemned by the judgment of God to exist in for eternity, not realizing they are in hell, perhaps not even perceiving that they are dead: "All get what they want, they do not always like it."[21] Yes, Lewis did assert the traditional, biblical model of hell defined by fire and pain and eternal punishment, but this is at a deeper level than the nihilistic, unchanging, diminished existence represented by the humans in *The Great Divorce* (and, we may speculate, *The Simpsons*). The condemned in the upper level of hell are held above the deeper violent, painful fires of hell (for example the lake of fire[22]), by the grace of God. Does this absolve God of the responsibility? The jury is still out—but not forever! Whatever decisions we make, we will be in heaven, or in hell, eternally: what we do in the here-and-now echoes through eternity.

VII. *THE SIMPSONS*: INDIVIDUAL RESPONSIBILITY: AN ALLEGORY OF PURGATION/PURGATORY

Let us consider *The Simpsons* further.

If the traditional understanding of purgatory/purgation is characterized by change leading to the completion of redemption (as distinct to the utter damnation of those in hell), is this so for all? Perhaps

20   *The Simpsons*, "And Maggie Makes Three," 6.13.
21   Lewis, *The Magician's Nephew*, 162.
22   Rev 19:20, 20:10, 20:14–15, 21:8

for some this might seem, in our temporal reality, to be the experience of a million years of confusion and suffering? And will there be regression and relapsing? And what of frustration, inertia, and rebellion that may lead to some never being redeemed, that is being *moved* (a temporal concept?) or *translated*, heavenward? Some may simply stay as they are and refuse to change, to be redeemed, drawn out of themselves by the graceful love of God?

Are the episodic tales in the (in)famous cartoon series *The Simpsons*, seen by millions on a daily basis, an analogy of this sort of purgation being undertaken by people held by the grace of God above hell's jaws. Do these lost souls find it impossible to understand the need for repentance. And if they do begin to repent, do they understand what to repent of? And, pertinently, would this regret lead to change in the right direction—that is, change in their beliefs about God (doctrine) and about their behavior (ethics) and themselves (theological anthropology). If they try to escape the existential crisis they are locked into, they are constantly reset (like rebooting a computer) to be as they were: this we may consider to be the condition, divinely imposed, of absolute *apokatastasis* (!).[23]

Do the characters illustrate something of the power of sin to entrap and lock people into themselves?—*homo incurvatus in se*? Perhaps some of the characters are a reversal of their lives in this reality; perhaps others are as they were in this life but worse, diabolically worse, as they refuse to move in their mind and heart towards Christ (a move still possible even if their religious and cultural heritage excluded any knowledge of Christian revelation), for this is the only valid change possible; other characters are a thin grey shadow of what they were when alive because they failed to commit in this life or to truly love, or take seriously the *nature* of choices, and the *responsibility* that went with decisions?

---

23   *Apokatastasis* (Greek) refers to the return, perfectly, to the original state, that is, reconstitution, restitution, or restoration to the original or primordial condition. In this instance, I am referring to, postulating, *eschatological apokatastasis*, that is return to the status at the point of death immediately after death from which the individual cannot, through his or her own efforts, escape.

5. Postmortem Status Purgatus: a Simpsons' Eschatology

VIII. *THE SIMPSONS*: INDIVIDUAL RESPONSIBILITY: CHILDREN/CHILDISH

So, humanity's self-willed beliefs and actions dictate the nature of the experience of this hellish purgation, but what of the ontic nature of the human, imprisoned, as it is, by an open-ended sentence, in an open prison, with no divinely imposed fences, walls, watchtowers, or guards? (C. S. Lewis postulated that the gates of hell are locked and triple-bolted from the inside by the inmates, whereas the gates of heaven are wide open.)[24] What of children? The cloying sentimentality of a Western definition of childhood as perfect innocence will lead modern liberals to exclude the possibility of children falling foul of the righteous judgment of God. (Does not childhood in many Western societies now appear to be a period of absolute self-centered indulgence where every child is to be feted as a prince or princess?) But in reality children are small adults, with all the strengths and flaws of adults. Well, there are three possibilities for the appearance of children in *The Simpsons*: *First*, "children as children": some children in this life on earth appear in this *postmortem status purgatus* as children; this constitutes a contradiction of a Pelagianist position regarding childhood. These are they who were corrupted in their immaturity by the adults who were supposed to care for them (these corrupting adults, family members, or simply friends, or strangers, are most likely in a much deeper level of actual hell: note, Mark 9:42; Matt 8:16; Luke 17:2). *Second*, "children as adults": some of the children from this life may appear in this Simpsonian *status purgatus* as childish and immature adults, these are those who, as children in the here-and-now, may have taken to themselves an adult-like superiority and power/authority over others, so here they are presented as incompetent and foolish, but domineering, adults, and can see no way out of their status purgatus. *Third*, "adults as children": some adults from our life appear as children in this *status purgatus*, because they suffered from a self-inflicted psychological condition we may call, can't-grow-up-won't-grow-up syndrome (!), they refused to take responsibility for their life and their actions and their decisions when alive.

---

24   See Lewis, *The Great Divorce*, 20–21.

IX. *THE SIMPSONS*: DEATH—HELL-BOUND

But some appear to escape: there are those who seem to die, an appearance decided upon by those around them because these individuals disappear from sight. Some characters do die, or given that they are all already dead and languishing in this *postmortem status purgatus*, they *appear* to die a second time, and move away in an instant. For example—

Maud Flanders

Maud Flanders, the wife of Ned "diddly" Flanders, the evangelical(ish) neighbor to *The Simpsons*, is killed at a race track, but perhaps in this *postmortem status purgatus* reality she simply slides further and deeper into hell. In life she was a judgmental gossip, someone who saw and decried fault in everyone—except herself; this is the sin of self-righteous judgmentalism writ large, when we are warned by Jesus, "Judge not, lest you be judged" (Matt 7:1–3). Far from repenting and turning (because of her religion she believes she does not need to change, she has done the repenting already) she becomes worse and worse, showing no true love of her neighbor or humility before the Lord. On one occasion she states, "That's right, I was at Bible Camp, I was learning how to be more judgmental."[25] Her religion shields her from God's loving forgiveness. The idea that she has simply descended deeper into hell is perhaps confirmed by the writer of a later episode where she makes an appearance, after this apparent death, as Satan's lover.[26]

Frank Grimes

Frank's story—in this *postmortem status purgatus*—is that he had it tough as a boy, really tough; crippled by illness, he achieves a moderate High School Certificate and a degree in nuclear physics by correspondence from his sick-bed. In our reality before his death Frank had probably been a healthy ambitious child of successful parents; as an adult, a high-flier, a great achiever, wealthy, but selfish: a Gordon Gekko![27] In the Simpson

---

25   *The Simpsons*, "Bart of Darkness," 6.1.

26   *The Simpsons*, "Treehouse of Horror XXII," 23.3.

27   Gordon Gekko, a fictional character in the 1987 film *Wall Street* and its 2010 sequel *Wall Street: Money Never Sleeps*, became a symbol in popular culture for unrestrained greed, characterized by a line he repeated, "Greed, for lack of a better word,

5. Postmortem Status Purgatus: a Simpsons' Eschatology

purgatory, through struggle, sweat, and tears, he achieves a lowly job at the same nuclear power plant that Homer works at, and is therefore driven and possessed by irrational anger and rage, envy and jealousy. He hates Homer because Homer seems to have everything easy when he has struggled for so little. In a rage of mimicry and hatred of Homer he accidentally kills himself, electrocuted, or so we are led to believe; in reality he has simply disappeared from sight and has been translated deeper into hell. We may postulate that Frank Grimes when alive in our world had been a wealthy businessman, politician, opinion-former, even with a touch of celebrity status, if then such a person had been a wealthy, successful, high-flier in our world, then what happens to "old Grimey" is reminiscent of a gospel inversion, evident from the parables: "Son, remember that in your lifetime you received your good things, while Lazarus received bad things, but now he is comforted here and you are in agony" (Luke 16:25). This should have taught him what was wrong with his life, and opened the way for such a person to turn and glimpse salvation, this should have opened his heart to Christ . . . but it did not, because he held out.

Dr Marvin Monroe

Marvin Monroe is the resident psychiatrist and therapist, an eccentric yet atypical character who died: we see his grave stone . . . but then he reappears in later episodes. Why?—what happened? Perhaps he sank deeper into hell, but began to repent? In later episodes it is stated he had been ill, very ill, thus he had disappeared from their sight. (But then all in this hellish state are ill at ease, dis-eased.)

X. *THE SIMPSONS*: THE SAVED—HEAVENWARD

Bleeding Gums Murphy

Bleeding Gums Murphy is perhaps an example of purgation and translation into heaven. A musician, a saxophonist, he is a loner—to his benefit—he is not corrupted further by those around him. As a young man

---

is good." See: https://en.wikipedia.org/wiki/Gordon_Gekko.

he would have been gregarious, influencing others, and being influenced to their bad effect. But no longer. Perhaps he has been in this purgatory for what seems to be an inordinately long "time," but he has now come to the point of exhaustion where he can see his own unworthiness, he now knows and understands his own un-righteousness, as he lays down his crown (Rev 4:10–11). There is no hint of judgmentalism left in him; or the moral corruption that characterized him, and his music, as a young man. At this point he appears to "die," ill in hospital, but is in reality, perhaps, translated to heaven: the movement as such is that they, the other residents of this purgatorial state, no longer see him. Lisa can see the light of Christ in him, but mistakes this for fashionable liberalism. So, out of the hundreds of characters in *The Simpsons*, is only one saved and translated to heaven? Does this compare to humanity in the here-and-now—only one in potentially thousands?

XI. *THE SIMPSONS*: THOSE WHO SUBSIST—PURGATORIAL

Ned Flanders

Ned Flanders was, perhaps, a Richard Dawkins type skeptic and atheist in this life, and in purgatory is reversed. But still, like his wife Maud, he can't get beyond human-centered religion: when alive he was an evangelical atheist; dead, an evangelical religionist? He represents all he mocked in this life, but fails to enact the Christian life in humility and repentance, while casually appearing to help others. Superficially he seems the archetypal nice American Evangelical Christian? The answer came in an episode where Bart and Milhouse break into the basement of Ned's house and find a shrine—a religious temple—to the 1960s pop group, The Beatles.[28] The room is full of icons and memorabilia, pseudo-religious artefacts, all in praise of The Beatles: Ned's Christian faith is shallow and is subservient to this pagan cult. When Homer asks Ned, "I never knew you were such a Beatles fan?" Ned shouts back at him, "Of course I am. They were bigger than Jesus!"[29] The door to this pagan shrine has

---

28 *The Simpsons*, "The Bart of War," 14.21.
29 The writers here are invoking a statement by John Lennon made to the media

5. Postmortem Status Purgatus: a Simpsons' Eschatology

a poster on the door—Beware of God. But which "god" is represented and worshiped by Ned's Beatles memorabilia? This demonstrates how our religious egotism may be at odds with the will of God, even if we claim to be Christian (Matt 7:21–23). Ned Flanders is an example, a warning, of the dangers of religion, self-generated, self-centered religion.

Ned is actually unmasked early on. When Homer trades (a Faustian pact?) his soul for a doughnut, the devil appears to conduct the transaction, appearing as Ned Flanders, with goat's legs, saying "It's always the one you least suspect."[30] So Ned is Satan pretending to be a Christian so as to lull the damned into believing they are right with God and give them false hope that they may one day be saved, though none of them realize they are in fact dead (!), and are lost souls. Ned is for some viewers an archetypal Christian; however, he has clearly been seduced by Satan. Yet his character has as many dis-analogies with Satan as analogies.[31] Ned is characterized by confusion and contradiction and is, we may postulate, one simple realization and repentance away from moving towards heaven? But fails.

Maggie Simpson

The Simpson baby, Maggie, was a young woman in this life who exercised enormous power over people, for little good. She suffered from can't-grow-up-won't-grow-up syndrome, corrupting other young women through an advice column, and so now is mute, and an infant, having acted as an irresponsible infant-like young woman in this life. As a baby she retains her IQ of 167 (shown on several occasion), likewise, as this one-year-old infant she shoots Mr. Burns—a reflection of how she destroyed people with words in this life. Perhaps this powerful twenty-something intellect

---

that they (The Beatles) were more famous than Jesus. (Lennon had originally made the remark in March 1966, published, in the *London Evening Standard* newspaper.) Ironically, Ringo Star (one of the surviving members of the group) commented recently on BBC News 24 that now, as an old man, when he walks along a pavement in London people sort of recognize him, but can't name him, or sometimes attribute him to The Beatles—or they identify him as one of the other Beatles (BBC News Channel, Wednesday June 12, 2013). John Lennon was murdered in 1980 by one of his fans: he inadvertently created the conditions of his own demise. The Beatles are clearly no longer more famous than Jesus.

30   *The Simpsons*, "Treehouse of Horror IV," 5.5.

31   Satan is real and a singular and personified, but is also legion; hence Ned is Satan, but equally is not. This reflects the confused nihilism of hell.

trapped in a one-year-old infant is the one person in this *postmortem status purgatus* that understands what is going on, that this divinely imposed condition of absolute *apokatastasis* leads to a running sequence they cannot through their own strength escape from: at the end of *The Simpsons Movie* Maggie speaks for the first time: one word spoken at the end of the film, which also defines the ontology of hell: "sequel"—that is, hell as an endless sequel, a sequence of living out their own religious empire, *ad infinitum*.

Lisa Simpson

Lisa Simpson (IQ of only 159; less than baby Maggie) would have been a forty-year-old fashionably liberal academic with an equally indulgent myopic liberal lifestyle grounded in sexual freedom and abortion, power, status, and authority. Lisa, the precocious politically correct eight-year-old, exhibits all the arrogance she did as a middle-aged professor-turned-politician in our reality; she tries but fails to control people for her own interest in the way she did with such Machiavellian skill as a senator before she died, shot by a fanatic, obsessed now by her own self-righteousness. In this state of hellish purgation she still fantasizes about being President of the United States,[32] of flirting with alternative religions: as a Buddhist (which she refers to as a godless religion: "no creator God, just the pursuit of enlightenment"[33]), flirting with pagan ideas (inventing earth deities and the like), and then becoming a Wiccan (an adherant of Wicca—the religious cult of modern witchcraft), joining a coven of three Wiccans, learning to cast spells.[34] Throughout all of her neo-gnostic ramblings and noetic wanderings she is insufferably precocious and judgmental, while convincing herself that she is nice, kind, and considerate, the perfect liberal.

Apu Nahasapeemapetilon

Lisa is in this *postmortem status purgatus* not for being a Buddhist but because her being a Buddhist is motivated by a desire to reject Christ (in addition to her many sins as an influential academic and politician). Apu Nahasapeemapetilon is Indian/Hindu; he is the workaholic proprietor

---

32   *The Simpsons*, "Bart to the Future," 11.17.
33   *The Simpsons*, "She of Little Faith," 13.6.
34   *The Simpsons*, "Rednecks and Broomsticks," 21.7.

5. Postmortem Status Purgatus: a Simpsons' Eschatology

of the Kwik-E-Mart, a popular convenience store in Springfield, but contrary to the Parable of the Sheep and the Goats he offers no charity—where charity would be a cost to himself—nor love of his neighbor. His store-keeping is corrupt, changing the sell-by dates on expired goods, profiteering to unacceptable limits, exploiting his customers to their detriment: all this places him fairly and squarely in this *postmortem status purgatus*, not primarily or necessarily because he is a Hindu, but because he is a bad, self-centered, adulterous, exploitative person! If he changed his behavior and attitude to his neighbors and customers, loving them at considerable cost to himself, then he might find he is drawn heavenward, being deemed acceptable to the resurrected and ascended Christ (Matt 25:31–46).

Marge Simpson

Marge Simpson failed to commit in this life or to truly love, or take seriously the nature of choice, or see moral realities: she constantly says, "Ah, my little boy," to her son Bart, regarding him as a misunderstood angel, and is blind or dismissive—consistently—to Homer's many faults and his abuse of other people outside of the home. She made fundamental mistakes in her youth, particularly in marrying Homer, but she can't face that single truth and thus hides from the truth that is Jesus Christ: the way, the truth, and the life. This hiding from the truth reflects the person she was in our reality, before she died, and thus she continues to live the lie in this hellish state.

Bart Simpson

Bart died as a fifty-six-year-old in our reality from decades of substance abuse, shielded behind childish irresponsibility, he had drifted from relationship to relationship, from job to job, never becoming anything in particular, never committing to anything or anyone and hence he is represented by a ten-year-old child suffering from chronic attention-seeking behavioral-deficit-syndrome, trying to be different all the time, taunting others, reveling in trying to escape the reality he is in. Bart as a drifter and wastrel acted out his years on earth with childish (not childlike) irresponsibility and thus is living in such a state of childish powerlessness in hell simply because he rejected the love of God in Christ, and thus is responsibility for his beliefs and actions. So some "children" in *The Simpsons* were actually adults in our reality, our life. In attempting to regain their adult status we see Bart and Lisa in some episodes where they have grown up: but they are both as bad as when they were alive, as adults, in the here-and-now, our reality.[35]

Ralph Wiggum

Ralph Wiggum is a strange little boy characterized by nonsensical sentences and bizarre behavior, yet he can come out with profound statements, he is simple-minded and apparently good natured, however, he claims to see little leprechauns who tell him to burn things. When the Simpson family are nice to him and praise him, a leprechaun appears on his shoulder and orders, "Now you know what you have to do, burn the house down, burn them all": thus speaks one of the few explicit appearance of a demon of hell who Ralph courts as his friend. Ralph nods in agreement.[36] So, was Ralph—when alive in our world—a twenty-five-year-old arsonist who committed suicide rather than be caught by the police? A young man who flunked school, was in and out of care, who could not commit to any job or relationship, developed from petty crime to arson as a way of getting back at society, once he developed the habit of burning he could not stop, he was addicted, indeed, possessed demonically.

Waylon Smithers

Waylon is Montgomery Burns' personal assistant—factotum—who through his infatuation (disordered love) for the old man is simply looking in the wrong direction: hellward rather than heavenward, therefore he simply does not want to be saved, does not want the glory offered by Christ for eternity. An extreme example of this turning away from heaven and salvation was seen in serial fornicators through the ages: perhaps the most recent being the case of the British TV/radio and pop-culture celebrity Jimmy Saville, who was obsessively possessed with fornicating with any kind of person of whatever age or identity (though specializing in children), numbering hundreds if not thousands? Waylon Smithers seems mild by comparison, but is not his focusing on inordinate attraction sufficient for his self-generated placement in this *postmortem*

---

35   *The Simpsons*, "Holidays of Future Passed," 23.9; *The Simpsons*, "Bart to the Future," 11.17; *The Simpsons*, "Lisa's Wedding," 6.19.

36   *The Simpsons*, "This Little Wiggy," 9.18.

5. Postmortem Status Purgatus: a Simpsons' Eschatology

status purgatus? Yet does he not have the chance to turn and repent, and accept a purging that will draw him into heaven?

Sex and Love in this Simpsonian Postmortem Status Purgatus?

Waylon Smithers—as with virtually all the characters—is an example of the demonic corruption of sexual attraction (*eros*); but also the virtual non-existence of true love, real love, that is, God-given *agape* in its various guises from pure charity to genuine selflessness, to actual self-sacrifice (John 15:13) amongst the inhabitants of this hellbound Springfield. (Likewise *agape*, is extremely rare in human society here on earth.) Waylon is clearly presented as a closeted homosexual, which leads him to focus on the debasement of love: yes, in terms of general human sin, a debasement of love regardless of sexual orientation and gender identity—that is a debasement to the exclusion of heaven and his salvation (as is the case amongst almost all of the inhabitants of this Simpsonian *postmortem status purgatus*). The best they can manage is a cloying sentimental attachment (essentially related to *storgē* and *philia*), which leads to argument, fractiousness, and ultimately domestic violence within families, or gossiping, back-stabbing, and hate-filled self-justifying vanity-driven jealousy in the work place and in social interactions generally. All this issues from debased sexual relations, and an abuse of their reproductive plumbing (!). How was it Shakespeare put it: knotting and gendering like toads in a barrel?[37] Or when separated from the love of God, that is love, the only true love, what, we may ask, is the end game in this exercise of *philia* and *storgē*, issuing as it does from *eros*?—

> . . . wooing, wedding, and repenting, is as a Scotch jig,
> a measure, and a cinque pace: the first suit is hot
> and hasty, like a Scotch jig, and full as
> fantastical; the wedding, mannerly-modest, as a
> measure, full of state and ancientry; and then comes
> repentance and, with his bad legs, falls into the
> cinque pace faster and faster, till he sink into his grave.[38]

Without the heavenward turn in life (generated by prevenient grace), keeping sex and relationships in their place, then there is only the grave

---

37 ". . . as a cistern for foul toads to knot and gender in! . . ." (Shakespeare, *Othello*, 4/2)

38 Shakespeare, *Much Ado about Nothing*, 2/1.

and hell to beckon. What is missing is selfless gift-love, giving even when it costs everything: the New Testament Greek word *agape*, and in the Hebrew for love, *ahava*, and in the Latin, *charitas*, the love of God.

XII. *THE SIMPSONS*: THE TAUNTS OF DEMONS

There are many faces of Satan in *The Simpsons*—not just old Ned (Flanders): evil is legion. Montgomery Burns, along with many other characters, might just be demonic (he alludes, on several occasions, to being Satan, though this might just be hopeful longings on his part). That is, are there, we may ask, really demons from hell masquerading as humans to taunt those in purgatory, with jibes and comments and temptations, but they cannot immediately and intimately harm without the individual's willed permission? The local minister, The Revd Lovejoy, is really a demon masquerading as a Christian minister. Superficially he appears to be a cynical religious professional who has lost all sense of vocation and love for God and lives out eternity in the hell of nihilistic pseudo-religion, but on a deeper level he is a demon of hell who through mimicking a Christian minister should alert those around him to where they've gone wrong—but these assorted humans fail to realize the truth about themselves and their situation. His wife likewise is a demon who persuades Maud Flanders to become like her, to join with her gossiping, back-stabbing, back-biting mission, which ensures Maud's ultimate damnation (her further translation into deeper hell). Lovejoy though his corrupted ministry mocks the very gospel he claims to represent and thus ensures his congregation fails simply to turn to the Light of the World and accept the change in them facilitated by the blood of the lamb, which would seal their redemption.

XIII. *THE SIMPSONS*: WHERE IS IT?

From what we have established, the question, "Where is the place of existence for these characters?" might seem spurious? We are duty-bound to ask the question, Does hell, or this state of purgation, actually exist, in the same sense that we take the reality we inhabit, while alive, to be real, corporeal, geographic? Is *The Simpsons*' Springfield, as a place of

5. Postmortem Status Purgatus: a Simpsons' Eschatology

residence, "hell" or "purgatory"? Well, it is certainly not heaven, though it is important to remember that for many what they desire to be heaven is in fact hell: to *1970s liberal Anglicans* and the Vikings[39] hell will seem like heaven to their confused way of thinking, hell is their deepest desire, although they see this hell as a fulfilment of the desire for heaven! The problem with a traditional concept of purgatory is that it seems to be a real place, geographically located. C. S. Lewis's solution was to posit that purgatory does not exist, as such, but if our ultimate goal is heaven, "time" spent in *purgation*, would be in heaven all along; however, by contrast, if we refuse the blood of the lamb, the "bleeding charity,"[40] then any experience of purgation was hell all along.[41] However, there is another salient point to consider, the physicality of this purgatory-hell is important to acknowledge because it indicates, it complements, a *real resurrection*, it posits a real spiritual-physical resurrection (1 Cor 15:35–58, in particular v. 44). If we marginalize, if we downplay, the physicality of *purgation*, this form of spiritual cleansing, looking back from a position of modern, enlightened superiority, dismissing it as a mediaeval myth, are we also marginalizing the actual and real resurrection? By contrast many religions posit a *postmortem* disembodied existence, of romantic souls immune from harm drifting in their own self-generated God-less fantasy world? Most of the inhabitants of *The Simpsons* appear to subscribe to this belief, this false hope.

XIV. RELIGION IN *THE SIMPSONS*

When C. S. Lewis wrote *The Great Divorce*, a speculative account of damned souls from hell visiting the fringes of heaven with the opportunity

---

39   For example, the Viking hall of the dead that the Danes, the Norsemen, took to be heaven, where they were to spend all their time feasting and whoring, drunken revelries and fighting, raping and killing, is in point of actuality a region in hell! But there were those amongst the Vikings who will love it because feasting, whoring, drunken, sadistic paraphilia, slaughtering, defined them utterly by the point of their death, at the utter loss of the *imago Dei* in them.

40   In a speculative conversation, with a hell-bound unrepentant sinner, Lewis posits that the crucifixion constitutes, quite literally, "bleeding charity." See Lewis, *The Great Divorce*, ch. 4, 19–23, specifically 21.

41   Lewis, *The Great Divorce*, ch. 9, 51–57, see specifically, 55. Also, see Sauter, *What Dare We Hope?*

to change and progress further into salvation and deep heaven,[42] he was working in the context of a nation that still, for better or for worse, rightly or wrongly, saw itself as Christian. However, *The Simpsons* is written against the backdrop of decades of religious syncretism in the West where officially there must be nothing contradictory or threatening to other religious tribes in an individual's religious practices and beliefs, all religions must get on with each other, and there must be no threatening truth, especially from Christianity! *The Simpsons* is obligingly obedient to this syncretistic apologetic mish-mash of religious sensibilities, though it singles out Christianity for especial veiled criticism.

Religion issues from *the fall*. Before humanity gorged its way into original sin it had a right relationship with God. Eating, metaphorically, of the fruit of the tree of the knowledge of good and evil meant that afterwards humanity invented this relationship in its own image, its own terms, its own interests: which is why most religion falls short of divine revelation, humanity constantly reinvented religion in its own image. This is an insight that we can also read from *The Simpsons*!

The main religion in *The Simpsons* is named as The Western Branch of American Reform Presbylutheranism;[43] as such it is Protestant, though all the world's main faiths make an appearance in one form or another. (Though any reference to Islam is veiled, probably for fear of jihadist death threats.) Religion in *The Simpsons* is almost comical: the nation of Israel has turned Judaism into a theme-park,[44] Bart claims that the tooth fairy is God's daughter,[45] Ned continues to debunk religion by inventing a religious theme park named "Praiseland"[46] (perhaps pointing out how much pop culture is inherently religious, or is it that much religion is no more than trivial popular culture?). Homer and Bart nearly become Roman Catholics,[47] but are pulled back by demonic *apokatastasis* (!); Bart sells his soul and then mystically regrets it: he can't identify a soul

---

[42] All but one of the visitors refuse the chance of heavenward salvation, and return to the hell they know and are so fond of.

[43] See, http://simpsons.wikia.com/wiki/Western_Branch_of_American_Reform_Presbylutheranism; also, https://en.wikipedia.org/wiki/Religion_in_The_Simpsons

[44] *The Simpsons*, "The Greatest Story Ever D'ohed," 21.16.

[45] *The Simpsons*, "Fat Man and Little Boy," 16.5.

[46] *The Simpsons*, "I'm Goin' to Praiseland," 12.19.

[47] *The Simpsons*, "The Father, the Son, and the Holy Guest Star," 16.21.

5. Postmortem Status Purgatus: a Simpsons' Eschatology

in himself, but is lost without it.[48] It is not so much religion *per se* that is criticized but Western/American attitudes towards religion. So does this reflects the approach to religion of lost souls in purgatory/hell? After his failed attempt to become a Roman Catholic, Bart demands love and peace from everyone, claiming he is founding a new religion; however, his followers then go on—generations later—to wage religious wars over exactly what Bart's teaching was: "love and tolerance," or "understanding and peace!"[49]

Marge Simpson is the one who cajoles her family into going to church, and behaving according to what she considers to be good Christian morality, but this is superficial. When it came to singing carols in a communal setting she comments, "Christmas carols only have one verse. I know there are more, but the second verse is where they get all weird and religious."[50]

Bart gets Principal Skinner sacked; Ned Flanders takes over as temporary head teacher, Superintendent Chalmers visits: Ned utters a brief mention of God over the intercom to all classrooms, Chalmers immediately fires Ned for reciting a school prayer—

> Flanders: ". . . Let's thank the Lord for another beautiful school day.
> Chalmers: "Thank the Lord! . . . That sounded like a prayer, . . . a prayer in a public school?! God has no place within these walls!"[51]

However, when God could be of use to advance his career, Superintendent Chalmers demands the children intercede for success in a national test fearful of poor results affecting him personally. He comments, "Get down on your knees, pray to your god, and ask him—no demand—he tell you the answer, and if he won't, he is no 'god' of yours."[52] So a "god-in-the-pocket" is acceptable in these purgatorial schools, a "god" firmly tethered on a leash?

Lisa, skeptic, Buddhist, pagan, Wiccan, intellectual atheist, feminist, card-carrying-intolerant-liberal, suddenly decides to believe in God when demons whisper into her mind ideas that flatter and compliment

---

48   *The Simpsons*, "Bart Sells His Soul," Series 7, Episode 4, first broadcast October 8, 1995.

49   *The Simpsons*, "The Father, the Son, and the Holy Guest Star," 16.21.

50   *The Simpsons*, "White Christmas Blues," 25.8.

51   *The Simpsons*, "Sweet Seymour Skinner's Baadasssss Song," 5.19. [SiC]

52   *The Simpsons*, "How the Test Was Won," 20.11.

her vanity and ego. She comments: "It all adds up. I am the gem that will bring world peace. How brilliant of God to remove my skepticism by making me the Chosen One!"[53] Earlier, Lisa invents a genetically-modified tomato that will solve world hunger; she imagines herself as a goddess in a hindu shrine in India being worshipped by those she has fed! [54] So, Lisa is held in hell-purgatory, we may say, by her messianic pretentions.

Homer Simpson's misunderstanding of atonement is partly why he is in hell-purgatory. He believed that if Jesus had fought back all would have been well: "If Jesus had had a gun he'd be alive today!" So, Jesus should have defended himself, gun's/weapons blazing to defeat those who sought his death![55]

The Simpsons mirrors the meaningless serendipity that in some quarters is seen to characterize Western popular religion since the 1960s: this is, in effect, what we may in humor call "A Beatles' Doctrine of Religion," and is found in *The Simpsons*. A Beatles' Doctrine of Religion (BDR) was implicitly founded by the popular music group The Beatles in 1967. Through their actions and witness, though their holidaying, they proposed and founded—directly in contradiction to the prevailing Christian religion and culture in Britain at the time—a lifestyle fantasy religion where each individual, whatever each desired, could invent its own religious mindscape and lifestyle to suit each heart's desire. The four members of The Beatles went on an open-ended, extended holiday (a latter day version of the Grand Tour for wealthy aristocrats?) to India where they stayed in an Ashram. This was at the height of their global fame, adoration, and worship (so-called "Beatlemania"). They spent the time taking mind-bending drugs and claiming they were meditating (though does not meditation involve a heightened consciousness, a clarity of mind, and a passivity not induced through chemical contamination?). Developing from the enormously successful pop-culture that The Beatles had championed, characterized by superficial trite little songs extoling romantic delusions, this so-called Beatles' doctrine of religion developed so that everyone could be as religious as they wanted to be (or not, as was each heart's desire!). But this had to be an inward, self-reverential religion that contradicted no one else, or—pertinently—did not threaten

---

53   *The Simpsons*, "Gone, Maggie, Gone," 20.13.
54   *The Simpsons*, "Duffless," 4.16.
55   *The Simpsons*, "Home goes to Prep School," 20.13.

5. Postmortem Status Purgatus: a Simpsons' Eschatology

or contradict the nation state and the beliefs, practices, and legislation of the government. Travelling abroad was an essential component of a Beatles' doctrine of religion. For example, the Bacchanalian annual (then twice-annual, etc.) "religious" holiday to the Mediterranean for sun worship, fornication with multiple partners, and drunken revelries, then as the "gods" blessed them with wealth (in the form of credit: debt) to Florida. However, this was for the laboring classes, the bourgeois, liberal, educated middle-classes gently meandered in their travelings to various Middle Eastern destinations, then to Thailand *et al*. Furthermore, according to a BDR, all religions are equal and must be regarded as of equal value, yet simultaneously they are equally of no value to the extent that any contradicting elements in world religions must be elided while simultaneously asserting no truth—that is the absolute truth of no absolute truth—so as to justify the tyranny of absolute relativism (!?). Ironically adherents, often twenty-something graduates suffering from "can't-grow-up-won't-grow-up syndrome" or thirty-somethings of independent financial means, would travel, say, to the Far East and expect the local populace to fully accommodate their (pseudo-)religious whims and practices, and not object, even if the BDR threatened and contradicted or insulted their centuries-old local religious practices.[56] We can see all of this in modern Western liberalism; we can also see it in *The Simpsons*.

When Homer's life appears threatened, he screams out to this panoply of BDR-constrained gods and goddesses, "Who's out there? Oh, I'm gonna die! Jesus, Allah, Buddha, I love you all!"[57] Various assorted, imagined divines (did Homer really understand and know what he was appealing to when he invoked the name of Jesus?), the non-existent gods and goddesses of *The Simpsons*, are all defined by the Uncle Albert Model of the Divine: that is, Uncle Albert, from the worldwide popular BBC television comedy *Only Fools and Horses*. Del Boy and Rodney can do whatever they like, Uncle Albert holds no restraints and constraints on his nephews' beliefs and behavior provided they listen to his interminable stories about his time as a merchant seaman during the World War Two. So, pay attention to the god/goddess of your own invention, listen to its stories, be religious in varying degrees, giving due attention to this divine

---

56 In 2015, in the spirit of Western pseudo-religious neo-colonialism, four graduates, from Canada and Britain, stripped naked atop of Mount Kinabalu in Malaysia, much to the disgust of the locals who regarded the mountain as sacred.

57 *The Simpsons*, "Screaming Yellow Honkers," 10.15.

Feuerbachian projection, and you can do what you like. This is the Uncle Albert Model of the Divine (UAMD), which underpins The Beatles' Doctrine of Religion. To demonstrate, the (surviving) Beatles dropped in occasionally on *The Simpsons*, just to make sure all was conforming to this BDR-UAMD?[58]

Although there is, superficially, a concept of equality/equal opportunities and accommodation of all in this Beatles-founded religion, Christianity must implicitly be regarded as less than equal by the proponents of a BDR because of its claim to superior revelation and to provide a systematic roadmap of life and death. Furthermore, a BDR has provided an official religious position for many Western nation states and governments: a politicized Beatles Doctrine of Religion underpins the British government, and is in effect to be labelled neo-pagan secular-liberal humanism. If the "gods" are to be an optional add-on: invent one, or claim to have discovered one; if you so desire, however, the one God of the Judeo-Christian tradition must go to be replaced by "gods" where each divinity is self-defined and of no threat to other people's "gods." The founding of a Beatles Doctrine of Religion occurred in 1967, the same year as the 1967 abortion act in Britain (and the liberalization/legitimization of homosexuality): sexual freedom raised to something of an intense emotional religious high was an essential component. And love?—love was a warm cozy feeling, essentially a cloying sentimental attachment issuing from the sexual freedoms: this form of love (reminiscent of the ancient Greek loves of *philia* and *storgē*, issuing from *eros*?), if generated, in turn legitimized the ever more bizarre forms of copulation and fornication that had generated this cloying sentimental attachment in the first place.

After their drug-fueled religious "grand tour" of an Indian Ashram, most of The Beatles abandoned what they took to be Hindu meditation, but continued with a tacit promotion of a Beatles Doctrine of Religion, which was intimately intertwined with lifestyle pop culture. George Harrison, The Beatles' lead guitarist, continued as a Hindu, patronizing

---

58   There are mentions of The Beatles in various episodes, however in terms of visitations, see: appearance by Ringo Star in, "Brush with Greatness," 2.18; appearance by George Harrison in, "Homer's Barbershop Quartet," 5.1 (a visitation reprised in "All Singing, All Dancing" 9.11); appearance by Paul and Linda McCartney in, "Lisa the Vegetarian," 7.5; appearance by John Lennon (who appears and comments from a fantasy pseudo-"heaven," in, "Treehouse of Horror XIX," 20.4.

5. Postmortem Status Purgatus: a Simpsons' Eschatology

the development of Hindu temples in Britain, but—in contradiction to the multi-faith neutrality that appeared to underpin a BDR—financed the Monty Python film, *The Life of Brian* centered on the song "Always look on the bright side of life," which trivialized and dismissed the cross and echoed a central tenet of a neo-pagan secular-liberal humanist dismissal of Christianity generally, the gospel specifically: just sit back and enjoy life while it lasts, hide in a pseudo-religious fantasy world. No wonder these people are hellbound. So why do people not perceive the warning in and of *The Simpsons*?

XV. DIFFICULTIES AND PROBLEMS WITH A DOCTRINE OF PURGATORY

Though intentionally humorous (a cutting and critical satire?), and drawing on the trivia of popular culture, this essay suggests that it is somewhat ironical that *The Simpsons* offers a similar analogous insight into humanity's teleology—the human's ultimate end, and the dangers of eschatology that people seek to hide from in self-generated fantasy worlds—that C. S. Lewis and J. R. R. Tolkien warned of in the mid-years of the twentieth century through their analogical narratives. This is a form of sub-creation (a term coined by Tolkien). Rhetorically we may ask, how does God use us as sub-creators to give intimations of what is to come?—and to *interpret* from others something of the nature of what is to come, that is, the pictures placed in the mind, given to a baptized imagination, of how our lives and actions will echo through eternity.[59]

Despite liberal sensitivities over judgment and eternal damnation, hell is an acceptable concept from an orthodox Christian perspective. However, asserting the need, soteriologically, of purgatory, or at least purgation, is considered for many a step beyond orthodoxy. James Sauer (writing from a Reformed perspective) notes: "I think the answers lie in the fact that the purgatorial idea, though doctrinally a heresy, contains a spiritual truth when applied to the human situation. There is something

---

59   It is these pictures that formed the basis of much of the work of the Inklings, for example, the picture of evil in J. R. R. Tolkien's *The Lord of the Rings* (1954 & 1955) and Charles Williams', *All Hallows' Eve* (1945) and *Descent into Hell* (1937), but especially C. S. Lewis's *The Great Divorce* (1945) and the dangers of damnation in *The Screwtape Letters* (1942), and the consequences of our decisions before God in *The Chronicles of Narnia* (1950–56).

in this false doctrine which reminds us of life. And there's the key."[60] Concerns are generally seen in four areas: ontological, biblical, theological and in grace.

First, ontological: is it real? And what do we mean by real? The problem with the traditional concept of purgatory is that it seems to be a real place, geographically located. This raises questions of location and geography. Purgation does not: we can assert a biblical precedent and justification for *postmortem* change (1 Cor 15:50–53), though purgation still raises paradoxical questions of time, of temporality.

Second, biblical: put simply, however much we can assert purgation, a place called purgatory is not biblical in the strict sense of the word, according to a traditional Protestant reading of the Bible, but, what about the witness of Maccabees?

> On the next day, as had now become necessary, Judas and his men went to take up the bodies of the fallen and to bring them back to lie with their kindred in the sepulchers of their ancestors. Then under the tunic of each one of the dead they found sacred tokens of the idols of Jamnia, which the law forbids the Jews to wear. And it became clear to all that this was the reason these men had fallen. So they all blessed the ways of the Lord, the righteous judge, who reveals the things that are hidden; and they turned to supplication, praying that the sin that had been committed might be wholly blotted out. The noble Judas exhorted the people to keep themselves free from sin, for they had seen with their own eyes what had happened as the result of the sin of those who had fallen. He also took up a collection, man by man, to the amount of two thousand drachmas of silver, and sent it to Jerusalem to provide for a sin-offering. In doing this he acted very well and honorably, taking account of the resurrection. For if he were not expecting that those who had fallen would rise again, it would have been superfluous and foolish to pray for the dead. But if he was looking to the splendid reward that is laid up for those who fall asleep in godliness, it was a holy and pious thought. Therefore he made atonement for the dead, so that they might be delivered from their sin. (2 Macc 2:39–46)

---

60   Sauer, "Purging a Problem," published online, Centre for Reformed Theology and Apologetics, http://www.reformed.org/index.html. See, http://www.reformed.org/webfiles/antithesis/index.html?mainframe=/webfiles/antithesis/v2n1/ant_v2n1_purging.html. Accessed May 29 2011.

Third, theological: what is the ontic nature of *postmortem* life? We scarce know little, save the threat of judgment, juxtaposed with the promise of Jesus' forgiveness: but what does the promise entail—salvation or damnation (we can glean clues from scripture, thankfully). The resurrection appearances make the question tantalizingly unanswerable, the precise nature of resurrection is unknowable, unquantifiable, but clues and hints are spread widely through scripture. We cannot know, we can only begin to glean intimations and understanding of the eschatological reality that we will inevitably face, by analogy, by word pictures, from the parables and sayings of Jesus: "The kingdom of heaven is like . . . ." Also, there is the: does not death leads to resurrection?—not disembodied souls wafting around in some pagan Elysium? Or is there a delay before the general resurrection?

Fourth, grace: the relationship between grace, the cross, sin, and salvation is focused onto one episode in the gospel, one moment of recognition: the good thief. We know not what this man's life has been; we know not of his relationship with God prior to his execution as a criminal, though he admits that his punishment is just, he has broken human law; yet, in a moment of recognition he is saved. In his rebellion, the thief on the other side—the so-called, bad thief—is damned. Grace does not need time (or does not appear to take time?). How do we regard the so-called good thief executed next to Jesus, and for that matter, the so-called bad thief? What soteriology is represented by deathbed conversions? What do these accounts tell us of the relationship between grace and the process of salvation? Is there a need for growth, sanctification, when even hardline Reformed Puritans, who regard purgatory as heretical, do not deny the need for sanctification. But does not the "either-or" problem remain?[61]

XVI. A PERSONIFICATION?

Professor Frink, the eccentric and bizarre scientist in *The Simpsons*, declared that he had discovered and could prove the existence of hell,

---

61   What we have not considered within this paper, as it is two doctrines that are considered somewhat outside of the Christian mainstream, though they would warrant consideration if this subject was taken further, is a doctrine of annihilationism and a doctrine of universalism. Annihilationists (or supporters of extinctionism/destructionism), will argue that after the final judgment some human beings and all the damned will be destroyed, they will cease to exist; universalists will argue that everyone will be saved, reconciled.

further that everyone went there.⁶² Well, all he did was hold a mirror up to himself and realize what had happened to him, and everyone in "Springfield": but he had totally lost sight of the beauty and wonder, the possibility and existence of heaven!—further, that there are people *in* heaven.

There is one character from *The Simpsons* that perhaps is the personification and embodiment of postmodern Western humanity—the so-called "Crazy Cat Lady." Eleanor Abernathy is presented as a deranged middle-aged woman surrounded by a large number of cats, her home is jam-packed full of hoarded junk, items she simply cannot throw away. Further, she is isolated from normal social interaction and intercourse. She appears to have lost the power of reason, and of coherent speech seen in her inability to communicate, except by throwing cats at other people: she simply mutters and screams gibberish, more pertinently, and in the biblical context, babble: "So the Lord scattered them from there over all the earth, and they stopped building the city. That is why it was called Babel, because there *the Lord confused the language* of the whole world. From there the Lord scattered them over the face of the whole earth" (Gen 11:8–9; *my emphasis*).

When eight years of age Eleanor Abernathy was clever and ambitious, the precocious, perfectly behaved school pupil who expressed the desire and ambition to be a lawyer and a doctor when she grew up, because, according to the feminist dictum, "a woman can do anything."⁶³ At sixteen she was studying for law school; at twenty-four years, an M.D. from Harvard Medical School and a J.D. from Yale Law School. However, by thirty-two years of age she is shown suffering from stress and tension, exhaustion, despite her successful career and her multi-million-dollar apartment: she is presented suffering from classic burnout. She turned to alcohol and became obsessed with her pet cat (presumably having exhausted several relationships that had been subordinate to her ambitions). By the time she turned forty, she had assumed her present state as a psychologically disturbed alcoholic, with what appears to be an unlimited supply of cats. There do appear to be moments of lucidity and intelligence, of "reason," in Abernathy—if she can get beyond herself and her sins.

---

62   *The Simpsons*, "How I Wet Your Mother," 23.16.
63   *The Simpsons*, "Springfield Up," 18.13.

5. Postmortem Status Purgatus: a Simpsons' Eschatology

When Mayor Quimby is recalled, she runs for the mayor's office. During a candidate debate, she is asked what public-policy issues are important to her. Unlike the other candidates (who act as stereotypical dishonest politicians), Abernathy discusses issues such as healthcare, economy, and public education in between her screams and gibberish (and a call for cats "in everyone's pants").[64]

After taking psychoactive medication there appears to be an improvement in her sanity and her ability to relate to other people. However, all is lost when Marge Simpson informs her that the medication is just sweets: Reese's Pieces (Peanut Butter Candy). Her medication helps her speak intelligibly, and is in effect a placebo, but once the ruse is exposed she reverts to her usual gibberish—so her problems are willful and psychological (?). Eleanor Abernathy is a lost soul, beyond redemption, beyond reason, and has placed herself outside of the love of God in Christ; as such she epitomizes many in this life in the West who hang by a thread above hell, who refuse to change, losing themselves in identity politics (defined by multiple "demons": work and ambition, sex and drugs and rock-and-roll, consumerism, relationships and homes . . . and social media) to bolster their delusions. Yet at the last moment they may turn to Christ and be forgiven (a deathbed conversion?), but this will require a clarity in their minds that will require them to relinquish the consumer-led lifestyle and delusions. Eleanor Abernathy is defined by a loss of reason, the loss of the ability to reflect on and stand outside herself.[65] That is the God-given ability to reason where reason, as C. S. Lewis noted, predates creation: "Reason is given before nature and on reason our concept of nature depends";[66] also, "Neither will nor Reason is the product of nature, . . . such Reason and Goodness as we can attain must be derived from a self-

---

64   See, https://simpsonswiki.com/wiki/Crazy_Cat_Lady#cite_note-Springfield_Up-1

65   For key episodic appearances of Eleanor Abernathy see: *The Simpsons*, "Girly Edition" 9.21; *The Simpsons*, "'I, (Annoyed Grunt)-bot' or, 'I, D'oh-bot'" 15.9; *The Simpsons*, "Treehouse of Horror XV" 16.1; *The Simpsons*, "Homer and Ned's Hail Mary Pass," 16.8; *The Simpsons*, "Springfield Up," 18.13; *The Simpsons*, "Home Away from Homer," 16.20; *The Simpsons*, "See Homer Run" is the 17.6; *The Simpsons*, "The Last of the Red Hat Mamas," 17.7. See also: *The Simpsons*, "Eeny Teeny Maya, Moe" 2.16; and, *The Simpsons*, "The Blue and the Gray," 22.13. For a compilation of the cat lady, showing her teleological descent into hellish madness, see: YouTube: https://www.youtube.com/watch?v=PXlmeE2jjrI.

66   Lewis, *Miracles* (2nd ed. 1960), 23.

evident Reason and Goodness outside ourselves, in fact, a Supernatural."[67] Therefore, for Lewis, religion is rational; reason is religious. Reason is of Christ, the Logos (John 1:1f.), the Word is reason: reasoning, reasoned. Eleanor Abernathy has willfully misused and then abandoned this reason and thus she has rejected Christ, her forgiving judge and her salvation. She appears to be truly a lost soul: lost of her own making.

XVII. UNIVERSAL SALVATION?

Perhaps the only doctrine to reconcile what we have described and asserted is a form of universalism. That is, not a liberal doctrine of universalism whereby all go to heaven, no; post-resurrection all get to be in eternity *where they wish to be*, where each life has led: for example, the Vikings in Valhalla, which they called heaven—the Viking hall of the dead that the Danes, the Norsemen, took to be heaven—where they were to spend all their time, *postmortem*, in feasting and whoring, drunken revelries and fighting, mutilating, raping, and killing. But is this in point of actuality a region in hell? Yet there were those amongst the Vikings who will love it because feasting, whoring, drinking, sadistic paraphilia, mutilation, and slaughter defined them utterly by the point of their death, to the severe degradation of the *imago Dei* in them. This is about the individual defining God's righteousness in its own image and desiring the consequences, but not fully appreciating precisely what those consequences are to be.

So, how do we define heaven? Simple: *we* don't. God created heaven and the conditions for being there. Most people have a twisted and distorted concept of heaven whereby they simply get to be and do whatever they feel most comfortable and satisfied doing: but is this not the precise nature of original sin repeated over and over again, *ad infinitum*?

Prior to the crucifixion-resurrection, the default position was that all were lost (with rare exceptions such as Elijah); now all are saved, all get what they want: hence *The Simpsons* languishing in purgation in the fringes of hell. All are saved—but to what existence? Perhaps all can claim to be saved—but some to heaven and some to hell. Such *postmortem status*, will seem to be hellish to many.

Perhaps the final word on salvation, universalism, and responsibility, lies with C. S. Lewis:

---

67   Lewis, "Bulverism," 227. Note Lewis capitalizes "Reason," "Goodness," and a "Supernatural."

Some will not be redeemed. There is no doctrine which I would more willingly remove from Christianity than this, if it lay in my power. But it has the full support of Scripture and, specially, of Our Lord's own words; it has always been held by Christendom; and it has the support of reason. If a game is played, it must be possible to lose it. If the happiness of a creature lies in self-surrender, no one can make that surrender but himself (though many can help him to make it) and he may refuse. I would pay any price to be able to say truthfully "All will be saved." But my reason retorts "Without their will, or with it?" If I say "Without their will" I at once perceive a contradiction; how can the supreme voluntary act of self-surrender be involuntary? If I say "With their will," my reason replies "How if they will not give in?"[68]

XVIII. CONCLUSION

This article illustrates an understanding of humanity's condition after death (*de statu hominis postmortem*), in many cases a disorder that may appear painful, agonizing, bewildering, lost, even though it is scripturally endorsed "change"; however, salvation may beckon (*Si purgatio fit, postmortem*): hence, *postmortem status purgatus*, that is the state, fixed within the context of purgation, following the *eschaton*—death, judgement, heaven, hell. As such, this conforms to the soteriology and eschatology of C. S. Lewis. Though by visiting *The Simpsons* we have an early twenty-first-century perspective! Some viewers regard *The Simpsons* almost like a soap opera—the program reflects humanity's public and private concerns, lifestyle issues. *The Simpsons* presents—for some—how people should live. In this, the comic element is played down and regarded as innocent. However, the comic element is important, indeed the *absurd* is very important. A general theme running through Dante's hell in *The Divine Comedy*, is that demons, and the evil that governs them, are absurd and comical, and should be laughed at rather than feared . . . or followed! To be absurd is to be illogical and irrational, bizarre. A contradiction in many ways of the reasoned and sound nature of creation, which God declared was good (Gen 1): evil is *absurd*, a contradiction—*alogos*. This is the path Lucifer set himself upon, rebelling against *El Shaddai*, *YWHW*,

---

68   Lewis, *Problem of Pain*, 96–97.

descending out of heaven into a hell, forming hell around him, welcoming those like "him" who rebel against the Lord and do not repent.

It may seem an exaggeration to label the inhabitants of Springfield and their ilk here on earth as evil, but they are a contradiction of God's will for their lives; they persist in their rebellion—however respectful and fashionable this mutiny may seem to some—and if evil is the surd-like contradiction of God then they are evil and reside *postmortem* where they are most suited. The *surd* in creation is the irrational element in the created order, the negative and destructive; essentially, today and historically (e.g., for the Greeks), a mathematical concept. But *surd* was invoked by theologians and philosophers in the patristic and mediaeval church for the irrational and contradictory, that which is destructive in the created order and in humanity—a use to complement its mathematical meaning.[69] The *surd* issues not directly at the command of God but exists as a possibility, as a consequence of creation: creation has the freedom to go its own way, to develop in ways contrary to the will of God. Yet, there is freedom to return, to haul down one's flag of tribal rebellion, to lay down one's crown before the throne (Rev 4:10f), to honor and acknowledge the Lord of creation, to recognize and admit, then repent of one's own silly little empire.

An irreconcilable dialectic stands between heaven and hell. Perhaps the occasional saved soul needs some change (1 Cor 15:50–53) to fully "move" into heaven, but it was already, from the point of death-judgment, in heaven, and perhaps our prayers will help its full translation. The lost souls in hell might look longingly at heaven, and wonder if they might change, even attempt through their own strength to "move" heavenward (Luke 16:19–31), but they are all along in hell from the point of death-judgment . . . and they will soon lose the ability to perceive and desire heaven as they sink deeper into their own depravity in their own hell. Any attempt to force a heavenward change will, as a *self-willed* thrust, not conform to the will of God. And like looking in a mirror, any move that appears away, forwards, is contradicted because you are looking at a reflection and really moving backwards, and deeper into the self-generated hell of your own de-humanized corruption. Those who get it

---

69   My acknowledgement the late John Austin Baker, theologian and bishop, who introduced me to this concept of the Surd, and the Surd-like, in creation, through a regular correspondence from c.1990 relating to my wife Hilary's epilepsy.

5. Postmortem Status Purgatus: a Simpsons' Eschatology

right are already in heaven; those who get it wrong are already in hell. Hell is, by definition, inconsistent and unintelligible?

Let go and let God.

This is the simplest thing to do; yet in reality the hardest and most seemingly impossible to do. *The Simpsons* adequately illustrates this, and the very real risks, *postmortem*, that humanity faces.

> *"Be not deceived; God is not mocked: for whatsoever a man soweth, that shall he also reap. For he that soweth to his flesh shall of the flesh reap corruption; but he that soweth to the Spirit shall of the Spirit reap life everlasting."*
> GAL 6:7–9 (KJV)

> *"All get what they want, they do not always like it."*
> C.S. LEWIS, THE MAGICIAN'S NEPHEW

6

The God of the Epileptic: *Postlapsarian* Exile, Affliction, and the Sufferance of Salvation

> *Now a word came stealing to me, my ear received the whisper of it.*
> *Amid thoughts from visions of the night, when deep sleep falls on*
> *mortals, dread came upon me, and trembling, which made all*
> *my bones shake. A spirit glided past my face; the hair of my flesh*
> *bristled. It stood still, but I could not discern its appearance.*
> *A form was before my eyes; there was silence, then I heard a voice:*
> *'Can mortals be righteous before God?*
> *Can humans be pure before their Maker?'"*
>
> JOB 4:12–17
>
> *"Truly, the fear of the LORD is wisdom;*
> *and to depart from evil is understanding."*
>
> JOB 28:28

SYNOPSIS

This paper examines the subject of theology and epilepsy, pertinently, how we try to explain epilepsy in the light of the love of God. Given its status as an affliction (a disability?), where is epilepsy leading (*telos*)? How does it stand in relation to the judgment (*eschaton*) of the triune God? How is it to be considered in relation to the self-revelation and forgiving judgment of God. Epilepsy can inform and shape—perhaps subtly, subliminally, implicitly—an individual's understanding of eschatology. (This will often seem to be different to the eschatological beliefs of the average academically impartial, seemingly disinterested and neutral, theologian whose brain is not epileptic.) An epileptic will often demonstrate certain nuanced details in his/her thought giving a more dynamic and truer understanding of the eschatological reality that humanity occupies, and the judgment that we all will face. In many instances, epilepsy can still be considered to be something of a taboo subject, along with death: as a seizure builds, the sufferer is gripped by a sense of crisis, which can affect anyone close by. More pertinently, does the condition of epilepsy allow the triune God to impart, to generate in the mind, a sounder eschatological understanding than many ordinary people demonstrate? This may be considered a particular interpretation of eschatology when most people do not concern themselves with the crisis of life and the risk of eternal judgment. Epilepsy can lift people out of a worldly complacency. Such beliefs are profoundly eschatological and, to a degree, dualistic: light and dark, heaven and hell, good and bad, ecstatic and nihilistic, either-or: in a word, dialectic. It may be speculated that this is why the marginalized, the afflicted, the suffering outcasts, saw Jesus and responded strongly, either one way or the other. Such people do not respond to Jesus with indifference. Post-seizure the world still remains the same, but there has been a change in the person, this is movement, either the movement towards salvation or, for some, a movement away from salvation into damnation.

Initially we need to establish certain methodological parameters between a theological-existential perspective and that of a Kantian closed-universe framework. The central question examined relates to cause: however much we analyze the mind-brain during seizures in terms of neurology, we still need to enquire into the cause and origin of the seizures theologically, more pertinently eschatologically. We can consider the account of Saul on the road to Damascus: a Spirit-enabled encounter with the risen and ascended Christ, which had a dramatic and cataclysmic effect on him (Acts 9:1–18). His symptoms are reminiscent of an epileptic seizure (phasing between *simple partial* and *complex partial*, between *consciousness* and *altered consciousness*) both in the attack on the road and in the details given at the point of his healing at the hands of Ananias: Saul/Paul's temporary blindness (an extended *postictal* period?) indicates the possibility of a seizure in the rear of the cerebral cortex (the outer layer of the brain), which processes information from the eyes before sending it to the temporal lobes at the front of the brain for interpretation, recognition, and so forth. This period of extended *postictal* appears to have generated *scintillating scotoma*, or conversely *retinal migraine* (the two conditions are similar but not the same), though both are often referred to by sufferers as *migraine aura*, and can occur—rarely—in both eyes simultaneously. A reading of John 9 (the man born blind) and Mark 9 (the exorcism of an epileptic boy) along with personal accounts of living with epilepsy (in accordance with the theological-existential methodology outlined) lead to the conclusion regarding our *postlapsarian* exile, and the role of affliction in the sufferance of salvation, drawing on the perceptions of the Franco-Jewish philosopher and Christian convert Simone Weil.[1]

---

1   For details of and access to all the works of art discussed here: http://www.cslewisandthechrist.net//toward-the-day.html
See also note at beginning of this book: Illustration.

6. The God of the Epileptic

I. INTRODUCTION

For a number of years now I have been exploring the relation between epilepsy and theology, more pertinently how we come to understand the phenomenon of epilepsy in the light of the love and self-revelation of God, but also in the context of how our minds work, how they are meant to be before God. Unlike many medical conditions that affect us, epileptic seizures, particularly on a daily basis, eat at that which is central to our very existence, threatening to overwhelm and destroy it: that is, our perception of reality, of life, our identity, our memory, continuity, our relationships, behavior, and crucially our beliefs. All epileptic seizures are a death, and are usually prefaced by a build-up in the mind of *krisis*, by a sense of judgment, and—if the seizure is survived— by rebirth/recovery. Just as it is impossible for a television camera to take a picture of itself, so too, unless we have recourse to revelation, it is impossible to use our mind-brain to try to understand what is going on in our mind-brain when it goes catastrophically wrong. How do we attempt to make sense of reality, life, and our relationship to the triune God—creator, redeemer and sanctifier—in the light of a condition such as epilepsy?

First, briefly, a few facts: Hilary and I met in December 1982; she was in hospital with her epilepsy at the time. We married six months later. During our life together we have carried her epilepsy before God in Christ: in this case, severe and intractable complex focal temporal lobe and generalized epilepsy (see table: brief glossary of epileptic seizures for types of seizure cited). The condition has slowly worsened as the years have passed. Apart from mild seizures on a daily basis, which disrupt, to a greater or lesser degree, her sense of continuity and identity, she has survived thirteen episodes of potentially catastrophic and fatal *status epilepticus*: a continuous state of epileptic seizures (sometimes for hours, sometimes for days; *status epilepticus* is to the brain the equivalent of a massive, near-fatal heart attack.) At the centre of this paper is a tool we use for virtually everything we do and are—the brain. The conclusion of the scientific/academic community is that the brain is "the most complex object in the known universe."[2]

2   Thomson, "Brain mysteries: A user's guide to the biggest questions of the mind," *New Scientist June 20, 2019*: https://www.newscientist.com/article/mg24232350-800-brain-mysteries-a-users-guide-to-the-biggest-questions-of-the-mind/?utm_medium=NLC&utm_source=NSNS&utm_campaign=2019-0620-GLOBAL-NSDAY&utm_content=NSDAY

TOWARDS THE DAY AFTER TOMORROW

II. REASON AND METHODOLOGY

If there is to be a method to our investigations it is to be found in Mark's Gospel, pertinently the exchange between Christ Jesus and the father of the epileptic boy (Mark 9:22b–24). The father asks Jesus, "'But if you are able to do anything, have pity on us and help us.' Jesus said to him, 'If you are able!—All things can be done for the one who believes.' Immediately the father of the child cried out [and said with tears], 'I believe; help my unbelief!'"[3] The father of the boy exhibiting what appears to be a *tonic-clonic* epileptic seizure does not stand calmly by assessing the situation and the suitability of Jesus to be who he is asserted to be, he does not isolate himself within a dispassionate, disinterested, calm, scientific mindset, he cuts through all such barriers between himself and the God-man standing before him and pleads, cries out, weeps, demands in his frustration and bewilderment. Others who approach Jesus adopt the social etiquette that is expected of good, well-born Jews: this man does not. This man cries out (the verb used is *krazō*, in this instance *krazas*), he weeps (*dakruon*), and pleads for understanding, healing, and the faith to meet the Christ's expectations. The words used are the same as in the record of Jesus before Lazarus' tomb where Jesus did not simply politely weep but wept with convulsions of grief, the verb implied that he was torn apart with grief, that he shuddered with grief. When Jesus calls Lazarus to come forth it is the same verb as used by the father of the epileptic boy, it is also the same verb used by the crowd who call for Barabbas to be freed not Jesus, and for Jesus to be crucified: the crowd scream out their demand, so did Jesus to Lazarus, so did the father of the epileptic boy to Jesus.[4]

---

3   (v. 22b) "'. . . but if you are able to do anything, have pity on us and help us.' (v.23) Jesus said to him, 'If you are able!—All things can be done for the one who believes.' (v.24) Immediately the father of the child cried out [and said with tears], 'I believe; help my unbelief!'" (A number of Greek scripts and the AV translation include the words in square brackets.)

(v. 22b) "*All eí ti dúnee boeétheeson heemín splangchnistheís ef heemás* (v.23) *Ho dé Ieesoús eípen autoó Tó Ei dúnee pánta dunatá toó pisteúonti* (v.24) *Euthús kráxas ho pateér toú paidíou élegen Pisteúoo boeéthei mou teé apistía*." Mark 9:22b-24, *Novum Testamentum Graece*, 119.

4   I am indebted to the Revd Jeffrey John for his observation on the language used by Jesus, particularly the power and emotion in the verb *kráxas*; his comments were in a sermon in a broadcast of choral evensong from St Alban's Cathedral, UK, (BBC R3, Sunday 18th March 2007): "Jesus mourns for his friend Lazarus . . . and you mustn't be misled by our polite English Bible translation into missing how extreme Jesus' mourning is. What the Greek says is that standing on the side of Lazarus' grave Jesus wept and wept, he kept on weeping. And it's not just that he was deeply moved and troubled in spirit,

6. The God of the Epileptic

This is not the dispassionate, disinterested aloneness that the Irish novelist and philosopher Iris Murdoch criticized as Kantian man: "Kant's man stands alone . . . defiant pride in the free power of his reason. His reason, it is true, is at that moment frustrated and conscious of its inability to achieve complete understanding; but there is nothing humbling or regrettable about this frustration."[5] Murdoch continued—

> The idea of life as self-enclosed and purposeless is of course not simply a product of the despair of our own age. It is the natural product of the advance of science and has developed over a long period. It has already in fact occasioned a whole era in the history of philosophy, beginning with Kant and leading on to the existentialism and the analytic philosophy of the present day.

Murdoch moves from a philosophical perspective to a dualistic, eschatological one:

> The chief characteristic of this phase of philosophy can be briefly stated: Kant abolished God and made man God in His stead. We are still living in the age of the Kantian man, or Kantian man-god. . . . How recognizable, how familiar to us, is the man so beautifully portrayed in the *Grundlegung*, who confronted even with Christ turns away to consider the judgment of his own conscience and to hear the voice of his own reason. Stripped of the exiguous metaphysical background which Kant was prepared to allow him, this man is with us still, free, independent, lonely, powerful, rational, responsible, brave, the hero. . . . The *raison d'etre* of this attractive but misleading creature is not far to seek. He is the offspring of the age of science, confidently rational and yet increasingly aware of his alienation from the material universe which his discoveries reveal. . . . It is not such a very long step from Kant to Nietzsche. . . . In fact, Kant's man had already received a glorious incarnation nearly a century earlier in the work of Milton: his proper name is Lucifer."[6]

---

as our reading said. It actually says that his guts were torn apart and that he heaved and shuddered with grief. And when he summons Lazarus to come forth he doesn't call, he screams, he bawls, he howls, as if he is shouting down death itself. It's the same verb as when the crowd howls for Barabbas to be set free."

5 Murdoch, "The Sublime and the Beautiful Revisited," 268–69.

6 Murdoch developed this critique in papers that came together for her seminal book *The Sovereignty of Good*: See "The Sovereignty of Good over Other Concepts," 77–78.

Kantian man has in effect created a monstrous Tower of Babel, a titanic illusion: *eritis sicut Deus*. The problem is that Kantian man has in many ways come to dominate medical science with its agenda based on scientific materialism, which in the case of epilepsy means Kantian man is groping in the dark effectively denying what is before him. Why?—because the brain and the mind are clearly more than mere flesh. We have to acknowledge a degree of duality between the mind and the brain even when such dualism is unpalatable. If there was no duality, no human being could commit suicide: according to the drive for survival the brain would not tolerate its own self-destruction: consciousness, self-consciousness, leads to a degree of duality. The mind is not the soul, let us get that clear, it is in many ways a modern theological heresy that mistakes the mind for the soul. As we shall see, perception, understanding, and identity are all crucial to our lives but are affected often with catastrophic results by seizures, and anti-convulsants merely suppress and distort so much of the mind's activity. And surgery, brain surgery, for epileptics in many cases may be considered as primitive as amputating a leg because you have a splinter in your toe.

Let us take this further by looking at William Blake's picture of *Newton* (1795).[7] This engraving of Newton embodies Blake's criticism of the single-minded, what may be considered blinkered, approach of some scientists and for that matter some who considered themselves to be deists in and from the eighteenth century. The picture is, in effect, a criticism of scientific materialism: we see the philosopher-scientist—represented, perhaps unfairly, by Isaac Newton—focusing relentlessly only on what he can measure, interrogate, and control. The philosopher-scientist is thereby isolated within the glorious wealth and fecundity, breadth and magnitude, of the world, a creation of which he is clearly a part, a creation he grows out of (Gen 2:7). The eyes are fixed on the tools of measurability represented by the dividers/compass, therefore he is oblivious in many ways to the creation he, Newton, is part of, much of which is beyond the blinkers of his method, indeed this methodology excludes whatever is not comprehensible and measurable by the intellect in the form of reason. (Or perhaps this truly is Murdoch's "Kantian Man.") For Blake, our use

---

7   William Blake (English poet and mystic, artist and printmaker, 1757–1827), *Newton*, 1795, copper engraving with pen and ink and watercolor, 460 x 600 mm, Tate Gallery, London.

6. The God of the Epileptic

of reason is as *fallen* as our will.[8] Reason, the misuse of reason, is turned in on itself, reason is now self-absorbed, self-serving: *homo incurvitas in se*—humanity turned in on itself, absorbed with and seemingly justified by itself. Blake is orthodox on this issue: reason for him was created to serve God, to frame creation with order, and to govern our desires, our passions, and hence our will; reason/order is therefore closely related to the role of Christ, the *Logos*, in creation. Newton (Murdoch's "Kantian Man") by comparison, for Blake, represents scientific materialism; he missuses his little compass/divider, his reason, and takes it to be a "god": human reason becomes god-like and excludes God. We may assert that so often anything outside of the range of the divider/compass of reason for a scientific materialist does not enter into scientific analysis or consideration, it is as though it does not exist. Blake's criticism was taken further by C. S. Lewis in the scathing portrait of scientific materialism in the form of Dr Weston in his cosmic trilogy; like Blake's work, Lewis used pictures, imagination, and mythology.[9] When in his middle years William Blake and his wife suffered from poor physical health, debilitating conditions that afflicted them, he wrote in a letter to a close friend, "The thing I have most at heart—more than life, or all that seems to make life comfortable without—is the interest of true religion and science (that is, inspired art and spiritual knowledge, revelations of Christ)."[10] So, for Blake (and for so many orthodox theologians) true science—and a true use of reason—is in spiritual knowledge, which is the revelation of Christ: *scientia* and *ratio*.

The philosopher Charles Taylor has commented how this disengagement with the object leads to an abstract isolationism, which has characterized the modern enlightened approach to reality.[11] Scientific rationalism disengages and to a degree loses itself in isolated abstraction. This is the effort to reduce the manifold diversity of relations in the perceived world—nature—or the field of experience to that which is

8   William Blake, *The Four Zoas*, §.ix, 180–87; §.i, 342, §.v, 235 §.viii, 453; §.ii, 109 & §.iv, 141 (unpublished illustrated manuscript), cited in Damon, *A Blake Dictionary*, 419.

9   Lewis *Out of the Silent Planet* (1938), *Perelandra* (1943) and *That Hideous Strength* (1945). See also, unpublished in Lewis's lifetime, Lewis, *The Dark Tower and Other Stories*.

10   Blake, "Letter to Thomas Butts, 10 January 1802." In Davis, *William Blake: A New Kind of Man*, 96–97.

11   Taylor, *Sources of the Self*. In this context see also Craig, *The Mind of God and the Works of Man* and Buckley, *At the Origins of Modern Atheism*.

manageable, that which science will reduce to a uniformity so that sense perception and human cognition *appear* satisfied, feel at home with what can be concluded. The object of investigation is not contemplated but interrogated in an attempt to find some unitary logical basis: this is the human will to know and control, decide and dominate. But this does not work with God, even when we have the effrontery to reduce God to an object; even when God wills himself to become an object—God's self-objectification in Christ—we err if we believe we can dissect and analyze. This was the fallacy of the so-called quest for the historical Jesus in the nineteenth century: any attempt to deconstruct the Christ will not work. This approach likewise does not work with epilepsy. With epilepsy you have to be involved; you can't rationally disengage. Being afflicted, whether as sufferer or carer, gives a qualification to understanding, which the healthy, the normal, simply lack. Has not Kantian man voluntarily excluded itself from this understanding?

III. CAUSATION 1:
THE COMLEXITY OF "WHY?"

We cannot look at epilepsy eschatologically without considering cause and effect, why and wherefore, responsibility and action: causation. Scientific materialism based on the misuse of reason will not really help us in understanding both the cause and effect of epileptic seizures. Therefore, we must turn to the self-revelation of God: Christ Jesus and the pneumatically authorized scriptures. So, what causes epilepsy? What do we mean by cause? What is the source or root, the origin, of seizures? From the closed perspective of scientific materialism, epilepsy is at its most basic an electrical malfunction in the brain. The electric impulses along the predefined synaptic pathways that make up our brain are considered to be the substance of our thoughts, the conscious thoughts in our mind: or more pertinently, are these synaptic pathways *vehicles* for our thoughts? From a reductionist perspective these electrochemical events are taken as the sole manifestation of "thought," but the functioning synaptic pathways do not so much constitute our thoughts, as provide a vehicle for our thoughts. We make these synaptic pathways as we grow and develop throughout our childhood, and add to them as memory patterns throughout our life. A leading international neurologist has commented that as each brain cell can have seven- to ten-thousand

6. The God of the Epileptic

synaptic connections with other brain cells (i.e., about one trillion neurons; ten quadrillion synapses), and given that, there is the seemingly infinite number of synaptic firing patterns—in potential—that form our thoughts, and then there is the strength of each firing that changes the subtlety and character of each thought, a nuanced infinity of strength variability: each human brain is therefore a creation of immensely greater complexity than the planet earth. In addition, it has been asserted, on the assumption that the universe is *finite*, that there are considerably more atoms in the human body than stars in the observable universe.[12] We are indeed awesomely created: "To see a world in a grain of sand," as William Blake put it.[13] But we are finite. General seizures are when there is an overload of electrical activity in a part of the brain that otherwise appears healthy; focal seizures are where there is damage or scarring in the brain. This scarring causes further seizure activity, which in turn overloads the flesh, the pathways in our brain, therefore there is further scarring. But what causes the malfunction? Is the reason internal to the human? Do our brains and mind occupy a closed universe where only what we perceive with our senses can act on us? Kantian man would believe this is so. However, the scriptures and church tradition points to a reality outside of our immediate sensory perception that can act on us, influence us, affect us, particularly in our minds.

---

12 "So, more galaxies or more cells? This is not a close call. Even using the highest estimate for galaxies (200 billion) and the lowest estimate for human cells (1 trillion), there are at least 800 billion more cells in your body than there are galaxies in the known universe." https://www.nytimes.com/2015/06/23/science/37-2-trillion-galaxies-or-human-cells.html.
See also, https://www.thoughtco.com/number-of-atoms-in-the-universe-603795.

13   William Blake, *Auguries of Innocence* (1789), the opening verse is as follows:

To see a world in a grain of sand,
And a heaven in a wild flower,
Hold infinity in the palm of your hand,
And eternity in an hour.

There are various nineteenth-century editions, however, for the complete poem see: https://www.poetryfoundation.org/poems-and-poets/poems/detail/43650

IV. CAUSATION 2: THE BLAME GAME

Theologically—eschatologically—where our judgment before God and our final destination is working out in the here-and-now, Jesus, in John 9:1-4, gives us a different explanation:

> As he walked along, he saw a man blind from birth. His disciples asked him, "Rabbi, who sinned, this man or his parents, that he was born blind?" Jesus answered, "Neither this man nor his parents sinned; he was born blind so that God's works might be revealed in him. We must work the works of him who sent me while it is day; night is coming when no one can work." John 9:1-4

The disciples question was theological—or, more pertinently, any answer would have to relate to theodicy. If Jesus had answered that this was so because the optic nerves had not formed properly, or offered some other scientific explanation, then this would have been no answer at all. Jesus answers, "Neither this man nor his parents sinned. He was born blind so that God's works might be revealed in him." Jesus responds to the prevailing social mores of the day—the Jewish belief that illness was the result of bad behavior, in a word sin, and that sin is measured by and in relation to the religious community. In his teaching Jesus often warns of the consequences of sin: suffering and death. But what do we make of inherited disease (or in today's terminology, genetic disease)? The Jews had an answer—the child's parents had sinned (or the child had sinned in the womb). But suppose the man's blindness is not directly linked to personal/individual sins: supposing the genuinely innocent can suffer?—that is innocence relative to the *fall*. You have a sense of this towards the end of The Book of Job, where Job argues with his tormentors that he is innocent; they argue back that he must have missed something somewhere along the line! So does this passage from John's Gospel offer another solution? "We must work the works of him who sent me while it is day; night is coming when no one can work" (John 9:4). Blame is not apportioned; but Jesus does assert that the situation must be geared towards the manifestation and declaration of the light: God's saving actions. Healing the man will bear witness. It is important in this context to remember the comments by Jesus about how the rain falls and the sun shines on the just and unjust alike: "But I say to you, love your enemies and pray for those who persecute you, so that you may be children of your

6. The God of the Epileptic

Father in heaven; for he makes his sun rise on the evil and on the good, and sends rain on the righteous and on the unrighteous" (Matt 5:44–45). Furthermore, Jesus's comments about a particular group of Galileans who fell afoul of Pilate and those killed when the tower of Siloam fell, questioning whether they were worse sinners than others, but stressing the need for repentance:

> At that very time there were some present who told him about the Galileans whose blood Pilate had mingled with their sacrifices. He asked them, "Do you think that because these Galileans suffered in this way they were worse sinners than all other Galileans? No, I tell you; but unless you repent, you will all perish as they did. Or those eighteen who were killed when the tower of Siloam fell on them—do you think that they were worse offenders than all the others living in Jerusalem? No, I tell you; but unless you repent, you will all perish just as they did." (Luke 13:1–5)

When Jesus confronts individual sinners he forgives them as they repent and warns them to sin no more: he sees the wider eschatological picture and the risks we all run of damnation without focusing on the individual degree of sinfulness in comparison to the religious community. Sin—therefore, for the Christ—is defined by and in relation to God, not necessarily by and in relation to the religious community in Jerusalem. Sin is defined eschatologically and none of us can escape judgment.

V. CAUSATION 3: *POSTLAPSARIAN* EXILE

So, this man was born blind, probably a congenital or genetic abnormality, or environmental factors affected the child's development in the womb. Epileptics can be born with a tiny group of malformed cells in a small, localized part of the brain: the damage occurring either in the womb or during birth. Over the years, during childhood, the damage will be extended after each tiny electrical storm in that tiny group of damaged or malformed cells. Are we to be dominated by our genetic fate? Is it the case that we must accept and live with whatever life's lottery, in the form of random genetic mutation, throws up?—whether our genetic heritage shines on us or rains, whether we are just or unjust? Christ's atoning sacrifice has wiped the slate clean, but we are still subject to the vagaries and vicissitudes of this reality, we willed it to be so through the *fall*: this is our *postlapsarian* inheritance. We are subject to the vagaries and vicissitudes of this reality (including what appears to be a random genetic lottery) *because of the fall*; we can see this as a punishment from God, but also as the natural by-product of our willful rebellion. And yet prior to the *fall* we would have been subject to the natural wasting and decay of nature and life: we got sick and died—"'tis the way of all flesh."[14] The separateness of the universe from God identifies creation as distinct, created, and as subject to entropy: randomness and decay in the universe is the rule in nature. We live in a universe where organisms are always getting more disordered: irreversible death and irreversible entropy mean the whole of reality is winding down. But since the *fall* is it fair to argue that this would have been at an increased rate compared to prior to the *fall*? Before the *fall*, the Holy Spirit would have potentially—selectively— healed people of cancer before the individual became aware they were ill, but whether healed or not, all would have been subject to the will of God. *Postlapsarian* humanity has distanced itself from the will of God—to a greater or lesser degree—and therefore has exposed itself to the dangers, the vagaries and vicissitudes of this reality *to a greater extent*. And then there is relative righteousness. Spiritual concupiscence both directly and indirectly governs our behavior, which is will and desire; this therefore influences the corruption of human nature: God may want to heal the rot in a sinners flesh, but the individual's willfulness—languishing East of Eden—may prevent it.

Is this what Jesus alludes to, albeit obliquely, in John 9:1-4? That because of the *fall* we find ourselves in the apparent randomness of this reality, the vicissitudinous vagaries with all the roll of the dice that this reality, this exile, throws at us, with the daily risks of infection, decay, exposure to natural forces like radiation that can sow the seeds of our demise? Such a verisimilitude of chaotic randomness implies that the seed of our demise may be sown as a butterfly flutters thousands of miles away, but this apparent chaos has led to the reality we occupy in all its breadth and wonder. Jesus does not sidestep the issue of why, he simply accepts that the man was born blind and loves him—and heals him as an example of the works of the Father. Then the neighbors question whether he has been healed; they question whether it is the same man who was the

14   The wording was made famous by a Victorian writer (Samuel Butler, *The Way of all Flesh*, 1903, written between 1873–74), but the phase was originally extracted from the Hebrew Bible: "to go the way of all the earth" (1 Kgs 2:2; cf, Josh 22:16).

blind beggar. Then the Pharisees get involved—the religious authorities. They question him, they question whether he ever was blind; then they get his parent in. All parties have to watch very carefully what they say lest they get banned from the temple, effectively excommunicated. The man cannot avoid their questioning. He is cast out of the temple into virtual exile by the authorities. He was marginalized, sworn at, despised and humiliated as a blind person, he was living the life of a beggar when he was blind because of the supposed sin; now he is totally disenfranchised, marginalized, an enemy amongst his own people. The Pharisees refuse to believe his testimony:

> The man answered, "Here is an astonishing thing! You do not know where he comes from, and yet he opened my eyes. We know that God does not listen to sinners, but he does listen to one who worships him and obeys his will. Never since the world began has it been heard that anyone opened the eyes of a person born blind. If this man were not from God, he could do nothing." They answered him, "You were born entirely in sins, and are you trying to teach us?" And they drove him out. John 9:30–34

The response of the Pharisees is to fall back on to the old idea that this man's blindness was because he was born in sin, to assert that he was entirely born in sin, in so doing they are acknowledging that he really had been blind and that he has now been healed, this despite their initial skepticism, their initial claims that he had not been blind—the logic and subtlety of this is lost on them. The blind man now has his sight, but it has cost him his community, he is like a boat adrift. But this kind of affliction is not new to him. As a beggar he was despised, humiliated, marginalized. Now he knows and believes in the Christ, despite the fact that he knew affliction intimately and will continue to know it.

Genesis 3 teaches us that humanity is one: through one man sin came. Therefore, the original sin committed is shared by all: one man's trespass led to condemnation for all (when Lucifer fell as an angel he did not take all the angels with him—only those who conspired with him). The crucifixion-resurrection changes this: by the one truly sinless human being (Christ Jesus) the *postlapsarian* curse is lifted. So why are we not restored to the *prelapsarian* condition? This raises important questions: How possible is it to glimpse this prelapsarian state? Is it possible through an act of grace and will to return? How did this prelapsarian state relate to our genetic inheritance? When Peter attempts to walk on water at Jesus' invitation (Matt 14:29–31) we have a glimpse of this prelapsarian ontology. Peter really believes, so he steps out, he walks towards the Lord. Then as the wind blows he *realizes* what he is doing; he *knows* he should not be able to walk on water, the will to know controls him, he starts to sink, to drown: the will to know negates his faith (as it did for Adam and Eve after they had tasted of the fruit of the tree of the knowledge of good and evil). We cannot escape this desire to know and control. However, not only was Peter protected as he walked, he was even immune—to a degree—from much of the effect of this reality, and his effect on this reality was limited from an environmental perspective. In a state of prelapsarian grace, would we have been so exposed to the vagaries and vicissitudes of this reality to the degree we now are? The Holy Spirit that hovered and moved over the waters in creation would have effected exactly which genes would and would not cut in and affect us, and would have given us an important degree of spiritual protection, in the womb and in our daily life. But we are now exposed to the full force of the winds of this reality so that genetically the rain falls and the sun shines in apparent randomness on the just and the unjust alike. To adapt and develop Thomist speculation, would an angel that passed through a nuclear reactor be irradiated, or immune to the danger? In our prelapsarian ontology, would we have been so exposed to the dangers of, say, radiation? The answer if we are to accept the conclusions of innumerable scientist is "yes." But this takes no account of miraculous intervention, which would have maintained protohumanity according to the will of God; and such miraculous intervention still goes on today—most of it un-notice, even by religious people. There always has been suffering and pain and death. The scientific data from all fields claims that as long as there has been sentient life there has been pain and suffering and death (though it is widely acknowledged that animals experience such pain in a markedly different way to us humans). I am asserting nothing that denies the scientific evidence, only stating the degree to which *postlapsarian* humanity is blind to the way healing and control and protection from the natural world can still be generated pneumatologically to an extent that was possible, and in all probability happened prior to the *fall*. This is a huge issue, which space prevents us analyzing in any depth.

Humanity—as the history of the last two thousand years has shown—will still continue on the path of its self-obsessed *fallen* willfulness, sure (as Peter demonstrated) in the knowledge of good and evil, right and wrong,

6. The God of the Epileptic

what should be and what should not, and thereby acting as if humanity was God (*eritis sicut Deus*): therefore we will suffer. But after the cross, suffering is still indiscriminate and arbitrary, random and meaningless, *to a degree*, affliction (as with the moral character of our lives) is now measured by Christ's cross, a cross that sanctifies and, yes, purifies, even when such affliction may be the result of a genetic lottery in the womb.

So, is epilepsy given to people as a punishment for sin by God?—or is it that in most cases we are subject to the vagaries and vicissitudes of this reality because of the fall? Even if the latter, individual sins can make the situation worse. And our openness to pneumatologically authored healing and protection measured by our righteousness and the will of God can make it somewhat better. We are exiled from paradise because of original sin, we live in *postlapsarian* exile, and hence, a genetic wildcard can cause these medical conditions because we willed it to be so: we would not live in innocence, protected to a large degree by the Holy Spirit, we were not satisfied with the divine beatific vision, we chose to take onto ourselves the mantle of decision, of the knowledge of good and evil, the result is that we are open to the effects of this reality in a way the angels are not. Languishing East of Eden does indeed relate to sin, but not directly to individually prescribed penal judgment that some Christians would like to believe in: we are all in the same situation together—exiled in a dangerous world, we are in a state of *postlapsarian* exile. Being East of Eden we are open to the dangers of genetic mutation: this genetic lottery can cause epilepsy. But then it is equally important to remember that many people bring epileptic seizures on themselves through misusing their brain: alcohol, drugs, head injuries (adventure sports, boxing, *et al.*), strobe-light effects (attending dance halls). One seizure may seem isolated, but then the brain is prone to further attacks and a pattern sets in. Yet this is only half the story. This only *begins* to explain cause.

VI. CAUSATION 4: POSSESSION

How do we assess/regard the scriptural claims that sometimes epileptic seizures are caused by demonic interference? Let's look at Mark 9:14–29, the account of the healing of an epileptic child. This narrative is placed between the transfiguration and the story of the disciples' preoccupation with their debriefing session, their professional grading, and their rewards: who will be the greatest amongst them! The boy's father describes to Jesus what appears to be a tonic-clonic epileptic seizure; however, his father prefaces his description with what is essentially a theological statement: ". . . he has a spirit that makes him unable to speak; and whenever it seizes him, it dashes him down; and he foams and grinds his teeth and becomes rigid; and I asked your disciples to cast it out, but they could not do so" (Mark 9:17b–18). If we follow the father's line of thinking this raises serious questions: Does so-called demonic possession *always* result in epileptic seizures? Are *all* epileptic-like seizures the result of demonic possession? Are all epileptics demon possessed? A more pertinent question must be, what is the extent to which the mind-brain is subject to supernatural influences—good or bad—outside of our control? When the boy is brought before Jesus we have a glimpse of classic first-century apocalyptic—eschatological—Judaism: the belief in the spiritual world of angels and demons, and the material world that parallels and reflects, in many ways, the spiritual realm, mirroring its conflicts (see the Book of Daniel and Ethiopic Enoch). Jesus addresses those around the boy: "You faithless generation, how much longer must I be among you? How much longer must I put up with you? Bring him to me." Jesus is angry probably because of their failure to heal, which is attributed to their (*postlapsarian*?) lack of faith. Jesus does not apportion blame onto the boy. This is important: the victim, the child, is not accounted responsible and therefore guilty. Neither for that matter does he blame the father. It is the disciples who receive the full brunt of his, yes, anger.

The boy's father pleads imploringly from the stress and frustration of years of caring; he speaks in desperation and bewilderment. He shouts, almost screams back, "I believe—help my unbelief!" (Mark 9:24b). Jesus responds: "When Jesus saw that a crowd came running together, he rebuked the unclean spirit, saying to it, 'You spirit that keep this boy from speaking and hearing, I command you, come out of him, and never enter him again!'" (Mark 9:25). What is happening here? First, Jesus does not just politely and with academic disinterestedly say, "Be healed that which is malfunctioning in this boy's brain"; neither, in this instance, does he say, "Go and sin no more." Jesus is *casting out*; the Son of God is *exorcising*: he is ordering the spirit to leave; and it obeys. This action is super- or preternatural. Second, he refers to it not as good or bad or even demonic but as that which prevents the boy from speaking and hearing, in fact that

6. The God of the Epileptic

which prevents the boy communicating. Third, the convulsions as such are regarded as a side issue. Epileptic convulsions are graphic, perturbing, and disturbing; however, Jesus sees beyond this: the crucial factors are possession and this inability to speak or hear. The spirit convulses the boy one last time and then leaves. The crowd take the child for dead: "Jesus took him by the hand and lifted him up, and he was able to stand." Jesus helped him, not the disciples, not the crowd, not even the boy's father: Jesus helped *him*—exorcised and cared for him when humanity failed the boy.

We have here a reality peopled by angels and demons—reality is therefore more than the sum total of that which is perceivable by the human senses. In Matthew 4:24 we read, "they brought to him all the sick, those who were afflicted with various diseases and pains, demoniacs and epileptics and paralytics, and he cured them." In this instance Matthew distinguishes between those possessed by demons and those who were epileptic. In the original Greek, Matthew clearly distinguishes demoniacs (*daimonizomenois*) from the moonstruck (*selēniazomenoi*) and both from the paralytics (*paralutikois*).[15] In the first century, a whole host of conditions associated with the brain and the mind were attributed to being moonstruck (*selēniazomenoi*). Therefore, mental conditions may or may not in biblical terms be triggered by external supernatural influences: we are not isolated individuals, closed off within this universe from anything

---

15   (v. 24) "*Kaí apeélthen hee akoeé autoú eis hóleen teén Suríɑn Kaí proseénengkan autoó pántas toús kakoós échontas poikílais nósois kaí basánois sunechoménous kaí daimonizoménous kaí seleeniazoménous kaí paralutikoús Kaí etherápeusen autoús.*" Matthew 4:24, *Novum Testamentum Graece*, 8. The Greek word, *seleeniazetai* (in this instance, *seleeniazomenous*), literally means "moonstruck!" In Jewish thinking at this time the idea was that what we term epilepsy was just one manifestation of mental illness or disturbance. This was caused by the moon which was considered to have demonic and malevolent, sinister, often spiteful and vindictive influences. This is reflected in the psalms—"The sun shall not strike you by day nor the moon by night" (Ps 121:6). Most translations of the Bible assume *seleeniazomenous* refers to those suffering from seizures; however, this does not in itself necessarily point to a diagnosis of epilepsy. The NIV translation at least holds this open: "News about him spread all over Syria, and people brought to him all who were ill with various diseases, those suffering severe pain, the demon-possessed, those having seizures, and the paralyzed, and he healed them" (Matt 4:24).The AV/KJV translates *seleeniazomenous* as "those which were lunatic" (note the etymology of the word luna-tic reflecting the idea of the influence of the moon). The NRSV and most other contemporary translations render, "epileptic."

"else" or "other," but, importantly, neither does this other reality prey on us all the time, and our relationship with God may protect us.[16]

Are we therefore at the mercy of every passing demon or spirit that wishes to play with our destruction, exploiting physical weaknesses in our brain to trigger seizures? Or worse—effecting our decisions and actions, which then have moral implications, one only has to think of many influential, important, and famous people who thought their belief system and actions were the result of their own autonomous decision making. Demonic influences may not be restricted to such graphic behavior as convulsions. Where is freedom and autonomy in this? Is this reminiscent of the Greek gods toying with humanity? Are we at the mercy of the elemental spirits, as Paul puts it, of the universe? What of the principalities and powers that Paul also speaks of? Where is God in all of this? We can be assured: "For I am convinced that neither death, nor life, nor angels, nor rulers, nor things present, nor things to come, nor powers, nor height, nor depth, nor anything else in all creation, will be able to separate us from the love of God in Christ Jesus our Lord" (Rom 8:38-39). We can belong to Christ or we can belong to that which we would fear being influenced by, owned by. Most people reading this passage from Mark's Gospel fear possession by such a demon and claim epilepsy as the one and only manifestation of demonic possession. However, it is important to remember that the boy's moral character was not changed to any great degree by the demon. Yes, it played with him, toyed with his body and even threatened his life, but the boy was not possessed in a more insidious way: such a demon would have had far more success with, say, Judas Iscariot, Pontius Pilate, Herod, where it only had to whisper ideas into the mind to ensure their path to destruction. However much harm the demon appeared to do to the boy in Mark's Gospel the child still had his right mind and moral character and had not made a willful decision to follow the path of evil in the way Judas Iscariot had, he had not made a willful decision to follow an evil path convinced utterly that such a path was the good. Imagine being assaulted and beaten-up by a robber on several occasions as you commuted to work; provided you do not become so overwhelmed with bitterness and a desire for revenge that

---

16 And then there are the self-generated demons/pseudo-demons of modern life—alcohol, drugs, tranquillizers, sex, power, ambition, status, greed . . . identity politics (?), these can all possess, all seize, all take possession rather than allowing the individual to simply live.

6. The God of the Epileptic

transcends justice, then you are relatively unscathed. However, imagine the same scene where the robber does not attack and beat you up but chats to you, takes you for a coffee, befriends you, eventually persuades you to join him in his unlawful activities. Which situation is worse? Which situation imperils your salvation? Therefore, demons invite us to indulge what appears good to us but is in reality destructive to others and then destructive to ourselves.

Evil may not always work directly on the individual but through people around us, thereby triggering seizures in one whose brain is vulnerable. Demonic influence and control can often appear, superficially, to be innocuous, justified, even fashionable, according to the social niceties, the eschatologically judgmental nature, of identity politics. However, consider: Hilary had a major complex partial seizure one morning several years ago. She was incapacitated for hours, and as usual I did all the housework, and looking after her. By late afternoon she had recovered sufficiently to want to do a little work in the front garden—5, 10 minutes, pottering, or so. I was suffering with a migraine but sat on the front doorstep, keeping an eye on Hilary. Two young women walked past. One commented to the other "Look the man sitting doing nothing while the women does all the work!" This immediately triggered another deep complex partial seizure in Hilary; I struggled to get Hilary back into the house. The remark seemed innocent and fashionable to the two women but was an instance of a "get behind me Satan" remark.[17] The demonically influenced/possessed young woman triggered a seizure in Hilary's already fragile state. Yes, this was a classic remark of feminist hegemonic tribalism, however a similar false judgement could have been uttered by a masonic man, or an identity politic "apparatchick" of a dozen or more persuasions. But this remark, and the judgementalist lie that drove it, triggered the seizure. This was not an isolated occurence; I could recount numerous instances (too many to be mere coincidences—often in an ecclesial context, particularly amongst 1970s Libeal Anglicans). But the one common factor in the assailant is the arrogant pride of self-belief and self-justification that contradicts the law of God and the Gospel. Hilary

---

[17] Peter took him aside and began to rebuke him. "Never, Lord!" he said. "This shall never happen to you!" Jesus turned and said to Peter, "Get behind me, Satan! You are a stumbling block to me; you do not have in mind the concerns of God, but merely human concerns." Matt 16:22–23

TOWARDS THE DAY AFTER TOMORROW

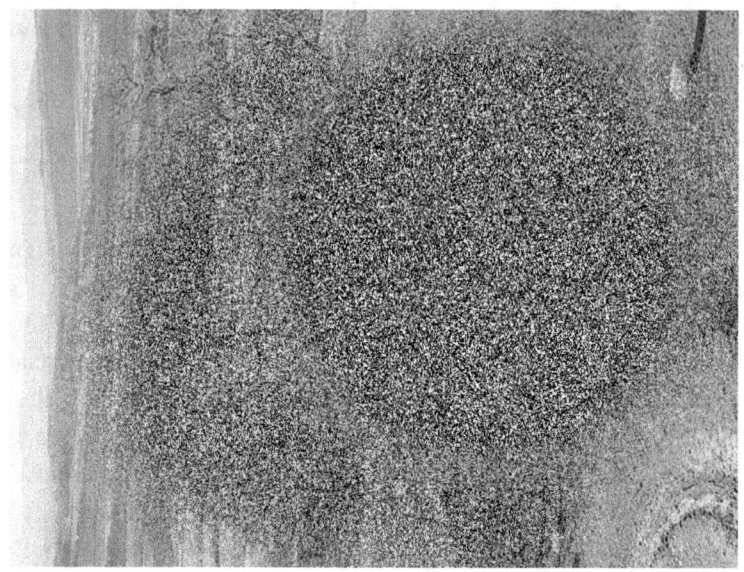

A "photoshoped" picture/graphic showing the effect of *scintillating scotoma* and its progress and potential permanency. The scaling pattern will appear to be vibrating with the tiny "scales" moving, like white noise on a TV with no transmission. What is happening is in the cerebral cortex (at the back of the brain, which processes visual input) not in the actual eyes.

6. The God of the Epileptic

was the innocent party before the LORD; the young women drifting deeper into a hell of her own making.

Provided we do not make a conscious decision to follow the path of evil, to heed the advice of such evil spirits, then demons can do us no real harm. The boy in Mark 9 was clearly not cooperating with this demon. One only has to think of how sane and normal, cool and calm most twentieth-century dictators—for that matter most politicians!— appeared: demons did not need to trigger something like epileptic seizures in them to ensure their full cooperation with evil.

Being in Christ does not necessarily inoculate us perfectly from the dangers of pain and suffering in this world, or from evil—and we must always remember that we live in a free and dangerous universe—the degree of protection, insularity, is directly in accord with, issuing from, our relationship with the Christ, that relationship is defined by our beliefs and ethics and our actions (works issuing from faith). Epilepsy defines frailty. It lays open our vulnerability. If we have established that the mind can be subject to forces from outside of what we take to be perceivable reality then not only bad forces but also good forces could act upon the mind and in turn upon the brain. And good forces, good spirits, could trigger an epileptic seizure in one who is prone to such attacks in the same way that more tangible triggers may cause an attack. If the brain, or part of the brain, has a weakness then something, even with good intention, may act as a trigger.

Consider the account of Saul on the road to Damascus: a Spirit-enabled encounter with the risen and ascended Christ had a dramatic and cataclysmic effect on him (Acts 9:1–18). His symptoms are reminiscent of an epileptic seizure (phasing between *simple partial* and *complex partial*, between consciousness and altered consciousness), both in the attack on the road and in the details given at the point of his healing at the hands of Ananias: Saul/Paul's temporary blindness (an extended period of *postictal* confusion?) indicates the possibility of a seizure in the rear of the cerebral cortex (the outer layer of the brain), which processes information from the eyes before sending it to the temporal lobes at the front of the brain for interpretation, recognition, and so forth. This period of extended postictal confusion appears to have generated *scintillating scotoma*, or conversely *retinal migraine* (the two conditions are similar but not the same), though both are often referred to by sufferers as *migraine aura*, and can occur—rarely—in both eyes simultaneously. This is a visual effect that precedes or sometimes follows on from a migraine, or accompanies a migraine.[18] Pertinently, it is sometimes part of *postictal* state (i.e., post seizure). The person will be normal, conscious, and looking, say at a house, but then a twinkling noise pattern (like white noise on a television screen that has lost signal) will start, sometimes in the center of the eye(s), or to one side, and grow to encompass the visual field and thereby effectively blind the person, though there may be some peripheral vision. This may be black-grey-white, or with some color.[19] The attack may last minutes or up to an hour; in rare occurrences it may last for several days—or weeks, or months, or years. After an episode of *status epilepticus*, Hilary, my wife, had this condition in the lower right-hand corner of her visual field (no more than around 3–4 percent of the visual field), in the right eye, continuously for six years!—It then simply disappeared. If it had been in the center of her visual field (like Saul?) then she would have been effectively blind.

What does the account tell us in the Acts of the Apostle? The key passage is when Ananias, several days after the conversion/seizure (on the road to Damascus) visits: "So Ananias went and entered the house. He laid his hands on Saul and said, 'Brother Saul, the Lord Jesus, who appeared to you on your way here, has sent me so that you may regain your sight and be filled with the Holy Spirit.' And immediately something like scales fell from his eyes, and his sight was restored" (Acts 9:17–18b).[20] The key here is the phrase, "something like scales (*hōs lepídes*)."[21] Sufferers of *scintillating scotoma* or *retinal migraine* have attempted to visualize in photographs or drawings the appearance of these *migraine auras*. The pictures produced often look like fine tiny, animated, scales that obscure

18   See, for a brief and succinct definition and description, Wikipedia: *Scintillating Scotoma*: https://en.wikipedia.org/wiki/Scintillating_scotoma and Retinal Migraine: https://en.wikipedia.org/wiki/Retinal_migraine

19   Google "migraine aura," selecting images, to see the variety and type; these are "photo-shopped" images made by people who suffer from this condition, and are therefore comparable by analogy.

20   (v. 17) "*Apēlthen dé Hananías kaíēlthen eis tēn oikían, kaí epitheís ep' autón tás cheíras eípen: Saoúl adelfé, ho kúrios apéstalkén me, Iēsoús ho oftheís soi en tē hodō hē érchou, hópōs anablépsēs kaí plēsthēs pneúmatos hagíou.* (v. 18) *kaí euthéōs apépesan autoú apó tōn ofthalmōn hōs lepídes, anéblepsén te kaí anastás ebaptísthē.*", (my emphasis) Acts 9:17–18b, *Novum Testamentum Graece*, 346.

21   (Acts 9:18)"*hōs lepídes*": Greek: *lepides*, "scales," "flakes," from lepis, or lepra, scaliness (hence leprosy): a literal translation (Nestle-Aland), "And immediately fell from eyes, his, as it were, scales."

6. The God of the Epileptic

what is being looked at. Saul came face-to-face with the resurrected Christ—God—and survived the encounter, but not unscathed. According to the Pentateuch (Exod 33:20; cf. Gen 32:30; 33:23; Judg 6:22; Isa 6:5), he should have died: clearly pain, disability, blindness here, is God's mercy!

In the case of the apostle Paul, the aura, the visual "scales," encompassed both eyes (what was happening was not in the eye or the optic nerve, but neurological, in the rear of the cerebral cortex, the visual processor) for three days, obscuring *all* his vision like an eclipse. This we may cautiously assert was perhaps *postictal status* (i.e., a continuous state of *scintillating scotoma* or *retinal migraine*); he could have remained like this for the rest of his life. But God sent Ananias to heal him. Was the apostle Paul an epileptic? Not necessarily so, for this was one attack, one seizure, yes, at a cataclysmic moment in his life, a point of crisis. This *scintillating scotoma* or *retinal migraine*, if it was such, may be considered to be an unfortunate side-effect issuing from his encounter with Jesus, which had triggered the seizure, phasing between *simple partial* and *complex partial.* Such a one-off seizure was triggered by an encounter with the Holy Spirit on the road to Damascus; the healing came at the hands of and from the holiness of Ananias, who was a channel, or conduit, for the Holy Spirit.

We may compartmentalize symptoms into classifiable conditions/diseases, but these are human structures imposed on the brain and the mind. When sinful humanity meets the divine, then something has to give, deep inside the complexity of our brains, with the ramifications that the mind is both independent of, yet intimately intertwined with the brain. If an epileptic is touched in such a way by the Holy Spirit then the frailty of a brain prone to epileptic seizures may result in an attack. A priest-monk of the Community of the Resurrection in Mirfield, Yorkshire, once commented to Hilary that perhaps God could do more through her with the epilepsy than without it! Hilary wrote about the perplexing question of self: "I still find it strange even now to hear from another what has occurred in epileptic activity and have no memory of it whatever; particularly if my behavior in this state has been bizarre, childlike, or not recognizing self, those around me, or the place, however familiar. It can be terrifying with hindsight." And again in another letter, ". . . I can't remember anything. It is akin to living with two selves, the first being God's gift initially without the epilepsy. The second self, that is possibly God's gift too, with the epilepsy, which is totally unpredictable—disturbances from mild to severe can occur without warning, or cancel memory—the first I know of their occurrence is when told, or finding myself in an unknown place which I eventually recognize as say . . . our house." This element of two gifts, a dual self, can sound disturbing to some but it may be that this is true of all of us, that there are two selves in all of us (Jung spoke often about the shadow self). It is just that in Hilary's case the epilepsy throws this into sharp focus.

A pertinent question a Jesuit priest put to me once was, did the boy in Mark's Gospel continue to have mild seizures after Jesus had cast out the demon? The demon had clearly worsened the boy's condition, and in exorcising Jesus may have given partial or complete healing to the brain *as well as casting out the demon*. Grace protects, but we continue to *fall* (*simil iustus et peccator*), if through sin we move away from the Lord's grace then we become more subject to the vagaries and vicissitudes of this reality; however, there is also a general debilitation in the aging process which will mean various parts of our bodies will ultimately fail—including our brains.

VII. KNOWING

Epilepsy in many ways exposes the delusions of epistemic certainty in much Enlightenment-led philosophy, that is, in the form of linguistics and epistemology, perception and knowledge. One only has to think of what perception, cognition, and knowing is like for an *idiot savant*. For example, in the film *Rain Man*, an autistic, *idiot savant* is presented accurately, who seemingly calculates without complex sums, without using time or cognition. Mozart, for instance, would sometimes wake up in a morning with a complete symphony in his mind; he could see it; all he had to do was write it down. I have noted similar events with Hilary, particularly when she is in complex partial seizures. This appears to be thinking outside of time. Many epileptics experience an eschatological crisis in the aura preceding a seizure. Several neurologists have voiced the opinion regarding the temporal lobes in the front of the brain that it was as if they were put there so we may know about God, so that God could communicate with us.[22]

Partial seizures do lead to what could be considered strange behavior: a complex partial seizure in an individual can resemble extreme dementia, yet the individual recovers his/her right mind—most of the

---

22   See: http://www.bbc.co.uk/science/horizon/2003/godonbraintrans.shtml.

6. The God of the Epileptic

time, unless the brain is permanently damaged, or the seizure progresses into *status epilepticus* (continuous, violent, full seizures, where the brain-body most often simple shakes itself to death). Yet if we conquer our fears when caring and observing, *complex partial seizures* can lead us to perceive some profound behavior in the relationship between God and the person suffering the seizure. I can recall four examples. (These are not isolated examples, these are a regular occurrence.)

First, in a state of complex partial seizure Hilary may be animated, focused, but exhibiting the automatistic form of altered consciousness like someone with dementia but characterized by the gauche awkward limb movements and facial expressions of someone with cerebral palsy: she may be highly active or passive, but not in her right mind—or so-called right mind. She entered a state like this once when we were in the chapel of an Anglican religious community in Oxford. The nuns did not mind but others regarded it as inappropriate behavior: Hilary was kneeling, her head and eyes darting all over the place, her face exhibiting an almost angelic holiness. She commented in fractured words and broken sentences saying, "Look, we can put them here!" and proceeded to mold little invisible "somethings" in her fingers and place them on the back of the chair in front. This went on for some time and fortunately the seizure did not progress into a deeper, more dangerous attack. Hilary's head flitted up-and-down, to-and-fro, looking around the chapel, smiling with joy and gently gurgling with fascination at the play of light from one or two candles in the evening light. Only as she came out of the seizure and normality returned did she adopt the behavior and etiquette normally expected of such a situation (evening prayer in a monastic chapel), and lucidly asked me in a puzzled voice what had happened, where she was, and so on, knowing that things were different, time had gone, and she remembered not. When an epileptic is in a state of altered consciousness they may in most instances mimic other people's behavior without seeming to make a conscious decision. Nobody in the chapel was doing anything remotely resembling what Hilary did in molding the little invisible "somethings" in her fingers. There was nothing in my knowledge of Hilary and her past behavior resembling this behavior. Was what she was doing in effect making an offering, a sort of prayerful presentation in her fingers as best she could under the circumstances of her altered consciousness? This was conscious behavior—but altered.

Second, in early September 2001, Hilary experienced a vivid dream that stayed with her for days: a powerful dream-vision of two jet airliners flying nose vertically in the air next to each other, their engines were on full-power, but this meant both planes stayed still, the thrust merely countering gravity. People on board the two planes were contacting loved ones by mobile phone to say farewell because they knew they would die—when the fuel ran out each plane in turn crashed slowly to the ground consumed in dust and fire. This dream was one week before 9/11. There were many instances the world over of people experiencing dreams and visions in the weeks before the attacks on America, which were prophetic: 9/11 has profound eschatological significance—it is an eschatological event from the Last Judgment breaking into our reality. Was this *krisis* brought about by the withdraw of grace? To adapt and extend a Barthian trope from his early work, 9/11 was in effect a moment from the *eschaton* that punctured our space-time reality, which reverberated and echoed out through our time. *A posteriori*, the effects are obvious, but the visions and intimations that people experienced were prior to the event (note how in Hilary's vision the cries of those doomed to die echoed through time). An epileptic brain is by definition more open to such intimation, to influence, to acceptance of visions than is the brain of Kantian man. But Kantian man would find a way to dismiss the significance and meaning let alone the existence of such visions simply by cordoning off, excluding.

Third, during a complex partial seizure, Hilary started talking, but it was all confused, no perceivable words or meaning, though there was clearly some sort of sentence structure. However, during the seizure she continued to write. On looking at the writing I realized that it was all written backwards: perfectly backwards, perfectly formed—not just the words placed in a backward order, but every letter was faultlessly inverted. The writing was perfectly, cursively, inverted, including, crucially, Hilary's flow and unique handwriting style. This would be a task that would take us mere normal mortals many minutes to complete even a simple sentence. However, in Hilary's case the writing had continued at the same speed as before with no change in style and cursive flow—and it did not look inferior to her normal handwriting. I then began to realize that some of her speech was perfectly inverted, backwards, like the writing.

Fourth, when Hilary was once wired up to a computer in hospital for seventy-two hours of video-recorded telemetry, they noted how a seizure would start but then her brain effectively firewalled the two affected

6. The God of the Epileptic

areas (a generalized seizure in the left-hand hemisphere of the cerebral cortex and a focal seizure in the right-hand hippocampus/temporal lobe), allowing a degree of normality, and certainly prevented the seizure going downhill into *status epilepticus*. In this "firewalled" state Hilary appeared superficially normal, but had no memory afterwards. The consultant commented that they were just beginning to observe and understand something of this phenomenon but, he added, all we do is knock out the brain, anaesthetize it, with anticonvulsants. Hilary has been through every possible anticonvulsant with only some degree of control achieved; some have actively worsened the condition.[23] Neurology is a very imprecise science, and wisdom dictates extreme caution. Do we all have this ability to firewall, to control, potentially catastrophic events in our brain? To what extent is this phenomenon pneumatologically authored/controlled? If so, how and when does it work, or fail? And where is the will of God in this?

Eschatologically epilepsy points to nihilism and chaos; *status epilepticus*—that is a continuous state of epileptic seizure lasting for hours until the person dies or, if s/he recovers, is brain damaged—is the ultimate path of epilepsy: the brain enveloped in a violent unstoppable electrical storm, the body writhing and convulsing, each sub-seizure rising and lowering into a nihilistic crescendo. *Status epilepticus* is eschatological, it is the withdraw of grace, and it can so easily kill. It also illustrates how without God sustaining creation teleologically all would collapse into chaos and then into nothingness.

VIII. AFFLICTION

Epileptic seizures may or may not be considered a disability, though such a classification is often to do with an individual's aims and objectives in life, and with lifestyle-identity politics: Icarus could have claimed that he was disabled because he clearly could not fly—properly! However,

---

23   One cannot help but think of the woman with the hemorrhage in Mark's Gospel and the evangelist's rather acerbic criticism of the doctors: "She had endured much under many physicians, and had spent all that she had; and she was no better, but rather grew worse" (Mark 5:26). It is interesting that Luke, the physician, does not include this quip against doctors in his gospel. In addition, one should not forget that over three million animals per year are the subject of medical experiments and then killed in vivisection clinics in the UK, in part, to produce new medicines like anti-convulsants, or to attempt to fight of dementia in brains that will ultimately fail.

epilepsy can be seen as an affliction: we have to acknowledge a distinction between suffering and affliction. The cross is not primarily about suffering: it is about affliction. This is a distinction that was made so well by the twentieth-century French Jewish philosopher who became a Christian, Simone Weil:

> In the realm of suffering, affliction is something apart, specific and irreducible. It is quite a different thing from simple suffering. It takes possession of the soul and marks it through and through with its own particular mark, the mark of slavery. Slavery as practised by ancient Rome is simply the extreme form of affliction. The men of antiquity, who knew a lot about the subject, used to say a man loses half his soul the day he becomes a slave.[24]

The vagaries and vicissitudes—to Aristotle, brute necessity—of this reality where we reside in *postlapsarian* exile hurl us around, for good or ill, whether we are just or unjust; but this does not deny the divine will for our lives. Weil noted how some people when afflicted may land at the foot of the cross; if so all they can do is look up and worship, accept God in Christ for what *he* is and what *he* has done; or they can rebel, they can reject the Christ and the suffering-affliction that comes to them. Even if they know not of the event of the crucifixion of Christ Jesus, God incarnate, in terms of cognitive knowledge, the reality—acceptance or rejection—holds true. Weil wrote:

> A blind mechanism taking no account of the degree of spiritual perfection, continually tosses people hither and thither and flings some of them at the very foot of the Cross. It is up to them only to keep, or not to keep, their eyes turned towards God through the upheaval.[25]

Furthermore, Weil often asserted that each person has "in a period of his or her life the possibility to take root in God": the point of conversion.[26] Hence, the body, the flesh, has an immense de-creative (Weil's term) importance in convincing us, when life gets difficult, when and if we

24   Weil, *L'Amour de Dieu et le Malheur (The Love of God and Affliction)*, in Weil, *The Simone Weil Reader*.

25   Weil, *L'Amour de Dieu et le Malheur*.

26   Weil, *The New York Notebook*, in *First and Last Notebooks*. See also Weil, *The Notebooks of Simone Weil Volume 1*. This is part of a two-volume translation of Weil's notebooks from the period c. 1933–41, trans Arthur Wills from, *Les Cahiers de Simone Weil Volumes 1–3*.

6. The God of the Epileptic

accept affliction, that this is not all there is to us: hence Weil's belief that without affliction we would be tempted to believe that we were in paradise. Affliction cuts deeply into the soul, it isolates the person from those around, it may lead to marginalization; like epilepsy, it sets the afflicted apart in a way that the healthy commenting in academic impartiality can never know or understand. Affliction resulting from a violent and abusive childhood sets the afflicted apart for life, even when this is hidden by a veneer of normality: "I am a reproach among all my enemies, but especially among my neighbors, and am repulsive to my acquaintances; those who see me outside flee from me" (Ps 31:11); however, such childhood affliction does, if the Spirit is allowed to work, equip one to care for someone with epilepsy in a way the normal, the healthy, cannot.

Talk of affliction naturally leads us to Job. The knowledge from the cross—*lignum crucis arbor scientiae* (the wood of the cross, is the tree of knowledge)—is a knowledge that does extend to those who do not suffer, those who have never experienced affliction, simply because they can know, can see, observe. Some may be able to empathize, but it is the failing of the human condition—part of our *postlapsarian* exile—that we can never really know, be a part of, another's affliction. This disables the healthy, the proud, when they attempt to preach to the afflicted as Job's detractors attempted to. God's answer at the close of the Book of Job is as oblique as Job's protestations of innocence are pertinent. We could assume that Job was unfortunate enough to come into contact with what appears to be leprosy. As a leper he was subject to the social mores of the day: rejection. We could therefore interpret his affliction as misfortune. However, on a deeper level, as the dialogue between God and Satan over Job illustrates, nothing is outside of the divine will. Job's misfortune and his affliction is an event, an occasion in time indelibly linked to God's actions in the world. It may be too easy simply to dismiss meaning, likewise too easy to blame suffering and affliction on personal/individual sins. If Job had been cared for, not marginalized, his questioning would not have been so fierce, but then his understanding of God would have been the poorer and he would have been more amenable to God's creation, he would have felt comfortable in this world. It is important to remember that what Job was suffering from primarily was not leprosy, or a physical illness, but *affliction*: *humiliation* and *marginalization* resulting from the self-righteousness, the religious self-righteousness, of those around him. Likewise the father of the epileptic boy (Mark 9) is more righteous in his despair before the Lord of heaven and earth than the disciples who failed to heal and then became self-absorbed in a reflective de-briefing over their status as religious professionals. Karl Barth noted how Job is more righteous in his puzzlement and in his questioning than his detractors:

> And do not regard it merely as a literary flourish if I say that Dostoevsky, by confronting the unteachable atheist Ivan Karamazov with the pure fool Alyosha, who has no arguments against his revolt, has perhaps done more for a real proof of God than Anselm and Thomas, Schleiermacher and Ritschl. If in the Book of Job it is the questioning Job who is in the right and not his friends (Job 42:7), this probably means that if there is any pointer to God or proof of God for us at all, it will be found where we come up against the mystery of God.[27]

Those who suffer affliction know this mystery of God on an intimate level. We may postulate that there is an intensity in this affliction that transcends cognitive knowledge. For example, does not an abused, broken, and suffering child living hundreds of years before the incarnation, on the other side of the world, know Christ in a way that transcends knowledge because of a degree of affliction shared with the Christ?

IX. CONCLUSION

What has this paper been about? Such a condition as epilepsy challenges Kant's closed universe (or more pertinently a post-Kant, closed universe), it points to the praeternatural, the supra-natural, to transcendence. Such a condition as epilepsy exposes the flaws within a Newtonian conception of the universe, of life, indeed the delusions of Kantian man. Such a condition as epilepsy affirms our *fallen* status and our utter dependence on the Savior, God incarnate, crucified and resurrected for our redemption: we cannot save ourselves, we are truly lost. This is reflected in the state of our mind-brain. What has this paper been about? It argues from the premise of how we find ourselves. This is not natural theology because

---

27 The comment was part of the so-called, Göttingen Dogmatics, lectures given 1924–25: «*Wenn im Hiobbuch unter den beteiligten Menschen der fragende Hiob Recht bekommt und nicht seine antwortenden Freunde [Hi. 42:7], so dürfte damit ausgesprochen sein, daß Hinweis auf Gott, Beweis Gottes, sofern dem Menschen solches überhaupt zusteht, da zu finden ist, wo wir auf Gottes Geheimnis stoßen.*» Barth, *Unterricht in der christlichen Religion 2, Zweite Band: Die Lehre von Gott/Die Lehre vom Menschen*, 4 Kapitel. Der Lehre von Gott, §.15 Die Erkennbarkeit Gottes, 46.

6. The God of the Epileptic

such a condition as epilepsy exposes the human predicament in a way that cosseted and closeted philosophical speculation will not: epilepsy is, admittedly, existential. But then Barth never shook of his existentialism, and after all is said and done, the Bible is existential.[28] Earlier we looked at Blake's philosophical portrait of Newton, it is now time to briefly note another work of art from the period of the Enlightenment: Goya's picture, *The Sleep of Reason Produces Monsters* (1799).[29] The illusion of clarity given to reason where it marginalizes revelation, where imagination, all that is transcendent, is ignored is all too clear: follow the progression of thought through from Kant into Schleiermacher and Hegel, then onto Feuerbach and Marx and you have the twin monsters of Nazism and Stalinism. The master copy of this etching in The Prado, Madrid, has the caption, "Fantasy abandoned by reason produces impossible monsters: united with her, she is the mother of the arts and the origin of their marvels":[30] imagination without reason dissolves into nihilistic confusion, so does reason when she abandons revelation. There is a salutary lesson here: revelation and reason must sit together, but, revelation places, situates, reason; reason does not confine, dictate the place for revelation.

It is only our familiarity with what we consider to be normal that makes the existential experience before the crucified Christ of one with epilepsy seem so different, so strange, but the disruption of identity

---

28 Eduard Thurneysen commented, in the context of a seventieth-birthday volume of correspondence and essays for Karl Barth, "Because his concern was with this message, or, as one could also say, because Karl Barth thinks not abstractly but concretely, which means on the basis of the Bible, and because biblical thinking is in itself existential thinking [«*und weil biblisches Denken in sich selber existentielles Denken ist . . .* »], Karl Barth's theological thinking was from the beginning directed to the life of humanity." See: Thurneysen, "die Anfänge," in Eduard Thurneysen (ed.), *Antwort—Festschrift zum 70 Geburtstag von Karl Barth*, 832.

29 Francisco Jose de Goya y Lucientes (1746–1828), *El Sueño de la Razon Produce Monstruos* (*The Sleep of Reason Produces Monsters*), Plate 43 of *Los Caprichos* (*The Caprices*), second edition, 1799, etching and aquatint, 18.1cm. x 12.2 cm. The eighty plates of the series Los Caprichos was privately published by Goya, being first advertised for sale in the Spanish newspaper *Diario de Madrid* in 1799 as a criticism of "human errors and vices." The subjects are often obscure, however they are a severe criticism of both political and religious figures, and are in many ways a precursor of the sort of acerbic criticism of religion-politics found later in the century in the writings of Søren Kierkegaard and Fyodor Mikhailovich Dostoevsky, then in the twentieth century in the work of Karl Barth and Dietrich Bonhoeffer.

30 "*La fantasia abandonada de la razon, produce monstruos imposibles: unida con ella, es madre de las artes y origen de sus marabillas.*"

must therefore be seen not as disabling, but enabling, *in Christ* (John 3: being born again—the old self/ego must die, must give way). What does observing epilepsy teach us? What do we learn and how do we grow through loving someone *in Christ* who endures intractable complex partial, focal, and generalized epilepsy?—that is, compared to Kantian man's impartial interrogation? In many ways this paper has been about the recognition of the sufferance of salvation: thus, noted the importance of Simone Weil's perceptions with regard to affliction. We may also note the apostle Paul's comments:

> We have this treasure in clay jars, so that it may be made clear that this extraordinary power belongs to God and does not come from us. We are afflicted in every way, but not crushed; perplexed, but not driven to despair; persecuted, but not forsaken; struck down, but not destroyed; always carrying in the body the death of Jesus, so that the life of Jesus may also be made visible in our bodies. For while we live, we are always being given up to death for Jesus' sake, so that the life of Jesus may be made visible in our mortal flesh. So death is at work in us, but life in you. 2 Corinthians 4:7–12

There is therefore a strong, very present eschatology in this paper. But is there a weak ecclesiology in this paper? Epileptics are so often people outside of the church, shunned, marginalized, whereas "normal" Christians either fear what they see, condemn—assuming that they are normal people, are whole, healed, and flawless, "un-*fallen.*" Or the "normal" people simply don't understand people with epilepsy and their carers, and categorize them as outside of their society and useful only to be gossiped about: the love of God for epileptics and their carers, to quote a phrase so often associated with Mother Teresa of Calcutta, is about loving until it hurts, and—like the boy in Mark 9—loving from the depths of our poverty, our inabilities. Mother Teresa also understood how the poor and afflicted, the marginalized and despised, actually qualified and legitimized the church—or not—according to the church's response to them.

I will end on a speculative note, suggesting that the Parable of Dives and Lazarus (Luke 16:19–31) can be read as an ecclesiological warning. Can we not see Dives as representative of the *ecclesia visibilis*; Lazarus as representative of the *ecclesia invisibilis*. Dives has everything in this life: health, wealth, status and power; he is ingratiated with the Roman oppressors, practices their religion (he wears the purple), whilst being

6. The God of the Epileptic

given a glorious Jewish funeral with paid mourners; he thinks he is caring for the poor by allowing Lazarus to sit at the gate to his city to beg. Lazarus has nothing: he is starving and destitute, sick and marginalized, shunned, ignored, even the dogs come to lick his sores—he is outside of religious society, he cannot be religious in the respectable sense. Upon death his carcass is thrown on the midden, the rubbish dump. But the roles are reversed eschatologically, dynamically: there is a compensatory factor at work here. This may appear dualistic, but if there is a dualism it is because humanity forges the distinction, pushes some people like the redeemed and saved Lazarus into an afflicted and marginalized state, whilst proudly reveling in their religiosity, like the condemned and lost Dives. No, this is not a weak ecclesiology. It is actually a very strong, very high, ecclesiology: our human efforts to define church come to nothing: Christ in judgment defines the church (to adapt Matthew 25, where the first person is Christ: "for when I was sick and afflicted with seizures and knew not my right mind you cared for me, you did not exclude me from your religion, you did not pass judgment on me, you were not afraid of the sight of my convulsion").

From the perspective of the carer, carrying epilepsy is like guiding a blind person along the top of a fog-bound cliff where the mists swirl and the ground keeps changing. This would be a task impossible without the intimations of the Holy Spirit: reliance on the Spirit is total and real, objectively. This fog-bound cliff is indeed the cloud of unknowing but must also be trusted implicitly. For those who are afflicted all they can do is wait on the Lord's grace, as Lazarus did, and wait in patient endurance (*en hupomone*[31] from the scriptures, used by Simone Weil), as Dives did not: love transforms affliction and suffering so that it becomes part of the *imitatio christi*, a privileged path of sanctification, the sufferance of salvation. For we are all held eschatologically by Christ's love for us, without which we would fall through all that we take for space and time and reality into nothingness. Perhaps only when we can fully understand the nihilism and nothingness inherent in our *postlapsarian* exile are we truly fit and prepared to go home: to walk the path home that Christ has opened up for us—hence the sufferance of salvation. We can never feel truly at home in this world, such a realization is part of our existential

---

[31] Steadfastness, constancy, endurance. In the New Testament, the characteristic of a man who is not swerved from his deliberate purpose and his loyalty to faith and piety by even the greatest trials and sufferings: a patient, enduring, sustaining, perseverance

krisis: but it is the God of the epileptic who saves, who redeems, who exorcises, who protects us from evil, who loves us in freedom, and who calls us home.

* * *

BRIEF GLOSSARY OF EPILEPTIC SEIZURES

An epileptic seizure is an electrical malfunction in the brain: the electrical flow along predefined neural pathways is interrupted, distorted, the pathways are overloaded resulting in seemingly chaotic electrical activity, which can have graphic and catastrophic implications. We use these pathways for thinking, therefore seizures affect profoundly us.

General seizures
General seizures are evidenced on electronic scanning devices as a general electrical storm in an area of the brain, but without a focal point.

Focal seizures
Focal seizures are evidenced on electronic scanning devices as a particular electrical storm in a part of the brain where there is discernable damage: a focal point (often in the temporal lobes at the front of the brain that interpret our sense perception and in many ways give us a mental model of the world, the reality, we inhabit). This focal point is usually scar tissue from inflicted damage, or scarring from previous seizures.

Postictal confusion
A period of confusion, puzzlement, intense questioning following a seizure: the confusion may last for up to an hour. The person is in their "right mind," so to speak, but appears not to cognitively "process" answers given in response to his/her questions, or fully perceive what has happened.

An absence (momentary simple partial seizure)—
A momentary loss of consciousness, a fracturing of the continuity of memory, perception, and identity, perhaps for less than a second; this may or may not be followed by confusion and a realization that something is wrong,

missing. There may be several momentary absences over, say, a morning, leading to debilitating confusion. (An absence seizure used to be called a *petit mal* seizure.)

Simple partial seizure
A simple partial seizure is an absence-like seizure lasting for several minutes, but where the person is conscious that something is happening this is often accompanied by hallucination, distortion of perception, etc.

Complex partial seizure
A complex partial seizure is the same as a simple partial seizure but with loss of consciousness or more pertinently the person exhibits changed or altered consciousness. The person may be animated, like someone who is sleepwalking. A complex partial seizure could last from a minute, to over an hour: the longer the seizure the more dangerous it becomes.

Atonic seizure
A drop attack: all muscle tone suddenly goes from the body and the person falls to the ground, with associated damage/bruising. (The brain is actually controlling and maintaining our muscle tone, posture, organs, and life functions all the time without our awareness, so to speak.) After a drop attack someone might then be in a simple or complex partial seizure, or will exhibit postictal confusion.

Tonic clonic seizure
A full, as distinct from partial, seizure: this is what used to be called, pejoratively, a "fit," the classic epileptic seizure where the body becomes rigid and jerks, often with foaming at the mouth, as a result of the intensity of the electrical storm(s) in the brain (see Mark 9): this used to be called a grand mal seizure.

status epilepticus
A continuous state of tonic clonic epileptic seizures, usually one phasing into another with perhaps a period of the seizure slowing for a few minutes, then building again. This *status* may last for hours or days: if the person recovers then s/he is usually brain-damaged; though in most cases death is the logical path as the seizures become unstoppable and the brain is wrecked.

SUDEP
An acronym for "sudden unexplained death from epilepsy," which may be related to a seizure or simply the brain "switching-off" for no discernable reason.

Vivid descriptions of seizures can be found in the highly charged theological novel *The Idiot*, by the Russian writer and prophet Fyodor Mikhailovich Dostoevsky, who himself was afflicted with epilepsy. A radio dramatization of *The Idiot* was presented on BBC R4 (radio 4) several years ago. This included one of the best dramatization of the pre-seizure state of a sufferer: see, https://www.youtube.com/watch?v=aB4sxAn1FFY. The pain and anxiety, the bewilderment, for the carer of a child with epilepsy was shown with insight, understanding, and profundity in a BBC drama, *The Lost Prince* (2003, dir. Stephen Poliakoff).

Conclusion:
A Negative *Telos*—
An Apophatic–Kataphatic *Eschaton*

If the aim of these essays was to demonstrate the diverse and divisive, socio-political and religio-cultural "*krises*" that bedevil humanity as it lurches teleologically into the *eschaton*, then perhaps these essays will stimulate and endorse discussion and a rekindling of a traditional/orthodox understanding of the *eschaton*. As such we may ask in conclusion what it is that characterizes, perhaps unifies, these human teleological "*krises*" leading upward to the *eschaton*? What trope can we propose to identify this chaos and contradiction? What underpins the confused and sometimes contradictory *teloi*, which humanity generates as it staggers through falling darkness towards its ultimate end in a character that is real and confused, arbitrary and conflicting, whilst convinced of the rightness of the moral relativism that it lives by and actively promotes to the detriment of others?

Theologically, perhaps the only sense that can be made out of this socio-political, religio-cultural confusion is *negation*. Primary in this understanding is Karl Barth's dialectic that identified God's "No" to our "Yes," and God's "Yes" to our "No."[1] This negation goes further. Barth's early development will illustrate this and serve to pull together what underpins these essays. If we think we are doing well and moving positively towards a good judgement... we are wrong; if we despair at our actions, and believe we are failing and it is impossible for God to bless us,

---

1 Barth's exposition of this particular dialectic may be found in *Church Dogmatics*, §.42 "The Yes of God the Creator," 325–407. See also, its origins, in *Römerbrief* (2nd ed.), 38 & 331. See also, generally, *CD* §§.28–31.

we are wrong. We are correct in our negativity, but we may be exonerated in judgement!

I. THE VINE AND THE BRANCHES

> I am the true vine, and my Father is the gardener. He cuts off every branch in me that bears no fruit, while every branch that does bear fruit he prunes[a] so that it will be even more fruitful. . . . No branch can bear fruit by itself; it must remain in the vine. Neither can you bear fruit unless you remain in me. I am the vine; you are the branches. If you remain in me and I in you, you will bear much fruit; apart from me you can do nothing. If you do not remain in me, you are like a branch that is thrown away and withers; such branches are picked up, thrown into the fire and burned. If you remain in me and my words remain in you, ask whatever you wish, and it will be done for you. This is to my Father's glory, that you bear much fruit, showing yourselves to be my disciples.
>
> JOHN 15:1–2, 4B–8

Early in his career as a minister and theologian, Karl Barth underwent a reordering of his beliefs—as we noted in the first of these essays—a *Wendung und Retraktation*. Further to this conversion we can consider Barth's concern for God's *aseity*—God's right, so to speak, to be God, independent from all that humanity seeks to impose on God in theological definitions and religious projections.[2] ". . . God is now seen as a reality complete and whole in itself apart from and prior to the knowing activity of human individuals."[3] Barth also commented that "world remains world, but God is God": «*Welt bleibt Welt ... Daß Gott Gott ist.*»[4] Therefore we must "recognize that God is God, "God as he is recognized in the life and word of Jesus," that "he is, from the ground up, from reason, something utterly different to all else . . . ."[5]

    2   For a full and detailed analysis of Barth's apophatism see Brazier "Barth's First Commentary on Romans (1919)—An Exercise in Apophatic Theology?" 387–403. See also, Brazier, *Barth and Dostoevsky* (2008) Ch. 2 The Apophatic Barth—God's Aseity, 19–28.

    3   McCormack, *Karl Barth's Critically Realistic Dialectical Theology*, 129.

    4   Barth "*Kriegszeit und Gottesreich*" (1915), 120f.

    5   «*Daß Gott Gott ist, «Gott so wie er im Leben und Wort Jesu zu erkennen ist", daß er «etwas von Grund aus Anderes ist als Alles Andre"*» (Barth's words in German parentheses). Herbert Anzinger, *Gaube und kommunikative Praxis*, 121.

Conclusion

> What concern to us is the God who was introduced to us once as the highest idea of ethics? The 'Father in heaven,' to whom Jesus points us is no Ideality, which lives from its opposition [antithesis?], no formal, unreal magnitude [entity?], that finally also belongs in this world, no idea of justice or love rivalling the ideas of ethics, but rather the reality, out of which our entire world has fallen. That God is our creator and origin in the other, for us, entirely new world, this would be the only positive thing that we can say. All our other speaking of God is a stammering, or it must if it should count seriously, exist in pure negation.[6]

If God's answer, for Barth, to our "Yes" is "No," and God's answer to our "No" is "Yes," does this constitutes a pruning, a constant temporal cutback and denial, a negation? This was a fundamental element in Barth's personal *telos*, foundational to the eschatology that characterized his work in *Der Römerbrief* and into his mature work in reordering theology back to the Christ and God's revelation. So what can this understanding tell us?

II. A KATAPHATIC-APOPHATISM; AN ASSERTION OF NEGATIVITY

In the context of humanity's reckless teleological careering towards the *eschaton*, and drawing on Barth's perceptions, we might consider how all our God-talk is a faltering stumble, a stammering, which can only be taken seriously if it is characterized by negation: an assertive negation, an apophatic assertion, thereby allowing God's revelation and purposes in Jesus Christ to permeate into us and thereby the disparate community that is the church: visible and invisible. This apophatism is not necessarily the negation found in Buddhist apophatism but a kataphatic apophatism that strips away all human pretentions, while asserting that *God is*. Following on from Barth, we must make space for the *Deus dixit*—the

---

6   The full text by Barth, quoted in Anzinger, is : «*Was soll uns der Gott, der uns einst als die höchste Idee der Ethik vorgestellt worden ist? Der «Vater im Himmel," auf den er [sc. Jesus] uns hinweist, ist keine Idealität, die von ihrem Gegensatz lebt, keine formale unreale Groß, die schließlich auch wieder in die Welt hineingehört, keine Idee der Gerechtigkeit oder der Liebe im Wetteifer der Ideen der Ethik, sondern die Wirklichkeit, aus der unsre ganze Welt herausgefallen ist. Daß Gott unser Schöpfer und Ursprung in der andern für uns ganz neuen Welt «ist, sei" das einzige Positive . . . , das wir sagen können. All unser sonstiges Reden von Gott ist ein Stammeln, oder es muß, wenn es ernst gelten soll, in lauter Negationen bestehen.*» Herbert Anzinger *Gaube und kommunikative Praxis*, 121–22 (Barth's words in German parentheses).

self-revelation of the *Deus abscondus* in Christ Jesus. Barth noted how he was not asserting "a mystical vacuum and not into a Buddhist nirvana," but rather how we must walk in this new life, this new relationship with the unknowable God.[7] Are we talking about distance?—a separation between the world and God in terms of *diastasis*, whereby two entities stand over against each other with no possibility of a synthesis (certainly not into a higher form of being in the worldly, or, we can assert, Hegelian sense)? For Barth this was *"thinking from or out of God."*[8] Such thinking was generated pneumatologically and was measured by its conformity to revelation.

Let us look a little more closely at Barth's comment from "Kriegszeit und Gottesreich" that «*etwas von Grund aus Anderes ist als Alles Ander.*» This is a difficult statement to comprehend: translating this in a manner that is quite close to the German in both vocabulary and syntax renders, "[*that God is*] *something other beyond ground(s), beyond reason(s), other as all*": therefore, God is from the ground-up, from reason, something utterly different to all else. Eschatologically, Barth wanted to avoid anthropomorphizing God, or encompassing God in spatial-temporal language, yet he also wanted to avoid reducing God to an abstract (Hegelian) idea. Thus he asserts that God *is* something, yet no *particular thing*; that God is no mere ethical ideal, indeed, the reality of God is utterly unlike anything we can conceive of or know. Is God beyond our concepts of reason, beyond the grounds of our thought systems, philosophies, and theologies? Or is Barth being intentionally paradoxical and dialectically ambiguous here? This is about human epistemic limitation and the inadequacy of language: linguistic negation through its apophatism asserts God's aseity and utter otherness in being. This is of fundamental importance in any attempt to understand the *eschaton* and humanity's teleological lurch into the darkness. Outside of Jesus Christ the most we can assert of God is «*ganz andere*» ("*entirely other*").

---

7   Barth, *Römerbrief* (1st ed.) (1919), 215, on Romans 6:1–14

8   « . . . [*e*]*in Denken von Gott aus.*» An idea drawn from Barth's discussions with Hermann Kutter. See, *Römerbrief* (1st ed.) (1919), 71f.; For an exposition see also, McCormack, *Karl Barth's Critically Realistic Dialectical Theology* (1995), 129–30.

III. APOPHATIC LANGUAGE AND CONCEPTS: ESCHATOLOGICAL NEGATIVITY . . . AN ASSERTION

If the *Deus dixit*, God's speaking through Jesus Christ, is the only intimation of eternity we can understand, then how does this play out in our understanding? We can in conclusion briefly look at how Barth expresses this in language and concept.

First, we can see negation used in relation to the knowledge of God and the doctrine of God. It is used for ensuring the distinctness, the wholly otherness of God beyond all human knowledge and understanding, beyond human categorization as an object or thing. God is not «*Ding in sich*» (*a thing in itself*),[9] not a metaphysical essence alongside other essences, not a second something, an-other, but the eternal, the transcendent, the pure «*Ursprung*» (origin) of everything that is. However, to say that God is no thing (i.e., no particular thing, as such) is not the same as saying God is *nothing* (*nothing at all*).[10] Within this context, for example, Barth uses the term *diastasis* (long before he discovered it also in the work of Kierkegaard) to express this critical distinction between God and this world: «*Welt bleibt Welt, das Gott Gott ist.*»

Second, we can see the use of negation as a refutation of the validity of natural theology, that is, the efforts made by men and women to define God, even invent gods, and attribute divine characteristics, without recourse to divine revelation, and thereby to define the *eschaton* in complimentary human terms. (It is important to remember that during the period following the publication of *Römerbrief* (1st ed.) Barth is still developing his skepticism of natural theology and it takes the form of a simple denial. This refutation does not have the theological explication that was to characterize his mature work.)

Third, there is the critical assumption that the churches and historical Christianity, human religiosity and piety (at best this is an organized religious response to the historical event of the incarnation and resurrection, at worst this is no more than religious projection), will always be subject to criticism and assessment—from the perspective

---

9   As used in *Römerbrief* (2nd ed.), 29–30 (ET, 51–53)

10   The subtlety of the English language here is not as clear in the German: «nein ding» (no thing) as compared to «nichts» (nothing), «Nichts» (nothingness) «gar nichts» (nothing at all).

of the gospel. Such a critique is negative because it looks critically, pessimistically, destructively on the religious efforts of humanity. All may not have served the gospel as they should have. Underlying this criticism is a belief in the aseity, sovereignty, and independence of God from humanity and human history. God in Christ is the final arbiter of whether human religion is acceptable or not, and on what terms, if any.

Fourth, we can see the emergence in the early lectures and addresses of a respect, under certain circumstances, for *negation as atheism – atheism as a negation*, a paradox. This is seen as the clearing away of all human conceptions and preconceptions, and especially projections. For example, Barth knew only too well that atheists might often have a better grasp of the truth of God than Christians immersed in religious culture.

Fifth and finally, there is negation in relation to the Christian life. Barth, like the apostle Paul, also uses negation as a characteristic of the Christian life (especially seen in both editions of *Der Römerbrief*). For example, to deny oneself and take up Christ's cross is a negation; Barth emphasizes in *Römerbrief* (2nd ed.) how love is defined in the negative in 1 Corinthians 13 (for example, *love is not* . . . , etc.). There is also the denial of this life as a paradoxical negation.[11] "This love is astonishingly negative and passive, different from all that we are otherwise accustomed to regard as love. Only in the great negations of 1 Corinthians 13 could it be adequately described: 'Love envieth not; love vaunteth not itself, is not puffed up, doth not behave itself unseemly, seeketh not her own, is not easily provoked, thinketh no evil.'"[12]

IV. WATCHING AND WAITING . . . STAYING

How do we approach the eschaton? What should define our *telos*? There is a clear reversal-inversion ethic or life principle in the gospel: those who exalt themselves will be abased; those who humble themselves will be exalted (*The Parable of the Pharisee and the Tax Collector*: Luke 18: 9–14). Those who are rich and powerful in this life will experience a reversal; those neglected and poverty struck will be rich in the next (*The Parable of Dives and Lazarus*: Luke 16:19–31). "Anyone who loves their life will lose

---

11   For example, 2 Cor 6:8b–10 & Matt 10:39
12   Thurneysen *Dostojewski* (1921), 65 (referring to 1 Cor 13:4b–5)

it, while anyone who hates their life in this world will keep it for eternal life." (John 12:25) So, does Barth's "Yes"/"No" dialectic reflects this? And today?—saints guide the way to heaven; celebrities suck people into hell? Writing on the life and commitment to Jesus of Jean Vanier, founder of L'Arche, the reporter Martin Bashir commented on Vanier's death,

> Jean Vanier devoted his life to what has been described as the upside down economics of Christianity: that the first shall be last. He embodied a principle first outlined in the New Testament by the Apostle Paul, who said, "When I am weak, then am I strong."[13]

So, we stay. We stand. If we try to be too positive (self-righteous), too lifestyle- and culture-assertive (*The Simpsons*), too domineering (identity politics), too destructive (war, conflict, slavery, abortion—mega holocausts), too active and busy (progress, success), too ambitious (status, wealth and power: feminists and freemasons) in trying to justify and advance ourselves, we fail and potentially condemn ourselves: this is a teleological conclusion we can read from these diverse essays. Our lives must be prophetic; we must challenge the world and all it stands for. If necessary we must stand and watch . . . and wait, look on that which others cannot bear. We sit: we stay. We serve. "If any one desire to be first, the same shall be last of all, and servant of all."[14] If necessary we must wait with the suffering of others and sit in the shadow of death (epilepsy). Watching and waiting—waiting on God—through the teleological chaos around us, as the *eschaton* beckons, we know not of the hour:

> On Good Friday Christians stay, helpless, looking into the loss and suffering of the Cross, like the women who were told to stay away when Jesus was dying. The women stood at a distance, pushed away from a horror, a spectacle, that was repulsive as it was politically astute. Sometimes all you can do is stay and wait . . . and cry out "How long, Oh Lord! How long!"[15]

---

13   BBC News website: https://www.bbc.co.uk/news/world-europe-48186136. Accessed May 10, 2019.

14   Mark 9:35; cf. Matt 20:26; 23:11; Mark 10:33–34; Luke 22:26

15   Right Revd Sarah Mullally, speaking on the "Thought for the Day" three-minute broadcast, as part of the *Today* news and current affairs radio program on BBC R4 (Mon–Fri, 06:00–09:00am; Sat, 0700–9:00). Broadcast, Good Friday 16th April 2019, 07:47–50. See, https://www.bbc.co.uk/programmes/p00szxv6. Archive of recordings: https://www.bbc.co.uk/programmes/p00szxv6/clips.

Select Bibliography

ARTICLES, LETTERS, AND PAPERS

Adam, Karl. "Die Theologie der Krisis." *Hochland* XXIII (1926) 271–86.
Aiken, Jane Andrews. "The Perspective Construction of Masaccio's 'Trinity' Fresco and Medieval Astronomical Graphics." In *Masaccio's Trinity*, edited by Rona Goffen, 90–107. Cambridge: Cambridge University Press, 1998.
Andrushko, Valerie A., Michele R. Buzon, Arminda M. Gibaja, Gordon F. McEwan, Antonio Simonetti, and Robert A. Creaser. "Investigating a Child Sacrifice Event from the Inca Heartland." *Journal of Archaeological Science* 38.2 (2011) 323–33.
Bainbridge, William S. "Extra-Terrestrial Tales." *Science* 279.5351 (1998) 671.
Barth, Karl. "The Architectural Problem of Protestant Places of Worship." In *Architecture in Worship the Christian Place of Worship (A Sketch of the Relationships between the Theology of Worship and the Architectural Conception of Christian Churches from the Beginnings to Our Day)*, edited by André Biéler, translated by Odette and Donald Elliott, 50–62. London: Oliver & Boyd, 1965.
———. "Barth writing to Eduard Thurneysen, 25. März 1918." In *Karl Barth–Eduard Thurneysen Briefwechsel Band I 1913–1921*, 388. Gesamtausgabe, Bearbeitet und herausgegeben von Eduard Thurneysen. Zürich: Theologischer Verlag, 1973.
———. "Barth writing to Eduard Thurneysen, 28. Dezember 1920." In *Karl Barth–Eduard Thurneysen Briefwechsel Band I 1913–1921*, 423. Gesamtausgabe, Bearbeitet und herausgegeben von Eduard Thurneysen. Zürich: Theologischer Verlag, 1973.
———. "Barth writing to Eduard Thurneysen, 3. Juni 1919." In *Karl Barth–Eduard Thurneysen Briefwechsel Band I 1913–1921*, 401. Gesamtausgabe, Bearbeitet und herausgegeben von Eduard Thurneysen. Zürich: Theologischer Verlag, 1973.
———. "Barth writing to Eduard Thurneysen, 7. Juli 1922 (Rundbrief)." In *Karl Barth–Eduard Thurneysen Briefwechsel Band I 1913–1921*, 528. Gesamtausgabe, Bearbeitet und herausgegeben von Eduard Thurneysen. Zürich: Theologischer Verlag, 1973.
———. "Barth writing to Eduard Thurneysen, June 20, 1921." In *Karl Barth–Eduard Thurneysen Briefwechsel Band I 1913–1921*, 497. Gesamtausgabe, Bearbeitet und herausgegeben von Eduard Thurneysen. Zürich: Theologischer Verlag, 1973.
———. "Biblical Questions, Insights and Vistas." Translated by Douglas Horton. In *The Word of God and the Word of Man*, 51–96. London: Hodder & Stoughton, 1928.

———. "Biblische Fragen, Einsichten und Ausblicke." Address delivered at the Aarau Student Conference, 1920. In *Das Wort Gottes und die Theologie*, 70–98. München: Kaiser, 1924.

———. "Der Christ in der Gesellschaft." (The so-called *Tambach Lecture*—address delivered at Die religiös-soziale Konferenz, The Conference on Religion and Social Relations, held at Tambach on the 25th September 1919). In Karl Barth, *Das Wort Gottes und die Theologie*, 33–69. München: Kaiser, 1924.

———. "The Christian in Society." The so-called *Tambach Lecture*—address delivered at Die religiös-soziale Konferenz, The Conference on Religion and Social Relations, held at Tambach on the 25th September 1919. Translated by Douglas Horton. In *The Word of God and the Word of Man*, 272–327. London: Hodder & Stoughton, 1928.

———. "Kriegszeit und Gottesreich" ("Wartime and the Kingdom of God") lecture given in Basle, Switzerland, 15th November 1915. Lecture from the Karl Barth archive in Basle, printed in Herbert Anzinger *Glaube und kommunikative Praxis* München: Kaiser, 1991.

———. "Nachwort." In *Schleiermacher-Auswahl, Siebenstern Taschenbuch 113–14*, 293. München: Siebenstern Taschenbuch, 1968.

Benhabib, Seyla. "The Generalized and the Concrete Other: The Kohlberg-Gilligan Controversy and Feminist Theory." In *Feminism as Critique*, edited by Seyla Benhabib and Drucilla Cornell, 90–103. Cambridge: Polity, 1987.

Boeing, Geoff. "Visual Analysis of Nonlinear Dynamical Systems: Chaos, Fractals, Self-Similarity and the Limits of Prediction." 4.4 (2016), 37. *Cornell University*. Open access article/paper. See: https://arxiv.org/abs/1608.04416

Bonting, Sjoerd. L. "Theological Implications of Possible Extraterrestrial Life." *Zygon* 38.3 (2003) 587–602.

Brazier, P. H. "A Theology of Death: The Slave Trade, the Holocaust and Abortion—The Delusions of Religious Atheism." *New Blackfriars* 92.1039 (2011) 285–307.

———. "Barth and Expressionism—Some Further Considerations." *Zeitschrift für dialektische Theologie*, 20.1 (Fall 2005), 34–52.

———. *Barth and Dostoevsky. A Study of the Influence of the Russian Writer Fyodor Mikhailovich Dostoevsky on the Development of the Swiss Theologian Karl Barth, 1915-1922*. Series: Paternoster Theological Monographs. Milton Keynes: Paternoster Press, 2008. (U.S. edition published by Wipf and Stock, Eugene, OR, 2008.)

———. "Barth's First Commentary on Romans (1919)—An Exercise in Apophatic Theology?" *The International Journal of Systematic Theology* 6.4 (2004) 387–403.

———. "C. S. Lewis and Christological Prefigurement." *The Heythrop Journal*, 48.5 (Sept 2007), 742–775.

———. "Review Essay: Hell and Damnation, Freedom and Responsibility. Joel Buenting, (ed.), The Problem of Hell: A Philosophical Anthology, and, Jordan C. Ferrier, Calvin and C. S. Lewis: Solving the Riddle of the Reformation." *Sehnsucht* Vol. 7/8 (2013-14) 123–33.

———. "The Just War Theory and the 9/11 Wars: A Biblical and Eschatological Consideration." *The Evangelical Review of Society and Politics* 6.1-2 (2012) 107–28.

———. "Towards an Understanding of the Ontological Conditions Issuing from Original Sin." *The Heythrop Journal*, 6 July 2016. Online: https://onlinelibrary.wiley.com/doi/abs/10.1111/heyj.12346.

Ceruti, Maria Constanza. "Human Bodies as Objects of Dedication at Inca Mountain Shrines (North-Western Argentina)." *World Archaeology* 36.1 (2004) 103–122.

D'Costa, Gavin. "The Impossibility of a Pluralist View of Religion." *Religious Studies* 32 (1996) 223–32.

———. Review of The Metaphor of God Incarnate by John Hick. *Religious Studies* 31.1 (1995) 136–38.

Diephouse, David J. "Hitler's Religion: The Twisted Beliefs That Drove the Third Reich." *Holocaust and Genocide Studies* 32.1 (2018) 121–22.

Douthat, Ross. "A Case for Hell." *New York Times*, 24 April 2011. Online: http://www.nytimes.com/2011/04/25/opinion/25douthat.html?emc=eta1. Accessed April 25, 2011.

Fossati, Lorenzo. "Risk vs Logic. Karl Barth and Heinrich Scholz on Faith and Reason: A Path through Philosophical Logic. From Arithmetic to Metaphysics." In From *Arithmetic to Metaphysics: A Path through Philosophical Logic (Philosophische Analyse/Philosophical Analysis)*, edited by Alessandro Giordani & Ciro de Florio, 119–34. Berlin: de Gruyter, 2018.

Fredrickson, B. L., and T. A. Roberts. "Objectification Theory: Toward Understanding Women's Lived Experiences and Mental Health Risks." *Psychology of Women Quarterly* 21.2 (1997) 173–206.

Hick, John. "The Possibility of Religious Pluralism: A Reply to Gavin d'Costa." *Religious Studies* 33.2 (1997) 161–66.

Jones, David. "Dunstan, the Embryo and Christian Tradition." *Triple Helix* 32 (2005) 10–18.

Lawton, Graham. "Uprooting Darwin's Tree." *New Scientist* 201.2692 (2009) 34–39.

Lewis, C. S. "De Descriptione Temporum." In *They Asked for a Paper: Papers and Addresses*, 9–25. London: Bles, 1969.

———. "Is Theism Important?" In *Undeceptions: Essays on Theology and Ethics*, 138–42. London: Bles, 1971.

———. "Modern Theology and Biblical Criticism." In *Christian Reflections*, 152–66. London: Bles, 1967.

———. *The Problem of Pain*. London: Bles, 1940.

———. "We Have No 'Right to Happiness.'" In *Undeceptions: Essays on Theology and Ethics*, 265–69. London: Bles, 1971.

Meacham, Steve. "The Shed Where God Died." Interview with Philip Pullman. *Sydney Morning Herald Online*. Dec 13, 2003.

Murdoch, Iris. "The Sovereignty of Good over Other Concepts." In *The Sovereignty of Good: The Leslie Stephen Lecture for 1967, 77–78*. 1970. Reprint, London: Routledge Classics, 2001.

———. "The Sublime and the Beautiful Revisited." *The Yale Review* XLIX (1959) 247–71.

Nagel, Thomas. "Moral Conflict and Political Legitimacy." *Philosophy and Public Affairs* 16.3 (1987) 215–40.

———. "Rawls on Justice." *The Philosophical Review* 82.2 (1972) 220–34.

Nussbaum, Martha. "Objectification." Philosophy and Public Affairs 24.4 (1995) 249–91.

Ottinger, Didier. "Beckmann's Lucid Somnambulism." In *Max Beckmann*, edited by Sean Rainbird, 129–55. London: Tate, 2003.

Pape, Robert A. "The Strategic Logic of Suicide Terrorism." *American Political Science Review* 97.3 (2003) 1–19.

Parsons, A. "On the Judges and the Christian Conscience." *Kensington Parish News*, St Mary Abbotts Parish Church Kensington, Spring 2011, 6.

Plato. "Theaetetus." In *Plato Complete Works*, translated by M. J. Levett, revised by Myles Burnyeat, and edited by John M. Cooper, 157–234. Indianapolis, IN: Hackett, 1997.

Ramsey, Paul. "No Morality without Immortality: Dostoevsky and the Meaning of Atheism." *Journal of Religion* 36 (1956) 90–108.

Reinhard, Johan. "A 6,700 metros niños incas sacrificados quedaron congelados en el tiempo." *National Geographic*, Spanish Edition, Nov 1999, 36–55.

Reinhard, Johan. "Sacred Mountains, Ceremonial Sites, and Human Sacrifice among the Incas." *Archaeoastronomy* 19 (2005) 1–43.

Sauer, James. "Purging a Problem." Online: Centre for Reformed Theology and Apologetics. http://www.reformed.org/index.html http://www.reformed.org/webfiles/antithesis/index.html?mainframe=/webfiles/antithesis/v2n1/ant_v2n1_purging.html. Accessed May 29 2011.

Seul, Stephanie. "'Herr Hitler's Nazis Hear an Echo of World Opinion:' British and American Press Responses to Nazi Anti-Semitism, September 1930–April 1933." *Politics, Religion & Ideology* 14.3 (2013) 412–30.

Schwöbel, Christoph. "Particularity, Universality and the Religions: Towards a Christian Theology of Religions." In *Christian Uniqueness Reconsidered: The Myth of a Pluralistic Theology of Religions*, edited by Gavin D'Costa, 30–45. New York: Orbis Books, 1990.

Sickler, Bradley L. "Infernal Voluntarism and 'The Deep Courtesy of Heaven.'" In *The Problem of Hell: A Philosophical Anthology*, edited by Joel Buenting, 163–78. Farnham, UK: Ashgate, 2010

Thurneysen, Eduard. "die Anfänge." In *Antwort—Festschrift zum 70 Geburtstag von Karl Barth*, edited by Eduard Thurneysen, 831–64. Zürich: Evangelischer Verlag AG, 1956.

Ward, J. "Impartiality is Biased." *Spectrum* 21.2 (1989) 105–9.

Weems, Reggie. "Universalism Denied: C. S. Lewis's Unpublished Letters to Alan Fairhurst." *Journal of Inklings Studies* 7.2 (2017) 87–98.

Wilson, A. N. "Religion of Hatred: Why We Should No Longer be Cowed by the Chattering Classes Ruling Britain Who Sneer at Christianity." *The Daily Mail.* April 11, 2009. Online: http://www.dailymail.co.uk/news/article-1169145/Religion-hatred-Why-longer-cowedsecular-zealots.html.

———. "Why I Believe Again." *The New Statesman*, April 2, 2009. Online: http://www.newstatesman.com/religion/2009/04/conversion-experience-atheism.

Wolterstorff, Nicholas. "Is It Possible and Desirable for Theologians to Recover from Kant?" *Modern Theology* 14.1 (1998) 1–18.

Wyheł, John van, and Mark J. Pallen. "The 'Annie Hypothesis': Did the Death of His Daughter Cause Darwin to 'Give up Christianity?'" *Centaurus* (International Journal of the History of Science and Its Cultural Aspects) 54.2 (2012) 105–23.

BOOKS AND PAMPHLETS

Alighieri, Dante. *The Divine Comedy, Vol. 1 Inferno*. Harmondsworth, UK: Penguin, 1984.

Anzinger, Herbert. *Gaube und kommunikative Praxis*. München: Kaiser, 1991.

Aquinas, Thomas. *Summa Theologiae*. 61 vols. Cambridge: Cambridge University Press, 2006.

Augustine of Hippo. *The City of God*. Translated by Henry Bettenson. Harmondsworth, UK: Penguin Classics, 1972.

Balthasar, Hans Urs von. *Cosmic Liturgy: The Universe according to Maximus the Confessor.* San Francisco: Ignatius, 2003.
———. *Karl Barth, Darstellung und Deutung seiner Theologie.* Köln: Hegner, 1951.
———. *The Theology of Karl Barth—Exposition and Interpretation.* Translated by John Drury. New York: Holt, Rinehart & Winston 1971.
Barr, James. *A Line in the Sand: Britain, France and the Struggle That Shaped the Middle East.* New York: Simon & Schuster, 2012.
Barth, Karl. *Das Wort Gottes und die Theologie.* München: Kaiser, 1924.
———. *Church Dogmatics.* 14 Vols. Translated and edited G. W. Bromiley and T. F. Torrance. Edinburgh: T. & T. Clark, 1936–77.
———. *Der Römerbrief (Erste Fassung 1919).* Herausgegeben von Hermann Schmidt, Gesamtausgabe 2. Akademische Werke. Zürich: Theologischer Verlag Zürich, 1985.
———. *Der Römerbrief (Zweite Fassung 1922).* Zürich: Theologischer Verlag Zürich, 1999.
———. *Dogmatics in Outline.* London: SCM, 1949.
———. *Dogmatiks in Grundriss.* München: Kaiser, 1947.
———. *The Epistle to the Romans.* Translated by Sir Edwyn Hoskyns. 1933. Reprint, Oxford: Oxford University Press, 1968.
———. *Karl Barth–Eduard Thurneysen Briefwechsel Band I 1913-1921.* Gesamtausgabe, Bearbeitet und herausgegeben von Eduard Thurneysen. Zürich: Theologischer Verlag, 1973.
———. *Unterricht in der christlichen Religion 2, Zweite Band: Die Lehre von Gott/Die Lehre vom Menschen.* Gesamtausgabe 20. Zürich: Theologischer Verlag Zürich, 1990.
———. *Wolfgang Amadeus Mozart.* ET 1956; foreword, John Updike. Reprint, Eugene, OR: Wipf & Stock, 1986.
Beattie, Tina. *The New Atheists: the Twilight of Reason and the War on Religion.* London, Darton, Longman & Todd, 2007.
Benton, Lauren. A. *Law and Colonial Cultures: Legal Regimes in World History, 1400–1900.* Cambridge: Cambridge University Press, 2002.
Benhabib, Seyla, and Drucilla Cornell, eds. *Feminism as Critique.* Cambridge: Polity, 1987.
Berthold, George C., ed. *Maximus Confessor: Selected Writings.* Classics of Western Spirituality. Mahwah, NJ: Paulist, 1985.
Besom, Thomas. *Of Summits and Sacrifice: An Ethnohistoric Study of Inka Religious Practices.* Austin: University of Texas Press, 2009.
Black, Edwin. *IBM and the Holocaust: The Strategic Alliance between Nazi Germany and America's Most Powerful Corporation.* Expanded ed. Washington, DC: Dialog, 2012. [Original ed., 2001]
Blake, William. *Auguries of Innocence* (1789): https://www.poetryfoundation.org/poems-and-poets/poems/detail/43650.
———. *The Four Zoas*, §.ix, 180–87; §.i, 342, §.v, 235 §.viii, 453; §.ii, 109 & §.iv, 141 (unpublished illustrated manuscript). In S. Fostrer Damon, *A Blake Dictionary*, 419–426. London: Thames & Hudson, 1973.
———. "Letter to Thomas Butts, 10 January 1802." In Michael Davis, *William Blake: A New Kind of Man*, 96–97. London: Paul Elek, 1977.
Bowden, John. *Karl Barth, Theologian.* London: SCM, 1983.
Bradley, Ian. *The Book of Hymns.* New York: Testament Books, 1989.
Brazier, P.H. *Barth and Dostoevsky: A Study of the Influence of the Russian Writer Fyodor Mikhailovich Dostoevsky on the Development of the Swiss Theologian Karl Barth,*

1915-1922. Paternoster Theological Monographs. Milton Keynes, UK: Paternoster, 2008.

———. *Dostoevsky: A Theological Engagement*. Eugene, OR: Pickwick, 2016.

———. *In the Highest Degree Vol I. Essays on C. S. Lewis's Philosophical Theology—Method, Content, & Reason*. Series: C.S. Lewis: Revelation and the Christ. Foreword, Gregory Hagg. Eugene, OR: Pickwick Publications, Wipf and Stock, 2018.

———. *In the Highest Degree Vol II. Essays on C. S. Lewis's Philosophical Theology—Method, Content, & Reason*. Series: C.S. Lewis: Revelation and the Christ. Foreword, Gregory Hagg. Eugene, OR: Pickwick Publications, Wipf and Stock, 2018.

Buckley, Michael J. *At the Origins of Modern Atheism*. New Haven, CT: Yale University Press, 1987.

Butler, Samuel. *The Way of all Flesh*. London: Grant Richards, 1903.

Buenting, Joel. *The Problem of Hell: A Philosophical Anthology*. Farnham, UK: Ashgate, 2010.

Burke, Jason. *Al-Qaeda: The True Story of Radical Islam*. London: Penguin, 2007.

Burke, Jason. *The 9/11 Wars*. London: Penguin, 2011

Busch, Eberhard. *Karl Barths Lebenslauf, Nach seinen Briefen und autobiographischen Texten*. München: Kaiser, 1975.

Bytwerk, Randall L. *Bending Spines: The Propagandas of Nazi Germany and the German Democratic Republic. Rhetoric & Public Affairs Series*. Ann Arbor, MI: Michigan State University Press, 2004.

Chaliand, Gerard. *The History of Terrorism: From Antiquity to al Qaeda*. Berkley: University of California Press, 2007.

Chesterton, G. K. *Orthodoxy*. 1908. Reprint, San Francisco: Ignatius, 1995.

Child, Francis James. *The English and Scottish Popular Ballads. 10 vols. 1882-98*. Reprinted in 5 vols. Dover Paperbacks. New York: Dover, 1965.

Cicero, Marcus Tullius. *De Officiis*. Translated by Walter Miller. Loeb ed. Cambridge: Cambridge University Press, 1913. See: http://www.constitution.org/rom/de_officiis.htm.

———. *The Nature of the Gods*. Translated and introduced by Patrick Gerard Walsh. Oxford: Clarendon, 2001.

———. *The Orations of Marcus Tullius Cicero, Volume IV: The Fourteen Orations against Marcus Antonius; The Treatise on Rhetorical Invention; The Orator; Topics; On Rhetorical Partitions, Etc.* Translated by C. D. Yonge. Wokingham, UK: Dodo, 2008.

Cochrane, Arthur C. *The Church's Confession under Hitler*. Pittsburgh: Pickwick, 1976

Cooper, Adam G. *The Body in St Maximus Confessor: Holy Flesh, Wholly Deified*. Oxford Early Christian Studies. Oxford: Oxford University Press, 2005.

Craig, Edward. *The Mind of God and the Works of Man*. Oxford: Oxford University Press, 1987.

Davis, Michael. *William Blake: A New Kind of Man*. London: Elek, 1977.

D'Costa, Gavin. *Christian Uniqueness Reconsidered: The Myth of a Pluralistic Theology of Religions*. Maryknoll, NY: Orbis, 1990.

———. *Christianity and World Religions: Disputed Questions in the Theology of Religions*. Chichester, UK: Wiley-Blackwell, 2009.

Davis, R. Chris. "Hitler's Theology: A Study in Political Religion." *Journal of Church and State* 56.1 (2014) 170–71.

Dawkins, Richard. *The God Delusion*. London: Bantam Press, Transworld, 2006.

Bibliography

Dostoevsky, Fyodor Mikhailovich. *The Brothers Karamazov*. Translated by Richard Pevear and Larissa Volokhonsky. London: Everyman's Library, 1990.

———. *Crime and Punishment*. Translated by Richard Pevear and Larissa Volokhonsky. London: Everyman's Library, 1993.

———. *Demons*. Translated by Richard Pevear and Larissa Volokhonsky. London: Everyman's Library, 1994.

Eberle, Matthias von. *Max Beckmann Die Nacht—Passion ohne Erlösung*. Frankfurt: Fischer Taschenbuch Verlag, 1984.

Erskine, Thomas. *Remarks on the Internal Evidence for the Truth of Revealed Religion*. Edinburgh: Waugh, Innes and Hamilton, 1820.

Finlan, Stephen. *Problems with Atonement: The Origins of, and Controversy about, the Atonement Doctrine*. Collegeville, MN: Liturgical, 2005.

Fischer, Simon. *Revelatory Positivism? Barth's Earliest Theology and the Marburg School*. Oxford: Oxford University Press, 1988.

Fukuyama, Francis. *The End of History and the Last Man*. New York: Free Press (Simon & Schuster), 1992.

Gardner, Brian, ed. *Up the Line to Death—The War Poets 1914-1918*. 1964. Reprint, London: Metheun, 1978.

Giordani, Alessandro, and Ciro de Florio, eds. *From Arithmetic to Metaphysics: A Path through Philosophical Logic (Philosophische Analyse/Philosophical Analysis)*. Berlin: de Gruyter, 2018.

Goffen, Rona. *Masaccio's Trinity*. Cambridge: Cambridge University Press, 1998.

Gray, John, *Seven Types of Atheism*. London: Allen Lane, 2018

Guite, Malcolm. Speaking on the BBC1 documentary *The Narnia Code*, broadcast on Thursday 16 April 2009. http://www.bbc.co.uk/programmes/b00jz2qp#broadcasts. Loc. 23:35.

Gunton, Colin E. B406, *A Selected Modern Theologian—Karl Barth, 2000-2001*. Recordings of a lecture course on Karl Barth at King's College London. Privately made and owned recordings.

———. *The Barth Lectures*. Transcribed and edited by P.H. Brazier. London: T. & T. Clark, 2007.

———. *Revelation and Reason Prolegomena to Systematic Theology*. London: T. & T. Clark, 2008.

Happé, Peter, ed. *English Mystery Plays*. London: Penguin, 1975. Online: http://quod.lib.umich.edu/c/cme/York/1:50?rgn=div1;view=fulltext.

Haught, John F. *God and the New Atheism: A Critical Response to Dawkins, Harris, and Hitchens*. Louisville: Westminster John Knox, 2008.

Hoffman, Bruce. *Inside Terrorism*. Columbia, SC: Columbia University Press, 1998.

Itzkowitz, Norman. *Ottoman Empire and Islamic Tradition*. 1972. Reprint, Chicago: University of Chicago Press, 1980.

Jüngel, Eberhard. *Karl Barth, A Theological Legacy*. Philadelphia: Westminster, 1986.

Kant, Immanuel. *Religion within the Boundaries of Mere Reason and Other Writings*. Translated and edited by Allen Wood and George Di Giovanni. Cambridge: Cambridge University Press, 1998.

Kelly, Edward F., Emily Williams Kelly, Adam Crabtree, Alan Gauld, and Michael Grosso. *Irreducible Mind: Toward a Psychology for the 21st Century*. Plymouth, UK: Rowman & Littlefield, 2006.

Kroeker, P. Travis, and Bruce K. Ward. *Remembering the End: Dostoevsky as a Prophet of Modernity*. Oxford: Westview Press Radical Traditions, 2001.

Lackner, Stephen. *Max Beckmann*. Crown Art Library. New York: Crown, 1984.

Langton, Rae Helen. *Sexual Solipsism: Philosophical Essays on Pornography and Objectification*. Oxford: Oxford University Press, 2009

Lawrence, T. E. *The Seven Pillars of Wisdom*. Ware, UK: Wordsworth Editions, 1997. Online texthttp://gutenberg.net.au/ebooks01/0100111h.html#book3.

Lewis, Bernard. *Islam and the West*. New York: Oxford University Press, 1993.

———. Istanbul and the Civilization of the Ottoman Empire.1963. Reprint, Norma, OK: University of Oklahoma Press, 1982.

Lewis, C. S. *Broadcast Talks. Reprinted with some alterations from two series of Broadcast Talks "Right and Wrong: A Clue to the Meaning of the Universe" and "What Christians Believe" given in 1941 and 1942*. London: Bles/Centenary, 1942.

———. *Christian Reflections*. London: Bles, 1967.

———. *The Chronicles of Narnia—Prince Caspian: The Return to Narnia*. London: Bles, 1951.

———. *The Chronicles of Narnia—The Horse and His Boy*. London: Bles, 1954.

———. *The Chronicles of Narnia—The Last Battle*. London: Bles, 1956.

———. *The Chronicles of Narnia—The Lion the Witch and the Wardrobe*. London: Bles, 1950.

———. *The Chronicles of Narnia—The Magician's Nephew*. London: Bles, 1955.

———. *The Chronicles of Narnia—The Silver Chair*. London: Bles, 1953.

———. *The Chronicles of Narnia—The Voyage of the Dawn Treader*. London: Bles, 1952.

———. *The Dark Tower and Other Stories*. London: Collins, 1977.

———. *The Great Divorce*. Bless: London, 1945.

———. *Mere Christianity. A revised and amplified edition, with a new introduction, of the three books Broadcast Talks, Christian Behaviour, and Beyond Personality*. London: Bles, 1952.

———. *Out of the Silent Planet*. London: Bodley Head, 1938

———. *Perelandra*. London: Bodley Head, 1943.

———. *The Screwtape Letters*. London: Bles/Centenary, 1942

———. *That Hideous Strength: A Modern Fairytale for Grown-Ups*. London: Bodley Head, 1945.

———. *Undeceptions: Essays on Theology and Ethics*. London: Bles, 1971.

Lutzer, Erwin W. *Hitler's Cross: How the Cross Was Used to Promote the Nazi Agenda*. 1995. Reprint, Chicago, Moody, 2016.

Mau, Jurgen, ed. *Sextus Empiricus. Sexti Empirici Opera, Vol III, Adversus Mathematicos. Series: Bibliotheca Scriptorum Graecorum et Romanorum Teubneriana*. Ancient Greek. 1961. Reprint, Berlin: de Gruyter, 2011.

Maximus the Confessor. *Ambigua, 2*. In *Patrologia Graeca*, edited by J. P. Migne. 161 Vols. Paris: Imprimerie Catholique, 1857–1966.

McCormack, Bruce L. *Karl Barth's Critically Realistic Dialectical Theology: Its Genesis and Development, 1909–1936*. Oxford: Oxford University Press, 1995.

Merriam-Webster Dictionary. Online: https://www.merriam-webster.com/dictionary/justice. Accessed Feb 20, 2017.

Murdoch, Iris. *The Sovereignty of Good. (Lectures 1962, 1966 & 1967)* , Reprint, London: Routledge Classics, 2001. [1970]

Nestle-Aland. *Novum Testamentum Graece*. Reprint, Stuttgart: Deutsche Bibelgesellschaft, 1995. [1979]
Nietzsche, Friedrich. *Twilight of the Idols*. Translated by Walter Kaufmann and R. J. Hollingdale. Harmondsworth, UK: Penguin, 1985.
Noel, Gerard. *Pius XII: The Hound of Hitler*. New York: Continuum, 2009.
Pastor, James F. *Terrorism & Public Safety Policing: Implications of the Obama Presidency*. Boca Raton, FL: CRC, 2009.
Pauck, Wilhelm. *Karl Barth: Prophet of a New Christianity?* New York: Harper, 1931. Online: https://archive.org/details/karlbarthprophet012001mbp.
Plato. *Plato Complete Works*. Translated, M. J. Levett, revised by Myles Burnyeat, and edited by John M. Cooper. Indianapolis, IN: Hackett, 1997.
———. *Plato in Twelve Volumes*. Translated by W. R. M. Lamb. London: Heinemann, 1955. Online: http://www.perseus.tufts.edu/hopper/text?doc=Plat.+Lach.+178a&redirect=true.
Podgorski, Daniel. "Free Will Twice Defined: On the Linguistic Conflict of Compatibilism and Incompatibilism." Online: *The Gemsbok*. See: https://thegemsbok.com/art-reviews-and-articles/philosophy-articles-friday-phil-free-will-determinism-compatibilism/
Pullman, Phillip. *His Dark Materials, consisting of Northern Lights, The Subtle Knife, and The Amber Spyglass*. London: Scholastic, 1995–2000.
Raabe, Paul, ed. *The Era of German Expressionism*. Translated by J. M. Ritchie. London: Calder, 1974.
Ray, John. *The Night Blitz*. Johannesburg: Cassel, 1996.
Reardon, Bernard, ed. *Liberal Protestantism*. London: Black, 1968.
Rogan, Eugene. *The Fall of the Ottomans: The Great War in the Middle East, 1914–1920*. Harmonsworth, UK: Penguin, 2016.
Rumscheidt, Martin. "The Correspondence between Harnack and Barth." PhD diss., McGill University, 1967.
Rupp, George. *Culture-Protestantism: German Liberal Theology at the Turn of the Twentieth Century*. Missoula, MT: Scholars/AAR, 1977.
Rychlak, Ronald J. *Hitler, the War, and the Pope*. Huntington, IN: Our Sunday Visitor, 2000.
Sageman, Mark. *Understanding Terror Networks*. Philadelphia: University of Pennsylvania Press, 2004.
Said, Edward W. *Orientalism*. Harmondsworth, UK: Penguin, 2003.
Salles, Ricardo. "Compatibilism: Stoic and modern." *Archiv für Geschichte der Philosophie* 83.1 (2001), 1-23.
Sauter, Gerhard. *What Dare We Hope? Reconsidering Eschatology. Theology for the Twenty-First Century*. London: Continnuum, 1999.
Saward, John. *Redeemer in the Womb*. San Francisco: Ignatius, 1993.
Schleiermacher, Friedrich. *Über die Religion: Reden an die Gebildeten unter ihren Verächtern (1799). On Religion: Speeches to its Cultured Despisers*, translated by Richard Crouter. Cambridge: Cambridge University Press, 1996.
The Septuagint. Dual language ed., compiled by Sir Lancelot C. L. Brenton. 1851. Reprint, Peabody, MA: Hendrickson, 1999.
Shakespeare, William. *The RSC Shakespeare: The Complete Works*. London: Palgrave Macmillan, 2007.

Solzhenitsyn, Aleksandr Isaevich. *Warning to the West*. New York: Macmillan, Hill & Wang, 1976.
Spieckermann, Ingrid. *Gotteskenntnis: Ein Beitrag zur Grundfrage der neun Theologie Karl Barths*. München: Kaiser, 1985.
Spink, Kathryn. *The Miracle, The Message, The Story: Jean Vanier and L'arche*. New ed. Darton, Longman & Todd, 2006. [1991]
Stapel, Wilhelm. *Der christliche Staatsmann—Eine Theologie des National-sozialismus*. Hamburg: Hanseatische Verlag, 1932).
———. *Die drei Stände Versuch einer Morphologie des deutschen Volkes*. Hamburg: Hanseatische Verlag, 1941.
———. *The Heiland*. 1932. Reprint, München: Hanser, 1953.
Sublimis Dei. Encyclical on "The Enslavement and Evangelization of Indians," issued by Pope Paul III, 29 May 1537. Online: http://www.papalencyclicals.net/Paul03/p3subli.htm.
Taylor, Charles. *Sources of the Self: the Making of the Modern Identity*. Cambridge: Harvard University Press, 1989.
The Jerusalem Talmud, Vol. IV. North Charleston, SC: CreateSpace, 2013.
The Statute of Virginia for Religious Freedom. Online: https://en.wikipedia.org/wiki/Virginia_Statute_for_Religious_Freedom.
Thurneysen, Eduard, ed. *Antwort—Festschrift zum 70 Geburtstag von Karl Barth*. Zollikon-Zürich: Evangelischer Verlag AG, 1956.
———. *Christoph Blumhardt*. München: Kaiser, 1926.
———. *Dostoevsky—A Theological Study*. Translated by Keith R. Crim. London: Epworth, 1964.
———. *Dostojewski*. München: Kaiser, 1921.
Tolkien, J. R. R. *The Lord of the Rings. The Fellowship of the Ring, The Two Towers, and The Return of the King*. London: Allen & Unwin, 1954 & 1955.
Vitz, Paul C. *Faith of the Fatherless. The Psychology of Atheism*. 2nd ed. San Francisco: Ignatius, 2013.
Webb, Stephen. *Re-figuring Theology—The Rhetoric of Karl Barth*. New York: State University Press of New York, 1991.
Weil, Simone. *L'Amour de Dieu et le Malheur (The Love of God and Affliction)*. In The Simone Weil Reader, edited by George A. Panichas, 439–468. London: Moyer Bell, 1977.
———. *Les Cahiers de Simone Weil Volumes 1–3*. Paris: Gallimard 1951.
———. *The New York Notebook*. In First and Last Notebooks, 67–332. Translated by Richard Rees. London: Oxford University Press, 1970.
———. *The Notebooks of Simone Weil, Volume 1*. London: Routledge & Kegan Paul, 1956.
Wikipedia. *Capacocha*. Online: https://en.wikipedia.org/wiki/Capacocha. Accessed Nov 30, 2016.
Williams, Charles. *All Hallows' Eve*. London: Faber & Faber, 1945.
———. *Descent into Hell*. London: Faber & Faber, 1937.
Wilson, A. N. *Against Religion*. London: Chatto & Windus, 1991.
Wolterstorff, Nicholas. *John Locke and the Ethics of Belief*. Cambridge: Cambridge University Press, 1996.

Select Mediaography

BRITISH BROADCASTING CORPORATION

BBC News (www), 4 March 2010. http://news.bbc.co.uk/1/hi/world/europe/8332276.stm. Accessed May 2010 and February 20, 2017.

BBC News (www). "Church of England bishops response to the Iraq war." http://news.bbc.co.uk/1/hi/uk/2659673.stm.

BBC News (www). Report on Sean Spicer, US politician, on chemical weapons. http://www.bbc.co.uk/news/world-us-canada-39573063; http://www.bbc.co.uk/news/world-us-canada-39580120

BBC R3 (radio). Choral Evensong from St Alban's Cathedral, UK, Broadcast Sunday 18th March 2007. http://www.bbc.co.uk/radio3/choralevensong/.

BBC R4 (radio) Thought for the Day, Revd Giles Fraser. Broadcast, Jan 1, 2018, 07:47–07:50. See, https://www.bbc.co.uk/programmes/p00szxv6

BBC R4 (radio) Thought for the Day, Right Revd Sarah Mullally. Broadcast, , Good Friday April 16, 2019, 07:47–07:50. See, https://www.bbc.co.uk/programmes/p00szxv6

BBC1 (TV) *Conspiracy*. Docu-drama, which accurately followed the one surviving copy of the minutes of the meeting at Wansee in 1942 when the Holocaust was planned and organized. https://en.wikipedia.org/wiki/Conspiracy_(2001_film); https://www.imdb.com/title/tt0266425/

BBC2 (TV) *The Narnia Code* (broadcast on Thursday 16 April 2009). http://www.bbc.co.uk/programmes/b00jz2qp#broadcasts.

THE CHURCH OF ENGLAND

The Church of England, *The Book of Common Prayer* (1662). http://justus.anglican.org/resources/bcp/1662/baskerville.htm

THE CHURCH TIMES

The Church Times website archive. M. Hill QC, "Judges should not be hand-picked," The Church Times, 7675, 23 April 2010. https://www.churchtimes.co.uk/

The Church Times website archive. M. Holness, "Christian teachers face legal action, warns barrister," The Church Times, 7630, 12 June, 2009.

The Church Times website archive. M. Holness, "Jewish school cleared," The Church Times, 7582, 11 July 2008. https://www.churchtimes.co.uk/

The Church Times website archive. P Ashworth, "Bishop Forster freedom-of-speech clause not necessary," The Church Times, 7564, 7 March 2008. https://www.churchtimes.co.uk/

The Church Times website archive. P Ashworth, "Council suspends officer over God-talk," The Church Times, 7620, 3 April, 2009. https://www.churchtimes.co.uk/

The Church Times website archive. S. Herbert, "Court rules Jewish school's admissions policy unlawful," The Church Times, 7633, 3 July, 2009. https://www.churchtimes.co.uk/

The Church Times website archive. Staff Reporter, "Bishops criticise 'secular' judgment," The Church Times, 7677, 7 May 2010. https://www.churchtimes.co.uk/

THE DAILY TELEGRAPH

The Daily Telegraph. Report on Dale McAlpine. http://www.telegraph.co.uk/news/religion/7668448/Christian-preacher-arrested-for-saying-homosexuality-is-a-sin.html

The Daily Telegraph, 4 May 2003. https://www.telegraph.co.uk/news/uknews/1429109/Campbell-interrupted-Blair-as-he-spoke-of-his-faith-We-dont-do-God.html

The Daily Telegraph, 9 May 2011. http://www.telegraph.co.uk/culture/tvandradio/bbc/8501819/BBC-producers-public-service-views-on-par-with-religion.html

ECOHR

The European Convention of Human Rights (ECOHR). https://www.echr.coe.int.

ENCYCLOPEDIA BRITANNICA

Sextus Empiricus Adversus Mathematicos (*Against the Mathematicians*). https://www.britannica.com/topic/Adversus-mathematicos

THE GEMBOK

Stanford Encyclopaedia of Philosophy. https://thegemsbok.com/

NEW SCIENTIST

Lawton, Graham , "Uprooting Darwin's Tree." *New Scientist*, January 21 2009. https://www.newscientist.com/article/mg20126921-600-why-darwin-was-wrong-about-the-tree-of-life/

Thomson, Helen, "Brain mysteries: A user's guide to the biggest questions of the mind." *New Scientist* June 20, 2019. https://www.newscientist.com/article/mg24232350-800-brain-mysteries-a-users-guide-to-the-biggest-questions-of-the-mind/?utm_medium=NLC&utm_source=NSNS&utm_campaign=2019-0620-GLOBAL-NSDAY&utm_content=NSDAY

THE NEW YORK TIMES

New York Times. 24 April 2011. Ross Douthat, "A Case for Hell." http://www.nytimes.com/2011/04/25/opinion/25douthat.html?emc=eta1
New York Times. 23 June 2015. Nicholas Bakalar, "37.2 Trillion: Galaxies or Human Cells?" https://www.nytimes.com/2015/06/23/science/37-2-trillion-galaxies-or-human-cells.html

PEOPLE MANAGEMENT MAGAZINE

People Management Magazine. http://www.peoplemanagement.co.uk/pm/articles/2011/04/maistry-v-bbc.htm

ROBERT KUNDA

http://robertkunda.com/2011/04/20/atheism-the-paper-tiger/

SEOP

Stanford Encyclopaedia of Philosophy. https://plato.stanford.edu/index.html/
Stanford Encyclopaedia of Philosophy. https://Compatibilism.edu/index.html/

THE SIMPSON'S

The Simpsons, "'I, (Annoyed Grunt)-bot' or, 'I, D'oh-bot.'" Series 15, Episode 9. First broadcast January 11, 2004.

TOWARDS THE DAY AFTER TOMORROW

The Simpsons, "And Maggie Makes Three." Series 6, Episode 13. First broadcast, 22 January 1995.
The Simpsons, "Bart Gets Famous." Series 5, Episode 12. First broadcast February 3, 1994.
The Simpsons, "Bart of Darkness." Series 6, Episode 1. First broadcast September 4, 1994.
The Simpsons, "Bart Sells His Soul." Series 7, Episode 4. First broadcast October 8, 1995.
The Simpsons, "Bart to the Future." Series 11, Episode 17. First broadcast March 19, 2000.
The Simpsons, "Duffless." Series 4, Episode 16. First broadcast February 18, 1993
The Simpsons, "Eeny Teeny Maya, Moe." Series 20, Episode 16. First broadcast April 5, 2009.
The Simpsons, "Fat Man and Little Boy." Series 16, Episode 5. First broadcast December 12, 2004.
The Simpsons, "Girly Edition." Series 9, Episode 21. First broadcast April 19, 1998.
The Simpsons, "Gone, Maggie, Gone." Series 20, Episode 13. First broadcast March 15, 2009.
The Simpsons, "Holidays of Future Passed." Series 23, Episode 9. First broadcast December 11, 2011.
The Simpsons, "Home Away from Homer." Series 16, Episode 20. First broadcast May 15, 2005.
The Simpsons, "Home goes to Prep School." Series 20, Episode 13. First broadcast March 15, 2009.
The Simpsons, "Homer and Ned's Hail Mary Pass." Series 16, Episode 8. First broadcast February 6, 2005.
The Simpsons, "How I Wet Your Mother, Series 23, Episode 16, first broadcast March 11, 2012.
The Simpsons, "How the Test Was Won." Series 20, Episode 11. First broadcast March 1, 2009.
The Simpsons, "I'm Goin' to Praiseland." Series 12, Episode 19. First broadcast March 28, 2001.
The Simpsons, "Lisa's Wedding." Series 6, Episode 19. First broadcast March 19, 1995.
The Simpsons, "Rednecks and Broomsticks." Series 21, Episode 7. First broadcast November 29, 2009.
The Simpsons, "Screaming Yellow Honkers." Series 10, Episode 15. First broadcast February 21, 1999.
The Simpsons, "See Homer Run." Series 17, Episode 6. First broadcast November 20, 2005.
The Simpsons, "She of Little Faith." Series 13, Episode 6. First broadcast December 16, 2001.
The Simpsons, "Springfield Up." Series 18, Episode 13. First broadcast February 18, 2007.
The Simpsons, "Sweet Seymour Skinner's Baadasssss Song." Series 5, Episode 19. First broadcast April 28, 1994.
The Simpsons, "The Bart of War." Series 14, Episode 21. First broadcast May 18, 2003.
The Simpsons, "The Blue and the Gray." Series 22, Episode 13. First broadcast February 13, 2011.
The Simpsons, "The Father, the Son, and the Holy Guest Star." Series 16, Episode 21. First broadcast May 15, 2005.
The Simpsons, "The Greatest Story Ever D'ohed." Series 21, Episode 16. First broadcast March 28, 2010.

Mediaography

The Simpsons, "The Last of the Red Hat Mamas." Series 17, Episode 17. First broadcast November 27, 2005.
The Simpsons, "This Little Wiggy." Series 9, Episode 18. First broadcast March 22, 1998.
The Simpsons, "Treehouse of Horror IV." Series 5, Episode 5. First broadcast 28 October 1993.
The Simpsons, "Treehouse of Horror XV." Series 16, Episode 1. First broadcast November 7, 2004.
The Simpsons, "Treehouse of Horror XXII." Series 23, Episode 3. First broadcast October 30, 2011.
The Simpsons, "White Christmas Blues." Series 25, Episode 8. First broadcast February 15, 2013.

THE TATE GALLERY OF LONDON

William Blake (English Poet and mystic, artist and printmaker, 1757–1827) *Newton*, 1795, copper engraving with pen and ink and watercolour, 460 x 600 mm, Tate Gallery, London.

UK GOVERNMENT'S OFFICE FOR STATISTICS

UK Government's Office for Statistics website for the 2001 census. http://www.statistics.gov.uk/CCI/nugget.asp?ID=460&Pos=1&ColRank=1&Rank=326

THE WEB GALLERY OF ART

The Web Gallery of Art is a searchable database of European fine arts and architecture (eighth-nineteenth centuries) currently containing over 44,800 images. https://www.wga.hu/.

Index of Names

Abel 76, 116–17
Abraham 36, 113
Adam and Eve 70, 202
Adams, Karl 41
Africa 17, 34, 89, 90, 94, 117, 146
Aikenhead, Thomas 88, 112
Ambrose of Milan (337/340–397) 125, 135
Amis, Martin (b. 1949) 81
Ananias 190, 207, 209, 210
Anselm of Canterbury (1033/4–1109) 217
Apollo 29
Aquinas, Thomas (1225–74) 102, 104, 125, 154, 236
Aristotle (384–322 BC) 52, 102, 104, 215
Augustine of Hippo (354–430) 73, 125, 135, 236

Balthasar, Hans Urs von (1905–1988) 48, 50–51, 73, 101, 237
Barabbas 192, 193
Baring-Gould, Sabine (1834–1924) 135
Barth, Karl (1886–1968) 1, 16–19, 41–74, 85–86, 108, 116–17, 144, 217–18, 225, 226, 227–31, 233–37, 239–42
Bass, Gary J. (1969) 129
Bashir, Martin (b. 1963) 231
Beatles, The 166–67, 176,–78
Beattie, Tina (b. 1955) 83, 237
Beckmann, Max (1884–1950) 53, 58, 61–62, 69–71, 235, 239–40
Berlin 42, 47, 92, 235, 239–40

Bethlehem 36, 37
Blair, Tony (b. 1953) 12, 147, 244
Blake, William (1757–1827) 1, 194–95, 197, 218, 237–38, 247
Blumhardt, Johann Christoph (1805–1880) 44–45, 242
Blumhardt, Christoph Gottlieb (1779–1838) 44, 46, 242
Bonhoeffer, Dietrich (1906–1945) 218
Bowden, John (1935–2010) 52, 237
Brunner, Emil (1889–1966) 64
Buddha 72, 177
Buenting, Joel 22, 155, 234–36, 238
Bultmann, Rudolf Karl (1884–1976) 64
Burke, Jason (b. 1970) 142–43, 238
Busch, Eberhard (b. 1937) 43, 60, 65, 238
Bush, George W. (b. 1946) 146–147
Bush, George, senior (1924–2018) 146–47

Cain 76, 116–17, 132, 136
Calvin, John (1509–1564) 22, 64–65, 87, 234
Christ 3, 8, 13, 15–17, 31–32, 34, 35, 44–47, 51–52, 54–56, 59, 61, 64, 66–72, 76, 80, 85–86, 88, 93, 96, 100–106, 110, 115–19, 127, 130–31, 133–35, 140, 142, 144–46, 149–52, 155–56, 158–59, 161–62, 165–66, 168–70, 183–84, 190–93, 195–96, 199, 201, 203, 206–207, 210, 215, 217–20, 227–29, 230, 234, 238
Jesus 4, 6, 8, 13–14, 16, 23, 27, 31–37, 44–47, 56, 61, 67–69, 71–72, 76, 85–86, 91, 93, 96, 101–103, 116,

Indices

122, 131, 133, 135–36, 140–42, 144–47, 150–51, 164–67, 169, 176–77, 181, 190, 192–93, 196, 198–202, 204–6, 209–11, 215, 219, 226, 227–29, 231
Yeshua 23, 76, 151
Cicero 85, 124, 238

Dante, Durante di Alighiero degli Alighieri (1265–1321) 155, 185, 236
Darwin, Charles Robert (1809–1882) 82, 97, 235–36, 245
David, King (ca. 1010-970 BC) 2, 27, 29, 32, 37, 60, 104, 133, 154
Davidman, Joy (1915–60) 2
Dawkins, Richard (b. 1941) 81–82, 107, 166, 238–39
Dives (& Lazarus) 160, 165, 219–20, 230
Dix, Otto (1891–1969) 58–59
Dodd, C. H. (1884–1973) 3
Dostoevsky, Fyodor Mikhailovich (1821–81) 9, 44, 46, 57, 88, 116, 217–18, 223, 226, 234, 236–40, 242
Douthat, Ross (b. 1979) 152–53, 235, 245
Dunstan, Revd Dr Gordon (1917–2004) 104, 109, 235
Dürer, Albrecht (1471–1528) 56, 59, 71, 72

El Greco (Doménikos Theotokópoulos 1541–1614) 56–57, 62, 71
Elijah 184

Fischer-Barnicol, Hans A. (1930–99) 43
Fraser, Giles (b. 1954) 133, 243
Fukuyama, Yoshihiro Francis (b. 1952) 4, 239

Gabriel 31, 32
Gekko, Gordon (1987 & 2010 film) 164–65
Geneva 43, 87, 88
Gentili, Alberico (1552–1608) 125

God 2–10, 12–20, 22, 24, 27, 31, 34, 36–37, 41–47, 50–57, 61–91, 93, 95–96, 101–8, 110, 113, 115–19, 121–22, 125–27, 132–33, 135–37, 142, 146, 148–59, 161–64, 167–69, 171–76, 178–79, 181, 183–93, 195–96, 198–204, 206, 210–12, 214–17, 219, 221, 225–36, 238–39, 242, 244 (See Jesus; Christ)
El Shaddai 3, 10, 36, 151, 185
LORD 27, 29, 121, 132, 142, 159, 189
Yahweh/YHWH 3, 10, 36, 132, 133, 137, 139, 140, 145, 146, 151, 185
Goethe, Johann Wolfgang von (1749–1832) 60–61
Gogarten, Friedrich (1887–1967) 64
Göttingen 51, 217
Grayling, A. C. (Anthony Clifford b. 1949) 81
Gray, John Nicholas (b. 1948) 81, 183, 239, 246
Gregory of Nazianzus' 102, 238
Grosz, Georg (1893–1959) 58–59
Grotius, Hugo (1583–1645) 125
Grünewald, Matthias (1470–1528) 54–58, 62, 64, 66, 68, 70–71
Guernica 144
Guite, Revd Malcolm (b. 1957) 83, 239
Gunton, Colin E. (1941–2003) 16–17, 45, 50–51, 73–74, 239

Harnack, Carl Gustav Adolf (1851–1930) 43, 48, 241
Harris, Sam 81, 239
Harris, Richard, Baron Harries of Pentregarth, 123
Harrison, George (1943–2001) 178
Haught, John F. (1942) 82, 239
Hegel, Georg Wilhelm Friedrich (1770–1831) 60, 64, 91–92, 218
Heidegger, Martin (1889–1976) 64
Henry VIII (1491–1547) 10, 12, 87
Herod 116, 206
Herrmann, Wilhelm (1846–1922) 43
Hirst, Damien (b. 1965) 74
Hitchens, Christopher (1949–2011) 81, 239

Indices

Hitler, Adolf (1889–1945) 69, 74, 91–92, 98, 118, 124, 235–36, 238, 240–41
Hoyer, Hermann Otto (1893–1968) 69

Iasiello, Louis (b. 1950) 129
Ibsen, Henrik Johan (1928–1906) 56
Isaac 36, 113, 194
Isaiah 27, 29, 118, 133
Isenheim 54–55
Israel 6, 35–37, 113, 133, 136–37, 142, 146, 174

Jefferson, Thomas (1743–1826) 90–91
John, Jeffrey (b. 1953) 192
Jeremiah 105
Job 189, 198, 216–17
John the Baptist 55–56, 64, 70–72, 105–6
Joseph 29–33
Judas 1, 180, 206

Kandinsky, Wassily (1866–1944) 58
Kant, Immanuel (1724–1804) 125, 193, 217–18, 236, 239
Karadzic, Radan (b. 1945) 123
Klinger, Max (1857–1920) 61
Kutter, Hermann (1863–1931) 43–44, 228

Lawrence, Colonel T. E. (Thomas Edward 1888–1935) 138–40, 240
Lazarus (& Dives) 160, 165, 192–93, 219, 220, 230
Lenin (Vladimir Ilyich Ulyanov 1870–1924) 60
Lennon, John Winston (1940–1980) 166–67, 178
Lewis, C. S. (1898–1963) 2, 12–13, 22, 107, 131, 150, 155–57, 159–61, 163, 173, 179, 183–85, 195, 234–36, 238, 240
Locke, John (1632–1704) 125, 242
Lorenz, Edward N. (1917–2008) 17
Lucifer 86, 185, 193, 201

Luke 6, 15, 20, 23, 27, 72, 105–6, 115, 141, 145, 157, 160, 163–65, 186, 199, 214, 219, 230–31

Malaysia 177
Marburg 42–43, 239
Marc, Franz Moritz Wilhelm (1880–1915) 58
Mark 3, 72, 136, 145, 157, 163, 190, 192, 203–4, 206–7, 211, 214, 216, 219, 222, 231, 236, 241
Marx, Karl (1818–83) 85, 124, 218
Mary 27–36, 55, 70, 87, 94, 103, 133, 150, 183, 235, 246
Matthew 41, 125, 135, 145, 205, 220
McCormack, Bruce (b. 1952) 44, 63, 226, 228, 240
Michelangelo di Lodovico Buonarroti Simoni (1475–1564) 56–57, 71
Mill, Stuart John (1806–73) 125
Molech 113
Mother Teresa of Calcutta (Anjezë Gonxhe Bojaxhiu 1910–97) 74, 219
Mozart (1756–91) 50, 64–65, 68, 71, 73, 211, 237
Mullally, Right Revd Dame Sarah Elisabeth (b. 1962) 231
Munch, Edvard (1863–1944) 56–58
Murdoch, Iris (1919–99) 193–95, 235, 240

Nazareth 8, 14, 16, 27–28, 86, 133, 145, 150–51
Newton PRS, Sir Isaac (President of the Royal Society) (1642–1726/27) 194–95, 218, 247
Niebuhr, H. Richard (1894–1962) 125
Niebuhr, Reinhold (1892–1971) 125
Niemöller, Friedrich Gustav Emil Martin (1892–1984) 134
Nietzsche, Friedrich Wilhelm (1844–1900) 59, 64, 91–92, 193, 241
Nolde, Emil (1867–1956) 58–60
Nuremberg 91, 98

Orend, Brian (b. 1971) 129

251

Indices

Owen, Wilfred Edward Salter (1893–1918) 62

Paul, Apostle (5–67) 6, 47–48, 61, 73, 92–93, 100, 105–6, 118, 125, 127, 136, 141, 152, 158, 178, 190, 206–7, 210, 219, 230–31, 236–37, 241–42
Saul of Tarsus 190, 207, 209–10
Penrose, Roger (b. 1931) 65
Peter 6, 55, 72, 135, 201–2, 239
Pilate 116, 199, 206
Plato (428/427 or 424/423 to 348/347 BC) 84, 124, 236, 241
Pope Paul III, papacy 1534–1549 (b. born Alessandro Farnese 1468–1549) 92–93, 242
Pufendorf, Baron von (1632–1694) 125
Pullman, Philip (b. 1946) 81, 107–9, 235, 241
Putin, Vladimir (b. 1952) 4

Raphael, Sanzio da Urbino (83–1520) 59, 71–72
Ritschl, Albrecht (1822–89) 43, 217
Rodin, François Auguste René (1840–1917) 56
Rome 11, 33–35, 55, 92, 98, 215

Safenwil 43, 45
Sassoon, Siegfried Loraine (1886–1967) 62
Satan 17, 86, 160, 164, 167, 172, 216
Saward, John (b. 1947) 101–3, 241
Schiller, Johann Christoph Friedrich von (1759–1805) 56–57
Schleiermacher, Friedrich Daniel Ernst (1768–1834) 43, 60–62, 72, 217–18, 234, 241
Shakespeare (bapt. 1564–1616) 171, 241
Simpson(s), The 21–22, 149–50, 152, 160,–70, 172–79, 181–85, 187, 231, 245–47
    Abernathy, Dr. Eleanor, MD JD (aka Crazy Cat Lady) 182–84
    Bleeding Gums Murphy 165

Burns, Charles Montgomery "Monty" 160–61, 167, 170–72
Chalmers, Superintendent Gary 175
Flanders, Maud 164, 166–67, 172
Flanders, Ned 164, 166–67, 172, 174–75, 183, 246
Frink, Professor John I.Q. Nerdelbaum Jr. 181
Grimes, Frank 164, 165
Lovejoy, Revd Timothy 172
Monroe, Dr Marvin 165
Nahasapeemapetilon, Apu 168
Quimby, Mayor Joe 183
Simpson, Bartholomew "Bart" 150, 164, 166, 168–70, 174–75, 246
Simpson, Homer 160–61, 165–67, 169, 174, 176–78, 183, 246
Simpson, Lisa 166, 168–70, 175–76, 178, 246
Simpson, Maggie 15, 161, 167–68, 176, 246
Simpson, Marge 161, 169, 175, 183
Skinner, Seymour 175, 246
Smithers, Waylon 161, 170–71
Wiggum, Ralph 170
Skarbimierz, Stanislaw of (1360–1431) 125
Solzhenitsyn, Aleksandr Isayevich (1918–2008) 9–10, 242
Stapel, Otto Friedrich Wilhelm (1882–1954) 64, 91–92, 242
Starr, Ringo (Richard Starkey b. 1940) 167, 178
Suarez, Francisco (1548–1617) 125
Syria 36, 101, 205

Taylor, Charles Margrave (b. 1931) 195
Thatcher, Margaret Hilda (1925–2013) 147
Thurneysen, Eduard (1888–1974) 1, 18–46, 56–58, 60, 66, 218, 230, 233, 236–37, 242
Tillich, Paul (1886–1965) 73, 125
Toledo 57
Trump, Donald John (b. 1946) 4
Tübingen 42

Indices

Uncle Albert 177–78

Valhalla 128, 151, 184
Van Gogh, Vincent Willem (1853–90) 56–58
Vanier, Jean (1828–2019) 231, 242
Vattel, Emerich de (1714–67) 125
Vitoria, Francisco de (1492–1546) 125

Wagner, Richard (1813–1883) 64, 92
Warnock, Helen Mary (1924–2019) 104
Webb, Stephen H. (1961–2016) 47–48, 52–53, 66–67, 242
Weil, Simone (1909–43) 190, 215–16, 219–20, 242
Williams, Charles Walter Stansby (1886–1945) 179, 239, 242

Index of Subjects

a/Abortion(s) 19, 20, 75, 79, 80, 83, 94, 95, 96, 97, 99, 100, 101, 102, 104, 107, 108, 109, 115, 117, 118, 168, 178, 231, 234
   abort(ed) 94, 108
   conception 31, 55, 76, 96, 101–3, 105, 113, 218
   d/Delayed animation/ensoulment 102–4
   embryo 95, 104, 114
   immediate animation 103–5
   postponed animation 102
abstract 4, 7, 65, 195, 228
absurd 150, 185
academic 1, 8, 52, 53, 150, 168, 191, 204, 216
ad infinitum 148, 168, 184
adult(s) 113–14, 163–64, 170
advent 41
aesthetic 54, 66, 68, 73
a/Afflict 1, 195, 205, 222
   a/Affliction 22, 24, 189–90, 201, 203, 215–21, 223
   Affliction 189, 215–16, 242
African(s) 31, 34–35, 89–90, 92, 95, 99–100, 104, 109, 114–15
Age of Reason 14, 76–77, 84, 90, 98, 123, 125, 127
aharît ha-yāmîm 6
alogos 150, 185

Al Qaeda 4 (See war)
altruistic 117, 133, 136
altruism 133
ambiguity 50
American(s) 2, 17, 21, 34–35, 90, 92, 99, 100, 102, 109–10, 118, 122, 142, 146–47, 152, 160, 166, 174–75, 235, 236
analogical 8, 159–60, 179
Anglo-Saxon 128
annihilate 109, 124
annihilation 90, 92, 109, 151
annunciation 32, 54
anthropology 23, 61, 76, 80, 92, 162
anti-Semitism 91
apartheid 90, 117
apocalypse 5, 8
apocalyptic 5, 6, 48, 133, 204
apokatastasis 162, 168, 174
apophatic 227
   apophatism 226–28
   kataphatic 227
argument 1, 2, 9, 60, 81, 86, 102, 106, 117, 143, 146, 153, 171
Aristotelian 92, 102 (See philosophy)
art 18–19, 41–42, 46, 47, 49, 52–57, 59–61, 64–74, 190, 195, 218, 241
artistic 18, 19, 42, 46, 47, 67, 68, 97, 138, 219, 247
ascension/ascended 3, 8, 169, 190, 209

253

Indices

Asian 92
Assertion 227, 229
Astrological 3
a/Atheism 9, 14, 61, 75–76, 81, 83, 86, 97–98, 108, 230, 236, 245
    atheist(ic) 9–10, 13, 75, 78, 81–82, 87–88, 107–8, 133, 153, 166, 175, 217
    atheists 9, 81, 97, 230
a/Atonement 36, 54, 72, 110, 151, 176, 180
    atoning 76, 110, 115, 118, 199
Aufhebung 50, 86
authority 8, 11, 15, 48, 84, 87, 116, 121, 124–26, 128, 130, 141, 163, 168
autonomous 10–11, 103, 107, 108, 114, 206
Ayin tahat ayin 140 (See war)
Aztec 3

Baha'i 3
b/Baptism 66–67, 80
Baptist 55, 56, 64, 70, 71, 72, 105, 106, 122
baptize(d) 29, 66, 92, 179
baptizer 66
Barthian 16, 86, 213
beauty 50, 54, 68, 73–75, 118, 182
beautiful 59, 73–74, 92, 175
b/Belief(s) 5, 7–9, 12, 13, 14, 19, 22–23, 43, 45–46, 70, 74–76, 81–87, 89, 91, 94, 96–97, 99–102, 108–11, 123–25, 148, 151–52, 155, 161–63, 169, 173–74, 177, 189–91, 198, 204, 206–7, 216, 226, 230
    believe 9, 14, 21, 44, 81, 106, 108, 110, 121, 151, 153, 165, 175, 192, 196–97, 201, 203–4, 216, 225
    believers 6, 9, 13 (See faith)
b/Bible 2–4, 6, 8–9, 15, 55–56, 78, 87–88, 90, 122, 137, 142, 145, 147, 164, 180, 192, 200, 205, 218
    biblical 6, 8, 20, 23, 55, 121, 123, 138, 143–44, 158, 161, 180–82, 205, 218
Blaue Reiter, Der 53, 58

body 10, 32, 55, 71, 79, 88, 90, 96–97, 101–5, 109, 117, 158, 197, 206, 212, 215–16, 219, 222–23
bourgeois 43–45, 59, 71, 107, 177
brain (See mind)
Brücke, Die 53, 58–60
Buddhist 3, 168, 175, 227–28

Capacocha 111–12, 242
    Qhapaq hucha 111–12
caste 89
catastrophic 5, 191, 194, 215, 221
categorical imperative 122, 144–47
causation 196, 198–99, 203
cause 61, 123–29, 190, 196, 203, 207
Celtic 13, 33, 88
chaos 3–5, 7, 17, 45, 58, 111, 200, 215, 225, 231
chaotic 2, 5, 200, 221
c/Children 28, 74, 81, 87, 89, 92, 95, 97–100, 107–14, 118, 135, 159, 163, 169–70, 175, 198 (See abortion)
    child 28, 33, 34, 36–37, 76, 80, 83, 94–96, 104–5, 107–9, 110–14, 158, 163–64, 169, 192, 198–99, 203–6, 218, 223
childbearing 109
childbirth 109
childhood 163, 196, 199, 216
Christianity 5, 12, 15, 43, 48–49, 62, 67, 70, 75, 77, 87, 110, 133, 146, 156, 174, 178–179, 185, 229, 231, 236–38, 240–41
Christian(s) 2, 3, 5–13, 16, 20–21, 49, 51, 55, 59–60, 64, 66–70, 72, 77, 79, 86–88, 91–94, 104, 107, 109–10, 114, 115, 121–23, 125, 127–28, 130–31, 133–37, 143, 146–48, 152, 155, 162, 166–67, 172, 174–76, 178–79, 181, 190, 203, 215, 230–36, 238, 240, 244
Christlikeness 24
c/Church(es) 6–8, 12, 14, 18, 42–44, 46–48, 50, 54–55, 66, 69, 71–72, 86–87, 92–93, 98–101, 103, 107–10, 115, 118, 121–222, 134, 145, 150, 175, 186, 197, 220, 227, 229
    Anglicans 51, 102, 109–10, 173

Indices

Church of England 10, 15, 21, 89, 92, 102, 109, 122, 134, 243
1970s Liberal Anglican(s) 1, 15, 102, 110, 130, 173
civilization 4–5, 35, 48–49, 62
civilized 6, 75, 139
cleansing 87–88, 90, 100, 155–57, 159, 173
compatibilism 149, 154, 241
concept(s) 5– 9, 18, 47, 57, 64–65, 73, 91, 104, 108, 115, 124–29, 139, 146, 152, 155–56, 162, 173, 178–80, 183–84, 186, 228–29
confusion 2, 67, 79–80, 91, 105, 153–54, 162, 167, 209, 219, 222–23, 225
contemplation 68–69
conversion(s) 93, 152, 181–83, 210, 216, 226, 236
corruption 166, 171, 186, 187, 200
creation 8, 17, 77, 82, 88, 105, 150–52, 179, 183, 185–86, 194–95, 197, 200, 202, 206, 215–17
crime 36, 62, 90, 95, 140, 154, 170
criminal 80, 91, 154, 181
crisis 4, 22–24, 42, 49, 52, 162, 189–90, 210, 212 (See *krisis*)
cross 16, 46, 54–55, 71–72, 110, 115, 118–19, 141–44, 146, 151, 155, 179, 181, 203, 215–16, 230
crucified 8, 23, 36, 45, 192, 218–19
crucifixion 8, 10, 46, 54–56, 110, 124, 150, 173, 184, 201, 216
culture 5, 11, 14, 21, 46, 52–53, 61, 71, 85, 88, 99, 115, 119, 126, 150, 164, 170, 174–79, 230–31, 244
cultural 5, 7, 15, 18–19, 42, 46–47, 49, 52, 63, 76, 79, 82, 84, 102, 109, 124, 142, 162, 225
curia 88

damnation 24, 146, 160–61, 172, 179–81, 190, 199 (See hell)
d/Dark 23, 50, 62–63, 81, 107–8, 190, 194–95, 240–41
darkened 62
darkness 7, 29, 61–62, 134, 225, 228
Darwinism 82

d/Death 3–5, 8–9, 16, 19–20, 22–23, 56, 62, 70, 74–78, 80–81, 83–84, 87–89, 91, 95–99, 109–10, 112, 114–18, 121, 129, 132, 144, 150, 152, 155–57, 159–62, 164, 173–74, 176, 178, 181, 184–86, 189, 191, 193, 198, 200–202, 206, 212, 219–20, 223, 231, 234–36, 239
die 3–5, 9, 36, 51, 56, 68, 71, 80, 88, 111–13, 117, 139, 158–60, 164, 166, 177, 213, 218–19, 227, 234–37, 241
mortem 76, 81, 93
defense (See war)
dehumanization/dehumanize(ing) 19, 76–78, 90, 94, 97–98, 100, 106, 117
delusion(s) 45, 75, 81–82, 115, 153, 176, 183, 212, 218
demon(s) 23, 44, 45, 113, 160, 170, 172, 175, 183, 185, 204–7, 211
daimonizomenois 205
demoniacs 205
d/Demonic 19, 45, 70, 74, 80, 101, 149, 171, 172–74, 203–7
despised 118–19, 201, 220
determinism 149, 154, 160–61, 241
Deus abscondus 227
Deus dixit 46, 54, 63, 65, 71–72, 74, 227, 229
Devil (See Satan)
d/Dialectic 6, 23, 50, 57, 66, 85–86, 103, 125, 130, 134, 137, 186, 190, 225, 231
dialectically 85, 228
dialectical theologians 63–64
Dialektische Theologie 19, 64
diastasis 228–29
antinomy 23, 57
antinomies 58
paradox 9, 22, 50, 103, 230
paradoxical 2, 23, 52, 86, 180, 228, 230
dina' de-malkhuta' dina' 133
disability 189, 210, 215
disaster 5, 153
disciple 55, 198
disciple(s) 198, 203–5, 217, 226
discriminate(ing) 106
discriminatory 96

Indices

disease 111, 113, 198
divinity 15, 44, 178
   divine(ly) 3, 6, 9, 13, 35, 67–68, 70, 73, 74, 77, 85, 101–2, 126, 132, 151, 162–63, 168, 174–77, 203, 211, 215–17, 229
docetic 103
dogma 130
domineering 77, 163, 231
dominion 62, 77, 78
dualistic 23, 116, 153, 190, 193, 220

earth 10, 17, 34, 41, 58, 66, 77, 89, 105, 114, 121, 155, 157, 163, 168–69, 171, 182, 186, 197, 200, 217 (See world)
ecclesia visibilis–ecclesia invisibilis 220
ecclesiology 220
   ecclesiological 67, 220
economic 48–49, 104, 126, 128, 145
encyclical 47, 92–93
enemy 20, 80, 93, 129, 141, 147, 198, 201 (See war)
   enemies 136, 141, 146, 148, 198, 216
Enlightenment 11, 14, 75–77, 84–92, 94–95, 97–98, 100, 105–11, 114–17, 119, 125, 127, 154, 212, 218
e/Epilepsy 22–24, 186, 189–91, 194, 196, 203, 205–7, 211–12, 215–16, 218–19, 220–21, 223, 231
   altered consciousness 190, 209, 212, 213, 222
   complex partial seizure 190, 207, 209, 210, 212–14, 219, 222–23
   convulsions/convulsing 192, 194, 204, 205, 206, 215
   e/Epileptic(s) 22–24, 189–194, 196, 203–5, 207, 209–10, 211–15, 217, 220–21, 223
   migraine aura 190, 209
   moonstruck 205
   neurons 197
   postictal 190, 209–10, 223
   retinal migraine 190, 209–10
   scintillating scotoma 190, 208–10
   seizure(s) 22–24, 189–92, 194, 196–97, 203–7, 209–15, 221, 222–23
   seleeniazomenous 205
   selēniazomenoi 205
   simple partial seizure 190, 209–10, 222
   status epilepticus 191, 209, 212, 214, 215, 223
   SUDEP 23, 223
   surd 150, 186
   synapses 197
   synaptic 196–97
   tonic-clonic 192, 204
equality 87, 90, 92, 100–101, 106, 115, 142, 178
   equal 90, 93, 96–100, 127, 142, 177–78
eritis sicut Deus 19, 88, 95, 116, 194, 203
e/Eschaton 2–8, 15–16, 19–20, 27, 42, 56, 70–71, 75–77, 80, 83, 86, 91, 101, 111, 114, 121, 144, 150–53, 185, 189, 213, 225, 227–31
   Consistent Eschatology 4
   end of all things 3, 4, 17
   end times 3, 5, 7, 16, 42
   eschatē 3
   eschatologically 11, 215, 228
   eschatological 18, 20–24, 41, 44, 45, 52, 54, 57–58, 63, 70–72, 74, 84, 101, 107, 118–19, 121–22, 136, 142, 145–49, 152, 162, 181, 189–90, 193, 199, 204, 212–13, 215, 234
   eschatological thinking 18
   eschatology 6, 16, 18–19, 22, 23, 41–42, 45, 63, 93, 116, 121, 159, 179, 185, 189, 190, 220, 227
   eschatos 3
   Futuristic Eschatology 4
   Inaugurated Eschatology 4
   over-realized 16, 18, 41
   process eschatology 63
   r/Realized eschatology 4, 6, 16, 18, 41, 93, 121, 159
   second coming 8, 144
   the day after tomorrow 3
   the end of days 6, 135
   Thoroughgoing Eschatology 4
eternal 3, 23, 35, 51, 132, 150–51, 158, 161, 179, 190, 229, 231
ethics 2, 10–11, 14, 43, 79–80, 82, 96, 104, 107–8, 114, 118, 122–24,

127–28, 130, 132, 144, 146–48, 150, 162, 207, 226–27
amoral 9, 147
ethical 1, 76, 128–30, 137, 228
ethically 124
moral 9, 10, 43–44, 92, 95, 109, 122, 145, 166, 169, 203–6, 225
m/Morality 9, 10, 11, 14, 74, 82, 110, 132, 148, 175, 236
ethnic 35, 90, 100
Europe 1, 5, 11, 18–20, 34, 42, 45–47, 49–50, 63, 87–89, 98, 107, 124, 127, 147
European(s) 13, 18, 62, 74, 90–92, 99, 244, 247
evangelical 13, 82, 97, 98, 155, 164, 166
evil(s) 17–18, 41, 45–46, 58, 70, 78, 80, 82, 86, 96, 106–9, 116–17, 121, 125, 127–28, 134–36, 141, 144–45, 147, 150, 154–55, 172, 174, 179, 185–86, 189, 199, 202, 203, 206–7, 221, 230
exile 190, 200–201, 203, 215–16, 221
existential 18, 24, 44, 48, 51, 58, 70, 95, 162, 190, 218–19, 221
existence 1
existentialism 51, 193, 218
e/Existentialist(s) 56, 70
exorcism 190, 211
exorcise 211
exorcising 204, 211
expressed 42, 46, 59, 81, 182
Expressionism 18–19, 41–42, 46–49, 51–54, 57–58, 60, 63, 69, 71, 74, 234, 241
Expressionist(s) 18, 41, 46, 48–50, 53–59, 59, 61–62, 69–70, 71–72
Expressionistic 18–19, 42, 46–49, 54–56, 59
expressive(ly) 58–59

faith 2, 5, 8–9, 12, 16, 49–50, 67, 70–71, 76, 81–82, 85, 87, 93, 110, 118, 135–36, 152, 160, 166, 179, 192, 202, 204, 207, 221, 244
faithful 1, 126
fall, the 8, 11, 19, 55, 59, 61, 80, 106, 108, 118, 136, 138, 149–50, 154, 174, 180, 198, 20–203, 211, 220–221 (See original sin)
fallen 2, 71, 83, 86, 118, 180, 195, 202, 218–20, 227
falls 3, 86, 149, 157, 171, 174, 189, 198, 202, 222
fell 1, 28, 29, 199, 201, 210
fate 3, 76, 92, 151, 160, 199
f/Feminism 8, 10, 109–10, 234, 237
f/Feminist(s) 11, 79, 83, 110, 175, 182, 231, 234
fertilization 102, 104
finite 197
First World War / WW1 18, 41–42, 45, 47–49, 58–59, 62–64, 74, 138 (See war)
force 126, 129–30, 135, 186, 202
forgive 15, 22, 95, 152
forgiven(ess) 10, 16, 22, 46, 52, 80, 118, 119, 153–155, 164, 181, 183
forgiving 6, 22, 80, 150, 151, 184, 189
f/Freemasonry 10–12, 85, 231
fundamentalism 83
fundamental 2, 9, 67, 83, 130, 169, 227, 228
fundamentalist 20, 83, 122, 130

genetic 198–201, 203
global 4–5, 20, 122, 146, 176
glory 54, 73, 75, 149, 170, 226
gnostic 102, 151, 168
g/Good, the 9–11, 15, 23, 57, 71–72, 76, 78, 87, 93, 96, 98, 101, 106–9, 117, 121, 125–28, 131, 135, 141–42, 153–54, 156, 165, 167, 170, 174–75, 181, 185, 190–92, 199, 202–4, 206–7, 209, 215, 225
g/Gospel 15, 23, 44, 49, 50, 55, 65, 69, 72, 78, 79, 92, 93, 100, 108, 109, 135, 140, 145–47, 152, 165, 172, 179–81, 214, 145, 192, 198, 206, 211, 214, 230
government(s) 4, 9, 12, 81, 91, 95, 98, 109, 121–23, 125, 127–28, 132, 147–48, 177–78
grace 46, 52, 88, 93, 106, 142, 160–62, 171, 180–81, 201–2, 211, 213–15, 221

Indices

Greek 3, 13, 30–34, 42, 57, 61, 67, 84, 101–4, 107, 119, 133, 158, 162, 172, 178, 192, 205–6, 209

hallucination 222
hate 59, 96, 106, 116, 141, 171
  hatred 32, 105, 117, 165, 236
heathen 67, 91 (See pagan)
heaven 3, 5–6, 8–9, 16, 21–23, 41, 61, 66, 72, 76, 114, 128, 141, 145, 149–52, 153–55, 157–58, 160–63, 165, 166–67, 170–71, 173–74, 178, 181–82, 184–87, 190, 197, 199, 217, 226, 231 (See hell)
  heavenward 162, 169–71, 174, 186
Hebrew(s) 2, 6–7, 17, 33, 36, 78, 89, 110, 113, 122, 132–33, 137, 139–40, 143, 146, 150–51, 172, 200 (See Jews; Judaism)
Hegelian 3, 228
hegemony 75, 127
h/Hell 3, 5–6, 8–9, 16, 21–23, 72, 76, 91, 93–94, 128, 142, 145–48, 149–51, 152–55, 157, 160–65, 167–70, 172–76, 179, 182–87, 190, 231, 234–36, 238, 242, 245 (See heaven)
  hellish 21, 153, 155–57, 161, 163, 165, 168–69, 18–84
heresy 5, 87, 179, 194
  heretic 87
  heretics 87, 116
heterodox 5
heteronomous 10, 11, 114
Hindu(ism) 1, 3, 168, 169, 176–79
history 3–4, 12, 17, 43, 69, 86, 110, 122, 131–32, 144, 146, 193, 202, 230
h/Holocaust(s) 19–20, 74–76, 89, 90–92, 94, 95, 96, 97, 98, 99, 100–101, 105–11, 114–17, 231, 234, 235, 237, 243
  mega-holocausts 19, 75–76, 89, 92, 95, 97–98, 100, 105–7, 109–10, 114–15, 117
holon/holos 103
holy 70, 121, 123, 125, 153, 180
homo incurvatus in se 162

human 3–5, 7–10, 13–17, 19, 22, 44, 50, 52–55, 58–62, 67–69, 71, 72, 74–76, 79, 82–86, 88–95, 96, 98–103, 105, 108, 109, 111, 113–14, 117, 123, 126, 132, 144, 148, 150–53, 156–57, 163, 166, 171, 179, 181, 189, 194–97, 200–201, 205, 211, 216, 218, 220, 225–30, 245
humanism 11, 12, 14, 107, 127, 130, 146, 178
humanist(s) 11–13, 44, 75, 79, 84, 88, 94, 99–100, 103, 106–10, 114–15, 122, 123, 130, 132, 147–48, 179
humanity 2, 4–9, 15–16, 19–22, 34, 36, 42, 46, 50, 57–59, 61–62, 66, 68–69, 72–73, 75–78, 80, 82–84, 87, 89, 91–93, 95, 96, 99–103, 105, 106, 107, 109, 114, 116, 118–19, 121, 149–52, 160, 163, 166, 174, 179, 182, 185–87, 189, 195, 200–203, 205–6, 211, 218, 220, 225–28, 230
humor 2, 150, 176
humorous 22, 149, 179

iconoclasm 46, 67, 69
  iconoclast(s) 18, 42, 46, 65, 66–68
idea(s) 4, 14, 17–18, 47, 63–68, 102, 115, 124, 135, 150–51, 164, 168, 175, 179, 193, 201, 205–6, 226–28
identity 4–5, 10–11, 13, 15, 23–24, 36, 66, 75, 80–87, 101, 115, 124, 170–71, 183, 191, 194, 206, 215, 219, 222, 231
  identity politics 4–5, 10, 13, 15, 24, 75, 80, 85–87, 115, 183, 206–7, 215, 231
ideologically 11, 122, 147
illegal 32, 113, 116, 125, 132
illness 22–23, 164, 198, 205, 217
illusion 70, 99, 108, 194, 218
imagery 61, 68
imagination 153, 179, 195, 219
imago Dei 150, 173, 184
imitatio christi 221
imminent 4, 128
  imminentize 4
imperialism 91

258

Indices

Inca 3, 76, 111–12, 114, 233–34 (See Capacocha)
incarnation 4, 8, 14–17, 101–3, 144, 146, 150, 193, 218, 229
  incarnated 8, 34, 72, 76, 101, 145
incomprehensible 74
individual 5, 9, 14, 22–24, 58, 65, 70, 79–80, 87, 93, 102, 114–15, 135, 152–53, 162, 172, 174, 176, 184, 189, 198–200, 203, 206, 212, 215, 217
infirmities 119
inheritance 200–201
inherited disease 198
innocent 84, 96, 113, 131, 135, 185, 198, 207
  innocence 83, 144, 163, 198, 203, 217
Inquisition 87–88, 116
  inquisitor 116
intellectual 5, 45, 81, 92, 97, 175
irrational 128, 132, 165, 185, 186
irresponsible 167–69
  irresponsibility 169
Isenheim Altarpiece 54, 55
Islam 20, 130–31, 140, 146, 174, 238, 240

Judaism 6, 174, 204 (See Hebrew)
Jew(s) 2, 6, 17, 20, 29, 30, 34–36, 75, 77, 91, 92, 94–96, 98–99, 100, 109, 114–15, 118–19, 124, 133, 134, 180, 192, 198
  Jewish 2, 6–7, 13, 29, 31, 34–36, 96, 98, 133, 190, 198, 205, 215, 220, 244
  Judeo 3, 6, 178
  Semitic 61, 91
  Star of David 29, 32
judge(d) 5–10, 15, 123, 140–45, 151–54, 158, 164, 180, 184
  judgment 3–6, 8, 16, 18–23, 41–42, 67–69, 71, 75–78, 80, 83, 85–86, 88, 91, 93, 101, 116–19, 12–22, 135, 145–146, 148–53, 157, 159, 161, 163, 179, 181, 186, 189–91, 193, 198–99, 203, 220, 244
jus ad bellum 121, 128
jus in bello 121, 128–29

justice 122, 126–27, 129, 132, 138–40, 155, 206, 227, 240
justification 19, 74, 76, 81, 101, 104, 117, 123–24, 128, 150, 180
  justified 48, 90, 96, 102, 107, 115, 122–24, 127–28, 147–48, 195
  justifying 110, 124, 171
just war theory(ies) 20–21, 121–29, 134, 135, 139, 147, 148, 234
  just war 20–21, 121–25, 127, 129, 131, 134–35, 139, 144, 147–48

Kantian Man 193–97, 214, 218–19
kataphatic 227
kerygmatic 50, 52–56
Kingdom of God 37, 234
King's College London 1–2, 19–22, 24, 45, 104, 142, 239
Kirchliche Dogmatik 19, 42, 47, 50–51, 53–55, 67–69, 73
knowledge 3, 63, 70, 78, 85, 89, 93, 106, 108, 129, 162, 174, 195, 202–3, 212–13, 216–18, 229 (See understanding)
  epistemic 212, 228
  knowing 44, 51, 212, 213, 226
  unknowability 54
krisis/krises 7, 18–19, 42, 48–49, 53, 70–71, 191, 213, 221, 225 (See crisis)

language 8, 16, 18, 41, 50–52, 182, 192, 228–29, 241
linguistic 228
literary 41, 57, 81, 217
Latin 84, 108, 156, 157, 172
law 9–10, 29–30, 35, 60, 83, 90, 94, 96, 106, 117, 127, 129, 130–36, 139–40, 145–46, 151, 154, 156, 180–82
  lawyer 85, 182
  Legality 132
  legislation 9, 11, 13, 83, 177
  legitimization 12, 107, 178
LGBTQ (etc.) 10, 15
l/Liberal 4–5, 11–15, 18, 21, 41–43, 45–46, 48, 53, 59, 63, 70, 75–76, 79, 81, 84, 88, 94, 96, 99–100, 102,–10, 114–15, 118, 122–23, 127, 130, 132,

259

Indices

146–48, 150, 151–53, 168, 173, 175–79, 184, 241
l/Liberalism 14, 44, 48, 71, 81, 166, 177
liberalization 97, 107, 178
life 1, 4–6, 9–10, 16, 21, 23, 42, 49, 57–60, 62, 67, 76–78, 80, 84–85, 91, 94–98, 101–5, 109, 113, 115, 126, 128, 135–36, 143–144, 149–52, 156, 160–67, 169–171, 177–81, 183–84, 187, 190–91, 193, 195–96, 199–202, 206, 210, 215–16, 218, 219–20, 223, 226, 228, 230–31, 245
lignum crucis arbor scientiae 216
Londinium 29, 31–32, 36
l/Love(s) 9, 23, 65, 75, 94–95, 107, 117, 133, 135–36, 141–42, 146, 160, 162, 164, 169–78, 183–84, 189–91, 198, 200, 206, 215, 220–21, 227, 230, 242
  agapé 133
  ahava 172
  eros 107, 171, 178
  philia 107, 171, 178
  storgē 107, 171, 178
Lucifer (See Satan)

Machiavellian 11, 92, 115, 131, 148, 168
Manichaean 76, 103
marginalized 23, 73, 190, 201, 217, 220
Marxist 3, 9, 62, 97, 98, 116, 130
materialism 194–96
mediaeval 42, 46, 54–55, 57, 64, 70, 123, 127, 173, 186
media studies 18, 21, 149
Ménières disease 13
merciless 63, 108
metaphor 53, 57, 108
metaphorically 108, 174
metaphysical 193, 229
migraine 190, 209, 210 (See epilepsy)
mind 22–23, 65, 84–85, 96, 134, 136, 162, 175–76, 179, 190–91, 194, 196–97, 204–7, 211–12, 218–20, 222, 245 (See epilepsy)
  brain 22–23, 31, 65, 113, 189–91, 194, 196, 197–99, 203–15, 218, 22–23, 245

consciousness 70, 82, 97, 112, 176, 190, 194, 209, 212–13, 222
mental 155–56, 205, 222
modern 4, 8, 21, 42, 45–47, 50, 54, 59, 64–65, 70, 87, 98, 101, 103, 108, 125, 132, 139, 151–52, 154, 163, 168, 173, 177, 194–95, 205, 241
  m/Modernism 14, 19, 42, 46–47, 69, 71, 127
  modernist 5, 14, 76, 82–83, 102, 150
Monothelitism 101
mortals 3, 189, 214
mother 27–28, 33, 55, 80, 95, 105–6, 112–113, 219
murder 62, 90, 126, 132, 138, 140, 145
music 46–47, 64–66, 68, 92, 166, 176
myth(s) 13, 64, 70, 81, 91, 95, 124, 173
  mythology 13, 64, 81, 91, 107, 195

Nacht, Die 53, 61–62, 138, 239, 241
narrative(s) 2, 15–17, 159–160, 179, 203
nation(s) 12–13, 89, 97–98, 121–24, 126, 128, 130–32, 134, 136, 137, 140, 142–43, 147, 174, 177, 178
National Socialism 64, 69, 92
  National Socialist(s) 3, 64–69, 72–74, 91–92, 98, 101, 134
  Nazi 69, 74, 91, 95, 98, 116, 236–38, 240
  Nazism 70, 219
n/Nativity 15–18, 27, 54
natural law 9, 127, 151, 156
nature 2, 23, 55, 58, 77, 81–82, 88, 96, 114, 117, 129, 144, 151, 157, 162–63, 169, 179, 181, 183–85, 195, 200, 207
negation 50, 62, 67, 135, 225, 227–29, 230
negative 53, 150, 153, 186, 230
negativity 4, 225, 227
neo-pagan secular-liberal humanism 11–14, 100, 107–10, 114, 122–27, 130, 146, 178–79
neo-Protestantism 18, 41, 43, 59
n/New a/Atheist(s) 81–86, 100, 106–10, 115, 237

Indices

New Testament 6, 8, 45, 133, 140, 172, 221, 231 (See Bible/biblical; Old Testament; Septuagint)
Newtonian 45, 218
night 1, 3, 28–29, 33, 61–62, 138, 147–48, 189, 198, 205
nihilism 10, 49, 59, 167, 215, 221
nihilistic 23, 150, 153, 160–61, 172, 190, 215, 219
Norse 3, 13, 34, 64, 91, 128 (See Viking)
nothing 5, 8, 18, 41, 70, 73, 79, 82, 85, 92, 96, 98, 105–6, 118, 123, 131, 133–34, 147, 153, 160, 174, 193, 201–202, 213, 217, 220, 226, 229
  nothingness 5, 157, 215, 221, 229
  no-thing 5
numinous 5

objectification 756, 77–79, 80, 83–84, 86, 90, 95–96, 100, 106, 108, 196
  objectified 78, 80, 83, 89, 94, 97, 108
  objectify 19, 78, 83
  objectifying 77, 78, 80, 94, 100
offensive 123, 135, 146
Old Testament 2, 6, 17, 113, 137, 140, 142 (See Bible/biblical; New testament; Septuagint)
ontology 76, 79, 101–2, 111, 150, 154, 161, 168, 180, 202
  ontic 5, 93, 157, 163, 180–81
  ontological(ly) 45, 72, 149, 180
oppression 48, 49, 87, 121, 130
original sin 8, 19, 54, 59, 80–82, 106, 108, 109, 131, 150, 154, 174, 184, 201, 203, 234 (see Fall, the; postlapsarian)
orthodox 5, 7, 16, 34, 48, 148, 179, 195, 225

pacifism 126
pacifist 145
pagan 11–14, 36, 61, 64, 67, 74, 76, 84, 88, 91, 100, 103–4, 107–8, 109–11, 114–16, 119, 122–24, 127, 130, 137–38, 140, 143, 146–48, 150, 155, 166, 168, 175, 178, 179, 181 (See heathen; neo-pagan secular-liberal humanism)
  p/Paganism 12–13, 20
  neo-pagan 11–13, 14, 100, 107–10, 114, 122–24, 127, 130, 146, 178, 179
painting(s) 47, 54–61, 69, 72
parable 2, 15–17, 22, 159
  p/Parable 2, 160, 169, 220, 230
  parabolic 2, 22
paralutikois 205
paralytics 205
parousia 7, 17
patristic 101, 125, 127, 186
peace 31, 34, 41, 98, 118–19, 123–25, 129–30, 134–37, 175–76
  pax romana 98, 124
  peaceful 126, 129, 147
Pelagianist 163
penal substitution 110, 115
people 2–4, 6, 8, 12–14, 17, 21–23, 28, 33, 35–36, 42, 44, 48, 50, 57, 62, 64, 67, 69, 71, 73, 74–76, 80, 83, 87–90, 91–94, 97–101, 104, 106, 111, 113, 117–19, 129, 131–34, 136, 138, 142–43, 145, 147–48, 150–52, 155, 161–62, 167–69, 178, 179–180, 182–85, 190, 200–203, 205–6, 209, 212–13, 215–16, 219–220, 231
  person(s) 2, 9, 12, 24, 36, 48, 57, 67, 72, 76, 78–79, 86, 95, 101–3, 114, 132, 140–41, 145, 149, 151–52, 154, 160, 165, 168–70, 190, 201, 209, 212, 214–16, 220–23
perception 3, 70, 130, 156, 158, 191, 194, 196–197, 212, 222
perspective 5, 7, 9, 10, 14, 20, 47, 54–55, 57–58, 62, 72, 79, 84, 108, 115, 122, 124–25, 127, 147–48, 179, 185, 190, 193, 196, 202, 221, 229
  vanishing point 57–58
philosophy 1, 13–14, 84–85, 103–4, 127, 193, 211–12, 241
  philosopher(s) 64, 81, 84–85, 102, 155, 190, 193–94, 195, 215
  philosophers 4, 78, 84, 90, 125–27, 139, 154, 157, 160–61, 186

Indices

philosophical(ly) 1, 3, 14, 18, 47, 104, 121, 126, 131, 193, 218
philosophically 151
picture 21, 50, 57–58, 62, 65, 68, 72, 179, 191, 194, 199, 208, 218
Platonic 53
pluralism 90, 153
  pluralistic 90
pneuma 197
  pneumatically 196
  pneumatologically 152, 202–3, 215, 228
political 4, 5–7, 10–12, 15, 19, 43, 59, 63, 83, 85, 87–89, 94, 96, 98, 102, 104, 124, 130–31, 137, 146, 160, 219, 225
  politic 10, 126
post-Christian 10–13, 109, 123, 148
p/Postlapsarian 22, 78, 80, 86–87, 107, 189–90, 199–204, 215–16, 221 (See original sin; fall, the)
postmodern 82, 85, 87, 97, 103, 109–10, 114–15, 148, 182
postmortem 4–5, 21, 71, 76, 150–52, 156, 159–61, 163–64, 168–71, 173, 180–81, 184–85, 186–87
postmortem status purgatus 21, 152, 149, 156, 160, 163–64, 168–71, 185
Praetorian(s) 29, 31–33
prayer 45, 66–67, 92, 175, 213
  pray 141, 175, 180, 198
progress 2–3, 7, 15, 49, 82, 174, 208, 212–13
p/Prophet 2, 9, 29–30, 43–44, 46–49, 58, 62, 105, 113, 223, 240, 241
proportion 55, 148
proposition(s) 2, 6, 15, 48, 75, 81–82, 86–87, 96–97, 102, 104, 127, 154, 160
Protestant 3, 43–44, 46, 48, 54, 57, 63–64, 66–69, 73, 87–88, 91, 94, 157, 174, 180, 233
Psalmists 105
p/Psychology 1, 65
  psyche 103
  psychological(ly) 3, 57–58, 81, 98, 163, 182–83
punishment(s) 80, 98, 110, 115, 118–19, 125–28, 130, 139–40, 142, 161, 181, 200, 203

purgatory 21, 149, 152, 155–61, 165–66, 172–73, 175–76, 179–81
purgation 21, 149, 152, 154–58, 161–63, 165, 168, 172–73, 179–80, 184–85
purgatorial 166, 175, 179
purging 152, 154, 156–57, 171, 180, 236

Rabbi(s) 28, 35–36, 198
racist 90–91, 109
Rastafarian 3
ratio 138, 143, 195
rational 1–2, 103, 184, 193
  rationalism 195
  rationalist 13
r/*Rātsach* 132–33
reality 17, 22–23, 44–45, 47–48, 53, 55–58, 62, 65–67, 71–72, 107, 128, 130, 140, 145–46, 150, 153–54, 157, 159, 161–66, 168–70, 172, 181, 187, 189, 191, 195, 197, 199–200, 202–3, 205–7, 211–13, 215–16, 221–22, 226–28
r/Reason 2, 14, 57, 61, 76, 77, 83, 84, 88, 90, 98, 123, 125, 126, 127, 144, 180, 182–85, 193, 194–97, 218, 219, 223, 226, 228, 235, 237, 238, 239
  reasonable 60, 89–91, 97
rebellion 10–11, 18, 41, 48, 116, 124, 138, 152, 155, 162, 181, 186, 200
reconciliation 20, 33, 110, 130, 135–36, 144–46, 148
  reconciled 135, 145, 181
Reformation 3, 19, 22, 69, 75–76, 84, 87–89, 93, 125, 234
Reformed 18, 41, 51, 63, 94, 179–81, 236
r/Religion(s) 4–6, 9, 11–14, 23, 43–44, 49–51, 53–54, 60–62, 64, 67, 72, 75–76, 81–92, 98, 107–10, 117–19, 126, 133, 151, 155, 164, 166–68, 172–78, 184, 195, 217, 219–20, 230, 234–36, 241–42, 244
  religio 7, 10–11, 19, 82, 84–85, 87–89, 92, 94, 96, 98, 102, 104, 122, 124, 146, 225
  religionist 83, 166

religiosity 18, 41, 44, 75, 84, 86, 108, 117, 220, 229
religious(ly) 2, 4-5, 7-14, 23-24, 35, 46, 49, 50, 52, 54, 58, 60-61, 63-64, 67, 69-70, 72, 75-76, 78, 81-91, 97, 101, 102, 107-12, 114, 116, 117, 122-24, 130, 133, 137, 142, 145, 150-51, 153, 160-61, 162, 166-68, 172, 174-79, 184, 198-99, 201-2, 212, 217, 219-20, 226, 229-30
Religious Atheism 19-20, 75, 234
Renaissance 13, 42, 46, 54-55, 57, 66, 70, 125
reparation 129, 137, 138-39, 143
repent 80, 118, 162, 165, 171, 186, 199
    repentance 149, 156, 162, 166-67, 171, 199
representation 58, 62, 160
republic 5
responsible 104, 130, 135, 150-51, 162, 193, 204
    responsibility 49, 72, 135, 150-51, 156, 161-63, 169, 184, 196
resurrection 8, 10, 14, 46, 54, 144, 146, 150, 152, 173, 180-81, 184, 201, 229
    resurrected 8, 45, 149, 152, 169, 210, 218
risen 3, 190, 209
retribution 135, 137-39, 144, 146
r/Revelation 2-8, 12-13, 46-47, 50-51, 54, 57, 65, 72-73, 85-86, 88, 93, 102, 130, 133, 137, 152, 154, 162, 174, 178, 189, 191, 195, 196, 219, 227-29, 238-39
    r/Reveal(ed) 2, 49, 193, 239
reverence 43, 68-69, 85
revolution(ary) 15, 18, 41, 62-63, 70, 79-81, 87, 102, 109, 116-17
rhetoric 52
righteous(ness) 19-20, 80, 83-86, 88, 116-17, 121, 122-23, 127, 132, 141-42, 145, 148, 151-53, 158-59, 163-64, 166, 168, 180, 189, 199-200, 203, 217, 231
    unrighteous 141, 151, 158, 199
Ritschlian 44

Roman 13, 17-18, 27-30, 32-37, 41, 45, 47-48, 61, 63, 67, 73-74, 76, 83, 85, 87, 92-93, 98, 111-12, 114-16, 124, 127-28, 142, 149, 151, 155, 174-75, 220, 226, 228, 234, 237
Roman Catholic 47, 83, 87, 92-93, 98, 112, 115, 124, 127-28, 155, 175
romanticism 49, 60
romantic(s) 60 ,65, 70, 72, 173, 176
Römerbrief, Der 18-19, 41-42, 47-48, 50-51, 53-54, 56-57, 61-62, 71, 227, 230, 237

sacrifice 33, 54, 74, 76, 89-90, 96, 110-15, 117-18, 171, 199
    sacrificial 76, 84, 89, 110, 114, 136
s/salvation 7, 11, 16-17, 22, 24-45, 49, 54, 72, 76, 86, 93, 102, 132, 142, 146, 151, 154, 157, 159, 165, 170-71, 174, 181, 184-85, 189-190, 207, 219, 221
sanctification 181, 221
Satan 17, 86, 160, 164, 167, 172, 207, 217
    d/Devil(s) 1, 116, 167
    Lucifer 1, 86, 185, 193, 201
scientific 82, 97-98, 104, 191-92, 194-96, 198, 202
    scientia 195
    scientist 65, 181, 194, 202
s/Scripture(s) 2, 8, 14, 20, 33-36, 104-6, 122, 123, 131, 137, 146, 181, 148, 185
sectarian 96
secular 4-5, 7, 11-14, 43, 49, 65-66, 75, 79, 94, 100, 103, 106-10, 114-15, 122-23, 127, 129-30, 132, 146-48, 178-79, 244
    secularization 114, 130
security 126
seizure(s) 22, 23, 24, 189, 190, 191, 192, 197, 203, 204, 207, 209, 210, 212, 213, 214, 215, 221, 222, 223 (See epilepsy)
self 4, 9, 11, 17, 19, 47-49, 54, 64, 70-71, 75, 78, 80, 82-83, 85-87, 97, 104, 106-7, 117, 123, 125, 129-30, 132-33, 137, 151-52, 157, 161-64, 167-71, 173, 176-79, 183, 185-86, 189, 191, 193-96, 202, 205, 211, 217, 219, 227, 231

Indices

self-denying 133
self-giving 133
self-justification 117, 207
selfless 172
Septuagint 77, 241 (See Old Testament)
sex(ual) 12, 14–15, 19, 27, 36, 49, 78–80, 83, 103, 107, 108–9, 131, 133, 151, 168, 171, 178, 183, 206
Shamans 34
shriven 149, 154
Simpsons, The 1, 21–22, 149–50, 152, 160–79, 181–85, 187, 231
sin(s) 8– 9, 16, 19, 33, 43–44, 46, 54–55, 59, 80, 90, 96, 106, 108–9, 116, 118, 125, 131–32, 134, 136, 150–51, 154–58, 162, 164, 168, 171, 174, 180–82, 184, 198–99, 201, 203–4, 211, 217, 244
sinned 118, 198
sinners 86, 155, 199–200, 201
sinning 109
slaughter(ed) 28–29, 32–33, 48, 75, 86, 89, 97, 100, 113, 118, 134, 141, 184
slavery 20, 90–92, 94, 99–101, 131, 215, 231
enslave(d) 34, 78, 89–90, 93, 99
enslavement 89, 93, 99, 115
enslavers 93, 99
slave(s) 20, 27, 35, 75, 89–91, 92, 95–96, 98–99, 100, 106, 114–15, 119, 142, 215
slave trade 19–20, 75, 90, 92, 99, 115
smitten 119
society 3, 7–8, 10–11, 14–15, 24, 43, 59, 71, 73–74, 82, 89, 94, 99, 114–15, 130, 140, 160, 170–71, 220
sociological 3, 43
Socratic 84
sōma 103
sorrows 118–19
space 1, 55, 63, 116, 118, 158, 202, 213, 221, 227
s/Spiritual 4, 14, 44, 96, 117, 134, 152, 155, 157, 173, 179, 195, 200–202, 204, 216
Stalinism 219
state 10, 12, 13, 17, 21, 30, 42, 57–58, 94–95, 97–98, 105, 110, 115, 125, 147, 153, 155–57, 160–62, 165–66, 168–69, 171–72, 177, 182, 185, 191, 201–3, 209–11, 212, 213–15, 218, 220, 223
state sanctioning 94, 95, 110, 115
status epilepticus (See epilepsy)
status quo 11, 18, 41
stewardship 77
sublimis Dei 92–93, 99, 242
suffer 1, 144, 147, 161, 198, 203,
s/Sufferance 22, 189, 190, 219, 221
sufferer 22, 189, 196, 223
suffering 23–24, 29, 37, 45, 54–56, 58–59, 87, 119, 129, 153, 155, 162, 169, 177, 182, 190, 198, 202–3, 205–7, 212, 215–18, 221, 231
suicide 49, 80, 99, 115, 130, 135, 170, 194
supernatural 4–5, 13, 15, 81, 204, 205
superstition 85
surrender 129–30, 185
Swiss Religious Socialism 43
synagogue 28, 35 (See Jew; Hebrew)
systematic 1–2, 7, 18, 21, 81, 83, 101, 178

Taliban 4, 131, 147
Talmud 96, 97, 242
technology 78, 84, 98–99
teleology 3, 22, 151, 179
teleological 7, 107, 183, 225, 227–28, 231
teloi 2, 7–8, 225
telos 2, 11, 21, 149–50, 152, 189, 227, 230
temporal 24, 55, 65–66, 162, 190–91, 209, 212, 214, 222, 227–28 (See time)
Ten Commandments 145 (See Jew; Hebrew)
terrorism 76, 87, 122, 129–30, 135, 137, 143–44, 147–48
Theism 8, 12, 13, 235 (See atheism)
theistic 13, 75, 81–83, 85, 87–89, 133
t/Theology 1–3, 7, 14–15, 17–19, 20–24, 42–45–48, 50–54, 63–64, 66–67, 71, 73–76, 81, 83–84, 87–88, 95, 100, 104, 109, 116–17, 121, 123, 127, 137,

142, 144, 180, 189, 191, 217–18, 226, 228–29
doctrinal 18, 21–22, 44, 74, 159–60
Systematic Theology 1, 19–22, 24, 142, 234, 239
theocracies 88
theocracy 88
theodicy 198
theologian(s) 3–4, 8, 16, 22, 41, 42, 47, 51, 63, 64, 73, 76, 101, 103, 110, 116, 125, 142, 153, 154, 157, 161, 186, 189, 195, 226
t/Theological 1, 2, 7, 14–15, 18, 19, 20, 21, 23, 41–42, 44, 46–47, 50–53, 55–56, 61, 63, 74, 76, 79–81, 83, 95, 101–2, 104, 106–7, 109, 123–25, 131, 149, 160, 162, 180–81, 190, 194, 198, 204, 218, 223, 226, 229, 234, 238, 239, 242
t/Theologically 59, 68, 71–72, 79, 95, 106, 190, 198, 225
theologies 16, 115, 228
theologoumena 4
time 1, 4–7, 9, 11–12, 16–17, 28–29, 34, 43, 50–52, 55–56, 62, 65, 67, 71, 92, 99–101, 102–4, 111–12, 113, 131, 144, 147–48, 152, 157–60, 164, 166, 168, 169, 173, 176–77, 180–82, 184, 191, 199, 205, 212–14, 217–18, 221, 223 (See temporal)
transcend(ed) 53, 55
transcendent 71, 144, 145, 219, 229
transgressions 1, 114, 118, 119
Transhumanist(s) 3–4
trial 42, 88, 123–24, 151
t/Tribalism 5, 10, 133, 138
tribal 7, 10–11, 19, 81, 85, 89, 91, 100–101, 106, 119, 124, 140, 146, 186
tribes 11, 13, 35, 88, 104, 126, 131–32, 136–38, 143, 146, 174
t/Trinity 22, 44, 55, 101, 145, 233, 239
triune 16, 22, 86, 150, 189–91
truth(s) 1–2, 8, 20, 49, 52–55, 57, 61, 73, 85, 90–93, 115–18, 169, 172, 174, 177–79, 230
axiom 9, 67, 86, 89, 103, 117, 137
axiomatic 97, 101, 106, 118

unbelief 9, 67, 86, 192, 204
understand(ing) 7, 9–10, 22–23, 33, 52, 43–44, 61–63, 73, 96, 106, 111, 118, 144, 151, 161–162, 175–177, 181, 185, 189–94, 196, 214–17, 220–21, 223, 225, 227, 228–29
unethical 9
u/Universal(ism) 16, 45, 76, 145, 150, 151, 236

vagaries 160, 199–200, 202–3, 211, 215
veneration 69, 84
vengeance 88, 105, 137–39, 141–42, 146, 148
vicissitudes 160, 199–200, 202–3, 211, 215
victim(s) 86–88, 94, 97—99, 105, 112, 114, 116–17, 137–38, 140–42, 144, 204
Viking 128, 146, 173, 184
violence 81, 110, 125–29, 134, 136, 139–40, 142–44, 153, 171 (See war)
virginal conception 31
visual 18–19, 41–42, 46–47, 54, 58, 65–66, 69, 71–73, 208–10

w/War(s) 2–3, 10, 12, 18–19, 20–21, 41–42, 44–45, 47–49, 53, 58–59, 62–64, 74, 80, 83, 90, 96, 98, 100, 115, 116–17, 121–39, 142–44, 146–48, 166, 175, 177, 231, 237, 239, 241, 243, 246
combatant(s) 129–30, 140, 144, 147
condemn 118, 142, 146, 159, 220, 231
conflict 20, 42, 121, 126, 129–31, 134–37, 140, 143, 231
conflicting 7, 126, 225
d/Defense 67, 123, 126, 129, 134–37, 139, 146, 148
defensive 98, 121, 135, 146
destroy 37, 42, 89, 95, 132, 138, 142, 191
destruction 20, 53, 67, 75, 77–78, 83, 89, 93, 121, 129, 134, 136, 139, 142–43, 148, 194, 206
hostile 114, 125
hostilities 124, 129, 137

Indices

kill 19, 75, 81–83, 86, 94–96, 100, 107, 110, 116, 131–32, 139–41, 144, 215
killing 44, 80, 83, 90, 98–100, 108–10, 115, 117, 126, 132, 138–39, 144, 147–48, 173, 184
Limited Defensive Response 20
manslaughter 132
milhemet hovah 133
milhemet mitsvah 133
milhemet reshut 133
militarist 145
military 122, 124, 127, 129–31, 136, 138, 142–43, 146–47
Nine-Eleven (9/11), "the Twin Towers" 20–21, 121–23, 137–43, 213, 234, 238
Pre-Emptive Absolute Response 20
w/War on Terror 121, 122, 123, 144, 146, 147
w/Warfare 124, 126, 128, 144
weapon(s) 19, 42, 113, 118, 134–35, 139, 148, 176, 243
Weimar Republic 47, 69
Western 4–5, 9, 11, 13, 20, 24, 33, 49, 75, 81, 84, 87, 94–97, 100, 105–7, 109, 112, 122, 124, 131–32, 142–43, 146, 151, 154, 160, 163, 174–78, 182, 234, 237
Wiccan 168, 175
w/Will 2, 3, 5–6, 8–10, 17, 20, 21–22, 27, 36–37, 41, 46, 48, 54, 58–59, 61, 64, 72–73, 75–76, 79–81, 84–87, 91, 95–96, 100–102, 105–6, 108, 110, 118–19, 121, 123, 126, 130–31, 133, 135–36, 138–39, 141, 144–46, 149–50, 152–59, 161–63, 167, 171, 173, 176, 179, 181, 183–86, 189, 195–96, 198–206, 208–9, 211, 214–20, 222–23, 225–26, 229–31, 241 (See fall; original sin)
willful(ly) 2, 21, 84, 93–95, 118, 156, 157, 183–84, 200, 206
witness 6, 45, 71, 150, 159, 176, 180, 198
womb 95, 102, 105–6, 113, 198–99, 202–3
w/Word of God 69

world 3–8, 10, 12–13, 15–17, 23–24, 34–35, 42–43, 47–49, 53, 57–58, 60, 62–63, 65, 67, 71–72, 77, 81, 94, 96–98, 108–109, 111–12, 114, 117–18, 122, 124, 135, 137–39, 142–43, 151, 153, 155, 165, 170, 173–74, 176–77, 179, 182, 190, 194–95, 197, 201–204, 207, 213, 216–18, 221–22, 226–31, 243 (See earth)
w/Worship 11, 66–69, 85, 111, 145, 149, 176–77, 216, 233
wounds 118–19

zeitgeist 18, 42, 46, 63–64, 73–75, 101, 108
Zoroastrianism 3
Zwischen den Zeiten 144

Sectional Contents

Introduction | 1
- I. The End Times: The Day After Tomorrow | 2
  - The Eschaton | 2
  - Multiple Ends | 3
  - What is Certain? | 5
  - Judeo-Christian Revelation | 6
- II. Aims and Objectives | 7
- III. Explanations, Qualifications | 7
  - The Authority of the Bible | 8
  - Creation, Fall, Incarnation, Resurrection, Second Coming, and the Four Last Things | 8
  - Atheism–Theism | 8
  - Law, the Moral Code, . . . and Human Responsibility | 9
  - Hegemonic Tribalism | 10
  - Neo-Pagan Secular-Liberal Humanism | 11
  - Liberal and Modernism | 14
  - 1970s Liberal Anglican | 15
- IV. Part One Towards an Understanding of the Arrival of the End Times | 15
  - A Delayed Nativity . . . What If? The Eschaton Prefigured | 15
- V. Part Two Towards an Understanding of the Emergence of the End Times | 18
  - Karl Barth: "Krisis," War, & Expressionism—An Eschatological Encounter | 18

Sectional Contents

        A Human Generated Eschaton: The Slave Trade, the Holocaust, and Abortion—The Delusions of Religious Atheism | 19

        The Just War Theory and the 9/11 Wars: A Biblical and Eschatological Consideration | 20

        A Simpsons' Eschatology: Towards an Understanding of Postmortem Status Purgatus—Eternal Life and Human Rebellion | 21

        The God of the Epileptic: Postlapsarian Exile, Affliction, and the Sufferance of Salvation | 22

PART ONE

TOWARDS AN UNDERSTANDING OF THE ARRIVAL OF THE END TIMES

1.
A Delayed Nativity . . . What If ? The Eschaton Prefigured | 27

    I.   A Biblical Holocaust | 27

    II.   Two Millennia Later | 29

    III. "Behold, a Virgin Shall Conceive, and bear a Son, and Shall Call His Name Immanuel" (Isaiah 7:14) | 30

    IV   First Visitors | 31

    V.   Exodus | 31

    VI. Refugees | 32

    VII. Magi | 34

    VIII. Migrants | 34

    IX. Arrival | 35

    X.   Ministry | 36

PART TWO
TOWARDS AN UNDERSTANDING OF THE EMERGENCE OF THE END TIMES

2.
Karl Barth:
"Krisis," War, & Expressionism—An Eschatological Encounter | 41

Synopsis | 41

- I. Introduction | 42
- II. Revolutionary Theology in the Making | 42
- III. Barth and Expressionism | 46
- IV. Why Expressionism? | 47
- V. Barth's use of an Expressionist Style, Trope, and Idiom | 50
- VI. Expressionism: the Visual Arts | 54
- VII. Matthias Grünewald and Hans Holbein the Younger | 54
- VIII. El Greco, Vincent Van Gogh and Edvard Munch | 56
- IX. German Expressionism 1. *Die Brücke* and *Der Blaue Reiter* | 58
- X. German Expressionism 2. German Romanticism | 60
- XI. German Expressionism 3. Max Beckmann | 61
- XII. *Zeitgeist* | 63
- XIII. Barth and Creativity | 64
- XIV. Barth the Iconoclast? | 65
- XV. Modernism? | 69
- XVI. Conclusion | 71

3.
A Human-Generated Eschaton:
Objectification in the Slave Trade, the Holocaust, and Abortion—
The Delusions of Religious Atheism | 75

Synopsis | 75

- I. Introduction | 76
- II. Creation and Objectification   77

Sectional Contents

III.	"Otherness:" Theological Objectification	79
IV.	The New Atheists and The New Morality	80
V.	The Modernist-Atheistic Sin	83
VI.	Religion as Unbelief	84
VII.	Enlightenment Death 1. Three Mega-Holocausts	87
VIII.	Enlightenment Death 2. A Pseudo-"Christian" Theology of Death	87
IX.	Enlightenment Death 3. Slavery: "Am I not a Man and a Brother?"	89
X.	Enlightenment Death 4. The Holocaust of God's Chosen People	91
XI.	Enlightenment Death 5. The Silence of the Aborted	94
XII.	Enlightenment Death 6. Defining Principles	97
XIII.	An Hypostatic Union 1. Without Confusion	100
XIV.	An Hypostatic Union 2. Immediate Animation	100
XV.	An Hypostatic Union 3. The Full Humanity of the Child-Person from Conception	105
XVI.	The Theological Roots of the Third Enlightenment Mega-Holocaust	106
XVII.	The Religious Roots of The Third Enlightenment Mega-Holocaust	109
XVIII.	*Qhapaq Hucha/Capacocha*: Inca Protectionist Child Sacrifice—the Eschaton Prefigured	111
XIX.	Cain and Abel	114
XX.	Conclusion	117

Sectional Contents

4.
The Just War Theory and the 9/11 Wars:
A Biblical and Eschatological Consideration | 121

    Synopsis | 121

    I.   Introduction | 122

    II.   Just War Theories 1. Aggression and Justification | 123

    III.   Just War Theories 2. A Thomist Theory | 125

    IV.   Just War Theories 3. The Just | 126

    V.   Just War Theories 4. A Roman Catholic Perspective—
           Jus Ad Bellum and *Jus In Bello* | 127

    VI.   Just War Theories 5. A Secular-Modernist Perspective? | 129

    VII.   Conflict | 130

    VIII.   War & Peace 1. Aggression and Sin—Sanity | 131

    IX.   War & Peace 2. Lordship and Obedience | 132

    X.   War & Peace 3. Justice | 133

    XI.   War & Peace 4. A Spiritual Battle | 134

    XII.   War & Peace 5. Reconciliation | 135

    XIII.   A Biblical Perspective 1. Doctrine, Principle, Axiom | 137

    XIV.   A Biblical Perspective 2. The Pagan Principle:
           Vengeance in Excess | 137

    XV. A Biblical Perspective 3. The Ancient Hebrew Principle:
           an Eye for an Eye | 139

    XVI.   A Biblical Perspective 4.
           The Christian Principle: Turn the Other Cheek | 140

    XVII.   A Biblical Perspective 5. The War Ethic for a War on Terror? | 142

    XVIII.   A War on Terrorism | 144

    XIX.   An Eschatological Perspective | 144

    X.   Conclusion | 146

Sectional Contents

5.
***Postmortem Status Purgatus*:**
A Simpsons' Eschatology:—Towards a Lewisian Understanding of Eternal Life and Human Rebellion | 149

    Synopsis | 149

    I.   Introduction | 150

    II.   Oh, Hell! . . . | 152

    III.   Purgatory or Purgation: *Postmortem Status Purgatus* | 154

    IV.   Purgatory or Purgation: "The Tree Lies Where it Falls" | 156

    V.   Purgatory or Purgation: Hold on a Moment . . . We Will all be Changed | 158

    VI.   An Infernal Analogy? | 159

    VII.   The Simpsons: Individual Responsibility: An Allegory of Purgation/Purgatory | 161

    VIII.   The Simpsons: Individual Responsibility: Children/Childish | 163

    IX.   The Simpsons: Death—Hell-Bound | 164

        Maud Flanders | 164

        Frank Grimes | 164

        Dr Marvin Monroe | 165

    X.   The Simpsons: The Saved—Heavenward | 165

        Bleeding Gums Murphy | 165

    XI.   The Simpsons: Those Who Subsist—Purgatorial | 166

        Ned Flanders | 166

        Maggie Simpson | 167

        Lisa Simpson | 168

        Apu Nahasapeemapetilon | 168

        Marge Simpson | 169

        Bart Simpson | 169

        Ralph Wiggum | 170

        Waylon Smithers | 170

        Sex and Love in this Simpsonian *Postmortem Status Purgatus*? | 171

    XII.   The Simpsons: The Taunts of Demons | 172

Sectional Contents

    XIII.   The Simpsons: Where is It? | 172

    XIV.   Religion in the Simpsons | 173

    XV.   Difficulties and Problems with a Doctrine of Purgatory   179

    XVI.   A Personification? | 181

    XVII.   Universal Salvation? | 184

    XVIII. Conclusion | 185

6.
The God of the Epileptic:
Postlapsarian Exile, Affliction, and the Sufferance of Salvation | 189

    Synopsis | 189

    I. Introduction | 191

    II. Reason and Methodology | 192

    III. Causation 1. The Complexity Of "Why?" | 196

    IV. Causation 2. The Blame Game | 198

    V. Causation 3. Postlapsarian Exile | 199

    VI. Causation 4. Possession | 203

    VII. Knowing | 212

    VIII. Affliction | 215

    IX. Conclusion | 218

    Brief Glossary of Epileptic Seizures | 222

Conclusion:
A Negative Telos—An Apophatic–Kataphatic Eschaton | 225

    I.   The Vine and the Branches | 226

    II.   A Kataphatic-Apophatism; an Assertion of Negativity | 227

    III. Apophatic Language and Concepts:
           Eschatological Negativity . . . an Assertion | 229

    IV. Watching and Waiting . . . Staying | 230